THE LATTER-DAY SAINT CENTURY

1901 – 2000

THE LATTER DAY SAINT CENTURY

RICHARD O. COWAN

Revised and updated edition of
The Church in the Twentieth Century

BOOKCRAFT

SALT LAKE CITY, UTAH

Cover Photo Sources

Courtesy *Deseret News*:
Photos of speaker at conference, Idaho Institute building, President Kimball with Tokyo Temple presidency, family, President Hinckley shaking hands with Church member

Courtesy Utah State Historical Society, all rights reserved:
Photos of First Presidency, women sewing, George Albert Smith

Courtesy LDS Church Archives, The Church of Jesus Christ of Latter-day Saints:
Photos of horsemen, Monticello Utah Temple

Courtesy Darrel Chamberlain:
Photos of Idaho Falls Idaho Temple, detail of St. Louis Missouri Temple

Courtesy John Luke:
Photo of angel Moroni

Courtesy Intellectual Reserve:
Photo of scriptures

All cover photos used by permission.

Library of Congress Catalog Card Number: 99-69149

ISBN 1-57008-693-1

First Printing of Revised Edition, 1999

Printed in the United States of America

Contents

Preface

The twentieth century has been an era of immense significance in the history of The Church of Jesus Christ of Latter-day Saints. Surely it would have been wonderful to live in the days of Joseph Smith and to associate with him personally. Likewise, to accompany the pioneers in their westward trek would have been an unforgettable experience. Yet the Church's challenges and opportunities of the twentieth century hold a unique excitement. The twentieth century will be remembered as an era of significant developments in Church structure, programs, and activities, as a time of great devotion and courage in the lives of Latter-day Saints, and as a period of phenomenal worldwide growth.

Writing contemporary history has definite advantages but also poses unique challenges. While there is an abundance of published sources such as newspapers, more reflective personal sources such as journals or correspondence are not as readily available. In some cases the researcher may have been intimately involved in the events described but lacks the perspective necessary to assess their long-term importance. Furthermore, writing about individuals who are still living requires particularly sensititive judgement. Despite these challenges, I have found the writing of this book to be an enjoyable experience.

My interest in this topic is long-standing. After finishing my Ph.D. in American history at Stanford University in 1961, I joined the religion faculty at Brigham Young University. In the mid 1960s, James B. Allen, of BYU's history department, encouraged my interest in recent Church history. Together we authored a small BYU Extension publication *Mormonism in the Twentieth Century.* About fifteen years later, Larry C. Porter, then chairman of the Department of Church History and Doctrine at BYU, assigned me to write a text on twentieth-century Church history and encouraged me to submit my manuscript for publication. The resulting book, *The Church in the Twentieth Century*, was published in 1985.

The Latter-day Saint Century is an update, revision, and expansion of this book. As the twentieth century draws to a close and because many significant developments have occurred since the earlier manuscript was prepared fifteen years ago, it seemed important and appropriate to prepare this new work.

I am indebted to many persons who have provided assistance, without which this work could not have been completed. I appreciated Bookcraft's commitment to publishing historical works such as mine. George Bickerstaff insightfully and graciously pointed out ways the original manuscript could be improved. Cory Maxwell encouraged me to pursue the project of revising my earlier work.

Several individuals have rendered important assistance as I prepared the manuscript of *The Latter-day Saint Century.* Patty Smith provided a computerized typescript of the earlier text. Heather Hobbs carefully reviewed *The Church in the Twentieth Century,* suggesting possible revisions. Vaughn Pickell, Jonathon Hart, Emily Zeigler, and Stacy Beal, my assistants in the office, worked closely with me in the revision process. At Bookcraft, Janna DeVore and

Peter Gardner have carefully edited the manuscript and provided many helpful suggestions. I am indebted to Bill Slaughter and April Williamsen at the Church Archives as well as to many others who helped locate photographs for the revision. I am grateful also to Randall Pixton for his hard work on the book's demanding design.

I am convinced that the Lord's hand can be seen not only in specific incidents where inspired guidance was obvious but also in the overall progress of His kingdom during the twentieth century. We do not need to look to the distant past to find examples of divine direction and assistance. It is my hope that this history of The Church of Jesus Christ of Latter-day Saints in the twentieth century will be a source of information, interest, and especially inspiration to all who read it.

1901 - 2000

I

The Dawning of the Twentieth Century

As the twentieth century began, Lorenzo Snow, fifth President of The Church of Jesus Christ of Latter-day Saints, presided over about 250,000 members. Many of these early Saints had personally experienced the hardships of pioneering in the deserts and had suffered through the persecutions that had been so common in the nineteenth century. Forty-three stakes and nineteen missions were functioning. Missionaries were teaching the restored gospel in the United States, Canada, western Europe, and the islands of the Pacific. But the Church's strength was still concentrated in just one area. All four temples were located in Utah. Because five out of six Latter-day Saints lived in the predominantly Mormon Intermountain area of the western United States, the Church's influence elsewhere was limited. The twentieth century would see The Church of Jesus Christ of Latter-day Saints expand far beyond these modest dimensions.

On Tuesday, January 1, 1901, the opening day of the new century, President Snow addressed a special New Year's Day audience in the Salt Lake Tabernacle. Having played a key role in the progress of the Church almost since its beginning, he now eagerly anticipated the future:

> I hope and look for grand events to occur in the twentieth century. At its auspicious dawn, I lift my hands and invoke the blessings of heaven upon the inhabitants of the

Pedestrians, carriages, and streetcars traverse Main Street in downtown Salt Lake City in 1903. (Photo courtesy Suzanna Broberg Langenheim)

HERALD.
NEWS
WORLD

> earth. . . . May righteousness increase and iniquity diminish as the years of the century roll on. May justice triumph and corruption be stamped out. And may virtue and chastity and honor prevail, until evil shall be overcome and the earth shall be cleansed from wickedness. Let these sentiments, as the voice of the "Mormons" in the mountains of Utah, go forth to the whole world, and let all people know that our wish and our mission are for the blessing and salvation of the entire human race. May the twentieth century prove the happiest as it will be the grandest of all the ages of time.[1]

Although President Snow's hopes have not yet been fully realized, he did see the Church take substantial strides toward fulfilling its worldwide mission.

Lorenzo Snow's Earlier Life

Lorenzo Snow was eighty-four years of age when he assumed the leadership of the Church. No other president had entered this office at such an advanced age. President Snow's long life had been filled with experiences that prepared him for his service as President of the Church.

Although opportunities for formal schooling were quite limited in frontier Ohio, Lorenzo Snow loved to read and yearned for an education. After completing one term in high school, he attended Oberlin College, a nearby Presbyterian institution. Lorenzo Snow was the first President of the Church to have had any college education. He taught school for a season in Ohio and would later organize the Polysophical Society to promote cultural refinement and learning among the early pioneers in Utah. This society was a forerunner of the Mutual Improvement Associations.

Lorenzo's first contact with the restored gospel came at the age of seventeen when he went to hear Joseph Smith preach in Hiram, Ohio, just four miles from Lorenzo's home. Four years later, he eagerly accepted his sister Eliza's invitation to visit her in Kirtland and attend the Hebrew school the Mormons were conducting. This gave him the opportunity to become personally acquainted with Joseph Smith and other Church leaders, and in June 1836 he was baptized.

Deep personal spirituality would characterize Lorenzo Snow throughout his life, and this trait was manifested early. Two or three weeks after his baptism, he became worried that he had not yet received "a *knowledge* of the truth of the work." It was his custom to retire each evening to a nearby grove of trees, "But," he reflected, "at this time I felt no inclination to do so. The spirit of prayer had departed and the heavens seemed like brass over my head." Nevertheless, he determined to pray as usual.

> I had no sooner opened my lips in an effort to pray, than I heard a sound, just above my head, like the rustling of silken robes, and immediately the Spirit of God descended upon me, completely enveloping my whole person, filling me, from the crown of my head to the

Major events in the life and administration of President Lorenzo Snow

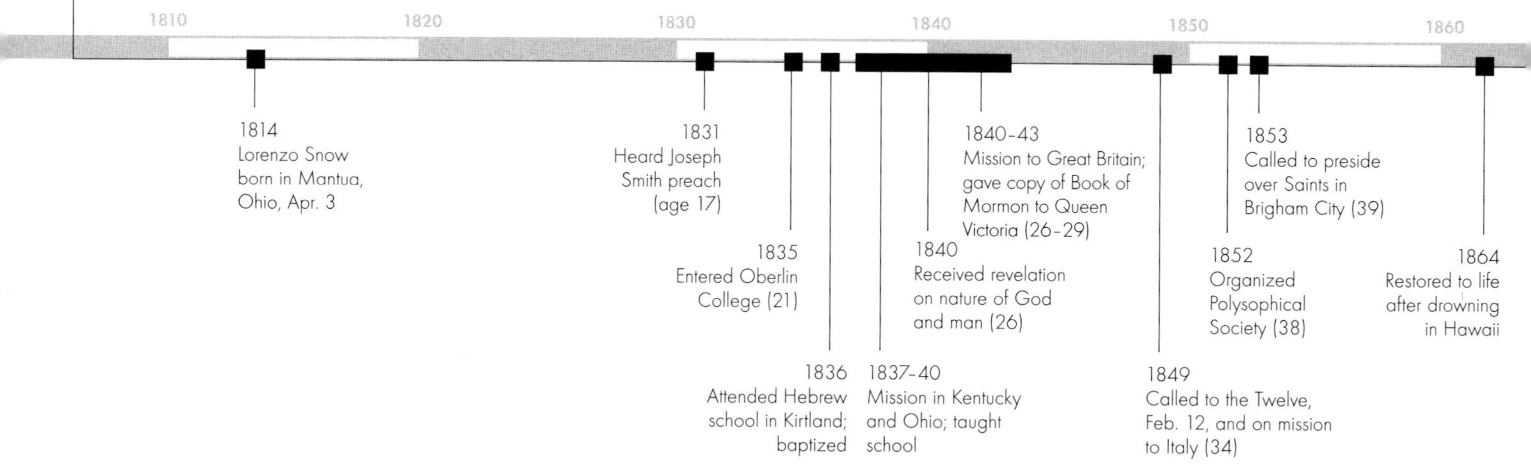
1810
1820
1830
1840
1850
1860
1814
Lorenzo Snow born in Mantua, Ohio, Apr. 3
1831
Heard Joseph Smith preach (age 17)
1835
Entered Oberlin College (21)
1836
Attended Hebrew school in Kirtland; baptized
1837–40
Mission in Kentucky and Ohio; taught school
1840
Received revelation on nature of God and man (26)
1840–43
Mission to Great Britain; gave copy of Book of Mormon to Queen Victoria (26–29)
1849
Called to the Twelve, Feb. 12, and on mission to Italy (34)
1852
Organized Polysophical Society (38)
1853
Called to preside over Saints in Brigham City (39)
1864
Restored to life after drowning in Hawaii

soles of my feet, and O, the joy and happiness I felt! No language can describe the almost instantaneous transition from a dense cloud of mental and spiritual darkness into a refulgence of light and knowledge, as it was at that time imparted to my understanding. I then received a perfect knowledge that God lives, that Jesus Christ is the Son of God, and of the restoration of the holy Priesthood, and the fulness of the Gospel. It was a complete baptism—a tangible immersion in the heavenly principle or element, the Holy Ghost; and even more real and physical in its effects upon every part of my system than the immersion by water; dispelling forever, so long as reason and memory last, all possibility of doubt or fear.[2]

Later, in Nauvoo, Lorenzo received by personal revelation a knowledge of man's potential destiny which he formulated into this couplet:

> As man now is, God once was:
> As God now is, man may be.[3]

After the pioneer trek to Utah, Lorenzo Snow was called in 1849 to the Quorum of the Twelve Apostles and appointed to open a mission in Italy. After only two weeks' preparation, he left his wives and families and traveled east with the first group of missionaries sent from the Rocky Mountain area. Elder Snow and his companions arrived in Italy in 1850. Missionary success did not come easily. Only after Elder Snow exerted his great faith in healing a young boy were the missionaries able to open the door, albeit just a crack, in Italy.

The Brigham City Cooperative Building. Elder Lorenzo Snow is standing at the far right. (LDS Church Archives)

In 1853 Brigham Young called Lorenzo Snow to preside over Latter-day Saint communities in the Box Elder area of northern Utah. He established his headquarters at Brigham City, which was named after President Young. He lived in this region for over forty years, although he did accept frequent assignments to travel elsewhere. Under his leadership, the Saints developed a series of cooperative enterprises that brought them prosperity. Here he

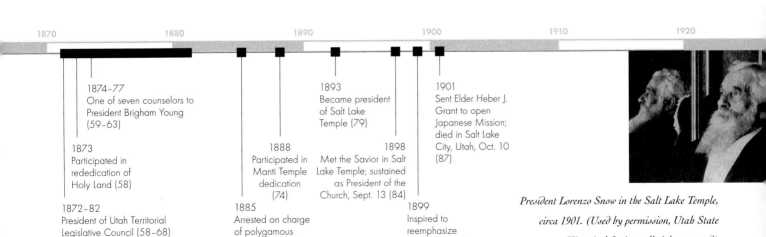

1870 1880 1890 1900 1910 1920

1872–82
President of Utah Territorial Legislative Council (58–68)

1873
Participated in rededication of Holy Land (58)

1874–77
One of seven counselors to President Brigham Young (59–63)

1885
Arrested on charge of polygamous cohabitation (71)

1888
Participated in Manti Temple dedication (74)

1893
Became president of Salt Lake Temple (79)

1898
Met the Savior in Salt Lake Temple; sustained as President of the Church, Sept. 13 (84)

1899
Inspired to reemphasize tithe-paying (85)

1901
Sent Elder Heber J. Grant to open Japanese Mission; died in Salt Lake City, Utah, Oct. 10 (87)

President Lorenzo Snow in the Salt Lake Temple, circa 1901. (Used by permission, Utah State Historical Society, all rights reserved)

gained valuable economic experience that would give him needed perspective when, as President of the Church, he would confront the challenge of an overwhelming debt.

Elder Snow accepted several assignments to travel overseas. This broadened his appreciation of the Church's worldwide mission. While filling a special assignment in Hawaii in 1864, Elder Snow appeared to have drowned when the small boat he was in capsized. After twenty minutes, his lifeless body was finally found and taken from the water. His companions administered to him and continued praying as they worked over him. Finally they felt impressed to apply mouth-to-mouth resuscitation, a life-saving technique not commonly known at that time, and his life was restored.

From 1872–73 he toured Europe and the Near East with a group of General Authorities and others. President Brigham Young instructed the group to "observe closely what openings now exist, or where they may be effected, for the introduction of the Gospel into the various countries you shall visit"[4] and to offer a dedicatory prayer in Palestine. On March 2, 1873, Elder Snow and the others ascended the Mount of Olives and, in compliance with President Young's instructions, offered a solemn prayer, blessing the Holy Land.

Spiritual experiences continued to characterize Elder Lorenzo Snow's ministry. On March 9, 1891, through his great faith in the power of the priesthood, he raised a young woman from the dead. Ella Jensen of Brigham City had been dead for two hours when he commanded her to "come back and live," declaring, "your mission is not ended." She lived to become the mother of eight children.[5] Upon the dedication of the Salt Lake Temple in 1893, Lorenzo Snow was made its first president. He enjoyed this calling until he was released upon becoming President of the Church in 1898.

Selection as President of the Church

Two important principles relative to succession in the Presidency of the Church were clarified as Lorenzo Snow assumed that office and during his administration. One of these points dealt with how soon the new President should take office, and the other defined how that person should be selected.

IMMEDIATE REORGANIZATION OF THE FIRST PRESIDENCY

Following the deaths of the first three Presidents of the Church, the Council of the Twelve Apostles presided for prolonged periods of times before the new President took office. As early as 1892, however, President Wilford Woodruff instructed that there should not be another of these lengthy "apostolic presidencies" following his death and so directed Lorenzo Snow, who would be his successor, to reorganize the First Presidency immediately. When Elder Snow asked, "President Woodruff, am I to receive this as a revelation?" he was told that he should.[6]

The authority of these instructions was later confirmed through a sacred experience Elder Snow had in the Salt Lake Temple. In 1898, as President Wilford Woodruff became critically ill, Lorenzo Snow grew extremely worried. The Church was unable to pay even the interest on its heavy debt. Elder Snow's son LeRoi recorded: "My father went to his room in the Salt Lake Temple . . . knelt at the sacred altar in the Holy of Holies in the House of the Lord and there plead to the Lord to spare President Woodruff's life, that President Woodruff might outlive him and that the great responsibility of Church leadership would not fall upon his shoulders. Yet he promised the Lord that he would devotedly perform any duty required at his hands. At this time he was in his eighty-sixth year."[7]

Elder Snow was in Brigham City when he received notice of President Woodruff's death on September 2, 1898. The Apostle immediately returned to Salt Lake City and went to his room in the temple.

> President Snow . . . repaired again to the same sacred altar . . . and poured out his heart to the Lord. He reminded the Lord how he plead for President Woodruff's life to be spared, that President Woodruff's days would be lengthened beyond his own; that he might never be called upon to bear the heavy burdens

The First Presidency, 1898–1901: (from left to right) George Q. Cannon, President Lorenzo Snow, and Joseph F. Smith. (LDS Church Archives)

> and responsibilities of the Church. "Nevertheless," he said, "Thy will be done. I have not sought this responsibility but if it be Thy will, I now present myself before Thee for Thy guidance and instruction. I ask that Thou show me what Thou wouldst have me do."
>
> After finishing his prayer he expected a reply, some special manifestation from the Lord. So he waited,—and waited—and waited. There was no reply, no voice, no visitation, no manifestation.[8]

Disappointed, he left the sacred room, and walked through the celestial room out into the large corridor. Here he received a glorious manifestation, which he later described to a granddaughter. She wrote:

> While we were still in the large corridor leading into the celestial room, I was walking several steps ahead of grand-pa when he stopped me and said: "Wait a moment, Allie, I want to tell you something. It was right here that the Lord Jesus Christ appeared to me at the time of the death of President Woodruff. He instructed me to go right ahead and reorganize the First Presidency of the Church at once and not wait as had been done after the death of the previous presidents, and that I was to succeed President Woodruff."

Then grand-pa came a step nearer and held out his left hand and said: "He stood right here, about three feet above the floor. It looked as though He stood on a plate of solid gold."

Grand-pa told me what a glorious personage the Savior is and described His hands, feet, countenance and beautiful white robes, all of which were of such a glory of whiteness and brightness that he could hardly gaze upon Him.

Then he came another step nearer and put his right hand on my head and said: "Now, grand-daughter, I want you to remember that this is the testimony of your grand-father, that he told you with his own lips that he actually saw the Savior, here in the Temple, and talked with Him face to face."[9]

On September 13, the Apostles met to discuss Church affairs, eleven days after President Woodruff's death. President Snow had not told anyone about his experience in the temple, desiring to see what the decision of the Twelve would be. Elder Francis M. Lyman referred to "President Woodruff's feelings, as expressed on different occasions during his administration, to the effect that whenever he died, the First Presidency of the Church should be organized without delay," and then declared that he was prepared to vote right then for a new President of the Church.[10] The others present concurred, and Lorenzo Snow was unanimously sustained to this calling.

President Snow then arose and acknowledged that "there was no use in his making excuses as to [his] inability, etc., to assume the vast responsibilities involved in the position to which he had been elected. He felt that it was for him to do the very best he could and depend upon the Lord. He knew the action taken by the Council was according to the mind and will of the Lord."[11]

SENIORITY AMONG THE TWELVE

As early as 1887 Elder Wilford Woodruff taught that following the death of a prophet, the senior Apostle is as much President of the Church when he is presiding over the Twelve as he is after the First Presidency is reorganized and that he would never be set aside in favor of somebody else.[12] President Harold B. Lee later explained that this is the case

The First Presidency and Quorum of the Twelve Apostles about 1899: (top row, from left) Anthon H. Lund, John W. Taylor, John Henry Smith, Heber J. Grant, Francis M. Lyman, George Teasdale, Marriner W. Merrill; (middle row, from left) Brigham Young Jr., George Q. Cannon, Lorenzo Snow, Joseph F. Smith, Franklin D. Richards; (bottom row, from left) Matthias Cowley, Abraham O. Woodruff (Rudger Clawson is absent from this photo). (Used by permission, Utah State Historical Society, all rights reserved)

because one's call as President of the Church actually begins when he is ordained and set apart as a member of the Quorum of the Twelve Apostles. "Each apostle so ordained under the hands of the President of the Church, who holds the keys of the kingdom of God in concert with all other ordained apostles, has given to him the priesthood authority necessary to hold every position in the Church, even to a position of presidency over the Church."[13]

"The moment life passes from a President of the Church," Elder Spencer W. Kimball testified, "a body of men become the composite leader—these men already seasoned with experience and training. . . . No 'running' for position, no electioneering, no stump speeches. What a divine plan! How wise our Lord, to organize so perfectly beyond the weakness of frail, grasping humans. . . . People talk about precedent. If it is precedent, it has become such by the repetition of the revealed order since the beginning."[14] This pattern has always been followed, and Elder John A. Widtsoe suggested that "should there be any deviation from the practices of the past, it would come by revelation to the President of the Twelve, who by virtue of his presidency, holds the keys of authority committed to this quorum of the priesthood."[15]

Because the senior Apostle becomes the next President of the Church, Lorenzo Snow knew it was important to clarify how that seniority was determined. An opportunity to do this came during his administration.

Brigham Young Jr., had been ordained an Apostle in 1864, and Joseph F. Smith received a similar ordination two years later. Because there were no vacancies in the Twelve at the time, however, these two men were not immediately sustained as members of the Quorum. In 1867 Joseph F. Smith was called to fill a vacancy in the Twelve, and a year later Brigham Young Jr., filled another vacancy in that same quorum. Thus when the President of the Twelve died in 1899, the question arose as to which of these two men was the senior Apostle.

At their regular Thursday meeting in the Salt Lake Temple on April 5, 1900, just before general conference, the First Presidency and the Twelve decided that "the acceptance of a member into the Council or Quorum of the Twelve fixed his rank or position in the Apostleship," and that "ordination to the Apostleship under the hands of any Apostle other than to fill a vacancy in the quorum, and authorized by the General Authorities of the Church, did not count in precedence."[16] Ordination to the Apostleship could be a strictly private matter, not widely known, while becoming a member of the Twelve is an official action that requires a sustaining vote from the body of the Church. Hence Joseph F. Smith ranked ahead of Brigham Young Jr., among the members of the Twelve. Finally, it was decided that "if the First Presidency were dissolved by the death of the President, his counselors having been ordained Apostles in the Quorum of the Twelve would resume their places in the quorum, according to the seniority of their ordinations into that quorum."[17]

Overcoming Church Debt

A major challenge facing the Church as Lorenzo Snow assumed the presidency was a staggering debt. This was a direct outgrowth of the Edmunds-Tucker Anti-Bigamy Act of 1887, which provided for the confiscation of Church property. Furthermore, the Church helped pay legal fees and court costs of those being prosecuted for living in plural marriage, and it assumed the responsibility of caring for the families of men who were imprisoned. At the same time, members became reluctant to make financial contributions to the Church, fearing that these funds would be seized by the government. Thus, "tithing receipts dropped from an average of more than $500,000 per year, during the 1880s, to a little more than $300,000 in 1890." Hence, "the long-run effect of the Edmunds-Tucker law was to throw the Church, which had previously enjoyed a creditor status, into a debt of at least half a million dollars."[18]

Other commitments during the 1890s swelled the debt even further. President Woodruff was anxious to complete the construction of the Salt Lake Temple, so a million dollars was spent on this project between 1890 and 1893. Church leaders had also encouraged local units to establish academies to meet the educational needs of the Saints. These schools continued to receive a substantial portion of Church appropriations. Expenditures for welfare also increased during the depression of the mid-1890s. The Church invested funds to develop essential Intermountain industries, but during the business slump they returned no profit. These difficult times led to yet another drop in the Church's tithing income. Thus the Church had to borrow in order to meet its obligations.

When Lorenzo Snow became President of the Church in 1898 he faced a debt of over $1.25 million, most of it owed to "gentile" (or non–Latter-day Saint) creditors. He therefore decided to sell bonds in order to meet the Church's debt. This move had at least three advantages: (1) It gained much needed time for Church leaders to seek a permanent solution. (2) Interest on the bonds was at a lower rate than the interest on the existing debt. (3) The bonds were sold to the Church's own members. President Snow preferred to borrow "among ourselves" rather than "go into the world." Three issues of a half million dollars each were planned. The first two series were issued in January 1899. Significant new developments, however, would make the third series unnecessary.[19]

PRESIDENT SNOW'S REVELATION ON TITHING

During the spring of 1899 President Lorenzo Snow was inspired to go to St. George in southern Utah and to take with him as many of the General Authorities as could be spared at Church headquarters. There he would receive by revelation the key to solving the Church's financial difficulties, providing the solid foundation for the growth that was to occur during the twentieth century. This vital revelation, however, did not come immediately. Upon arriving in St. George, President Snow paced the floor, having "the most painful and anxious expression on his face that I had ever seen," his son later recalled. "Why have I come to St. George?" the President worried aloud. "Why have I come here?"[20]

It was at the St. George Tabernacle in the spring of 1899 that President Lorenzo Snow received a revelation on the law of tithing. This revelation and the Saints' willingness to recommit themselves to tithe-paying brought the Church out of debt by 1906. (LDS Church Archives)

At the special conference held in the St. George Tabernacle on Wednesday, May 17, 1899, President Snow seemed uncertain as he began to speak. "All at once father paused in his discourse," his son recalled. "Complete stillness filled the room. . . . When he commenced to speak again his voice strengthened and the inspiration of God seemed to come over him, as well as over the entire assembly. His eyes seemed to brighten and his countenance to shine. He was filled with unusual power. Then he revealed to the Latter-day Saints the vision that was before him. . . . He told them that he could see, as he had never realized before, how the law of tithing had been neglected by the people."[21]

The President stressed that faithful compliance with this law would become the means of releasing the Church as well as individual members from the burden of debt. "The word of the Lord is: The time has now come for every Latter-day Saint, who calculates to be prepared for the future and to hold his feet strong upon a proper foundation, to do the will of the Lord and to pay his tithing in full. That is the word of the Lord to you, and it will be the word of the Lord to every settlement throughout the land of Zion."[22]

Referring to the prolonged drought in southern Utah, President Snow assured his listeners that if they would pay an honest tithing they could with faith plant their crops for the coming season. "He promised them, in the name of the Lord," his son recalled, "that the clouds would gather, the rains from heaven descend, their lands would be drenched, and the rivers and ditches filled, and they would reap a bounteous harvest that very season."[23]

Later that evening President Snow reflected: "Now I know why I came to St. George. The Lord sent me here, and he has a great work for me to perform. There is no mistake about it. I can see the great future for the Church and I can hardly wait to get back to Salt Lake City to commence the great work."[24]

On his way back home, President Snow visited various communities, where he repeated his exhortations for the Saints to honor the law of tithing. Upon arriving in Salt Lake City he found the annual conference of the Young Men's and Young Women's Mutual Improvement Associations in session. At a meeting of the Young Men's officers on May 30, President Snow gave an impressive discourse on tithing that those who were present accepted by formal resolution as "the word of the Lord to them, which they promised to accept and obey themselves, and would do all in their power to get the whole membership of the Church to do likewise."[25] President Snow was visibly affected. He arose and said: "Brethren, the God of our fathers, Abraham, Isaac and Jacob bless you. Every man who is here, who has made this promise, will be saved in the celestial kingdom. God bless you. Amen."[26]

A solemn assembly of priesthood leaders convened in the Salt Lake Temple on July 2. "The call for this assembly did not originate in his own mind," President Snow's son testified, "but as a command from the Lord who revealed it in vision." All the General Authorities were present, and all forty stakes were represented. During the session, which lasted from 10 A.M. to 7 P.M., each of the eighteen speakers referred to the renewed tithing revelation, which was again accepted as "the word and will of the Lord through President Snow to the Church."[27]

As a whole, the Saints in southern Utah faithfully accepted President Snow's challenge and gave much more than one-tenth of their income to the Lord's work. After some anxious weeks, the rains came and the crops were saved. Similarly, as the Saints in all areas of the Church faithfully complied with the law of tithing, the promised blessings were realized. The burden of debt was overcome. By 1907 Joseph F. Smith, Lorenzo Snow's successor, would announce that the increased tithes had enabled the Church to pay all its obligations. Since that time the Church has been able to remain free from debt, and tithing has continued to be the largest source of financial support.

Worldwide Mission of the Church

At the dawning of the twentieth century, President Lorenzo Snow was impressed with the urgency of proclaiming the gospel to all the world. To this end, in 1901 he appointed Elder Heber J. Grant of the Quorum of the Twelve to open a mission in Japan. Elder Grant selected three others to accompany him on this mission. Because of formidable cultural and language barriers, however, the fruits of

Elder Heber J. Grant dedicates Japan for the preaching of the gospel on Sunday, September 1, 1901. Accompanying Elder Grant on this wooded hillside south of Yokohama are (from left) Horace S. Ensign, Alma O. Taylor, and (far right) Louis B. Kelsch. (Used by permission, Utah State Historical Society, all rights reserved)

the Elders' labors were meager. Only after eighteen long months of tedious language study did the first pair of missionaries venture out among the Japanese people. Speaking in general conference upon his return in 1903, Elder Grant admitted, "To be perfectly frank with you, I acknowledge I have accomplished very little indeed." Only three converts had been baptized. "At the same time," he continued, "I have assurance in my heart there will yet be a great and important labor accomplished in that land."[28] These early missionaries had laid a foundation upon

which future growth would be built, although the work would not flourish in that land until after World War II.

President Snow regarded opening the mission in Japan as only the beginning of the Church's increased missionary efforts. He also had in mind carrying the gospel to Russia and Austria as well as to the republics of Latin America.

ROLE OF THE TWELVE AND THE SEVENTY

President Lorenzo Snow believed that two particular groups of the General Authorities had a special responsibility to take the lead in accomplishing the Church's worldwide mission. In 1901 he declared: "Here are the apostles and the seventies, their business is to warn the nations of the earth and prepare the world for the coming of the Savior. . . . We have started in this direction by sending Brother Grant over to Japan, but this is only a start. . . . Whether he will accomplish much or not matters not in one sense; it is for the apostles to show to the Lord that they are his witnesses to all the nations, and that they are doing the best they can."[29]

During the nineteenth century's era of colonization, Church leaders, particularly the Twelve, had become intimately involved in the administration of local Church affairs. But President Snow now became concerned at the amount of time the Twelve Apostles and also the Seventy were spending with auxiliary organizations such as the Young Men's Mutual Improvement Association. In his last public discourse President Snow stressed that the stake presidents should take on these local responsibilities because the Twelve and the Seventies were called, "*by the appointment of the Almighty, to look after the interests of the world*. The seventies and the twelve apostles are special witnesses unto the nations of the earth."[30]

Under the direction of these Church leaders, missions were organized in various parts of the world to carry on the work of preaching the gospel. In earlier decades, the Church's corps of proselyting missionaries was composed primarily of married men who left home to preach for relatively short periods of time. By the 1890s, however, young unmarried elders were much more common among the missionary ranks.

Although wives had sometimes been called to accompany their husbands into the mission field during earlier years, none had been officially designated as missionaries. In 1897, for example, Elizabeth Claridge McCune went with her family to Europe. She was not called as a missionary, but Lorenzo Snow blessed her, promising that "thy mind shall be as clear as an angel's when explaining the principles of the Gospel."[31] While there, she created many opportunities to share the gospel. The following year, President George Q. Cannon referred to the good work Elizabeth had done in England and announced, "It has been decided to call some of our wise and prudent women into the missionary field." The first sister to be officially set apart was Harriet Maria Horsepool Nye, wife of Ephraim H. Nye, then serving in San Francisco as president of the California mission.[32]

Inez Knight (pictured here) and Lucy Jane (Jennie) Brimhall were called by the First Presidency in 1897 as the first single lady missionaries. (Photographic Archives, Harold B. Lee Library, Brigham Young University, Provo, Utah)

Shortly afterwards the First Presidency approved the call of two single young women from Provo to become the first "lady missionaries." Lucy Jane (Jennie) Brimhall and Inez Knight were set apart to serve in the British mission. "Although we do not always have clear sailing and have even been forced to seek protection from mob violence in a police station, receiving the slurs of the mob and even spat upon by the enemy, together with rocks and sticks from their

Joseph F. Stimpson taught this Sunday School class in Kofu, Japan. This picture, taken in 1908, reflects some of the small successes enjoyed by early missionaries to Japan. (LDS Church Archives)

hands, yet we rejoice in the work," Sister Knight wrote from the mission field.[33] The Sisters filled a niche that the Elders could not, being invited to Manchester to visit with investigators "who entertained prejudiced ideas concerning Utah's women."[34]

Many of these new missionaries had the benefit of special missionary preparation courses at the Church's academies. Their work was further strengthened by a new series of tracts, "Rays of Living Light," authored by Elder Charles W. Penrose. These tracts formed the basis of "cottage meeting" discussions on gospel topics.

While responsibility for local Church activity was being shifted more squarely onto the shoulders of stake presidents and bishops, steps were being taken to make those units more efficient. Before the turn of the century, some stakes had been very large, having as many as twenty thousand members. The entire Salt Lake Valley, for example, was covered by one single stake. By 1904 this area had been divided into six stakes. Churchwide, the average stake soon had only about five thousand members, a figure which would remain fairly constant throughout much of the twentieth century.

A NEW EMPHASIS ON THE "GATHERING"

Consistent with President Snow's worldwide vision was a new understanding of the Saints' responsibility to "gather." During the nineteenth century, Mormon migration patterns had been dominated by a geographical gathering of thousands of converts from the nations of the earth to the centers of Latter-day Saint colonization in America. Early revelations proclaimed the importance of gathering: "Wherefore, prepare ye, prepare ye, O my people; sanctify yourselves; gather ye together, O ye people of my church, upon the land of Zion. . . . Go ye out of Babylon; gather ye out from among the nations" (D&C 133:4, 7). Such injunctions held great appeal for the Saints in the Old World. Many of them lived in grimy industrial cities, while others struggled to earn their living as landless tenant farmers. Most belonged to small, persecuted Mormon branches which typically met in dingy and inadequate rented halls. While most were leaving unsatisfactory economic conditions behind, many appear to have been motivated primarily by the desire to help establish Zion in the promised land.

Revelations given through Joseph Smith had anticipated that the "gathering" would have two phases. At first, the Saints were to be "gathered in unto one place" (D&C 29:8); however, the time would come when there would no longer be just one gathering place, but "other places" or "stakes" would be appointed for the "strength of Zion" (see D&C 101:20–22). This latter phase, typical of the twentieth century, would be more spiritual than geographical (see D&C 133:14). Though remaining in their homelands, Saints would "gather" out of the wicked world and become identified with the Saints.

Church leaders began discouraging geographical gathering during the 1890s, a decade of particularly severe economic depression in America. As historian Frederick Jackson Turner noted, 1890 had marked the end of the frontier and of readily available free land in America. Most immigrants, therefore, congregated in the cities; many failed to find work, became discouraged, and wanted to return home.[35]

At about the turn of the century, the General Authorities emphasized that instead of gathering into one place, now the important task was to build up the "other places" around the world.[36] "It looks to me that our minds ought to extend somewhat," President Snow challenged, "get out of the beaten track, and a little change be made."[37]

This advice would be reiterated in a 1921 editorial in the *Millennial Star*, the Church's British magazine: "The Counsel of The General Authorities to the yet ungathered Saints is not to flock Zionward under existing conditions; but to remain in the countries where they now dwell. . . . Such as have home and employment especially, should stay and help build up the Lord's work in the various missions and conferences and branches, strengthening the hands of the elders and other missionaries labouring among them."[38] The Church's counsel was reinforced by restrictive immigration laws adopted by the United States during the 1920s.

Lorenzo Snow presided over the Church for only three years. Nevertheless, his brief administration brought significant developments with far-reaching impact. Not only did his Presidency straddle the turn of the century, but it can be regarded as an era of transition for several other reasons: He was the last President to come from the same generation as the Church's founding prophet, Joseph Smith. He helped define the inspired principles that would continue to guide succession in the Presidency of the Church. Through him, the Lord called for a rededication to tithe-paying. President Snow proclaimed the Church's worldwide mission and took steps to achieve it.

Nevertheless, the transition was not yet complete. Many key developments were to take place during the administration of President Joseph F. Smith, who would see much progress, prosperity, and reform. However, he would also witness the resurgence of anti-Mormon agitation. These attacks were at least in part an outgrowth of the Progressive Era in America.

The Church in the Progressive Era

The opening years of the twentieth century are known in United States history as the Progressive Era. Under the leadership of United States president Theodore Roosevelt, reform legislation sought to remedy such problems as unregulated monopolies, the wasting of natural resources, and unclean conditions in food-packing plants. The press's sensational exposés of slums and a variety of other social evils earned the nicknames "yellow journalism" or "muckraking." This reform era had its roots just before the turn of the century, so it overlapped the administrations of Church Presidents Lorenzo Snow and Joseph F. Smith. In this setting, the elections to the United States Congress of two General Authorities, Elders B. H. Roberts and Reed Smoot, sparked a revival of earlier agitation against the Mormons.

The Saints' Involvement in Politics

The roots of nationwide anti-Mormon feelings go back at least to the midpoint of the nineteenth century. As part of the Compromise of 1850, Utah had been made a territory rather than a state. This meant that its key officials were appointed by the president of the United States rather than being elected by the people. Then, in 1852, the Church made the first public announcement of plural marriage. This practice became the focal point of attacks directed against the Latter-day Saints. The federally appointed officials allied themselves with the small

United States president Theodore Roosevelt in Salt Lake City in 1903. Roosevelt, a steadfast friend of the Saints, helped create a better public image for the Church. (LDS Church Archives)

RGETTS BROS

non-Mormon, or "gentile," minority in Utah to form the Liberal party and to effectively dominate the political scene. In response, the Mormon majority formed the People's party to preserve whatever vestige of local self-government they could. With political issues drawn along these lines during the later nineteenth century, the Church as an institution inevitably found itself involved in politics.

A series of anti-bigamy laws culminated in the Edmunds-Tucker Act of 1887. This harsh law not only punished those convicted of polygamous living but also restricted the Saints' participation in elections, disincorporated the Church as an institution, and provided for the seizure of its assets. In 1889 the United States Supreme Court upheld this law as constitutional. This posed a dilemma for the Latter-day Saints, who believed that the practice of plural marriage had been divinely revealed (see D&C 132), but who had been instructed to obey "the law of the land which is constitutional" (D&C 98:5). While praying for guidance, President Wilford Woodruff was shown that the work of the Church would be disrupted by its enemies if the practice of plural marriage continued. Hence, in 1890 he issued his inspired Official Declaration or Manifesto, declaring: "Inasmuch as laws have been enacted by Congress forbidding plural marriages, which laws have been pronounced constitutional by the court of last resort, I hereby declare my intention to submit to those laws. . . . And I now publicly declare that my advice to the Latter-day Saints is to refrain from contracting any marriage forbidden by the law of the land."[1]

A brief era of goodwill toward the Mormons followed the termination of plural marriages, and the long-sought-for goal of Utah's statehood now appeared attainable. Church leaders therefore disbanded the People's party and urged the Saints to identify themselves with one or another of the national political parties. With the ending of both polygamy and the Mormon political party, the way was cleared for Utah, January 1896, to be admitted into the Union as the forty-fifth state.

From the early days of the Church, Latter-day Saints had been taught to seek and uphold wise and good men (see D&C 98:10); and with the obtaining of statehood, they looked forward to becoming more involved in the political process. Because the Saints dominated the population of the new state, there were concerns that the Church and its leaders, general or local, would continue to dominate politics. For example, there were Church members who, "upon hearing a rumor that a candidate was the preference of some general authority, perceived it as a religious obligation to vote for that candidate whether his views corresponded to their interests or not."[2] Church leaders were sensitive to these concerns, so sought to monitor the involvement of Church officers in politics. In April 1896 they issued a "political manifesto." It declared "that before accepting any position, political or otherwise," that would interfere with a Church leader's carrying out his religious responsibilities, he should first consult with his ecclesiastical superiors to determine if he could "take upon himself the added duties and labors

Major developments in the Church, 1887–1917

1880 1890

1887
Edmunds-Tucker Law provided for confiscation of Church property and barred polygamists from voting or holding office

1890
President Woodruff's Manifesto announced the end of plural marriages

1896
Utah admitted as a state of the Union

1898
Lorenzo Snow became President of the Church

and responsibilities of the new position." Nevertheless, the manifesto insisted, "we do not in the least desire to dictate to them concerning their duties as American citizens."[3]

THE ROBERTS CASE

In this setting Utah democrats urged Elder Brigham H. Roberts, a member of the First Council of the Seventy, to run for Congress. Although Utah's constitution provided that new plural marriages should forever be prohibited, there was a general unwritten understanding that men who had already entered into plural marriage prior to the 1890 Manifesto would not be subject to prosecution and would not be required to abandon their plural families as long as they did not marry any additional wives. Elder Roberts had married all three of his wives before 1890, so party leaders were confident that there would be no problem. His nomination in 1898, however, brought the charge of a "reversion to polygamy." Protestant ministers led the attack, accusing the Church of a breach of faith by again attempting to control politics and by renewing the approval of polygamy. Church leaders emphatically denied these charges, and Roberts won the election easily.

His opponents, however, promoted a nationwide campaign against him. When he arrived in Washington, his right to a seat in Congress was challenged. A "monster" petition claiming over seven million signatures was presented, and the nation's newspapers and magazines were full of articles attacking Roberts and the Mormons. By a ratio of about five to one the House of Representatives voted for Roberts's exclusion, an action rarely taken in American history. It was evident that the Latter-day Saints had not yet been fully accepted and were still under the necessity of convincing the nation of their good faith. Elder Roberts was convinced that "the

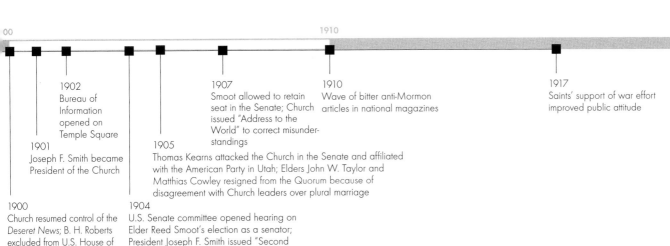

The election of Brigham H. Roberts, a member of the Council of the Seventy who had plural wives, to the U.S. House of Representatives in 1898 sparked nationwide controversy. (LDS Church Archives)

1900
Church resumed control of the *Deseret News*; B. H. Roberts excluded from U.S. House of Representatives

1901
Joseph F. Smith became President of the Church

1902
Bureau of Information opened on Temple Square

1904
U.S. Senate committee opened hearing on Elder Reed Smoot's election as a senator; President Joseph F. Smith issued "Second Manifesto" banning all new plural marriages

1905
Thomas Kearns attacked the Church in the Senate and affiliated with the American Party in Utah; Elders John W. Taylor and Matthias Cowley resigned from the Quorum because of disagreement with Church leaders over plural marriage

1907
Smoot allowed to retain seat in the Senate; Church issued "Address to the World" to correct misunderstandings

1910
Wave of bitter anti-Mormon articles in national magazines

1917
Saints' support of war effort improved public attitude

real cause of this anti-'Mormon' crusade was a fight for the political control of Utah on the part of the 'crusaders'" and that "their concern about the alleged evils of polygamy was mere pretense."[4]

THE SMOOT CASE

Elder Reed Smoot was elected to the United States Senate by Utah's Republican legislature in January 1903. Formerly a businessman in Provo and Salt Lake City, he had become a member of the Quorum of the Twelve Apostles in 1900. Even though he had obtained a "leave of absence" from his ecclesiastical duties, his election immediately revived the old charges of a violation of the proper separation of church and state. As they had done in the case of Elder Roberts four years earlier, Salt Lake City ministers, editors, and others mounted a nationwide campaign; and protests against Reed Smoot poured into the Senate from all parts of the country. However, Elder Smoot was sworn in as a senator and allowed to take his seat. Nevertheless, the Committee on Privileges and Elections was authorized to conduct a thorough investigation of the whole affair and to determine whether or not he was qualified to remain in the Senate. In the resulting hearings, not only Smoot, but the whole Mormon Church was subjected to intense scrutiny—perhaps "the longest and most thorough investigation of any religious body in the history of the United States."[5]

President William Howard Taft (left) and Senator Reed Smoot share the same car in a parade in Salt Lake City. (Used by permission, Utah State Historical Society, all rights reserved)

The committee's chairman was Senator Julius C. Burrows of Michigan. His grandfather had been a member of the Church during the days of the Prophet Joseph Smith and had marched with Zion's Camp in 1834, but was subsequently excommunicated. This family background may have added to Senator Burrow's prejudice against the Latter-day Saints.[6]

The Smoot hearings did not get under way until January 1904. A parade of witnesses levied a variety of charges against the Mormon senator, notably that the practice of polygamy had not been abandoned and that the Church still dominated life in Utah. The accusation of polygamy was easily dismissed, as Elder Smoot was a monogamist. Nevertheless, Smoot was alleged to be a member of a "self-perpetuating body of fifteen men" (the First Presidency and the Twelve) who controlled Utah's economy and politics and secretly encouraged the continued practice of plural marriage. He was also accused of having taken a secret oath of disloyalty to the United States. Senator Smoot responded by emphazing the legality of his election. Numerous and varied witnesses were called by both sides. Even Church President Joseph F. Smith was required to testify. For three days he frankly admitted that he was still living with his plural wives (whom he had married before the 1890 Manifesto) and answered other prying questions about his personal life and sacred aspects of his religion. He stressed that Latter-day Saints are not obligated to accept as doctrine the political opinions of prominent Church leaders. President Smith believed that, when his testimony began, all the senators except one were unfriendly, but that he had won the respect of several others before he was through.

The committee's hearings dragged on for two and a half years; a report of the proceedings filled more than thirty-four hundred pages in four large volumes. As with the Roberts case, the press widely reported the hearings, but unfortunately it generally emphasized only the more sensational aspects of the testimony and those which were less favorable to the Church. Finally, in June 1906, the committee concluded that Reed Smoot was not entitled to serve as a senator. Eight committee members, including Burrows, voted for this majority report. A minority of five others, however, believed that no just grounds had been found to disqualify or expel Smoot.

A 1910 rally at the county building in Provo in support of the seating of U.S. senator Reed Smoot. The participants show their displeasure with Frank J. Cannon, editor of the Salt Lake Tribune, *who authored a number of editorials and magazine articles that sharply criticized Smoot and the Church. (Used by permission, Utah State Historical Society, all rights reserved)*

*Elders Matthias F. Cowley (pictured here) and John W. Taylor, members of the Quorum of the Twelve, believed that polygamy could still be practiced outside of the United States. Because of their persistence, Church leaders eventually asked for their resignations from the apostleship. (*Deseret News *photo)*

Six months passed before the Senate chose to consider the committee's report. From December 13, 1906, to February 20, 1907, Reed Smoot's fate was debated in the Senate. One senator is reported to have quipped: "I don't see why we can't get along just as well with a polygamist who doesn't polyg as we do with a lot of monogamists who don't monog!"[7] A two-thirds vote was required to approve the committee's recommendation to oust Smoot. When the vote was taken, twenty-eight voted in favor of the recommendation, forty-two voted against, and twenty abstained. Thus Elder Smoot had received the support of 60 percent of those voting. They had determined that he personally was not guilty of any criminal offense and anticipated that his influence as an Apostle might be an advantage to the Republican party in Utah.[8] Reed Smoot went on to a distinguished thirty-year career in the Senate, earning the respect of his colleagues with his personal integrity and hard work. He would play a particularly influential role as chairman of the Senate Finance Committee.

Revival of Anti-Mormon Agitation

Even though Elder Reed Smoot had been allowed to retain his seat in the Senate, the prolonged debate demonstrated that certain questions continued to trouble the general public. The elections of Roberts and Smoot provided the occasion for a revival of attacks directed against the Church and its members. In the spirit of the Progressive Era, "muckraking" journalists dwelled on what they called the twin relics of Mormonism—polygamy and hierarchy. *Polygamy*, of course, referred to the alleged continuation of plural marriages, and *hierarchy* to the undue influence Church leaders were accused of exerting over secular affairs, including political and economic concerns. The phrase "twin relics" was borrowed from a plank in the 1856 Republican party platform that promised to eradicate "the twin relics of barbarism—slavery and polygamy."

THE QUESTION OF CONTINUED POLYGAMY

It was only natural that the practice of plural marriage would be difficult for many Mormons to give up. Since it had become so much a part of the belief and personal lives of the individual members of the Church, it was not to be expected that everyone involved would suddenly change their feelings, even though the change of practice had been required by the President of the Church.

Mormon polygamy had been a prominent topic in the Smoot hearings, but Church witnesses emphasized that no new plural marriages were being authorized and that by 1902 there were only 897 polygamous families, in contrast to the 2,451 that had existed in 1890. The Senate committee's investigation, however, disclosed that new polygamous marriages actually had been performed by certain leaders of the Church since the Manifesto. Specifically involved were two Apostles, John W. Taylor and Matthias F. Cowley. Both men believed that the Manifesto applied only to members of the Church living within the United States.

As a result, just a few weeks after his appearance before the Senate committee in Washington, President Smith, at the 1904 April conference, issued an official statement sometimes called the "Second Manifesto": "I hereby announce that all such marriages are prohibited, and if any officer or member of the Church shall assume to solemnize or enter into any such marriages he will be deemed in transgression against the Church and will be liable to be dealt with, according to the rules and regulations thereof, and excommunicated therefrom."[9]

This new statement specifically stressed that the ban on plural marriage applied worldwide and that no new plural marriages would be authorized anywhere, even in the Mormon colonies of Mexico and Canada. President Smith also directed that the 1890 Manifesto be included in the Doctrine and Covenants; this answered critics who had pointed out that the Doctrine and Covenants included the revelation authorizing plural marriages but did not include the declaration suspending them. The problem remained, however, as some members, including Elders Cowley and Taylor, still refused to accept the new position as binding. In October 1905 the First Presidency took the very unusual step of asking for their resignations. Elder Taylor acknowledged that he was out of harmony with the General Authorities' interpretation of the 1890 Manifesto. He held that: "the term, 'laws of the land' in the manifesto meant merely the laws of the United States," so that the prohibition against polygamy did not extend worldwide. He conceded that this broader interpretation had "been given by President Woodruff and others" but insisted that their views were not "binding upon me or the Church, because it was never presented for adoption by 'common consent,' as was the manifesto itself."[10]

Several groups continued to insist that plural marriage was an essential doctrine and continued to perform such marriages. On several subsequent occasions during the twentieth century, the First Presidency denounced these so-called fundamentalists, and the Church's policy has been to excommunicate anyone practicing plural marriage.

ALLEGED CHURCH INFLUENCE

Thomas Kearns was a leading source of anti-Mormon agitation. Kearns, a non-Mormon, served as a senator from Utah along with Reed Smoot. In 1904 Kearns played a key role in organizing the American Party in Utah, of which he became a major financial backer. This was actually a revival of the old anti-Mormon Liberal party. Reasons for organizing the new party came from charges in the Reed Smoot hearings of continued polygamy and Church interference in politics. Supporters of Kearns and the American Party, however, did not do well in that year's election.

Early in 1905, in a speech made to the Senate near the end of his term, Thomas Kearns bitterly attacked Mormon leaders, branding them as a "monarchy" that dominated the political, business, and social life in Utah and secretly permitted their "favorites" to continue taking plural wives. The reason for Kearns's bitterness, historian B. H. Roberts

Thomas Kearns, a non-Mormon U.S. senator from Utah, led anti-Mormon attacks in Utah by organizing the American Party and purchasing the Salt Lake Tribune, *which almost daily published attacks against the Church. (LDS Church Archives)*

believed, was President Joseph F. Smith's refusal to help reelect the senator.[11] Ironically, Kearns was now attacking the very ecclesiastical influence that he himself had unsuccessfully attempted to gain.

Kearns had also purchased the *Salt Lake Tribune*. After the 1904 election, he named Frank J. Cannon as editor, who earlier had been an influential Mormon but was now an embittered enemy of the Church. Under their leadership, the *Tribune* defamed the Church and specifically President Joseph F. Smith on an almost daily basis. Some commented that the infamous *Nauvoo Expositor* was "holy writ" when compared to the *Tribune*.

Another Salt Lake paper, the *Deseret News*, was a key medium through which the Church answered these attacks and proclaimed its message. While President Lorenzo Snow had generally desired to sell businesses in which the Church had earlier invested, he saw the value of maintaining an active interest in this newspaper—especially amidst the discussions surrounding Elder Roberts's election to the House of Representatives. Charles W. Penrose, an experienced and capable journalist, served as the paper's editor. The *Deseret News* came to be recognized as the Church's official newspaper voice, and Penrose (who became a member of the Quorum of the Twelve in 1904) made a substantial contribution in defending the Church.

By 1906 the value of having Reed Smoot in the Senate had become apparent, but some still questioned the wisdom of his running for reelection. Charles W. Nibley, who would soon become Presiding Bishop of the Church, raised some of these doubts with President Joseph F. Smith as they stood on the deck of a ship en route home from Europe. After listening to Nibley's points, President Smith emphatically brought his fist down on the rail and insisted, "If I have ever had the inspiration of the spirit of the Lord given to me forcefully and clearly it has been on this one point concerning Reed Smoot, and that is, instead of his being retired, he should be continued in the United States Senate." Nibley promptly retracted his concerns.[12]

SOME LINGERING ATTACKS

Many of the charges published in the *Salt Lake Tribune* were picked up by national periodicals. The years 1910 and 1911 brought a revival of anti-Mormon writings. Four popular magazines particularly involved were *Pearson's*, *Everybody's*, *McClure's*, and *Cosmopolitan*. Sensationalized denunciations of the Church and its leaders demonstrated a generally antagonistic view of the Latter-day Saints. A particularly negative series of articles appeared in *Cosmopolitan* during 1911. The first of these, entitled "The Viper on the Hearth," was headed with an illustration of a huge snake coiled around a defenseless family. The writer asserted that the viper was the Mormon Church, preparing for the time when it could inflict a fatal strike on the family structure of America and take over the nation both politically and economically. Another cartoon in the series depicted President Joseph F. Smith as the head of a huge octopus whose tentacles were reaching out to grasp education, industry, the government, and so on.

Published in nationally circulated magazines, such articles did much to hurt the Church's image. They were often filled with obvious distortions of the facts. For example, the writer of "The Viper on the Hearth," who claimed to have spent several months among the Mormons researching his articles, asserted that the Saints believed that Urim and Thummim were two "stenographic angels" who aided Joseph Smith in translating the Book of Mormon.[13]

President Smith chose not to respond to such charges, but insisted that he bore "no malice" toward those who spoke "only evil of the Latter-day Saints. . . . I forgive them for this. I leave them in the hands of the just Judge."[14]

OPPOSITION OVERSEAS

In Europe the Church also lacked general public acceptance. Negative stories circulated by the clergy and printed in newspapers created suspicion and ill will. Missionaries frequently reported being criticized, being driven out of town, and even having stones thrown at them. In 1906, the German government decreed that Mormon teachings were "subversive of morality" and ordered the Church to withdraw from the country. This forced the eight thousand German Saints to conduct the Church activities in Germany themselves. By 1910, however, a few missionaries had returned to various parts of Germany.

A special conference directed by Elder Rudger Clawson of the Twelve convened in Berlin on July 21, 1910. "The hall was crowded with saints and friends, but the occasion was greatly marred by the entrance of several police who unceremoniously and defiant to politeness interrupted President Clawson's speech and closed the meeting."[15] The German members were permitted to leave, but the missionaries, the mission president, and even Elder Clawson were held and then banished from the country.

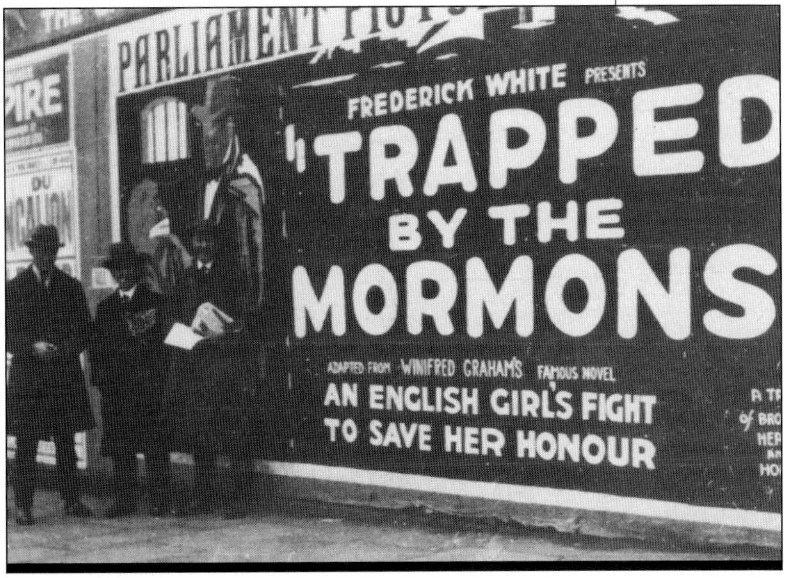

Missionaries pose by the side of an advertisement for Trapped by the Mormons, *a 1922 film that depicted Mormon missionaries as evil men trying to seduce young women away from their homes. (LDS Church Archives)*

In Europe as in America, the supposed continuation of plural marriages was a popular theme in attacks against the Church. Reports from the American "muckraking" magazine crusade reached Great Britain at a time when British conservatives were speaking out against the erosion of traditional Victorian virtues. British Latter-day Saints shared conservatives' concerns over growing immorality, abortion, and divorce. Ironically, certain crusaders made Mormons their symbol of immoral living, and the evils of polygamy became a central theme of their lectures and rallies. Some novels and movies followed the fictional plight of an innocent young heroine kidnapped by, and then rescued from, a crafty American missionary. In a few isolated areas emotions ran so high that anti-Mormon rallies turned to violence. Mud and rocks were hurled at chapels in Birkenhead and Nuncaton, a branch president was tarred and feathered, and missionaries were harassed out of town. In the face of such agitation, the level of convert baptisms dropped during the second decade of the twentieth century. Nevertheless, there were some sympathetic newspapers willing to publish the Church's response to such attacks. The *London Evening Times*, for example, carried a statement by the First Presidency explaining the Church's basic teachings and its stand on emigration and plural marriage.[16]

Efforts to Create More Favorable Attitudes

The magazine crusade, together with earlier sensational publicity during the Roberts and Smoot elections, reinforced the negative public attitudes about Mormons and Mormonism that had lingered from the nineteenth century. That had been an era of ignorance and persecution. There had been almost no contact between the main body of the Latter-day Saints and the public as a whole. In such a setting, misrepresentations were accepted as fact because most people had no personal experience with Mormons to suggest otherwise. During the opening years of the twentieth century, however, the Church took steps to remedy the problem, resulting in some improvement.

THE FIRST BUREAU OF INFORMATION

At the turn of the century, even those who came to Salt Lake City might not hear the truth about the Latter-day Saints. Hotel operators would send employees with carriages to meet incoming trains

The Tabernacle Choir at a performance in New York City in 1911. The choir's eastern tour helped turn the public's attention away from the mounting criticism in national magazines. (LDS Church Archives)

Temple Square in Salt Lake City soon after the Bureau of Information opened in 1902. The Bureau of Information was created to counter the negative popular image of the Church. (LDS Church Archives)

and vie for guests. These hack drivers made quite a business of filling visitors with wild tales about the Mormons. Both community and Church leaders were concerned about the negative image this practice created. Discussions among members of the Young Men's Mutual Improvement Association general board and the First Council of the Seventy resulted in the specific recommendation that a "bureau of information" be established on Temple Square to provide correct information to those visiting the city. In 1902 the First Presidency approved this project and assigned the Seventy to take charge of it. The first building was an octagonal structure measuring twenty feet across and costing six hundred dollars. About two dozen volunteers staffed the bureau; during the year they distributed Articles of Faith cards and other literature to 150,000 visitors. At last visitors to Salt Lake City were learning about the Mormons from the Mormons themselves.

A new nine-thousand dollar building was erected in 1904. Popularity of the guided tours of Temple Square continued to grow, and in 1906 free organ recitals were added. As the number of visitors continued to increase, ever more commodious facilities were provided.

THE "ADDRESS TO THE WORLD"

In April 1907, just a few weeks after the Senate finally voted to allow Elder Reed Smoot to retain his seat, the Church took another step in presenting its case to the public. The First Presidency's sixteen-page "Address to the World" was adopted by unanimous vote in general conference. This powerful yet conciliatory statement emphatically denied the charges made against the Church, and clearly set forth its major doctrines, ideals, and aspirations. It declared that Mormonism respected the sanctity of marriage, that it opposed tyranny, that its tithes were not used for the benefit of the leaders, that the Church believed in and upheld constitutional governments, and that the Church had long since abandoned plural marriage. A group of Utah ministers published a review criticizing the Church's address, but their efforts received little attention and had minimal effect.[17]

SOME POSITIVE SIGNS

When, in 1911, the Mormon Tabernacle Choir accepted an invitation to sing at an exposition in New York City, an eastern tour was planned. Thus, at the peak of the "magazine crusade," the choir presented more than four dozen concerts in twenty-five cities, spending ten days at Madison Square Garden in New York City and having an appearance at the White House in Washington, D.C. The choir was well received, and favorable comments by music critics helped contribute to an improving image of the Latter-day Saints.

An important opportunity to present correct information about the Church came when the editors of *Americana* magazine invited Elder B. H. Roberts to respond to some false information published earlier in their *American Historical Magazine.* Theodore Schroeder, an attorney who led anti-Mormon attacks in Salt Lake City, had revived the "long-discredited" theory that Joseph Smith had based the Book of Mormon on a historical romantic novel written in about 1812 by Solomon Spaulding.[18] The editors were so pleased with Elder Roberts's response that they invited him to prepare a more thorough explanation of the Church's origins and history. When Elder Roberts discussed the scope of the proposed project with them, they agreed to expand their magazine from a bimonthly to a monthly publication and to devote most of its space to the Mormon articles. Roberts's history appeared serially from 1909 to 1915 and was later published in book form.[19]

The former president of the United States, Theodore Roosevelt, also advanced a more positive view of the Latter-day Saints when, in 1911, he published a letter in *Collier's* magazine describing his favorable relations with the Saints. He characterized the allegation that he had made political deals with the Mormons as being so "ludicrous that it is difficult to discuss it seriously." He also strongly proclaimed the virtues of the Saints, "whose standard of domestic life and morality and whose attitude toward the relations of men and women was as high as that of the best citizens of any other creed; indeed, among these 'Mormons' the standard of sexual morality was unusually high."[20] In Great Britain, an investigation initiated by Home Secretary Winston Churchill put to rest false reports that had been circulating about the Mormons in that land. The interest of such influential individuals as Roosevelt and Churchill augured well for a growing spirit of fairness in dealing with the Church and its members.

Another reflection of the changing situation was a statement made in 1916 by Charles C. Goodwin. Goodwin, who in earlier years as editor of the *Salt Lake Tribune* had been an outspoken enemy of the Church, wrote: "A more kindly and benevolent man has seldom held an exalted ecclesiastical position in these latter days than President Joseph F. Smith. . . . To his people he is a great spiritual leader. To men at large he is a man of wide sympathies, great business acumen and a born leader of the great institution of which he is the head."[21]

Thus the opening years of the twentieth century saw The Church of Jesus Christ of Latter-day Saints overcome problems that had persisted for years—debt, political exclusion, and a poor public image. But this was not all. At the same time there were many other positive and far-reaching developments in the Church taking place under the leadership of President Joseph F. Smith.

Joseph F. Smith and an Era of Transition

President Joseph F. Smith led the Church during most of the twentieth century's first two decades. His administration as well as his personal life represented important links with the past and the future.

Joseph F. Smith's Earlier Life

Joseph F. Smith was born in Far West, Missouri, on November 13, 1838, in the midst of one of the most bitter periods of anti-Mormon persecution. His parents were Hyrum and Mary Fielding Smith. Within his first year, the Saints had been driven from Missouri and had commenced to build the city of Nauvoo in Illinois. He was only five years old when his father, Hyrum, and his uncle, the Prophet Joseph Smith, were martyred in Carthage Jail. The impression of this personal tragedy would remain with him throughout his life.

In 1848 he helped his widowed mother drive an ox team across the plains to Utah, performing most of the duties of a man. On one occasion their oxen were lost and could not be found despite a diligent search. While praying for help, his mother suddenly arose from her knees and began walking toward a nearby river, even though she had been told that her oxen had been seen earlier in the opposite direction. She found them in a deep gulch by the riverbank, perfectly concealed from view. "This circumstance," Joseph later reflected, "was one of the first practical and positive demonstrations of the efficacy of

A 1920s photograph looking south on downtown Salt Lake City and the Salt Lake Valley. Notable buildings include (from left to right) the Utah State Capitol Building, the Church Administration Building, the Hotel Utah, and the Salt Lake Temple. (Used by permission, Utah State Historical Society, all rights reserved)

prayer I had ever witnessed. It made an indelible impression upon my mind and has been a source of comfort, assurance and guidance to me throughout my life."[1]

After arriving in Utah, the family settled on a farm just southeast of Salt Lake City. The heavy responsibilities carried by Widow Smith weakened her physically, and she died in 1852, leaving her children orphaned.

Two years later, a fifteen-year-old Joseph was called to fulfill a mission to the Hawaiian Islands. As Elder Parley P. Pratt set the youth apart, he promised him that he would learn the Hawaiian language "by the gift of God as well as by study."[2] In fulfillment of this blessing, Joseph was able to learn the language in only three months. "My desire to speak was very strong," he later recorded; "it was present with me night and day, and I never permitted an opportunity of talking with the natives to pass without improving it. I also tried to exercise faith before the Lord to obtain the gift of talking and understanding the language."[3] He declared that he could teach the gospel and perform ordinances "with greater ease" in Hawaiian than he could in English. During his three years in Hawaii the young missionary had to overcome severe and prolonged illness, but had the opportunity to heal the sick, cast out devils, and to preside over several branches of the Church. These trying as well as rewarding experiences helped him to develop an even stronger faith in his Heavenly Father and a lasting love for the Hawaiian people.

Joseph F. Smith was ordained an Apostle in 1866 and served in the leading councils of the Church for more than fifty years. (Used by permission, Utah State Historical Society, all rights reserved)

During the following decade, he served a mission to Britain and another to Hawaii. He also married, went to work in the Church historian's office, and obtained a position in the territorial legislature.

In 1866, at the age of only twenty-seven, Joseph F. Smith was ordained an Apostle by President Brigham Young, and served briefly as one of his special additional counselors. When a vacancy occurred in the Twelve the following year, Elder Smith was sustained as a member of that quorum.

During the next decade and a half, Elder Joseph F. Smith was called to preside over settlements in Utah and Davis counties respectively, to serve twice as president of the European Mission, and to direct the work in the Endowment House. One of his most interesting assignments came in 1878. He was appointed to go east with Elder Orson Pratt to

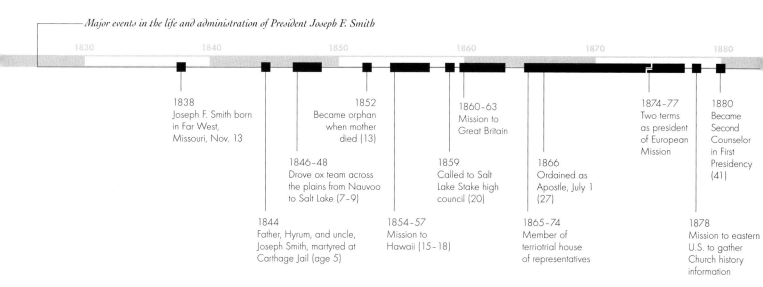

Major events in the life and administration of President Joseph F. Smith

1830 · 1840 · 1850 · 1860 · 1870 · 1880

- 1838 — Joseph F. Smith born in Far West, Missouri, Nov. 13
- 1844 — Father, Hyrum, and uncle, Joseph Smith, martyred at Carthage Jail (age 5)
- 1846–48 — Drove ox team across the plains from Nauvoo to Salt Lake (7–9)
- 1852 — Became orphan when mother died (13)
- 1854–57 — Mission to Hawaii (15–18)
- 1859 — Called to Salt Lake Stake high council (20)
- 1860–63 — Mission to Great Britain
- 1865–74 — Member of terriotrial house of representatives
- 1866 — Ordained as Apostle, July 1 (27)
- 1874–77 — Two terms as president of European Mission
- 1878 — Mission to eastern U.S. to gather Church history information
- 1880 — Became Second Counselor in First Presidency (41)

gather up records and data relative to the early history of the Church. They first went to Missouri, where they visited the temple site in Independence and had several valuable conversations with David Whitmer, one of the Three Witnesses to the Book of Mormon, in nearby Richmond. They visited Elder Smith's birthplace in Far West and stopped at other places in Illinois before going on to Kirtland, Palmyra, the Hill Cumorah, and New York City. On their way back west, they contacted Elder Smith's cousin, Joseph Smith III, the president of the Reorganized Church. This trip heightened Joseph F. Smith's interest in Church history sites, many of which he was later instrumental in purchasing.

When the First Presidency was reorganized in 1880, three years following the death of Brigham Young, George Q. Cannon became the First Counselor and Joseph F. Smith the Second Counselor to President John Taylor. These same two men later served as counselors to Presidents Wilford Woodruff and Lorenzo Snow, the only time that the same two individuals served as counselors to three Presidents of the Church.

Unfortunately, Joseph F. Smith's service in the First Presidency was seriously hampered by the persecution of the Saints over their practice of plural marriage. (He had married six wives and eventually became the father of forty-three children, plus five who were adopted.) Because of the Edmunds-Tucker Act, he had to go into "exile" or "retirement" from 1884 to 1891. During this trying period he visited outlying settlements and otherwise served the Church as best he could. In 1888, for example, he was sent to Washington, D.C., to represent the Church there. He was accompanied by Charles W. Penrose, the editor of the *Deseret News.* Because of the intense prejudice against Mormons, the two men had to travel under assumed names—President Smith being known as Jason Mack (the name of his great-uncle) and Brother Penrose as Charles Williams. During an interview, Grover Cleveland, the president of the United States, counseled them that if the Mormons would do away with the doctrines of prophets and revelation, abandon the practice of plural marriage, and become like everybody else, all difficulties would disappear. The brethren agreed that the predicted result would follow if they did what the president said, "but to follow such counsel was to destroy the Church and bring to naught the work which the Lord planted in the earth never again to be taken away or destroyed."[4]

Joseph F. Smith did not come out of hiding until the proclamation of amnesty in 1891. At the October 1891 general conference the complete First Presidency was seated together on the stand for the first time in seven and a half years. The changing attitude toward the Saints during the 1890s was reflected in the fact that Joseph F. Smith, who had so recently spent seven years in exile, was now invited to participate in the convention called to draw up a constitution for the new state of Utah. However, this decade was only a brief lull in the storm of anti-Mormon persecution, which became the primary challenge facing Joseph F. Smith during his presidency.

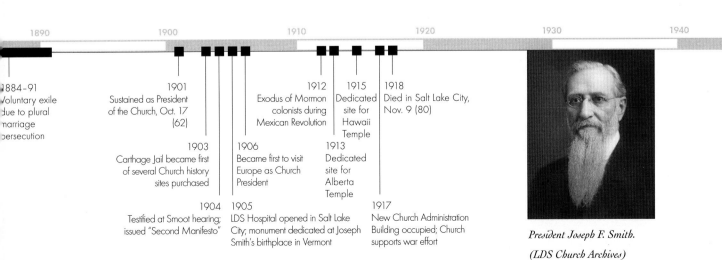

1890 1900 1910 1920 1930 1940

1884–91 Voluntary exile due to plural marriage persecution

1901 Sustained as President of the Church, Oct. 17 (62)

1903 Carthage Jail became first of several Church history sites purchased

1904 Testified at Smoot hearing; issued "Second Manifesto"

1905 LDS Hospital opened in Salt Lake City; monument dedicated at Joseph Smith's birthplace in Vermont

1906 Became first to visit Europe as Church President

1912 Exodus of Mormon colonists during Mexican Revolution

1913 Dedicated site for Alberta Temple

1915 Dedicated site for Hawaii Temple

1917 New Church Administration Building occupied; Church supports war effort

1918 Died in Salt Lake City, Nov. 9 (80)

President Joseph F. Smith.
(LDS Church Archives)

The Sacred Grove, near Palmyra, New York, where God the Father and Jesus Christ appeared to fourteen-year-old Joseph Smith. Early on in the twentieth century, the Church purchased the Smith homestead, which included the Sacred Grove. (LDS Church Archives)

President Lorenzo Snow died on October 10, 1901. Just one week later the Apostles met and sustained Joseph F. Smith as the sixth President of the Church. He and his counselors were sustained at a special conference that convened in the Tabernacle on November 10.

Renewed Prosperity Opens Opportunities

Being the father of a large family taught Joseph F. Smith prudent financial practices. This, plus his experience as counselor to three former Church Presidents, helped prepare him to direct the financial affairs of the Church.

As the Saints faithfully continued to pay their tithes, the Church was able to pay off all its debt by the end of 1906. It was with justifiable pride that President Smith could announce at the following April general conference: "Today the Church of Jesus Christ of Latter-day Saints owes not a dollar that it cannot pay at once. At last we are in a position that we can pay as we go. We do not have to borrow any more, and we wont have to if the Latter-day Saints continue to live their religion and observe the law of tithing. It is the law of revenue to the Church."[5] This ushered in a period of prosperity that enabled the Church to undertake activities not possible when the Saints were saddled with the burden of debt.

The Carthage Jail in Illinois, where a mob killed the Prophet Joseph Smith and his brother Hyrum. The purchase of the jail and the surrounding acres in 1904 represented the first of many important Church history sites acquired by the Church under the administration of President Joseph F. Smith. (LDS Church Archives)

SIGNIFICANT HISTORICAL SITES

The fact that Joseph F. Smith had personally lived through many significant events undoubtedly intensified his interest in Church history. During his administration the Church for the first time had the funds to begin purchasing important historical sites. These acquisitions would help new generations of Latter-day Saints more fully appreciate their religious heritage and spiritual roots.

The first site purchased was Carthage Jail in Illinois, where the Prophet Joseph Smith and his brother Hyrum had been martyred in 1844. When Joseph F. Smith visited the site of his father's murder, he remarked to Presiding Bishop Charles W. Nibley, "Charley, I despise this place. It harrows up my feelings to come here."[6] Nevertheless, under his direction two acres including the jail were purchased on November 5, 1903, at a cost of four thousand dollars.

The Church also purchased the one hundred acres that constituted the Smith homestead in Manchester township near Palmyra, New York. This property included the Sacred Grove, where the Prophet received the First Vision in 1820. It also included the Smiths' frame home, which was just being built in 1823 at the time Moroni appeared to the young Prophet in the family's original log home just down the road. In 1915 the Church called newlyweds Willard and Rebecca Bean on a mission to Palmyra for "five years or longer." They actually remained twenty-four years. Living in the Smith home, they overcame opposition and gained respect for the Church at its birthplace.[7]

Through four separate transactions between 1905 and 1907 the Church purchased the homestead of the Mack family (Joseph Smith's maternal ancestors) and some adjoining property, totaling 283 acres. This included the site of the Prophet's birth. A "memorial cottage" or small visitors' center was constructed on the site. Nearby, an imposing monument of polished Vermont granite was erected to honor the Prophet Joseph Smith, one foot in height for each of his thirty-eight-and-a-half years. It was dedicated by President Joseph F. Smith on December 23, 1905, the one-hundredth anniversary of the Prophet's birth.

Another significant acquisition was in Independence, Jackson County, Missouri, identified by revelation as the center place for the latter-day Zion. A tract of twenty-five acres was acquired on April 14, 1904. It was part of the original sixty-three acres

Missionaries in 1911 pose before the monument of the birthplace of Joseph Smith. President Joseph F. Smith dedicated the monument in 1905, on the centennial anniversary of Joseph Smith's birth. (Used by permission, Utah State Historical Society, all rights reserved)

purchased by the Saints in 1831, and it lies adjacent to the temple site Joseph Smith dedicated there. A chapel and a mission home for the Central States Mission were subsequently erected on this property. The Church also established Zion's Printing and Publishing Company here. From this publishing house countless tracts, pamphlets, books, and other religious literature were furnished to the Latter-day Saint missions of North America. This operation continued until the 1940s, when it was consolidated with the Deseret News Press in Salt Lake City.

The final Church history site purchased during the twentieth century's first decade was at Far West in northern Missouri. Here, under unusually trying circumstances, the Twelve had dedicated a temple site in 1839 in compliance with a revealed command of the Lord.[8]

These sites not only helped Latter-day Saints appreciate their own heritage, but they also enabled the Church to reach nonmembers with the message of the Restoration. At several of these locations, visitors' centers, known as "bureaus of information," were patterned after the successful effort on Salt Lake's Temple Square.

President Joseph F. Smith also encouraged the work of the Church historian's office. For example, Elder B. H. Roberts, one of the assistant Church historians, was assigned to annotate and update Joseph Smith's narrative as originally published in Church periodicals during the 1840s and 1850s. Roberts explained that the resulting seven-volume work was more in the nature of a chronological account than a history written "in the ordinary way."[9] Because Joseph Smith's work was a compilation of "personal journal annals" and of early primary documents, it was often referred to as the *Documentary History of the Church*, abbreviated *DHC*.[10] It's official title, however, was simply *History of the Church*, now more commonly abbreviated *HC*. This work should not be confused with the multivolume publication of Elder Roberts's *Americana* articles containing more traditional historical analysis and scholarship; these appeared at the time of the Church's centennial in 1930 under the title *A Comprehensive History of the Church.* "Though B. H. Roberts did not claim professional status as a historian," his biographer points out, "he is probably best known for the writing of history, which consumed much of his life."[11]

IMPORTANT BUILDING PROJECTS

The Church's building program particularly benefitted from the new era of prosperity. New buildings included many local meetinghouses as well as several key structures at or near Church headquarters. In 1905 the William S. Groves Latter-day Saints Hospital opened in Salt Lake City. Construction was financed primarily by general Church funds, to which was added a substantial donation from the estate of Dr. Groves. This facility was the first in what would become a system of Church-operated hospitals during the twentieth century.

To finance charitable enterprises such as the LDS Hospital, as well as the Church's religious programs, President Joseph F. Smith followed the policy of making selected investments. For example, the Church maintained or acquired control of the *Deseret News,* Zion's Savings Bank and Trust Company, Utah-Idaho Sugar, and Beneficial Life Insurance Company. It also purchased about 25 percent of the ZCMI stock. In 1919 the Deseret Sunday School Union Bookstore and the Deseret News Bookstore combined to form the Church-operated Deseret Book Company.

An ambulance of the William H. Groves Latter-day Saints Hospital. The hospital, established in 1905, was the first of several Church-operated hospitals. (Deseret News *photo)*

Among the many building projects completed in downtown Salt Lake City in the early decades of the twentieth century was the impressive Hotel Utah. (LDS Church Archives)

One of the Church's largest and most controversial investments during this period was in the construction of the Hotel Utah, which opened across the street from Temple Square in 1911. Speaking in general conference, President Smith justified the Church's interest in this venture. He quoted an 1841 revelation and explained that the Hotel Utah would fulfill a function similar to that specified for the Nauvoo House—it would be a "resting-place for the weary traveler, that he might contemplate the glory of Zion" (D&C 124:60). Responding to criticism that liquor was sold in the hotel, President Smith explained that the hotel was operated by an independent corporation, and took the occasion to urge the Saints to continue to faithfully observe the Word of Wisdom.[12] In 1910, just behind the Hotel Utah, the Church opened the Deseret Gymnasium to meet the recreational needs of the Salt Lake community and the Saints in general.

One of the Church's most critical building needs was for adequate office space. For many years the work of the General Authorities, auxiliaries, and other Church organizations had been conducted from offices scattered around downtown Salt Lake City. The new Bishop's Building, dedicated in 1910 and located directly across the street from the Salt Lake Temple, provided accommodations for the Presiding Bishopric and most of the auxiliary organizations. Seven years later the Church Administration Building was opened at 47 East South Temple Street. This handsome five-story granite structure featured fine marble and woodwork

Completed in 1917, the Church Administration Building provided much-needed office space for General Authorities and other Church leadership. (Used by permission, Utah State Historical Society, all rights reserved)

interiors. Although some critics described this building as too lavish, it provided dignified accommodations for the General Authorities and symbolized the Church's strength and stability. It also provided badly needed space for the Church historian's office and the Genealogical Society.[13]

The Saints Abroad

President Joseph F. Smith shared President Lorenzo Snow's understanding of the Church's worldwide mission. As he continued to encourage the Saints to remain and build up the Church in their homelands, Latter-day Saint missions and branches expanded abroad. This expansion was reflected in Joseph F. Smith's becoming the first President of the Church to visit Europe.

During several weeks in 1906, he visited the missions in the Netherlands, Germany, Switzerland, France, and England. President Smith's visit did much to strengthen the Church in these lands. Inspirational events bolstered the Saints' faith. In Rotterdam, Holland, he gave a blessing restoring full sight to a faithful eleven-year-old boy who had declared that he believed "the Prophet has the most power of any missionary on earth" and that if "he will look into my eyes I believe they will be healed."[14]

President Smith returned to Europe in 1910. He also traveled to the Hawaiian Islands (four times), Canada, Mexico, and various stakes in the western United States. During these trips he dealt with special problems faced by the Saints in different areas, gave counsel, and even selected sites for temples.

DIFFICULTIES IN MEXICO

President Joseph F. Smith's administration witnessed events that would have a far-reaching impact on the future of the Church in Mexico and in adjoining sections of the United States. During the last decades of the nineteenth century, Latter-day Saints seeking a haven from the anti-polygamy persecution then raging north of the border had established colonies in northern Mexico. Furthermore, a mission had been established in Mexico City where a few small branches were organized. Nevertheless, because of clerical opposition in Mexico and the Saints' problems at home, the mission had been closed in 1891.

By the turn of the century, conditions seemed right for reopening the mission in Mexico. The Latter-day Saint colonies had become well established and were prospering; their young people, who by this time could speak Spanish fluently and were well acquainted with the Mexican culture, were now available for missionary service. Therefore in 1901, with the approval of the First Presidency and under the immediate supervision of the Juarez Stake, the mission in Mexico City was reopened.

During the next ten years, the work prospered. The missionary force increased to twenty. President Anthony W. Ivins of the Juarez Stake made frequent visits to the mission, and a total of six members of the Twelve came from Salt Lake City to visit the mission during those years. Local men and women were called and trained as leaders. Rey L. Pratt, who became mission president in 1907 and would preside

Mormon colonists flee their homes in northern Mexico as contending revolutionary armies maraud the area in 1912. (LDS Church Archives)

for nearly a quarter century, became a beloved leader for the Mexican people.

By 1911, when the mission's membership exceeded a thousand, President Pratt observed that "prospects were never brighter for the spreading of the gospel in this land."[15] But the whirlwind of revolution and anti-American sentiment had been unleashed, and within a very short time it would disrupt the Church's progress in Mexico.

Francisco "Pancho" Villa, a Mexican revolutionary, led attacks against U.S. citizens in northern Mexico and in New Mexico. The violent circumstances led the Saints to evacuate the Mormon colonies in 1913. (Used by permission, Utah State Historical Society, all rights reserved)

By August 1913 it was necessary to evacuate the missionaries once again, and the Mexican Saints were left alone to take care of themselves. In San Marcos, about fifty miles northwest of Mexico City, for example, Rafael Monroy, a comparatively recent convert, was given the responsibility of serving as branch president. Just two years after the departure of the missionaries, however, the brutal forces of revolutionary conflict and religious prejudice struck down the leadership of the small branch. Because President Monroy and his cousin Vincente Morales were accused of being members of a rival faction and because they would not deny their testimony of the gospel, they were viciously shot by a revolutionary mob.

These forces had also brought trouble to the Mormon colonists in northern Mexico. In 1912 as the revolution swirled around them, the Saints were grateful for what they regarded as divine protection. Once, when Pancho Villa's army was approaching the Mormon settlement at Colonia Dublan, the Saints "were in great fear." A member of the bishopric recalled: "Two opinions were voiced, to make an exodus to the mountains or to go to the small garrison at Nuevo Casas Grandes for protection." Bishop Anson B. Call "had the right for inspiration, and he finally told us to go to our homes, turn out all lights, and retire with a trusting faith that the Lord would answer our prayers." During the night, Pancho Villa and his army came to a nearby vantage point where he thought he could see lights throughout the area. Concluding that an opposing army had already occupied the town, he "ordered his men to turn left and beat a new road over the prairie. . . . No doubt, Villa's soldiers would like to have continued their pillage and murderous acts."[16]

Mexican Mission leadership and Mexican converts posing with Apostle Richard R. Lyman (center) in 1925. Elder Rey L. Pratt (third from left) became a beloved leader to Spanish-speaking converts in Mexico and the United States while serving as president of the Mexican Mission from 1907 until his death in 1931. (LDS Church Archives)

On another occasion Bishop Call was falsely accused of betraying one of the revolutionaries and was condemned to be shot. A firing squad stood him against a tree, cocked and aimed their rifles, and their leader began counting, "una, dos," and just before uttering the final "tres" gave Call a chance to save his life if he would agree to pay two hundred pesos. The bishop regarded this as a literal fulfillment of a promise made to him by Apostle Anthony W. Ivins: "They may rob you of all you possess and put you to every test that the enemy of righteousness can imagine, but they shall not have power to take your life."[17]

When rebels confiscated the Saints' arms, stake leaders ordered an evacuation of women and children by a special train to El Paso on July 26. The men followed a few days later in a mile-long wagon caravan. By February 1913, as the revolutionary crisis began to cool in the area of the colonies, some of the Saints began returning to Mexico while about half remained permanently in the United States.

During later years the colonists' superior schools and advanced

Rafael Monroy (left) with family members circa 1913–14. A revolutionary mob killed Monroy, president of the San Marcos Branch, and his cousin in 1915 in part because they would not deny their testimonies of their newfound faith. (LDS Church Archives)

agricultural methods would attract favorable attention for the Church. Furthermore, when the Mexican government began enforcing laws prohibiting foreign clergy from functioning, most of the missionaries in Mexico and almost all of the mission presidents, as well as the leaders in the Church's growing school system, would come from these colonists who had become Mexican citizens. In this way, the Mormon colonies provided the strength that would enable the Church in later years to grow throughout Mexico and elsewhere in Latin America.

The difficulties in Mexico had a positive impact beyond the borders of that nation, leading to Church expansion in the southwestern United States. Exiled families provided new vitality and leadership to Latter-day Saint congregations in Arizona, New Mexico, and Texas. Furthermore, in 1915 the First Presidency assigned Rey L. Pratt to take charge of proselyting among the Spanish-speaking peoples in the United States. This would become an important missionary field.

TEMPLE SITES

President Joseph F. Smith inaugurated the construction of the first two temples away from the centers of Mormon colonization in Utah. He recognized the need for these sacred edifices to bless Church members living in foreign lands: "They need the same privileges that we do, and that we enjoy, but these are out of their power. They are poor, and they can't gather means to come up here to be endowed, and sealed for time and eternity, for their living and their dead."[18]

During his first visit to Europe, President Joseph F. Smith made an important prophetic statement. At a conference in Bern, Switzerland, in 1906, he stretched out his hands and declared: "The time will come when this land [Europe] will be dotted with temples, where you can go and redeem your dead."[19] He also explained that temples would be built in diverse countries of the world. Interestingly, a half century later, the first Latter-day Saint temple in Europe would be dedicated in the very city where President Smith made his prophecy.

One of the new temples was located in Cardston, Alberta, Canada. In 1888, when Elder John W. Taylor had dedicated Cardston as a location for Latter-day Saint colonization, he had declared, "I now speak by the power of prophecy and say that upon this very spot shall be erected a Temple to the name of Israel's God, and nations shall come from far and near and praise His high and holy name."[20] Later, President Joseph F. Smith sent Presiding Bishop Charles W. Nibley to Canada to recommend the best possible sites for a temple. He brought back photographs of four locations. President Smith thoughtfully studied the pictures and, pointing to one of them, said, "I feel strongly impressed that this is the one."[21] He had selected the same site Elder Taylor had dedicated years earlier. President Joseph F. Smith dedicated this site in 1913 and construction commenced on the temple.

He also dedicated a site for a temple in Hawaii, where he had served as a missionary many years before. Following a meeting at mission headquarters in Laie, June 1, 1915, he invited Elder Reed Smoot and Bishop Charles W. Nibley to join him for an evening walk into the nearby tropical grounds. While they were strolling, President Smith unexpectedly confided to Elder Smoot and Bishop Nibley, "I feel impressed to dedicate this ground for the erection of a temple to God, for a place where the peoples of the Pacific Isles can come and do their temple work."[22] Elder Smoot reflected, "I have heard President Smith pray hundreds of times. . . . But never in all my life did I hear such a prayer. The very ground seemed to be sacred, and he seemed as if he were talking face to face with the Father. I cannot and never will forget it if I lived a thousand years."[23] Construction on both temples was well under way at the time President Smith died in 1918.

World War I and the Church

World War I broke out in Europe in 1914. The United States, however, did not become actively involved until three years later, after Germany had sunk several American vessels in an undeclared submarine war. On April 6, 1917, the United States officially entered the conflict.

Members of the Church in America believed the war was being fought for noble purposes. U.S. President Woodrow Wilson had declared that it was a war for the purpose of preserving democracy, liberty, and peace. Because these sentiments seemed to agree with long-expressed feelings of the Church, members responded quickly to the call to arms.

In Utah, where most of the Saints still lived, a total of 24,382 enlisted, far exceeding the quota assigned to the state. Six of President Joseph F. Smith's sons served in the uniform of their country. The Red Cross asked for $350,000—and received $520,000. When the government began to sell Liberty bonds, Utahns were requested to raise $6,500,000; they purchased $9,400,000 worth.

It was the custom for each state to raise a volunteer military unit. Utah provided the 145th Field Artillery Regiment. The great majority of its approximately fifteen hundred officers and men were Latter-day Saints, including the unit's chaplain, Elder B. H. Roberts of the Seventy. Six hundred members of this modern "Mormon Battalion" saw duty overseas.

The Church, as an institution, also participated officially in the war by purchasing $850,000 in Liberty Bonds. In addition, auxiliary organizations purchased bonds with their own funds, amounting to nearly $600,000, and women of the Relief Society actively participated with the

(Above) Elder B. H. Roberts, one of the First Seven Presidents of the Seventy, served in World War I as the chaplain of the 145th Utah Light Artillery in France. (Below) Major Hugh B. Brown, right, trains Canadian soldiers for duty in World War I. The patriotism displayed by Utah and the Church helped improve outsiders' perception of the Latter-day Saints. (LDS Church Archives)

Relief Society president Bathsheba W. Smith, surrounded by officers, circa 1905. In 1910, Emmeline B. Wells (standing, right) would become president and later lead the Relief Society's homefront activities during WWI. (Used by permission, Utah State Historical Society, all rights reserved)

Red Cross. Sisters in America developed meatless and wheatless menus, filled in on the farm, planted gardens, and bottled fruit for the Relief Society emergency cupboard.[24]

The Church was uniquely prepared to help provide food for the starving peoples of war-torn Europe. For years the Relief Society had been storing wheat in preparation for just such an emergency, so it was able to sell over two hundred thousand bushels to the United States government. The sisters put this money into a special wheat fund for future charitable purposes. The American press praised the Saints' prompt and patriotic response to the war emergency, countering negative impressions lingering from the anti-Mormon magazine crusade of earlier years.[25]

Overseas Saints also responded to the calls of their own countries. Sisters in Britain volunteered to sew and knit clothing for the soldiers at the front.[26] Further, a newspaper in Pudsey, England, praised the local Saints: "The Pudsey branch has . . . a record of patriotism which will be hard to beat, as every man of military age, with the exception of those engaged in government and munition work has enlisted. Whatever we may say about the so-called 'Mormons,' we must admit that they are certainly 'very patriotic at Pudsey.' "[27] On the other side of the conflict, German Latter-day Saints fought willingly for their fatherland, seventy-five giving their lives.

The Church's April general conference had been in session when the United States officially entered the war in 1917. In his opening address, President Joseph F. Smith reminded the Saints that even in the face of conflict, the spirit of the gospel must be maintained. He declared that even in war the people should "maintain above all other things the spirit of humanity, of love, and of peace-making." He instructed prospective soldiers to remember that they were "ministers of life and not of death," and that they should "go forth in the spirit of defending liberties of mankind rather than for the purpose of destroying the enemy."[28]

An improved popular attitude toward Latter-day Saints, financial stability, acquisition of historic sites, and construction of key Church buildings were only some of the lasting contributions of President Smith's administration. The Church also made significant refinements in its priesthood and auxiliary programs, and launched several important publications. These, too, would have a long-lasting impact.

Programs and Principles

The opening decades of the twentieth century witnessed a major expansion and reform in both priesthood and auxiliary programs. These innovations were built on foundations that had been laid during the previous century. The Church also standardized the schedule of basic local meetings, which would be followed for most of the twentieth century.

The structure of the Church was not restored all at once. By April 6, 1830, the date the Church was organized, duties for only four priesthood offices had been outlined by revelation (see D&C 20:38–67). The remainder of the Church's organization and programs were added piecemeal over an extended period. For example, the first stake was established at Kirtland, Ohio, in 1834, but the first wards were not created until five years later in Nauvoo, Illinois.

The auxiliary organizations developed later, primarily while Brigham Young presided over the Church. Although the first Relief Society had been organized at Nauvoo in 1842 to care for the needy and strengthen community morals and Sunday Schools had met irregularly in both Kirtland and Nauvoo, neither of these organizations was formally established Churchwide until the 1860s. At that time President Young directed Eliza R. Snow to promote the establishment of a Relief Society in every branch of the Church, and Elder George Q. Cannon headed the first "union" organization of the formerly independent local Sunday Schools. President Young personally

Crowds on Temple Square commemorate the jubilee celebration of the founding of the Mutual Improvement Association. The MIA underwent significant changes in the early decades of the twentieth century. (Deseret News *photo*)

JUBILEE
1925

organized in 1869 the Young Ladies Department of the Cooperative Retrenchment Association, (forerunner of the Young Women's Mutual Improvement Association) and in 1875 a similar association for the Young Men to provide intellectual and cultural development.

Aurelia Spencer Rogers started the first Primary in 1878, the year following Brigham Young's death, to provide weekday religious training for children. A fifth auxiliary organization, the Religion Class, was organized in 1890 to provide religious instruction for children one afternoon each week. Eventually these two organizations would be combined.

Even though priesthood quorums and auxiliary associations were established during the nineteenth century, the programs sponsored by these organizations underwent substantial development and expansion during the years immediately preceding and following the beginning of the twentieth century. A person who had been active in the Church prior to 1890 might scarcely be able to recognize the programs that developed during the following two or three decades. These changes not only affected the work of the priesthood and the auxiliaries but also had an impact on the Saints' basic meeting pattern.

Developments in Sacrament and Fast Meetings

The scriptures have directed that members of the Church meet together often to instruct and strengthen one another and to partake of the sacrament (see Moroni 6:5–6; D&C 20:75; 43:8; 59:9–10). Although the basic objectives have remained constant, the pattern of these meetings has changed over the years to meet varying needs and conditions.

In 1852, Brigham Young directed the Saints "to meet each Sabbath at 10 a.m., and 2 p.m.," and indicated that "in the evening, the several quorums of the priesthood would assemble to receive instructions." Each Thursday, they were to meet at 2 P.M. "for prayer and supplication." In addition, a special fast meeting was to convene at 10 A.M. on the first Thursday of each month.[1] On this occasion the Saints were asked to bring offerings to the bishop for the relief of the poor.

In some of the larger centers, such as Salt Lake City and Provo, it became customary to hold just one worship service at a central location on Sunday afternoons, and the sacrament was administered in these community-wide meetings rather than in the separate wards. In 1894, however, Church leaders directed that the administration of the sacrament should be moved to the regular Sunday evening services held in each ward.[2] Thus, the ward sacrament meeting became a familiar Churchwide practice.

By 1896, new patterns of life made a shift in the fast day advisable. During pioneer times, the Saints generally had lived in agricultural communities where most people were of the same faith, making a midweek fast meeting possible. By the end of the century, however, an increasing number lived in urban centers and worked for non-Mormon employers, making it awkward to disrupt their workday to attend a fast meeting. The First Presidency

Significant changes in Church organizations and publications, 1880–1921

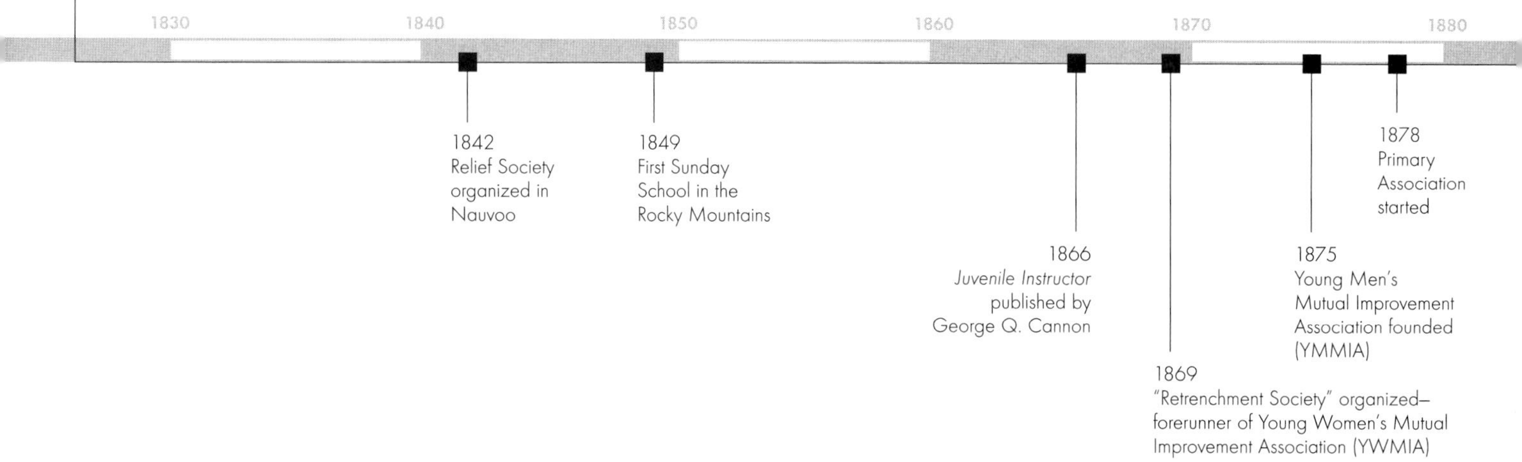
1830
1840
1850
1860
1870
1880
1842
Relief Society
organized in
Nauvoo
1849
First Sunday
School in the
Rocky Mountains
1866
Juvenile Instructor
published by
George Q. Cannon
1869
"Retrenchment Society" organized–
forerunner of Young Women's Mutual
Improvement Association (YWMIA)
1875
Young Men's
Mutual Improvement
Association founded
(YMMIA)
1878
Primary
Association
started

concluded that "Thursday as a day of fasting and prayer in the Church no longer serves the object for which it was intended." Therefore, the monthly fast day was shifted to the first Sunday, to be devoted to "the administration of the Sacrament, to the bearing of testimony by the members of the Church, to the blessing of children and the confirming of members in the Church."[3]

Relief Society general board in 1916, a time when this organization was unfolding educational programs and launching its own magazine. (Used by permission, Utah State Historical Society, all rights reserved)

Auxiliary Expansion

The Church's auxiliary organizations were most affected by the developments during the opening years of the twentieth century. Although specific changes varied from one organization to another, they generally involved an improvement in teaching methods and materials directed to specific age groups, a greater emphasis on the scriptures rather than on secular materials, and a greater role for each organization's general leaders.

OPPORTUNITIES FOR LEARNING

During the nineteenth century the Latter-day Saints had been in the forefront of educational development. The School of the Prophets in the 1830s, for example, had been one of the nation's first adult education programs. At the dawning of the twentieth century the Saints were again in the lead as several of the Church's organizations commenced new instructional programs especially for adults.

During the nineteenth century the Relief Society had stressed "compassionate service" and had emphasized sewing or other projects directly related to assisting the needy. In 1902, however, the Society inaugurated a greater emphasis on education including a special eight-month nursing course on how to care for the sick and Mothers' Classes, which led to a broader curriculum a few years later. At first, local

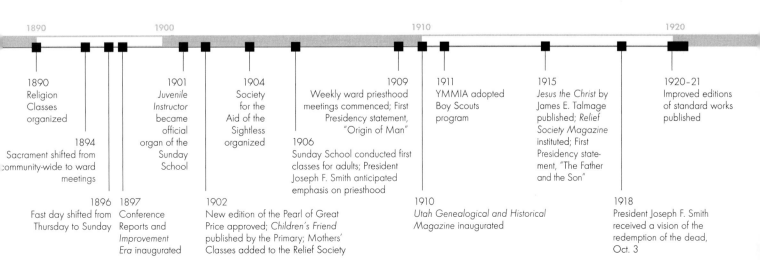

1890 1900 1910 1920

1890 Religion Classes organized

1894 Sacrament shifted from community-wide to ward meetings

1896 Fast day shifted from Thursday to Sunday

1897 Conference Reports and *Improvement Era* inaugurated

1901 *Juvenile Instructor* became official organ of the Sunday School

1902 New edition of the Pearl of Great Price approved; *Children's Friend* published by the Primary; Mothers' Classes added to the Relief Society

1904 Society for the Aid of the Sightless organized

1906 Sunday School conducted first classes for adults; President Joseph F. Smith anticipated emphasis on priesthood

1909 Weekly ward priesthood meetings commenced; First Presidency statement, "Origin of Man"

1910 *Utah Genealogical and Historical Magazine* inaugurated

1911 YMMIA adopted Boy Scouts program

1915 *Jesus the Christ* by James E. Talmage published; *Relief Society Magazine* instituted; First Presidency statement, "The Father and the Son"

1918 President Joseph F. Smith received a vision of the redemption of the dead, Oct. 3

1920–21 Improved editions of standard works published

Relief Societies provided their own study materials, but in 1914 the general board began providing uniform lessons for these weekly classes. The pattern soon developed to study theology the first week of the month, followed by homemaking, literature, and social science in the successive weeks of the month.

Even after the turn of the century the Sunday School remained an organization for children. The first class for adults, the Parents' Class, was not inaugurated Churchwide until 1906, four years after the Relief Society had instituted its Mothers' Class. David O. McKay had a profound impact on Sunday School development in this era. As a young returned missionary at the turn of the century, he was called to be a member of the Weber Stake Sunday School superintendency and to give particular attention to instruction. He introduced refinements in teaching methods, such as having teachers define goals and outline lessons to achieve them, using teaching aids, and making practical application of lessons to daily life. Under his direction, the stake developed courses for specific age groups. In 1906 David O. McKay was called to the Council of the Twelve and also became a member of the Sunday School general superintendency; in this position he was able to promote these improvements throughout the Church, and improved lesson materials were published.

The general board of the Deseret Sunday School Union, circa 1906. David O. McKay (center) served as superintendent, introducing improved curriculum and innovations in teaching style for the Sunday School. (LDS Church Archives)

At this same time, other organizations were also starting to provide educational opportunities for the Saints. Priesthood quorums commenced regular lesson work, seminaries were inaugurated for high school students, and college-level classes were added to several Church schools.

IMPROVED ACTIVITIES

During the nineteenth century the Young Men's and Young Ladies' Mutual Improvement Associations had followed similar but separate paths of development. Originally the two MIAs met separately, consistent with the wishes of Brigham Young, who did not want the sessions to degenerate into "courting meetings." Following the turn of the century, the move to unite the two associations gained impetus, and by 1914 joint meetings had become the rule. At first, MIA meetings emphasized lectures on theology, science, history, and literature. Formal classwork had been introduced in about 1890, but until after the turn of the century just one large class was held for all ages. Several local groups, however, felt the need to separate the younger and older members. By 1903 the practice of conducting separate junior and senior groups had been implemented Churchwide. In 1911 the Young Men's organization adopted the growing Boy Scout program, and the Church eventually became one of the largest sponsors of this international movement. In 1913 the Young Ladies adopted the Campfire Girls summer program, but they replaced it the following year with the Church's own year-round Beehive Girls program. Later years saw the formation of other age-group programs to better serve the needs of the youth. As the Sunday School and especially the priesthood quorums expanded their theological study, this

Boy Scouts from Troop 6 in Santa Monica, California, proudly wear their uniforms, circa 1938. The Young Men's Mutual Improvement Association adopted the Boy Scout program in 1911, becoming one of its largest sponsors. (LDS Church Archives)

topic was dropped from the MIA.

As more and more Latter-day Saints moved into cities, Church leaders became concerned that the new environment and increased leisure would erode traditional virtues and family life. As a response, in 1916 the First Presidency launched the Social Advisory Committee to focus the work of the Church's own auxiliaries and to coordinate these efforts with other public or private agencies. Committees at both the general and local levels sought to enhance activities both for youth and adults.[4] Church leaders placed increasing emphasis on modesty, chastity, and marriage within the faith. Leaders encouraged the youth to avoid pool halls, card games, non-LDS dances, and Sunday sports. The wards, which were at the center of Mormon community life, sponsored more picnics, excursions, and other well-supervised recreational activities. The MIAs also expanded their music, dance, speech, drama, and sports activities.

Similarly, the Primary Association enhanced its educational and activity programs for children. Special class names and emblems were introduced to increase interest: boys became known as "Trail Builders" and girls as "Home Builders."

As the other auxiliary organizations began structuring their classes for specific age groups, they increasingly adopted centrally prepared, uniform lessons. The opening years of the twentieth century also brought a greater emphasis on regional conventions and general auxiliary conferences for the training and motivation of local workers. All these developments tended to strengthen the role of each auxiliary's general board.

The Priesthood Reform Movement

At the height of this rapid auxiliary expansion, President Joseph F. Smith looked forward to a time when the priesthood would again occupy a position of preeminence. At the April general conference in 1906 he declared:

> We expect to see the day, if we live long enough (and if some of us do not live long enough to see it, there are others who will), when every council of the Priesthood . . . will understand its duty; will assume its own responsibility, will magnify its calling, and fill its place in the Church. . . . When that day shall come, there will not be so much necessity for work that is now being done by the auxiliary organizations, because it will be done by the regular quorums of the Priesthood. The Lord designed and comprehended it from the beginning, and He has made provision in the Church whereby every need may be met and satisfied through the regular organizations of the Priesthood. It has truly been said that the Church is perfectly organized. The only trouble is that these organizations are not fully alive to the obligations that rest upon them. When they become thoroughly awakened to the requirements made of them, they will fulfill their duties more faithfully, and the work of the Lord will be all the stronger and more powerful and influential in the world.[5]

Elder J. Golden Kimball, a member of the First Council of the Seventy for over forty-six years, was a colorful and beloved leader of the Saints. At the April general conference in 1906, Elder Kimball urged the priesthood quorums to increase their effectiveness. (Used by permission, Utah State Historical Society, all rights reserved)

Speaking at the same conference, Elder J. Golden Kimball of the First Council of the Seventy assessed even more bluntly the need for a revival of priesthood activity: "The auxiliaries have been urged forward with greater enthusiasm . . . [and] these organizations are to the front. The Priesthood quorums are apparently weary in well doing. . . . They have become lax in their work and let loose their hold. While the auxiliary organizations have taken the right of way, the Priesthood quorums stand by looking on awe-struck. . . . So the auxiliary organizations are going away up the hill and we, the Priesthood quorums, stand down in the valley and look on."[6]

At this time, priesthood meetings were being held at varying intervals, often monthly and sometimes only during the winter, when men were not involved in time-consuming farmwork. Furthermore, all the quorums within a given ward did not usually meet at the same time, but on various weeknights. With such infrequent and irregular meetings, priesthood quorums' effectiveness declined. By the beginning of the twentieth century, Church leaders lamented that less than half of Latter-day Saint men were active in their priesthood quorums. The leaders suspected that one problem was the growing popularity of fraternal lodges. They believed that these needs—spiritual and temporal—should be met by the Church, and that the priesthood quorums themselves should provide true brotherhood.

The revival of priesthood activity appears to have started among the Seventies, whose quorums at this time were organized throughout the stakes of the Church. In 1907 President Joseph F. Smith reminded them of their unique responsibility to be prepared for missionary service. He told them they should not depend on the auxiliaries or Church schools for their knowledge of the gospel, but make their own "quorums schools of learning and instruction, wherein they may qualify themselves for every labor that may be required at their hands."[7] In November of that same year, Elder B. H. Roberts of the First Council of the Seventy announced the "New Movement" among the Seventies. It would include study of *The Seventies Course in Theology* each Sunday morning. "To become a Seventy," he declared, "means mental activity, intellectual development, and the attainment of spiritual power."[8] The *Improvement Era* magazine became the official vehicle through which monthly instructions were received by these priesthood quorums. The success of these efforts among the Seventies attracted admiration and led to a broadening of the reform movement.

WEEKLY WARD PRIESTHOOD MEETINGS

In 1908, to give direction to the revitalization of the priesthood and specifically to provide lesson materials for Aaronic and Melchizedek Priesthood quorums, the First Presidency appointed a General Priesthood Committee. Apostle David O. McKay soon became committee chairman, and other General Authorities served as committee members.

One of the committee's far-reaching recommendations was for the inauguration of weekly ward priesthood meetings. The First Presidency concurred, pointing out that these weekly meetings would get priesthood bearers into the habit of regular activity and strengthen them through improved lesson materials. Furthermore, bishops would be able to meet the priesthood heads of all ward families each week. "We like the idea of these weekly reunions of the fathers of the ward with their sons and associates," the Presidency concluded.[9]

At first these ward priesthood meetings were scheduled for Monday evenings. This schedule, however, interfered with evening chores, especially in farming areas, so Sunday morning gradually became the preferred time.

The General Priesthood Committee increased the effectiveness of these ward meetings by providing uniform courses of study to be used throughout the Church. In 1923, this committee was released and responsibility for the Melchizedek Priesthood was assigned directly to the Council of the Twelve; responsibility for the Aaronic Priesthood was assigned to the Presiding Bishopric.

AARONIC PRIESTHOOD AGE GROUPINGS

Another important accomplishment of the priesthood reform movement was systematizing ordinations to offices in the Aaronic Priesthood at specified ages. As early as 1877, the First Presidency had endorsed the practice of ordaining young men to the lesser priesthood to give them needed experience before they received the higher or Melchizedek Priesthood. Although it had become typical to ordain boys to the office of deacon at age twelve, no ages were fixed for ordination to subsequent offices. In 1908 the General Priesthood Committee recommended that deacons be ordained at twelve, teachers at fifteen, priests at eighteen, and elders at twenty-one, thus giving young men three years' experience in each Aaronic Priesthood office. Standardizing the ages of ordination enabled the committee to more effectively plan the program for each priesthood group. The concept of set ages for ordination has continued even though some of the ages have been modified.

Home Evenings Encouraged

As early as the days of Brigham Young, the First Presidency had instructed parents to gather their families together "if not every day, at least as often as they can" in order to "interrogate them respecting their associations, their words, actions . . . , and teach them the principles of the gospel."[10]

In 1909 the Granite Stake in Salt Lake City, Utah, inaugurated a weekly home evening. Two thousand stake members attended the special meeting where the plan was announced. Church President Joseph F. Smith addressed the group and declared that the "inspiration" of the stake presidency in "setting apart at least one evening in a week for the especial use and benefit of the families of the Saints, is of the greatest importance."[11] The success of this activity undoubtedly contributed to the First Presidency's recommending a similar program Churchwide six years later.

In 1915 President Joseph F. Smith and his counselors issued instructions which subsequently became the frequently quoted charter for the Church's emphasis on the family: "We advise and urge the inauguration of a 'Home Evening' throughout the Church, at which time fathers and mothers may gather their boys and girls about them in the home and teach them the word of the Lord." In this way, parents "may thus learn more fully the needs and requirements of their families. . . . This 'Home Evening' should be devoted to prayer, singing hymns, songs, instrumental music, scripture-reading, family topics and specific instruction on the principles of the gospel, and on the ethical problems of life, as well as the duties and obligations of children to parents, the home, the Church, society and the nation." The Presidency also suggested that activities should be adapted for younger children and that light refreshments might be served. In conclusion, the First Presidency promised: "If the Saints obey this counsel, we promise that great blessings will result. Love at home and obedience to parents will increase. Faith will be developed in the hearts of the youth of Israel, and they will gain power to combat the evil influence and temptations which beset them."[12]

Doctrinal Direction in an Era of Confusion

The early twentieth century was a period of heated debate between religious fundamentalists, who held to traditional biblical teachings, and "liberals" or modernists. Many asked where the Mormons stood. The Church was fortunate to have the leadership of President Joseph F. Smith, an unusually able and inspired teacher of gospel fundamentals. A compilation of his sermons and writings is found in the volume entitled *Gospel Doctrine*, and Church members still look to his teachings for helpful definitions of basic gospel concepts. President Smith and his counselors in the First Presidency issued several "doctrinal expositions" clarifying the Church's stand on key issues of the day.

Perhaps the most heated and prolonged discussions centered on the creation of the earth and the theory of organic evolution. In their 1909 statement, "The Origin of Man," the First Presidency quoted Genesis 1:27 and affirmed that "All men and women are in the similitude of the universal Father and Mother, and are literally the sons and daughters of Deity."[13] The Presidency labeled the concept that "Adam was not the first man upon this earth, and that the original human being was a development from lower orders of the animal creation" as "the theories of men. The word of the Lord declares that Adam was 'the first man of all men' (Moses 1:34), and we are therefore in duty bound to regard him as the primal parent of our race."[14]

Other discussions questioned the traditional concept that the Trinity, or Godhead, consisted of three persons in one. The First Presidency's 1916 exposition, "The Father and the Son," explained that the scriptures apply the title *Father* to members of the Godhead "with plainly different meanings" which should be carefully segregated. God is Father as the literal parent of our spirits. Jesus Christ also may be called Father as Creator of this earth, as the Author of Salvation to those who abide in His gospel, and as the representative of God the Father by divine investiture of authority. Concerning the Savior's status as the Son and as our Elder Brother, the First Presidency affirmed: "He is essentially greater than any and all others by reason (1) of His seniority as the oldest or firstborn; (2) of His unique status in the flesh as the offspring of a mortal mother and of an immortal, or resurrected and glorified Father; (3) of His selection and foreordination as the one and only Redeemer and Savior of the race; and (4) of His transcendent sinlessness."[15]

During these years, a group of particularly capable Latter-day Saint scholars further contributed to gospel understanding. One of these was James E. Talmage, who as a young man had taught science at Brigham Young Academy and later had served for several years as president of the University of Utah. In 1899 he delivered a very popular series of lectures on the Articles of Faith. So many attended that the lectures had to be moved from a smaller room to the

Elder John A. Widtsoe, a member of the Quorum of the Twelve Apostles, and his family having a family home evening, circa 1912. In 1915, weekly "Home Evenings" were initiated Churchwide at which families were to enjoy scripture study, singing, activities, and light refreshments. (Photographic Archives, Harold B. Lee Library, Brigham Young University, Provo, Utah)

Assembly Hall on Temple Square. His material was later published in book form by direction of the First Presidency. This work has been translated into over a dozen other languages and continues to be accepted by Church members as an essential exposition of Latter-day Saint theology.[16]

Rather interesting circumstances surrounded the publication of a second important work by James E. Talmage. In 1911 certain individuals gained unauthorized access to the Salt Lake Temple and took photographs of its interior with primitive flash camera equipment. They then offered to sell these pictures to the Church for $100,000. Otherwise, they threatened to sell the photographs to publishers in New York as part of a plot to expose temple rituals. The First Presidency recognized this as attempted blackmail so promptly published in the *Deseret Evening News* an account of the plot together with pictures of the temple's interior. Dr. Talmage, who later that year would become a member of the Twelve, then contacted Church officials, suggesting that a scholarly explanation of the history and nature of temple service accompanied by high-quality photographs on good paper be published in book form. The Presidency invited him to prepare this text. The result was *The House of the Lord*, published in 1912.[17]

Elder James E. Talmage of the Quorum of the Twelve Apostles. A scientist, public speaker, and author, Elder Talmage was greatly respected for his ability to teach the gospel. His written works include The Articles of Faith, The House of the Lord, *and* Jesus the Christ. *(LDS Church Archives)*

Between 1904 and 1906, Dr. Talmage gave a series of lectures on the life of the Savior and the significance of His mission. As early as 1905, the First Presidency expressed an interest in having these lectures published in book form. In 1914 they asked Elder Talmage to prepare the manuscript "with as little delay as possible." For the next seven months he carried his regular responsibilities as a member of the Twelve but devoted every spare minute he could to this project. He was given a room in the Salt Lake Temple's east center tower where he could work on the book without the usual interruptions. "I have felt the inspiration of the place," Elder Talmage later reflected, "and have appreciated the privacy and quietness incident thereto."[18] In weekly sessions, the entire manuscript was read to a group composed of all the available General Authorities, who gave their approval before publication. Elder Talmage "was deeply aware of the magnitude of his task and he approached it in a spirit of reverent awe."[19] He regarded this as "the outstanding book of all he had written, or would ever write."[20]

Jesus the Christ came off the press in the fall of 1915. The First Presidency announced that they had commissioned this work and urged that it "be read and studied by the Latter-day Saints in their families" as well as in priesthood quorums, auxiliaries, and Church schools.[21]

Beginning in 1907, Elder B. H. Roberts's *Seventies Course in Theology* kindled a more intense interest in gospel study. Another key contributor to gospel understanding was John A. Widtsoe, an immigrant convert from Norway. Like Talmage, he drew from personal gospel study and his training as a scientist when he wrote *A Rational Theology* in 1915. Dr. Widtsoe became a member of the Twelve six years later. These and other scholarly works of the period have continued to be recognized as key volumes in a Latter-day Saint's library.

A marvelous revelation received by President Joseph F. Smith only a few weeks before his death was a fitting climax to these contributions to gospel understanding. The President had been deeply affected by the death of his Apostle son, Hyrum, in early 1918. Just over eight months later on October 3, 1918, while President Smith was reflecting on Christ's Atonement, he opened his Bible and read in 1 Peter 3:18–20 and 4:6 about the Savior's preaching to the spirits in prison. While he was pondering these passages, the Spirit of the Lord rested upon him and he saw in vision the "hosts of the dead" who were gathered in the spirit world. He saw the Savior appear to them and preach the gospel to the righteous. He was shown that the Lord commissioned others to continue this work, and that faithful elders in the present dispensation would also preach to the dead after leaving mortality. In this way, all the dead may be redeemed. This "Vision of the Redemption of the Dead" was presented by President Smith to the First Presidency and the Twelve, who accepted it unanimously. In 1976 this revelation was officially added to the standard works and soon afterwards designated as section 138 in the Doctrine and Covenants.

Key Developments in Official Church Publications

Ever since 1820, when a biblical passage led Joseph Smith to the Sacred Grove, the printed word has played a key role in the unfolding of the Lord's work. As Elder Mark E. Petersen later declared: "Our publications and communication system is positively essential, vital, and basic to the life blood of the Church."[22] The early years of the twentieth century brought a variety of important developments in Church literature. With the rapid expansion of priesthood and auxiliary programs, Church organizations published new lesson outlines and either inaugurated magazines or made greater use of existing ones to help promote their programs. These years even brought important improvements to the published editions of scriptural works.

DEVELOPMENTS IN PERIODICALS

Although Latter-day Saints had actively published newspapers and magazines as early as 1831, most of the best known publications of the twentieth century dated from the years immediately preceding or following the turn of the century. While most nineteenth-century publications had been sponsored

Development of Church Periodicals in the Early Twentieth Century

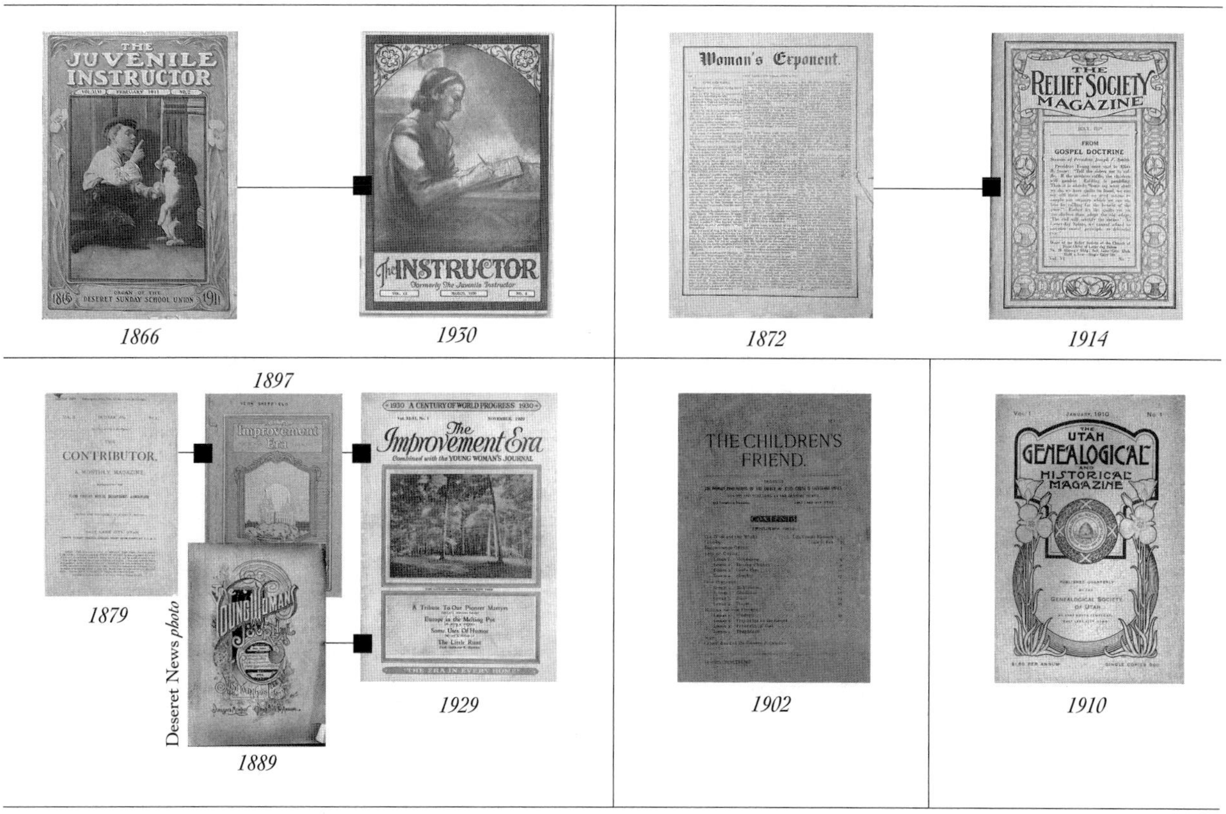

All courtesy LDS Church except as noted

Helen Keller reads from a braille copy of the Book of Mormon held by President Heber J. Grant in 1941. Created in 1904, the Society for the Aid of the Sightless published scriptures, hymns, manuals, and other Church literature in braille for blind members. (Photo courtesy Manuscripts Division, J. Willard Marriott Library, University of Utah)

by private individuals or groups, those dating from the early twentieth century were published by specific Church organizations, particularly the auxiliaries.

When the *Juvenile Instructor* was inaugurated in 1866, it had been a personal project of Elder George Q. Cannon, who saw the magazine as a means of teaching the gospel to the youth of the Church. This publication is credited as being the first magazine for children published between the Mississippi River and the Pacific Coast. Following Elder Cannon's death in 1901, the Deseret Sunday School Union purchased the magazine from the Cannon family and made it the Sunday School's official organ. As the Sunday School added adult classes, the magazine's scope broadened accordingly; the word *Juvenile* was finally dropped from the title in 1930.

In 1897 the Young Men's Mutual Improvement Association replaced its *Contributor* with a new periodical entitled the *Improvement Era.* Joseph F. Smith of the First Presidency and B. H. Roberts of the First Council of the Seventy were editors, and Elder Heber J. Grant of the Twelve was the business manager. In 1929 this magazine would be merged with the *Young Woman's Journal*, which had been published since 1889 by the Young Ladies's MIA. Gradually, the enlarged *Improvement Era* came to be recognized as the basic Church magazine for adults.

Albert Talmage, brother of Apostle James E. Talmage, published a braille magazine and directed the Church's programs for the blind during the opening decades of the twentieth century. Here, aided by his sister, he prints an issue of the monthly Messenger for the Sightless. *(*Improvement Era *photo)*

Beginning in 1872, a group of women, some of whom were members of the Relief Society general board, began publishing the *Woman's Exponent.* This journal continued until 1914 when the Relief Society began supplying lesson materials to be taught in its weekly meetings Churchwide; this provided the basis for launching its own official *Relief Society Magazine* the following year.

Two other organizations launched periodicals during the first decade of the twentieth century. These were the *Children's Friend*, started by the Primary Association in 1902, and the *Utah Genealogical and Historical Magazine*, a quarterly published by the Genealogical Society beginning in 1910.

LITERATURE FOR THE BLIND

In 1904 the Society for the Aid of the Sightless was created under the direction of President Joseph F. Smith. It was charged with the responsibility of publishing literature for the blind, "aiding in their education, endeavoring to improve their condition, becoming interested in all that pertains to their welfare," and cooperating with others as opportunity came to work for these ends through education and legislation.[23]

The lack of braille scriptures, hymns, or lesson materials was a substantial obstacle that prevented blind Latter-day Saints from becoming fully involved in the mainstream of Church activity. Largely through the efforts of Albert M. Talmage (a blind brother of the Apostle James E. Talmage) and his wife, Sarah, the society worked to fill this void. Beginning in 1912, a monthly braille periodical, *The Messenger to the Sightless*, published materials of religious and general interest.

Publishing the Book of Mormon in braille was an important and challenging project for Albert and Sarah Talmage. They had to prepare metal printing plates by hand. They thoroughly moistened the special braille paper before embossing the dots by means of their hand-operated press. They then hung completed pages to dry on clotheslines that had been strung around their home. These pages were distributed piecemeal to eagerly waiting readers. By the early 1930s, however, only the first half of the Book of Mormon had been brailled. At this point the Church decided to have the entire book

President Heber J. Grant with party at a commemoration of the centennial of Joseph Smith's finding the plates in the Hill Cumorah. (LDS Church Archives)

embossed by a national braille publisher, and in 1936 the book appeared in seven large braille volumes. Copies were sent to Latter-day Saint missions around the world and were loaned to interested readers.[24] Since then, the Doctrine and Covenants, the Pearl of Great Price, and a few other Church books have also been released in braille. Priesthood and auxilary lessons as well as other Church literature have been made available both in braille and recorded forms.

THE STANDARD WORKS

The three books that the Latter-day Saints accept as scripture in addition to the Bible had all been published in the nineteenth century. The Book of Mormon was published one month before the Church's organization in 1830. The Doctrine and Covenants, which contained a selection of revelations received by Joseph Smith together with seven of his "Lectures on Faith" appeared in 1835. The Pearl of Great Price, a selection from the revelations, translations, and narration of Joseph Smith, was first published in 1851 by Elder Franklin D. Richards, president of the British Mission, in order to make these choice materials more accessible to the Saints abroad.

The present verse divisions, together with improved historical notes and cross-references prepared by Elder Orson Pratt, were features of new editions of the Doctrine and Covenants in 1876 and of the Book of Mormon in 1879. A similar new edition of the Pearl of Great Price was prepared by James E. Talmage in 1902. On October 10, 1880, the Church in general conference voted to accept the Doctrine and Covenants and the Pearl of Great Price "as revelations from God to the Church of Jesus Christ of Latter-day Saints, and to all the world."[25]

A new edition of the Book of Mormon appeared in 1920, and new editions of the Doctrine and Covenants and the Pearl of Great Price the following year. These were the work of a committee headed by Elder George F. Richards, and many of the revisions were the work of Elder Talmage. Improvements in these new editions included printing the text in two columns to make reading easier, adding headings or superscriptions to introduce and summarize the contents of each chapter or section, amplifying footnotes, and adding an index to each of these three scriptural works. The new edition of the Book of Mormon also included an account of its origin, an analysis of the various sets of plates from which it was translated, a chronology, and a new pronunciation guide. Useful additions to the Doctrine and Covenants included a brief history of its beginnings, together with a chronological summary of its contents. Errors in existing editions were corrected to make the text conform to the wording in the *History of the Church*, which had been edited recently by Elder B. H. Roberts. The 1921 edition of the Doctrine and Covenants also omitted the "Lectures on Faith," which formerly had been published along with the revelations. This action was taken because this material was "never presented to nor accepted by the Church as being otherwise than theological lectures or lessons." Furthermore, some teachings in the "Lectures on Faith," notably that on the nature of the Holy Ghost, had been misunderstood.[26]

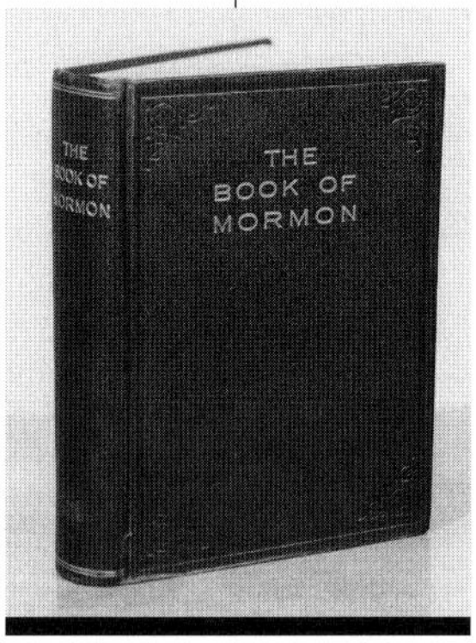

The 1920 edition of the Book of Mormon. The new edition included an index, footnotes, and descriptive headings. (Deseret News *photo)*

Thus the opening years of the twentieth century brought significant developments in scriptures, other publications, and Church activities in general.

5

Heber J. Grant Begins His Administration

The year 1918 marked a major turning point in the course of world and Church events. For the world, it brought an end to World War I and a turning to peace. For the Church it brought a change in leadership. Within two weeks of the November 11 armistice, President Joseph F. Smith died and Heber J. Grant became the Church's seventh president. President Grant was not sustained publicly for several months, however. Because of the serious flu epidemic, the general conference normally held in April was not convened until June 1, 1919. On that occasion President Grant was sustained in a solemn assembly. He would preside longer than any other president except Brigham Young. His twenty-seven-year administration stretched from the conclusion of World War I to the end of World War II.

Heber J. Grant's Earlier Life

For younger Church members, Heber J. Grant represented a personal link with the early leaders of the Restoration. He was the son of Jedediah M. Grant, a New York convert who became the first mayor of Salt Lake City and a counselor to President Brigham Young. Heber's mother, Rachel Ivins, had been sealed to Joseph Smith after his death and at the time of her marriage to Jedediah. Thus, in terms of eternal family relationships, Heber J. Grant considered himself a son of the Church's first prophet, a heritage which he valued highly.[1] He was the first Church President to be born after the Saints' exodus to the

Elder Heber J. Grant with his wife, Emily, in Venice, Italy, in 1906. Elder Grant, who would become the seventh President of the Church, was then serving as president of the European Mission. (LDS Church Archives)

Rocky Mountains, being born in Salt Lake City in 1856, just nine years after the Mormon pioneers had arrived there. As a boy, Heber was very close to Brigham Young's family and became well acquainted with the great colonizer.

Heber was not to enjoy the companionship or counsel of his earthly father. Jedediah died suddenly at the age of forty, only nine days afer Heber's birth. A talented, faithful, and persistent mother would be the major guiding light of Heber's childhood and youth. Rachel supported herself and her son by sewing and taking in boarders. Sometimes she worked at her foot-powered sewing machine for so many hours that her legs would give out, and she would have Heber help by working the treadle with his hands. Through such experiences young Heber learned lessons of thrift and industry, which would be important virtues to teach the Saints during the Great Depression of the 1930s.

His mother was convinced that Heber was a child of destiny. She cherished promises made to him during his childhood by Heber C. Kimball and Eliza R. Snow. To this end she admonished him: "Behave yourself, Heber, and some day you will be an apostle."[2]

OVERCOMING DIFFICULTIES

At the youthful age of seventeen, Heber J. Grant outlined what he hoped to accomplish in his life, and then he persisted until he had achieved his goals. Ralph Waldo Emerson's words became a favorite motto: "That which we persist in doing becomes easier for us to do; not that the nature of the thing itself has changed, but that our power to do is increased." This principle was carried out repeatedly in the life of Heber J. Grant. For instance, he overcame physical frailty to develop his skill as a baseball player. When he joined a baseball club, he was permitted to play only with much younger boys, but he determined that one day he would play on a championship team. "I spent hours and hours throwing the ball against Bishop Edwin D. Woolley's barn, which caused him to refer to me as the laziest boy in the Thirteenth Ward," Heber admitted. "Often my arm would ache so that I could scarcely go to sleep at night. But I kept on practicing."[3] With this diligence Heber ultimately was able to play on the team that took the Utah Territory championship and defeated champion teams from neighboring areas. He also overcame the problem of poor handwriting, eventually winning prizes at fairs and obtaining a coveted position as a bookkeeper because of his excellent penmanship.

Being tone-deaf, he was challenged by his inability to sing. Nevertheless, he was determined to practice. After becoming a member of the Twelve, he humorously admitted: "Upon my recent trip to Arizona, I asked Elders Rudger Clawson and J. Golden Kimball if they had any objections to my singing one hundred hymns that day. They took it as a joke and assured me that they would be delighted. . . . After I had sung about forty times, they assured me that if I sang the remaining sixty they would be sure to have nervous prostration. I paid no attention whatever to their appeal, but held them to their bargain and sang

Major events in the life and administration of President Heber J. Grant

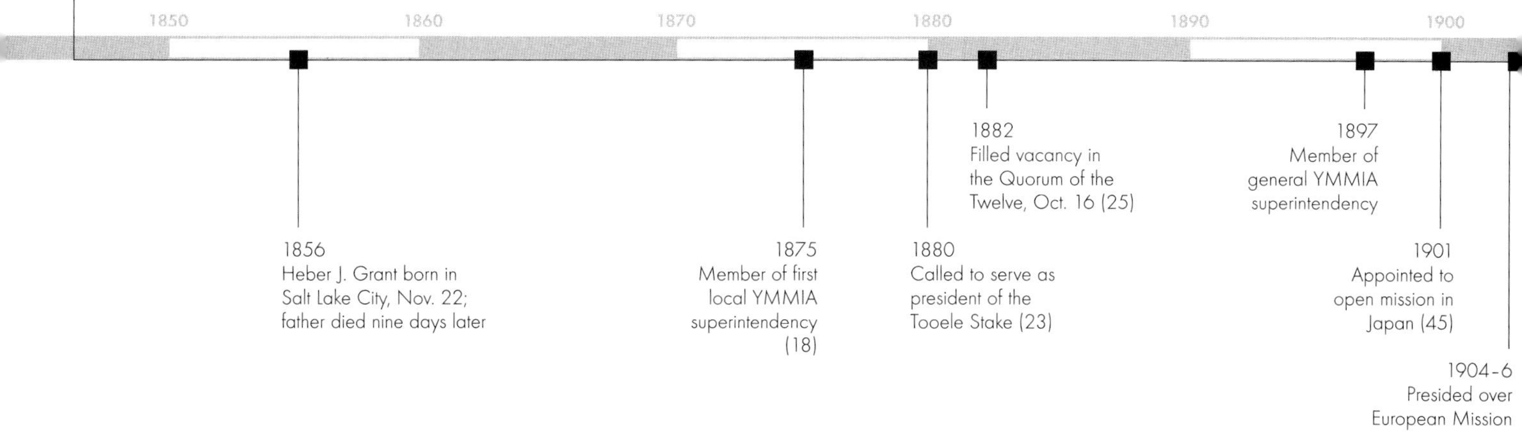
1850
1860
1870
1880
1890
1900
1856
Heber J. Grant born in Salt Lake City, Nov. 22; father died nine days later
1875
Member of first local YMMIA superintendency (18)
1880
Called to serve as president of the Tooele Stake (23)
1882
Filled vacancy in the Quorum of the Twelve, Oct. 16 (25)
1897
Member of general YMMIA superintendency
1901
Appointed to open mission in Japan (45)
1904-6
Presided over European Mission

the full one hundred."[4] Many years later he must have derived some personal satisfaction when he learned that because he had been seated close to the microphone during a radio broadcast from the Tabernacle, listeners seemed to hear him singing a solo accompanied by the choir and organ.[5]

Important Church responsibilities came to Heber at a young age. When the first Mutual Improvement Association was organized in the Salt Lake Thirteenth Ward in 1875, eighteen-year-old Heber J. Grant was made a member of its superintendency. He subsequently helped pioneer this movement throughout the Church. At age twenty-three he was called to be president of the Tooele Stake in western Utah; he accepted this call even though it required him to move away from Salt Lake City at just the time he was getting established in his business career. Then, two years later, he was called to fill a vacancy in the Council of the Twelve Apostles.

CALL TO THE APOSTLESHIP

Heber J. Grant had come in from Tooele to attend the October 1882 general conference. As he entered Temple Square, he met his good friend George Teasdale who remarked, " 'Brother Grant, I am delighted to see you. You and I are going to be'—and he stopped suddenly and his face turned red," President Grant later remembered. "But the Lord gave me the balance of the sentence. The balance of Brother Teasdale's sentence was—'sustained this afternoon as apostles of the Lord Jesus Christ to fill the vacancies in the Quorum,' and that went through me like a shock of electricity." But at that conference the vacancies were not filled. "I do not believe any mortal man ever more humbly supplicated God during the next few days to forgive him for his egotism than I did for thinking I was to be chosen an apostle."[6] But within a week, President John Taylor published a revelation which read in part: "Thus saith the Lord to the Twelve, and to the Priesthood and people of my Church: Let my servants George Teasdale and Heber J. Grant be appointed to fill the vacancies in the Twelve."[7]

Even though this call was preceded by a spiritual premonition and came in the form of a written revelation, still Elder Grant did not feel comfortable in his new position. "I was too young, too inexperienced and really unworthy of such a great honor. The adversary tried to convince me that I should resign. On more than one occasion when I would testify of my knowledge that Jesus is the Savior it seemed—although I did not hear a voice—as though I was told: 'You lie. You have never seen the Savior, and you have no right to testify of him.' " A few months later he was traveling through the Navajo Indian reservation in Arizona and was feeling very depressed. "All at once I stopped the mule I was riding, and . . . I seemed to see a council in heaven, where they were discussing the fact that the general conference of the Church had adjourned and that no choice had been made to fill the two vacancies in the quorum of the Apostles. A general discussion ensued," Elder Grant beheld, "and the Prophet and my father favored sending a revelation that I should

1910 1920 1930 1940 1950 1960

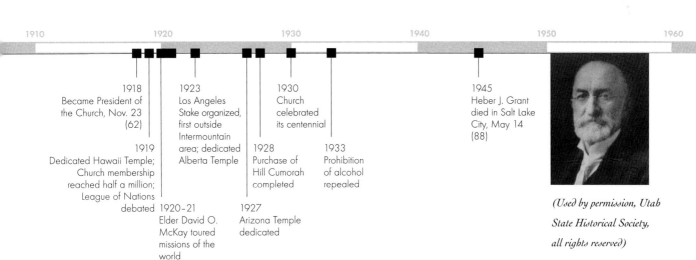

1918 Became President of the Church, Nov. 23 (62)

1919 Dedicated Hawaii Temple; Church membership reached half a million; League of Nations debated

1920–21 Elder David O. McKay toured missions of the world

1923 Los Angeles Stake organized, first outside Intermountain area; dedicated Alberta Temple

1927 Arizona Temple dedicated

1928 Purchase of Hill Cumorah completed

1930 Church celebrated its centennial

1933 Prohibition of alcohol repealed

1945 Heber J. Grant died in Salt Lake City, May 14 (88)

(Used by permission, Utah State Historical Society, all rights reserved)

Heber J. Grant (standing, fifth from left) with family members and missionaries in Japan, circa 1902. His daughter Mary is seated on the far left, and his wife, Augusta, is seated second from the left. Although the early work in Japan bore few fruits, it laid the groundwork for future missionaries to this land and to other foreign missions. (Used by permission, Utah State Historical Society, all rights reserved)

be one of the two persons chosen to fill those vacancies. I had with me a copy of the revelation to John Taylor calling George Teasdale and myself to the apostleship, and I took it out of my pocket and sat there and wept for joy."[8]

In 1877 Heber J. Grant married Lucy Stringham, and in 1884 he married Emily Wells and Augusta Winters. This thrust him into the midst of difficulties caused by the anti-polygamy persecution of the late nineteenth century. By the time he became President of the Church, however, only Augusta was still living. Despite the many demands placed on his time as a General Authority, Heber J. Grant was consistently a considerate husband and devoted father. His ten daughters and their families always had an important place in his life.

Elder Grant's 1901 appointment to Japan was one of the most challenging assignments he ever received. The ability to converse in Japanese did not come easily to him but required much tedious effort. After returning home from two years in Japan, he was sent to preside over the European Mission for three more years. These experiences did much to round out his personal understanding of the opportunities as well as the challenges facing the Church worldwide, preparing him for his role as prophet.

President Grant's Character and Teachings

President Grant delegated much of the detailed administrative responsibility for ecclesiastical programs to his capable counselors, leaving him more time to make important contributions in the realms of business affairs and personal relations. Heber J. Grant was at home with the financial leaders and chief executives of many of the nation's largest corporations. They were his personal friends who welcomed him warmly and listened as he related faith-promoting experiences or spoke of the Saints' aspirations. These businessmen "found in President Grant a man of simple faith, one whose utter frankness bespoke an honesty that could be relied upon implicitly."[9] With them, he often discussed important matters while enjoying his favorite game of golf. These contacts were not only an important force in developing a more favorable attitude toward the Church and its members but were also vital in securing aid during periods of financial difficulty.

President Heber J. Grant, a physical-fitness enthusiast, often transacted Church business while golfing with ecclesiastical and business associates. Pictured here are (from left) Stephen H. Love, James H. Wattis, President Grant, President Charles W. Nibley, and Elder Reed Smoot. (LDS Church Archives)

Heber J. Grant's ability to make friends, to deal with people both great and small, and to show concern for the individual were important qualities of his life. A close associate, Joseph Anderson, observed that "he had no special interest in the accumulation of money except for the good he could do with it." For example, "no one will ever know how many mortgages on homes of widows he paid out of his own funds."[10] He loved to present good books to his associates or even to casual acquaintances, each year distributing scores, or probably hundreds, of volumes in this way.

"Keep the commandments" was an oft-repeated admonition by President Heber J. Grant. He frequently advocated the principles of tithing and abstinence from liquor and tobacco as taught in the Word of Wisdom. Concerning tithing he declared: "I believe that people are blessed in proportion to their liberality. I am not saying that they always make more dollars," but they will "increase in the faith and in the testimony and the knowledge of the divinity of the work in which we are engaged." Furthermore, he added, "I believe that to those who are liberal the Lord gives ideas, and they grow in capacity and ability more rapidly than those that are stingy."[11]

On the subject of the Word of Wisdom he testified: "There is absolutely no benefit to any human being derived from breaking the Word of Wisdom, but there is everything for his benefit, morally, intellectually, physically, and spiritually, in obeying it."[12] In 1931 the First Presidency lamented the efforts of "conspiring men" (D&C 89:4) in the tobacco industry seeking to "fasten the cigarette habit upon our boys and girls. . . . We feel constrained," the Presidency concluded, "to call upon all Saints to be faithful in observing the warning contained in this revelation [the Word of Wisdom], that they may enjoy the wonderful promises made by the Lord to those who walk in obedience to His commandments."[13] President Grant increasingly emphasized observance of the Word of Wisdom as an appropriate measure of worthiness for baptism, priesthood advancement, and temple privileges.

President Grant did not depend on his resources and judgment alone, but on divine support and guidance as was illustrated in an experience he had just after becoming President of the Church. For two months he pondered over who should fill the vacancy he had left in the Quorum of the Twelve. As he considered those whom he regarded as worthy and qualified, he returned again and again to the name of Richard W. Young, a military officer, lawyer, businessman, stake president, and lifelong friend. Finally, with the approval of his counselors, President Grant wrote Young's name on a slip of paper, intending to present this nomination at the regular weekly meeting of the First Presidency and the Twelve in the temple.

Biographer Francis M. Gibbons records, "President Grant removed the paper with the name written on it, fully intending to present him to the council for approval. But for a reason he could never fully explain, he was unable to do so; instead, he presented the name of Melvin J. Ballard, president of the Northwestern States Mission, a man with whom he had had very little personal contact."[14] This was a valuable lesson to President Grant, and confirmed the counsel he had received from President Joseph F. Smith just before that prophet's death: "The Lord bless you, my boy, the Lord bless you: you have got a great responsibility. Always remember this is the Lord's work and not man's. The Lord is greater than any man. He knows whom He wants to lead His Church, and never makes any mistake."[15]

Opened in 1922, the Primary Children's Hospital was located in this house on North Temple Street across from Temple Square for thirty years. (LDS Church Archives)

Temporal Concerns and Current Issues

Latter-day Saints regard their religion as embracing a total way of life. They accept the President of the Church as Prophet not only to the Saints but to the whole world. Hence there is no hard line between that which is spiritual and that which is temporal, or between that which is religious and that which is secular. It is no wonder, then, to find the Church involved in what may be regarded as temporal or secular matters. During President Heber J. Grant's administration, for example, the Church launched several programs for the temporal benefit of the Saints, and its leaders found it necessary to speak out on a variety of current issues.

Along with the Social Advisory Committee launched in 1916,[16] two new Church agencies were particularly interested in seeking remedies for some rather diverse social problems. In 1919 the Relief Society organized its Social Service Department to promote maternal health and child welfare, working in cooperation with public social welfare agencies. This department played a key role in supervising the adoption of children. The Relief Society's general board conducted a special summer course at Brigham Young University in 1920 followed by 126 local institutes to teach scientific methods in family welfare work.

Then, in 1922, the Primary Association opened a hospital in Salt Lake City. This project resulted from the desire to help crippled children on the part of Primary President Louie B. Felt and her counselor May Anderson. They studied the latest methods used in children's hospitals in the eastern United States. The Church remodeled and equipped a large house on North Temple Street across from Temple Square to provide the first home for the Primary Children's Hospital.

Throughout the twentieth century, Church leaders have taken stands on "moral issues" and urged the Saints to fulfill their responsibilities as good citizens by prayerfully considering and supporting worthy candidates and causes, and by being involved in the political party of their choice. President Heber J. Grant, for example, had been very active in Democratic party politics during his earlier life. He therefore had strong opinions on most political issues. As President of the Church, however, he was very cautious in expressing his personal feelings. He respected the principle of the separation of church and state, and he did not want to offend faithful Church members who might hold views opposite to his own. Nevertheless, there were many issues on which the Church felt compelled to take a stand, although it refrained from declaring a position on others.

THE LEAGUE OF NATIONS

An issue on which the Church did not take a stand was the question of America's joining the

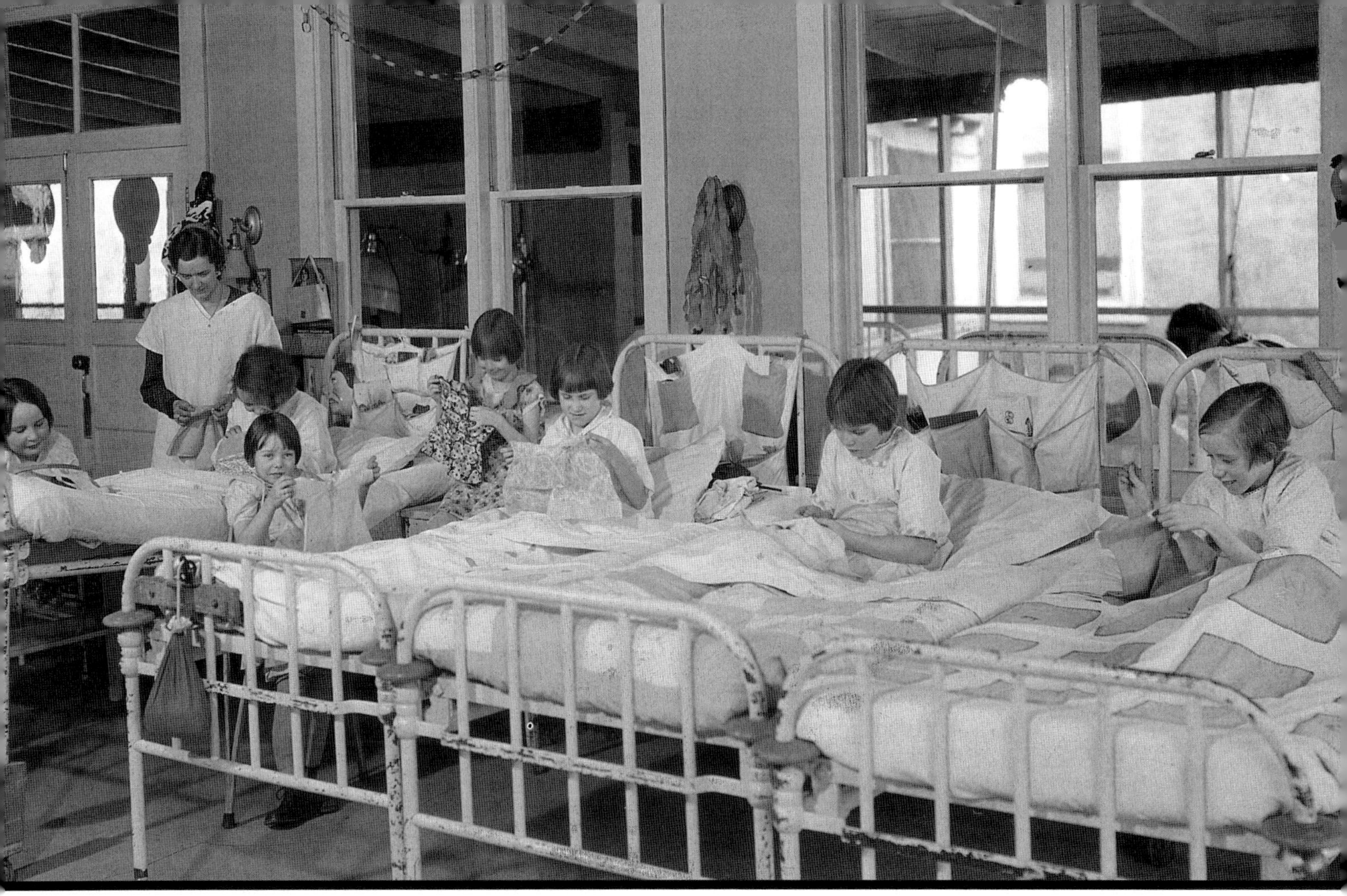

Children at Primary Children's Hospital. (LDS Church Archives)

League of Nations following the close of World War I. During 1919 United States President Woodrow Wilson was urging the importance of joining the league as the only effective means of preserving the peace so recently won. President Wilson had the support of the members of his Democratic party in the Senate, but most Republican senators favored entry into the league only if there were certain "reservations" or amendments made which they believed were necessary to protect America's sovereignty. Elder Reed Smoot was one of these "Reservationists" and spoke out in opposition. A large group of Church leaders, notably Elder B. H. Roberts, on the other hand, were open in their support of the league. Both sides recited passages from the Book of Mormon to support their respective positions. Speaking at a stake conference on September 21, 1919, President Grant acknowledged that he favored joining the league, but clearly stated that this was his personal belief and not the official stand of the Church. "I regret exceedingly," he declared, "that the standard works of the Church of Jesus Christ of Latter-day Saints have been brought into this controversy."[17] President Grant had his remarks published with the report of the general conference which convened two weeks later. Soon afterward the Senate defeated the treaty that would have involved the United States in the League of Nations and this question faded as a topic for debate. That Heber J. Grant did not allow differences on this issue to divide him from his brethren is reflected in his subsequent calling of three men as counselors—Charles W. Nibley, J. Reuben Clark Jr., and David O. McKay—who had questioned the wisdom of joining the league.[18]

COMMUNITY STANDARDS

During the 1920s, President Grant and his counselors had the occasion to speak out on a number of matters affecting the moral standards of the community. In 1925 when the demand arose to legalize betting on horse races, the First Presidency declared: "The Church has been and now is unalterably opposed to gambling in any form whatever. . . . It is opposed to all practices the tendency of which is to encourage the spirit of reckless speculation."[19] The following year Church leaders also condemned card playing as a waste of time which "brings no good, bodily, intellectually or in any way, and sometimes leads your children to become gamblers, because they become expert card-players."[20]

The wider availability of automobiles during the 1920s created new pressures on proper Sabbath observance. In 1928 the First Presidency insisted that "the Lord's day is a holy day—not a holiday." It should not "be given over to pleasure seeking." The Saints were encouraged to "utilize that portion of Sunday not appointed for meetings in promoting family association in the home." The Presidency also discouraged "more traveling than is necessary. . . . Let all unnecessary labor be suspended and let no encouragement be given by the attendance of members of the Church at places of amusement and recreation on the Sabbath day. If Sunday is spent in our meetings and in our homes greater blessings will come to our families and communities."[21]

THE REPEAL OF PROHIBITION

Because Latter-day Saints accept the Word of Wisdom (see D&C 89) as revelation from God, no other political issue of the early twentieth century touched the standards and beliefs of Mormonism more than did the question of prohibiting the manufacture or sale of alcoholic beverages. The question of prohibition had become a hot political issue in Utah as early as 1908. Senator and Apostle Reed Smoot advocated "local option," the position of the national Republican party, which held that each locality should be free to decide whether or not to outlaw liquor. Most Latter-day Saints favored total national prohibition. Perhaps the most vocal spokesman for this point of view was Heber J. Grant, then a member of the Council of the Twelve. His position was based on strong personal convictions, two of his close friends having died in early manhood after taking up tobacco and alcohol habits. The Church, however, did not officially endorse either local option or outright prohibition at that time. President Joseph F. Smith declared: "We endorse any movement looking to temperance."[22] In 1917 the Utah legislature approved prohibition for the state, and by 1920 the Eighteenth Amendment to the United States Constitution made it the law of the land nationwide.

The benefits of prohibition were accompanied by some problems. Bootleggers illegally produced and sold alcoholic beverages, and much of this traffic came to be dominated by criminal gangs. As the 1920s progressed, the demand for repealing the prohibition amendment increased. President Heber J. Grant rejected these demands. The Eighteenth Amendment, he argued, was "one of the greatest benefits that has come to the people of the United States."[23] He countered arguments of increased crime saying that the few who break the law should not receive more consideration than the millions who benefit from it. He believed there had been a dozen times more drinking before prohibition went into effect. Millions of homes were thus being spared from the wreckage of drunkenness.

During the early 1930s, various Church organizations gave renewed emphasis to living the Word of Wisdom. Each week during the 1931–32 season, the young people of the Church recited the following slogan in their Mutual Improvement Association meetings: "We stand for Physical, Mental and Spiritual Health through Observance of the Word of Wisdom." Observing the Word of Wisdom's centennial on February 27, 1933, helped focus still more attention on this principle. Throughout the Church this revelation had been the theme of all meetings of the previous Sunday.

Thus the anti-prohibition planks in the 1932 platforms of both major political parties were diametrically opposed to the stand being taken by the Church. Although both parties opposed a "return of the saloon," the Republicans advocated states' rights in dealing with the problem while the Democrats openly declared: "We advocate the repeal of the Eighteenth Amendment."[24]

The heavy Democratic victories (including victories in Utah) were at least in part a vote for the repeal of prohibition. After the election, the campaign against prohibition accelerated. By February 1933 the Twenty-first Amendment, which would repeal the Eighteenth, had passed both houses of Congress. By the fall of that year, thirty-three of the necessary thirty-six states had already ratified the new amendment. A special November election was called for to elect delegates to conventions that would decide whether or not Utah and some other states would provide the three remaining votes necessary to ratify the repeal. As the election drew closer, the pace of the campaign intensified. Numerous articles appeared in the Church's *Deseret News* and monthly magazines. At the October general conference, President Heber J. Grant reported receiving an unsigned postcard begging him not to talk about the Word of Wisdom again. Undeterred, President Grant responded: "I request each and every Latter-day Saint within the sound of my voice to read what I said about the Word of Wisdom just six months ago. Every word that I said I meant, and among other things I said I hoped and prayed that we as a people would not vote for the repeal of the Eighteenth Amendment. Really, I was almost tempted this morning to read my whole sermon over again, and let it go at that."[25] He actually went on to give a longer talk on the same topic.

Because the candidates' stand on prohibition was openly stated, the results of the special November election confirmed that Utah and two other states would vote for repeal. Clearly, many of the Utah Saints failed to follow their Church President's counsel. Salt Lake City, for example, defeated prohibition by a margin of better than three to one. These facts were trumpeted widely in the national press. On December 5 conventions met in the three ratifying states. The convention in Utah prolonged its proceedings to allow Pennsylvania and Ohio to vote first. Thus Utah, a majority of whose population were Latter-day Saints, deliberately gained the distinction of being the final state needed to ratify the Twenty-first Amendment repealing prohibition. Upon receiving word of the vote in Utah, the pro-liquor forces in New York City staged a parade featuring a banner proclaiming "Thank God for Utah!"

The defeat of prohibition was a keen disappointment to Church leaders and was a recurring theme in their talks for at least a decade. In 1935 Elder George F. Richards of the Council of the Twelve expressed these sentiments: "It has been a source of great regret to me that prominent, leading, faithful men in this Church have felt justified in voting in favor of the return of liquor as against the expressed will of the President of the Church, who I believe expressed the mind and will of God unto this people."[26] As late as 1941, President Grant lamented that the Saints' devotion did not extend far enough for them to pay any attention to his counsel. He wrote: "Many of them have such a bad case of politics that they ought to have a provision attached to their singing of 'We Thank Thee, O God, for a Prophet'—provided he keeps his mouth shut politically."[27] The following year he declared in conference: "May I never live long enough that when I am in favor of a thing and all the brethren are in favor of it, such as was the case when we were opposed to bringing whiskey back, that Utah and the Mormons will be in opposition to us."[28] In 1943 Elder George Albert Smith lamented that "in a state where we could have retained what we had, there were enough Latter-day Saints, so called, . . . who paid no attention to what the Lord wanted, ignored what He had said through his prophet, and what is the result? Such delinquency as we have never known." He was convinced that the Saints "are paying the penalty and will continue to do so until they turn away from their foolishness and desire with all their hearts to do what our Heavenly Father desires us to do."[29]

The repeal of prohibition in 1933 did not end the Church's involvement with the liquor question. Utah and several other states chose to have liquor sold only in state-operated stores. Over the years various business interests advocated making alcoholic beverages available in restaurants, but the Church, in concert with several non-Mormon groups, opposed all such "liquor by the drink" proposals.[30]

Geographical Expansion

Within the first few months of President Heber J. Grant's administration, Church membership passed five hundred thousand. Three-fourths of these Saints still lived in the essentially rural Intermountain area in western America. The next few years, however, would bring a definite geographical expansion. Evidences of this trend included the growing number of Latter-day Saints in major cities, the dedication of new temples, and the increased personal involvement of General Authorities in supervising and directing the Church's progress worldwide.

EXODUS FROM THE INTERMOUNTAIN AREA

Following the close of World War I, thousands of Latter-day Saints left the traditional centers of Mormon colonization in Utah and Idaho. The basically agricultural economy of the semiarid Intermountain West did not share in the general prosperity of the 1920s. Furthermore, the coming of the tractor and other machinery reduced the need for manpower, thus lessening the number of jobs available on the farm. This resulted in an exodus, especially of younger people, from these areas seeking improved economic opportunities in major metropolitan centers, particularly in southern California. This outward flow would be increased during the 1930s by the severe impact of the Great Depression in the Intermountain West. The Latter-day Saints therefore were part of the continuing westward movement and the prevailing rural-urban shift of the general population. Church activity came to play a new and important role in the lives of these transplanted Saints. Though living in large cities, they found through their branches or wards the close friendships and associations they had enjoyed in the small towns left behind. Some found that the move to a new environment occasioned a spiritual awakening. Howard W. Hunter, who came to California as a young man in the 1920s, later reflected, "I think of this period of my life as the time the truths of the gospel commenced to unfold. I always had a testimony of the gospel, but suddenly I commenced to understand."[31]

The Washington, D.C., Chapel (top) and the Hollywood Stake Center symbolized the growing strength of the Church in areas outside the Intermountain West. (LDS Church Archives)

In 1920 there were 3,967 Church members in California; during the next ten years this number soared to 20,599, and by 1940 the total reached 44,784. During these same twenty years, the portion of all Latter-day Saints living in the Pacific Coast states increased from 2.8 percent to 10.9 percent.

While most nineteenth-century migrations of the Saints had been encouraged or even sponsored by the Church, the movements during the twentieth century were the results of individual decisions. At least some of the Saints leaving the Intermountain area wondered if they were doing the right thing. A group in Santa Monica, California, for example, asked President Heber J. Grant in 1921 if they were out of harmony with Church policy because they had not officially been sent to live there. President Grant answered their letter in person during one of his frequent visits to the Golden State. He assured them that at that time a Mormon settlement in Santa Monica was in accordance with Church policies.

The formation of new stakes was clear evidence of Latter-day Saint growth in widely scattered urban centers. In 1844 Joseph Smith had declared: "I have received instructions from the Lord that from henceforth wherever Elders of Israel shall build up churches . . . there shall be a stake of Zion. In the great cities, as Boston, New York, etc., there shall be stakes."[32] In 1923 and 1927 stakes were established in Los Angeles and San Francisco, respectively, and during the next decade stakes were organized in several other prominent cities throughout the United States: New York, 1934; Honolulu, 1935; Chicago, 1936; Portland and Seattle, 1938; Denver and Washington, D.C., 1940. The construction of substantial chapels also was further evidence of Latter-day Saint growth

Choir at the dedication of the Alberta Temple in Canada in 1923. (LDS Church Archives)

in these urban centers. Examples included the beautiful Hollywood (Los Angeles) Stake Center and the Washington, D.C., Chapel, dedicated in 1929 and 1933, respectively. Not only did these buildings provide adequate facilities for Church activities, but they were attractive places where the Saints could bring their nonmember friends.

Not all Church members leaving the Intermountain area went to large cities. Many joined the thousands already scattered throughout the United States and Canada. Organization of the Church's first branch in Alaska during 1938 was symbolic of this diffusion. In some areas nearly half of the members lived too far from the nearest chapel to participate in any group programs. Providing meaningful activity for these scattered Saints was a challenge. To relieve this problem, several missions sponsored regional colonies where the scattered Saints might gather. Kelsey in northeast Texas, for example, flourished as a Mormon colony during the first decades of the twentieth century.

The dispersion of Church membership was reflected by the location of the first three temples dedicated during the twentieth century. In contrast to the previous four temples, all located in Utah, these new structures were located far from the headquarters of the Church. Construction of the Hawaii and Alberta temples had begun under the leadership of President Joseph F. Smith, but they were dedicated in 1919 and 1923, respectively, by President Heber J. Grant. In 1921 President Grant selected the site for a temple in Mesa, Arizona; he dedicated that beautiful structure six years later. These three imposing buildings attracted much favorable comment and symbolized the Church's commitment to continued activity and growth in these scattered areas.

DEVELOPMENTS ABROAD

As missionary work revived following the close of World War I, the General Authorities felt the need to have at least one of their number become personally acquainted with conditions in all parts of the world. President Grant therefore assigned Elder David O. McKay of the Quorum of the Twelve to undertake an inspection tour of the Church's far-flung missions and schools. At the time of this appointment, Elder McKay was serving as general superintendent of the Sunday School, as head of the Church's educational system, and as chairman of the committee assigned to correlate priesthood and auxiliary activities. Assigned to be his companion was Hugh J. Cannon, editor of the *Improvement Era* and a former missionary to Germany and stake president. Elders McKay and Cannon were set apart for their tour by President Heber J. Grant on December 2, 1920, and traveled approximately fifty-six thousand miles during the next thirteen months. They visited the Church's missions in the Pacific, dedicated China for the preaching of the gospel, experienced the unique challenges in the non-Christian lands of southeast Asia, witnessed firsthand the Jewish-Arab tensions in the Holy Land, and finally toured the missions of Europe before returning home. Their report gave the General Authorities an unprecedented worldwide vision of the Church's challenges and opportunities, enabling them to weigh the needs of one area against those of another.

On Christmas Day, 1925, Elder Melvin J. Ballard (center) dedicated the continent of South America for the preaching of the gospel. (LDS Church Archives)

By 1924 the outlook for missionary work in Japan had become quite bleak. Since the mission had opened in 1901, only 174 converts had been baptized. Linguistic and cultural differences were now compounded by a growing sense of Japanese nationalism. The 1924 United States immigration law greatly restricted the number of Oriental individuals who could enter the country and was very offensive to the Japanese. These and other conditions led President Heber J. Grant, who had opened the mission twenty-three years earlier, to withdraw missionaries from Japan. Although the accomplishments of the mission may have appeared meager, there were some lasting contributions. The Book of Mormon and other Church literature had been translated into Japanese. There were a few active Saints who worked to keep the Church organization functioning and who remained faithful during the dark years that would follow. Some of them would be present to help reestablish the Church in Japan following World War II.

While proselyting was being closed in Asia, missionary work in South America was about to begin. The first gospel seeds were sown not by missionaries from North America but by immigrants from Europe, and not among South America's Spanish-speaking majority but among a German-speaking minority. Following the close of World War I, a large number of Germans left Europe in quest of a better future in South America, particularly in Argentina and southern Brazil. Wilhelm Friedrichs, a Latter-day Saint convert, and his family arrived in 1923. Emil Hoppe, whom Friedrichs had helped convert in Germany, followed soon afterward. Friedrichs and Hoppe eagerly shared the gospel with other German immigrants, and soon several families were interested. Friedrichs reported his activities to the First Presidency and requested that missionaries be sent to Argentina.

In the fall of 1925 Church leaders sent Elder Melvin J. Ballard of the Quorum of the Twelve to South America to open a mission there. He was accompanied by two members of the First Council of the Seventy—Elder Rulon S. Wells, who spoke fluent German, and Elder Rey L. Pratt (then serving as president of the Mexican Mission), whose knowledge of Spanish and of Latin American culture would prove essential. Upon their arrival in Buenos Aires, they were greeted by the Friedrichs and Hoppe families with tears of gratitude. Early on Christmas

J. Vernon Sharp poses with an Aymara chief and his wife in Ollanttaitambo, Peru, located near Macchu Picchu, in 1927. When Elder Melvin J. Ballard dedicated South America for the preaching of the gospel in 1925, he prayed that the promises made to the descendants of Lehi might soon be fulfilled. (LDS Church Archives)

As part of the 1930 centennial celebration, a pageant called "The Message of the Ages" was performed in the Tabernacle and, as depicted here, on the steps of the Utah State Capitol Building. (Deseret News *photo*)

morning 1925, Elder Ballard and his companions went to a secluded grove of weeping willows near the banks of Rio de La Plata. On this beautiful summer morning the group knelt and Elder Ballard offered a prayer dedicating South America for the proclamation of the gospel. He especially petitioned that promises made to the descendants of Lehi might soon be fulfilled. Just before returning home a few months later, Elder Ballard prophesied that the work would grow slowly at first, but that eventually thousands would be baptized. Within a few years, missionary work had spread into southern Brazil, but the full realization of Elder Ballard's prophecies would not come until after World War II.[33]

Church leaders continued to counsel European Saints to remain in their homelands and build up the Church there. Despite this counsel, many remembered the earlier ideal of "gathering to Zion" and believed that they could escape poverty by immigrating to America. Therefore the years 1923 to 1930 witnessed the heaviest emigration the German Mission had ever experienced up to that time. Consequently, Church membership in Europe grew very slowly, increasing from 25,500 in 1920 to only 28,000 a decade later. There was, however, at least one new area into which the gospel was introduced during these years; Czechoslovakia was opened to missionary work in 1929.

The Church's Centennial

The decade of the 1920s witnessed a series of centennial observances. At the April general conference in 1920, Church leaders marked the one-hundredth anniversary of Joseph Smith's vision of the Father and the Son by stressing the authenticity of his testimony and by paying tribute to his work. A cantata entitled "The Vision," prepared for the occasion by Evan Stephens, was also presented. In 1923 and 1927 Saints and missionaries from the eastern states gathered at the Hill Cumorah and the Sacred Grove near Palmyra, New York, to commemorate the Angel Moroni's visits and Joseph Smith's receiving the gold plates there one hundred years earlier. In 1928 the Church completed the purchase of 283 acres that included the entire Hill Cumorah. Two years earlier, the Church had purchased the Peter Whitmer farm near Fayette, New York, where the Church was organized in 1830. In 1937 the Church would purchase a portion of the Martin Harris farm near Palmyra and would also begin to acquire property in Nauvoo, Illinois, including the former temple site.

All these celebrations reached a climax with the centennial of the Church's organization. George Albert Smith, then a member of the Twelve and interested in Church history, chaired the committee that planned this event. Because huge crowds from all over the Church had poured into Salt Lake City desiring to attend one of the centennial general conference sessions, a fourth day was added to the usual three-day format. The opening session on Sunday morning, April 6, 1930, the one-hundredth anniversary of the Church's organization, was the highlight. President Heber J. Grant read the First Presidency's centennial message to the peoples of the world, bearing witness to the divine mission of the Savior and to the latter-day restoration of His Church through the Prophet Joseph Smith. The message called on Church members around the world "to rededicate their lives to the service of the Master and the establishment of his kingdom upon the earth."[34] Church leaders were sustained in a special manner normally reserved for "solemn assemblies" where a new Church President is being installed; each priesthood group sat in an assigned area on the main floor in the Tabernacle and stood as a body to vote when its turn came. When the voting was concluded, the entire congregation stood and rendered the hallowed Hosanna Shout by waving white handkerchiefs as they shouted in unison: "Hosanna, Hosanna, Hosanna to God and the Lamb; Amen, Amen, and Amen." Because the Saints identified this ritual with such special events as temple dedications, the shout, like the special manner of voting, added impressively to the spirit and solemnity of the conference.

The Church's seven temples were illuminated at night for the first time during conference week, symbolizing "the joy of the people that the work of the Lord had successfully completed its first century."[35] A centennial pageant, "The Message of the Ages," opened in the Tabernacle that Sunday evening. A working force of fifteen hundred persons included the cast, the Tabernacle Choir, and an orchestra. The pageant reviewed how the gospel, known to ancient prophets, was restored in the latter days.

These centennial observances reinforced the Latter-day Saints' interest in Church history. During the Sunday afternoon session of conference, Elder B. H. Roberts presented the several large volumes of his *A Comprehensive History of the Church*, which was being published as an official part of the centennial celebration. He indicated that this work contained the sermon he would like to preach and the testimony he would like to bear on the occasion of the Church's centennial. The six volumes represented in book form the history originally written by Elder Roberts for *Americana* magazine between 1909 and 1915. Two of Elder Roberts's associates in the Church historian's office were also making significant contributions; Elder Joseph Fielding Smith's *Essentials in Church History*, which had been published in 1921 as a lesson manual for the Melchizedek Priesthood quorums, would continue to be the most popular single volume of Church history for more than half a century. Andrew Jenson had compiled eight hundred large manuscript volumes, about half giving histories of specific local units and the remainder being the day-by-day "Journal History of the Church." At the time of the Church's centennial, Jenson was completing publication of his multivolume *Latter-day Saint Biographical Encyclopedia* and was condensing his histories of Church units for publication in a single reference volume to be known as the *Encyclopedic History of the Church*.

The opening years of Heber J. Grant's administration, then, saw a substantial geographical expansion in Church membership at the same time as the series of centennial observances was focusing the Saints' attention on their heritage. But there were other developments occurring during these same years. One of the most important of these was a redefinition of emphasis in the Church's educational program.

6

Charting the Course of the Church in Education

*L*atter-day Saints have always been interested in education, believing that knowledge has eternal significance. To support this commitment are such scriptural passages as: "The glory of God is intelligence, or, in other words, light and truth" and "It is impossible for a man to be saved in ignorance" (D&C 93:36; 131:6). While the foregoing passages refer primarily to spiritual attainment, the following injunctions refer more specifically to the importance of gaining a broad education: "And I give unto you a commandment that you shall teach one another the doctrine of the kingdom. . . . Of things both in heaven and in the earth, and under the earth; things which have been, things which are, things which must shortly come to pass; things which are at home, things which are abroad. . . . Yea, seek ye out of the best books words of wisdom; seek learning, even by study and also by faith" (D&C 88:77–79, 118). "Study and learn, and become acquainted with all good books, and with languages, tongues, and people" (D&C 90:15). "Obtain a knowledge of history, and of countries, and of kingdoms, of laws of God and man, and all this for the salvation of Zion" (D&C 93:53). During President Heber J. Grant's administration, however, serious questions were raised concerning whether or not the Church should sponsor an educational program and, if so, what direction it should take.

The Saints had organized the School of the Prophets in Kirtland, one of the earliest programs for adult education in the

Students talk outside the institute of religion building at the University of Idaho in Moscow, Idaho. Under the direction of J. Wylie Sessions, this institute became a prototype for others at college campuses throughout the nation. (Deseret News *photo*)

Brigham Young University and surrounding community in the 1920s. (Photographic Archives, Harold B. Lee Library, Brigham Young University, Provo, Utah)

United States. Upon arriving in the Great Basin they quickly established local elementary schools and the territorial University of Deseret. Near the end of his life, Brigham Young launched two schools—Brigham Young Academy at Provo in 1875 and Brigham Young College at Logan the following year. A system of "academies" or Church high schools, grew to more than two dozen schools from Canada to Mexico during the following decade. To promote and give direction to these schools, the Church organized its board of education in 1888.

A Time of Transition

By the end of the nineteenth century, forces were at work that would drastically change the character of the Latter-day Saints' educational efforts. The increasing number of non-Mormons in Utah led to the passage in 1890 of a territorial law forbidding religious instruction in public schools and providing for the establishment of public high schools. Therefore, during that same year the Church founded Religion Classes to provide weekday religious instruction that would supplement the secular learning children were receiving in public elementary schools. These classes convened in ward buildings after school, generally one afternoon each week. Thus, this new auxiliary functioned side by side with the similar program of the Primary, which had been organized twelve years earlier. While the Primary emphasized activity, the Religion Class concentrated on instruction. Then, as religious instruction was eliminated from the University of Deseret (which was renamed the University of Utah in 1892), several of the Church's academies began to add college-level courses, particularly in the field of teacher education. In the 1890s, college students began to outnumber high school students at the Brigham Young Academy, and in 1903 it was renamed Brigham Young University.

With the growth of free, tax-supported high schools, enrollment declined in the LDS academies, where students were required to pay tuition. President Joseph F. Smith was quite concerned over

Major developments in Church education, 1870–1940

1870 — 1880 — 1890 — 1900

1875
Brigham Young Academy founded

1888
Church Board of Education organized

1890
Religion Classes created for elementary school students

this trend. He explained that the Church continued to spend a substantial share of its tithing funds to maintain Church schools so that "true religion undefiled before God the Father, may be inculcated in the minds and hearts of our children while they are getting an education, to enable the heart, the soul and the spirit of our children to develop with proper teaching, in connection with the secular training that they receive in schools."[1]

Nevertheless, enrollment continued to decline, and by 1911 there were more Latter-day Saint youth attending public rather than Church schools. The Church therefore inaugurated a part-time religious education program similar to the Religion Classes, but for high school students. The first "seminary" was opened in 1912 at Granite High School near Salt Lake City. This was done on recommendation by the Granite Stake presidency. Joseph F. Merrill, the member of the stake presidency in charge of education, had based his ideas for the new program on religious seminaries he had seen in Chicago.[2] The new program quicky proved to be an effective way to supplement the secular education students were receiving in public high schools, and within a few years several more seminaries were opened, primarily in Utah. Thus, in the early twentieth century, the Church was conducting two distinct types of educational programs: (1) full-time academies that provided secular as well as religious instruction; and (2) Religion Classes and seminaries that supplemented secular instruction in public schools.

A Decade of Decision

The Church needed to decide whether to emphasize its full-time schools or its part-time religious education programs. In 1919 three members of the Twelve were appointed to give direction to education. Elder David O. McKay, a former principal of one of the Church's academies and a recently appointed general superintendent of the Sunday School, became commissioner, with Elders Stephen L Richards and Richard R. Lyman as assistants. Adam S. Bennion was named superintendent of Church schools that same year.

In 1920 the Church took the first step toward discontinuing its full-time schools. The board of education adopted the following recommendations of Commissioner McKay: (1) Most of the academies should be closed because they were supported by funds from all over the Church but benefitted only a relatively limited area. (2) A few of the academies, where college-level courses had already been incorporated—Dixie Academy in St. George, Brigham Young College in Logan, Weber Academy in Ogden, Snow Academy in Ephraim, all in Utah; and Ricks Academy in Rexburg, Idaho—would become Church junior colleges, stressing "normal" or teacher-education programs. (3) Courses leading to a four-year degree would be concentrated at Brigham Young University.[3] By 1923 nine other academies were closed and their buildings made available to the state at a nominal cost. Also, high school courses were eliminated from the junior colleges.

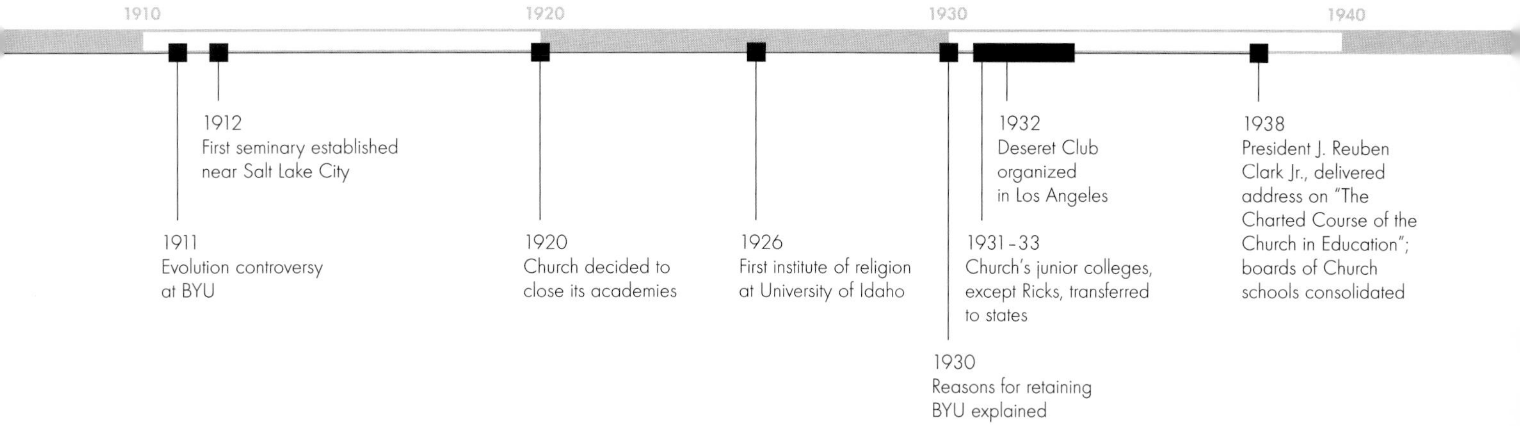
1910
1920
1930
1940
1912
First seminary established
near Salt Lake City
1911
Evolution controversy
at BYU
1920
Church decided to
close its academies
1926
First institute of religion
at University of Idaho
1932
Deseret Club
organized
in Los Angeles
1931–33
Church's junior colleges,
except Ricks, transferred
to states
1930
Reasons for retaining
BYU explained
1938
President J. Reuben
Clark Jr., delivered
address on "The
Charted Course of the
Church in Education";
boards of Church
schools consolidated

The next major step in reshaping the Church's educational program came following a series of key board of education meetings during February and March 1926. President Heber J. Grant identified the underlying cause for this reappraisal of the Church's activities in education when he declared: "I am free to confess that nothing has worried me more since I became president than the expansion of the appropriation for the Church School system. With the idea of cutting down the expense, we appointed three of the Apostles as Commissioners; but instead of cutting down, we have increased and increased."[4] In 1925 the Church had spent $958,440.67 for education, which amounted to 25.9 percent of its total tithing expenditures.[5]

Members of the board wondered: (1) Does the Church receive sufficient benefit from spending eight times as much on educating students in a Church school as compared to those in seminary? (2) Could the Church spend its funds better elsewhere? (3) Can the Church afford to compete with the growing number of public junior colleges? (4) Can the Church afford to operate Brigham Young University on the same level as "the richly endowed universities of our land?" (Some of these questions continued to be asked in later decades.)

The First Presidency from 1934–45: (from left) J. Reuben Clark Jr., Heber J. Grant, and David O. McKay. (Used by permission, Utah State Historical Society, all rights reserved)

At the conclusion of these discussions the board decided to continue establishing seminaries wherever they were needed and wanted and to "withdraw from the field of the junior colleges" since the states made provisions to operate their own schools. Brigham Young University was to concentrate on upper division work, especially the preparation of teachers, and to work toward becoming a superior, though not necessarily large, Church university.[6]

The first school to close was the Latter-day Saints College in Salt Lake City. After 1931 only two departments continued, becoming the LDS Business College and the McCune School of Music. The former college's campus, located just behind the Hotel Utah on the block east of Temple Square, provided badly needed space for the Genealogical Society library and for administrative offices of the auxiliaries and other Church organizations.

The board offered the facilities of other Church junior colleges to the respective local governments at a minimal cost, with the understanding that these schools would be kept open. Under such an agreement Snow College in Ephraim was transferred to the state of Utah in 1932, as were Weber College in Ogden and Dixie College in St. George the following year. Gila College in Thatcher, Arizona, was transferred to the county in 1933. When Ricks College property was offered to Idaho, however, the state declined to assume this added economic burden. The Church therefore appropriated funds to maintain Ricks College as a Church-owned junior college.[7] The board decided to retain Brigham Young University as part of the Church's educational program for three reasons explained in 1930 by Commissioner Joseph F. Merrill: (1) BYU was where students could be trained as teachers for Church seminaries as well as for public schools. (2) Faithful scholars at a Church university could interpret the discoveries of science and the results of research in the light of gospel truths. "When men find that we are learned in their science and philosophy they have respect for us, one that ignorance could never command. How can we be assured a group of scholars, familiar and sympathetic with our doctrines and ideals, scholars able and ready to be our advocates and defenders . . . unless we have a university?" (3) The Church felt it needed "a university that shall hold up Latter-day Saint ideals so high in the educational world that all students in all schools of all grades may see the beauty thereof, and perhaps be influenced by them."[8]

Thus by 1930 the Church had definitely placed its emphasis on part-time religious education. The Church continued to operate the Juárez Academy and elementary schools in its northern Mexican colonies. Missions also operated several small schools in the South Pacific; one of the largest of these, the Maori Agricultural College in New Zealand, however, closed following a disastrous earthquake in 1931.

The Juárez Academy in Colonia Juárez, Mexico, was one of the few schools that the Church continued to operate after 1930. (LDS Church Archives)

Emphasis on Seminaries and Institutes

While the Church was taking steps to close most of its full-time schools, its part-time programs of religious instruction were expanding. For example, seminary enrollment grew from about five thousand in 1922 to nearly thirty thousand a decade later. The relative economy of these part-time programs would become increasingly attractive as the Great Depression of the 1930s tightened restrictions on Church funds. By 1938, seminary enrollment had reached 38,939. Typically these classes were offered in Latter-day Saint communities, mostly in Utah and southern Idaho, but a few scattered classes were also offered in Colorado, Nevada, and Wyoming.[9]

These seminary classes were conducted on a "released-time" basis. This meant that students took seminary instruction much the same as any other class during their regular school day. Over the years there have been several inconclusive challenges to this system. One of these came in 1930 when the state high school inspector charged that the principle of separation between church and state was being violated because high school credit was granted for religion classes and because public funds helped bus students who spent one hour of their day

The Maori Agricultural College rugby team in 1926. The college was one of several schools operated by the Church in the Pacific. It was closed, however, in 1931 following an earthquake. (LDS Church Archives)

Payson, Utah, Seminary in 1926, at a time when the Church was expanding its part-time programs for religious education. (LDS Church Archives)

in seminary. In response, Commissioner Joseph F. Merrill pointed out that giving credit for Bible courses taught in private schools was an accepted practice and that seminaries actually reduced public educational costs by providing classes for many students one hour each day.

Finally, the state board of education ordered that the seminaries be operated as completely separate units but approved granting high school credit for some seminary classes.[10] Most local school boards supported the LDS seminary program. Ironically, only in Salt Lake City did the board reject the released-time concept, resulting in seminary classes being held early in the morning before school hours. Consequently, in Salt Lake City seminary enrollment was only 10 percent of the high school-aged youth, while the average in released-time areas was 70 percent.

A similar part-time religious education program, originally called Collegiate Seminary, had developed on the university level. It began in 1926 when the First Presidency appointed J. Wylie Sessions to go to the University of Idaho in Moscow "to take care of our boys and girls" there, and "to see what the Church ought to do for our students attending state universities." Sessions, who had a background in education but not in religious instruction, analyzed any information he could find about what other groups were doing to get religion onto college campuses. He particularly patterned his program after the religious "foundations" at the University of Illinois. The name "Institute of Religion" was suggested by a non-Mormon friend in Idaho. Sessions believed that classes with solid academic content, along with well-planned social activities and an attractive, well-equipped building, were all essential in competing successfully for the students' time.[11]

By 1929 similar programs had been established on two other campuses, and during the 1930s, institutes spread to a total of seventeen locations, including all major schools in the Intermountain states as well as the University of Wyoming and locations in California. Sessions personally supervised the inauguration of the program and the erection of facilities at several of these locations.

Unusual circumstances led to the establishing of institutes in southern California. In 1935 the University of Southern California invited the Church to send a representative to instruct academic classes on Mormonism in its school of religion. Elder John A. Widtsoe of the Council of the Twelve, a former university president, received this assignment. Following the 1935–36 school year, G. Byron Done was appointed to succeed Elder Widtsoe and to become director of the institute in Los Angeles. In order to promote the institute programs and to provide additional social contacts for students, Done inaugurated "fireside chats," informal gatherings on Sunday evenings that treated topics of current interest.

The institutes provided an opportunity to integrate religious instruction with the secular university studies. By 1938 there were approximately four thousand students enrolled.

A companion program, the Deseret Club, had its beginning in southern California. A group of leading Latter-day Saints in the area felt the need to bring students together for intellectual and social activities within the influence of Latter-day Saint ideals and standards. The Deseret Club was formally organized in 1932 at the campus of the University of California at Los Angeles (UCLA). The club soon spread to other Los Angeles college campuses. When Elder Widtsoe was in the area, he recognized the value of the Deseret Club in the lives of LDS students, and in 1936 he was instrumental in bringing it under that official sponsorship of the Church Board of Education. Eventually, Deseret clubs came to be organized on campuses where there were not enough Latter-day Saint students to justify establishing the full institute program.[12]

Worldly Scholarship and the Gospel

LDS educational leaders during the twentieth century have stressed the importance of scholarly preparation for faculty members, especially in the Church's schools. President George H. Brimhall of Brigham Young University had been eager to strengthen the school's faculty and to expand its curriculum. Between 1907 and 1909, therefore, he hired four new teachers who had advanced degrees from leading universities of the nation; one of these was the first Ph.D. to teach at BYU. These teachers, however, enthusiastically presented speculative theories as the product of the most current scientific research. Students were confused when these ideas came into conflict with traditional gospel teachings. Following a careful investigation in 1911, the Church's superintendent of schools concluded that these professors treated the Bible as only "a collection of myths [and] folk-lore" with "some inspiration," rejected the idea of miracles, and questioned the historicity of the Restoration. Despite the First Presidency's 1909 affirmation that Adam, "the primal parent of our race," was divinely created in the image of God, these men presented "the theory of evolution . . . as a demonstrated law."[13] Even though a majority of collegiate students supported these teachers, following an investigation by the Church Board of Education in 1911, they were asked to resign. Many predicted that this action would lead to the demise of BYU. In response, President Brimhall asserted, "If the life of the college depends on any number of men out of harmony with the brethren who preside over the Church, then it is time for the college to die."[14] He believed that he could have sided with the professors and received much popular acclaim, but added, "I would rather be a Moses on the mount with all of Israel against me, than Aaron at the altar of the Golden calf with all of Israel dancing around and praising me."[15]

President Joseph F. Smith was concerned that inexperienced students were not always equipped to determine whether or not a given theory was true, and that discussions of such topics only left the young people "in an unsettled frame of mind." He explained that "the conclusion that evolution would be best left out of discussion in our Church schools" was not any indication of how much of this theory may be true or false. While the Lord has not revealed the *"modus operandi"* employed in creating the world, President Smith declared, He has revealed the "simple and effectual way of serving Him" and there need be no speculation about this. President Smith was also concerned that speculation on modern theories would undermine the unity that should exist among members of the Church.[16]

Academic scholarship, particularly in the field of religion, received increasing emphasis in the later 1920s and 1930s. With the expansion of seminaries and the inauguration of the institutes of Religion, Church educational leaders felt the need to provide more adequate training and curriculum materials for the teachers in these programs. Instruction in theology was expanded at Brigham Young University. In 1930 Guy C. Wilson, who had opened that first seminary nearly two decades earlier, became the first full-time religion teacher at BYU. Special summer courses were offered for seminary and institute teachers, and from 1930 to 1933 noted scholars in biblical and religious studies came to BYU as guest lecturers. At the same time, several promising graduate students were encouraged to seek advanced degrees at noted centers such as the Chicago Divinity School. By the mid-1930s, however, an increasing number of Church members and leaders were concerned over teachers of religion being trained by non–Latter-day Saint scholars and were worried that higher criticism of the scriptures and other "humanistic" ideas were creeping into what was being taught. These concerns led the General Authorities to give much closer supervision to the Church's educational system, especially to religious instruction. Two members of the Twelve were assigned to interview all faculty members at Brigham Young University to determine their loyalty to the Church and its teachings. As a result of this attention, several teachers felt uncomfortable and left BYU to accept positions elsewhere.[17]

President J. Reuben Clark.
(Deseret News *photo*)

Two new counselors called to the First Presidency during the 1930s played a key role in giving important direction to education as well as to other Church programs. J. Reuben Clark Jr. and David O. McKay became counselors to President Heber J. Grant in 1933 and 1934, respectively. Following a quarter century's distinguished diplomatic career, President Clark had become undersecretary of state and was serving as the United States ambassador to Mexico at the time of his call to the First Presidency. And perhaps none have come into the Presidency with a richer background in Church service than did David O. McKay, who had fulfilled significant priesthood, Sunday School, correlation, education, and missionary assignments.

In 1938 J. Reuben Clark Jr., representing the First Presidency, outlined the objectives of the Church's educational activities and specified the qualifications for teachers therein. His address, "The Charted Course for the Church in Education," was delivered at a special summer gathering of teachers at Aspen Grove in Provo Canyon near the BYU campus and has become an oft-quoted classic.

President Clark began by citing "some of the more outstanding and essential fundamentals underlying our Church school education." He declared that there are "two prime things which may not be overlooked, forgotten, blinked, shaded, or discarded." The first of these is "that Jesus Christ is the Son of God, the Only Begotten of the Father in the flesh, the Creator of the world, the Lamb of God, the sacrifice for the sins of the world . . . and that because of His death and by and through His resurrection every man born into the world since the beginning will be likewise literally resurrected." President Clark insisted that these truths "must all be honestly believed in full faith, by every member of the Church." The second truth that must likewise be accepted and taught is "that the Father and the Son actually and in truth and very deed appeared to the Prophet Joseph in a vision in the woods; that other heavenly visions followed to Joseph and to others; that the Gospel and the holy Priesthood after the Order of the Son of God were in truth and fact restored to the earth from which they were lost by the apostasy of the Primitive Church; that the Lord again set up His Church, through the agency of Joseph Smith; that the Book of Mormon is just what it professes to be; that to the Prophet came numerous revelations for the guidance, upbuilding, organization and encouragement of the Church and its members; [and] that the Prophet's successors, likewise called of God, have received revelations as the needs of the Church have required." President Clark stressed that these realities "must stand, unchanged, unmodified, without dilution, excuse, apology, or avoidance; they may not be explained away or submerged. Without these two great beliefs the Church would cease to be the Church," and, he stressed, those who do not believe them cannot be regarded as Latter-day Saints.

Then, speaking more directly to teachers, President Clark continued: "The youth of the Church, your students, are in great majority sound in thought and in spirit. The problem primarily is to keep them sound, not to convert them. The youth of the Church are hungry for things of the spirit; they are eager to learn the Gospel, and they want it straight, undiluted. . . . Doubt must not be planted in their hearts. Great is the burden and the condemnation of any teacher who sows doubt in a trusting soul."

He warned that "there is neither reason nor is there excuse for our Church religious training and teaching facilities, unless the youth are to be taught and trained in the principles of the Gospel, embracing therein the two great elements that Jesus is the Christ and that Joseph was God's prophet. The teaching of a system of ethics to the students is not a sufficient reason for running our seminaries and institutes. The great public school system teaches ethics."

The basic requirement for one who would teach gospel principles is, he said, "a personal testimony of their truthfulness. No amount of learning, no amount of study, and no number of scholastic degrees, can take the place of this testimony, which is the *sine qua non* of the teacher in our Church school system." A teacher lacking such a testimony, President Clark insisted, does not have "any place in the Church school system."

In conclusion, President Clark instructed teachers that "your chief interest, your essential and all but sole duty, is to teach the Gospel of the Lord Jesus Christ as that has been revealed in these latter days. You are to teach this Gospel using as your sources and authorities the Standard Works of the Church, and the words of those whom God has called to lead His people in these last days. You are not, whether high or low, to intrude into your work your own peculiar philosophy, no matter what its source or how pleasing or rational it seems to you to be. To do so would be to have as many different churches as we have seminaries—and that is chaos."[18]

Organizational developments also reflected the General Authorities' continuing interest in education and their desire to have more direct supervision of Church schools. Brigham Young University, Ricks College, and the LDS Business College each had previously been under separate boards of trustees. To achieve "a more centralized control," these local boards were released in 1938, and all units were brought under the direct supervision of the General Church Board of Education. This board consisted of General Authorities and a few others.[19] This increased supervision helped keep the educational system as a powerful spiritual force in the Church. Unlike many other universities in the nation that started as church-related schools but gradually became merely secular institutions, Brigham Young University continued to relate the learning of the world to the revealed truths of the gospel.

Attainments in Education

Latter-day Saints understandably pointed with pride to their educational attainments. Census data in 1940 indicated that Utah, where Church members represented the majority of the population, had the highest level of educational attainment of any state in the Union: young adults in Utah had completed an average of 11.7 years of school compared to 11.3 in the next two highest states and a national median of 10.3 years.[20] The *Improvement Era* reported with interest the results of studies conducted by E. L. Thorndike of Columbia University. He found that Utah had the highest proportionate number of persons listed in *Who's Who* and *American Men of Science*. Thorndike concluded that "the production of the superior men is surely not an accident, but is closely related to the kind of persons living in the area."[21]

The Great Depression and the Church Welfare Plan

One of the most powerful influences on the direction of Church history during the twentieth century was the Great Depression of the 1930s. During the 1920s speculation in stocks drove prices increasingly higher. But, during the fall of 1929, as optimism cooled, a wave of selling drove stock prices downward. On October 29, "Black Tuesday," the bottom fell out of the market and millions lost their savings. As people stopped buying unnecessary goods, many businesses failed. In the semiarid Mountain West, where most Latter-day Saints still lived, the impact on mining and agriculture was especially devastating. In 1932 unemployment in Utah reached 35 percent, compared to a national peak of 24.9 percent. During these years, average personal income in the Beehive State fell by 48.6 percent.[1]

The Church as an institution also felt the brunt of the Depression, but the Latter-day Saints did not share in the slump in religious activity experienced by most other denominations. A serious problem, however, was the decline in tithes, the Church's major source of income. Even though the amount of tithes dropped substantially, the number of those paying their tithing decreased only slightly. The drop in tithing income brought a corresponding decline in expenditures, falling from $4 million in 1927 to only $2.4 million in 1933.[2]

The Church was able to preserve its financial solvency through careful economizing. Nevertheless, this was accomplished only

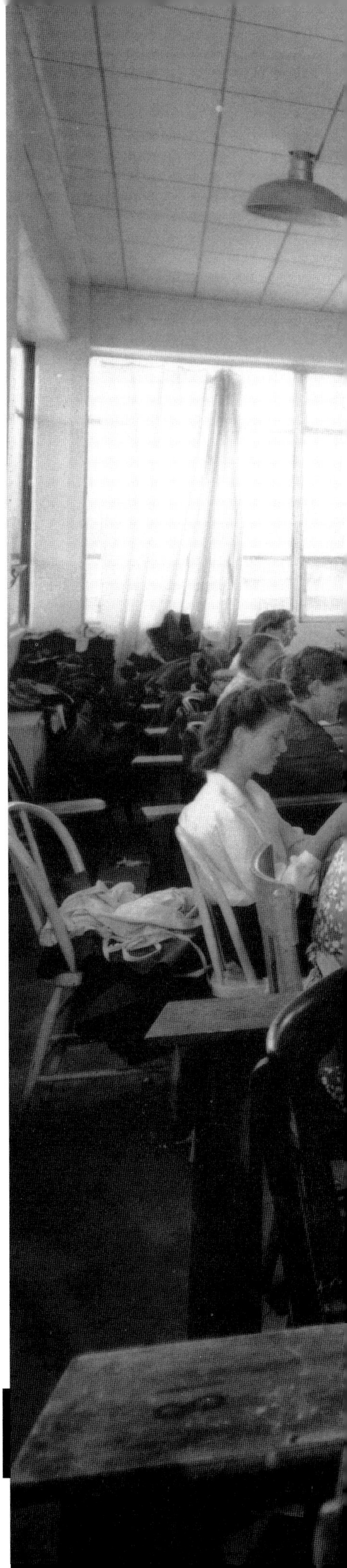

Women at work in the Salt Lake City Church Welfare Plant. (Used by permission, Utah State Historical Society, all rights reserved)

through curtailing worthwhile activities. Expenditures for building dropped most sharply, local congregations often postponing or even deciding not to build badly needed chapels. Also, many members had to put off the blessings of serving missions.

The New Deal

In the midst of these difficulties, the 1932 United States elections were of special interest to the leaders and members of the Church. Elder Reed Smoot, whom President Grant regarded as a staunch defender of prohibition, was up for reelection to the Senate. In the presidential race, the Republicans praised Herbert Hoover's handling of the Depression, while the Democrats and their candidate, Franklin D. Roosevelt, promised a "new deal" for the "forgotten man." The result was a landslide victory for the Democrats that swept most Republicans, including Senator Smoot, out of office. During the "one hundred days" following Roosevelt's inauguration in 1933, Congress enacted a series of sweeping measures giving the federal government power to combat the Depression. New Deal agencies regulated wages and hours, curbed unfair competition, subsidized and regulated farm production, constructed dams and hydroelectric generating plants, put more than 1.6 million youth to work at camps across the country, and provided aid to the needy.

As these programs got under way, they had the general support of most Latter-day Saints; and Church leaders encouraged cooperation with the government's efforts to create jobs and thereby relieve suffering. Elder Stephen L Richards called on the Latter-day Saints to support the government's policies. "It is true that we may entertain some different views, and we have the right to our opinion," he conceded, "but in an emergency an army follows its commander." He urged the Latter-day Saints to support, "not only the form of government under which they live, but [also] those who preside over them."[3]

Although Church leaders, notably Elder B. H. Roberts, generally approved of the New Deal during its first years, they did, nevertheless, voice some reservations. Perhaps the greatest worry to Church leaders was that some of the Saints might succumb to a "dole mentality." President Grant sadly acknowledged that many were saying: "Well, others are getting some government relief, so why should not I get some of it?" "I believe that there is a growing disposition among the people," he said, "to try to get something from the government of the United States with little hope of ever paying it back. I think this is all wrong."[4] Elder Stephen L Richards lamented: "The practice of 'sponging' on the government is perverting the finest virtues of American citizenship—self-respect, self-reliance and integrity."[5] Another concern was the government's accumulation of debt in order to finance relief programs. The United States national debt, which had peaked at $25.5 billion at the end of World War I, had dropped to $16 billion by 1930. As New Deal programs multiplied, however, the debt doubled by 1936, reaching

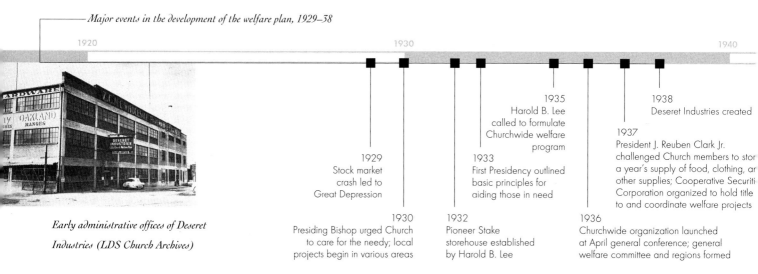

Major events in the development of the welfare plan, 1929–38

1920 — 1930 — 1940

1929
Stock market crash led to Great Depression

1930
Presiding Bishop urged Church to care for the needy; local projects begin in various areas

1932
Pioneer Stake storehouse established by Harold B. Lee

1933
First Presidency outlined basic principles for aiding those in need

1935
Harold B. Lee called to formulate Churchwide welfare program

1936
Churchwide organization launched at April general conference; general welfare committee and regions formed

1937
President J. Reuben Clark Jr. challenged Church members to stor[e] a year's supply of food, clothing, an[d] other supplies; Cooperative Securiti[es] Corporation organized to hold title to and coordinate welfare projects

1938
Deseret Industries created

Early administrative offices of Deseret Industries (LDS Church Archives)

Unemployed men line up outside a registration office in 1931. It has been estimated that during the Great Depression some four to five million Americans were without work. (UPI photo)

$33.8 billion. This expansion of the federal government's role raised yet other concerns. J. Reuben Clark Jr., sustained in 1933 as President Grant's counselor, emphasized the declaration that the Lord had "established the Constitution of this land, by the hands of wise men" (D&C 101:80). He believed that the inspired Constitution's greatest contribution was the separation of powers by which the executive, legislative, and judicial branches of government checked one another and yet worked harmoniously together. He feared that the New Deal was upsetting this balance as well as the proper division of power between the national government and the states.[6]

Guiding Principles

As the Great Depression of the 1930s spread economic suffering throughout the world, Latter-day Saint leaders were not left without guidance as to how they should respond to the crisis. From the beginning the Lord had commanded, "Thou shalt love thy neighbour as thyself" (Leviticus 19:8; Matthew 22:39), a principle which the Apostle James designated "the royal law" (James 2:8). When the Lord gave this commandment to the children of Israel He also instructed them to provide for the poor (see Leviticus 19:10). During His earthly ministry the Savior linked helping the poor with becoming perfect (see Matthew 19:21). In the present dispensation the Lord again commanded His Saints to remember, visit, and administer to those in need (see D&C 44:6; 52:40). He has vigorously condemned those who are able but refuse to help their less fortunate brethren (see Mosiah 4:16–18; D&C 56:16; 104:18).

In 1834 the Lord declared that it was His purpose to care for His Saints but cautioned, "it must needs be done in mine own way" (D&C 104:15–16). Three years earlier He had revealed His "own way." The Saints had been commanded to consecrate their property to the bishop for the care of the poor. Each individual then received a stewardship based not only on his or her family's needs but also on their circumstances (such as abilities or talents) and on their "just" wants (see D&C 42:30; 51:3; 82:17). All were expected to work to the extent of their ability for what they would receive (see D&C 42:42; 68:30–31; 75:29). Individuals felt not only the usual economic pressures but also a religious or spiritual obligation to develop or magnify their stewardships for the benefit of others. Any surplus beyond a family's wants and needs was transferred to the bishop's storehouse for the good of the whole group. Latter-day Saints often refer to living this law of consecration as the united order.

As Church leaders contemplated the needs of the Saints during the Depression they could also look back at the examples of at least two groups who had lived according to the united order—Enoch's city of Zion and the Book of Mormon people following the Savior's visit to America (see Moses 7:13–19; 4 Nephi 1:2–5; 15–17). Early Christians may also have lived this principle (see Acts 4:32–35).

Even before the Depression decade, the Church had an ongoing welfare program. During the 1920s the Presiding Bishopric and the Relief Society general board were especially active in finding employment for the jobless, maintaining a storehouse, and in other ways aiding the needy.[7] As economic conditions grew worse, therefore, the Church was able to build on already existing foundations. In 1930 Presiding Bishop Sylvester Q. Cannon declared that "it is our business . . . to see to it that none of the active members of the Church suffers for the necessities of life." He explained that the object was to "help people to help themselves," aiding them to become independent rather than depending on the Church for assistance.[8]

Local leaders were innovative as they sought solutions to the economic distress of their members. The Granite Stake in Salt Lake City put the unemployed to work on various stake projects; they operated a sewing shop where donated clothing was renovated, and helped secure food for the needy through cooperative arrangements with nearby farmers. The Pioneer Stake, also in Salt Lake City, was probably hardest hit by the Depression. Under the leadership of its young stake president, Harold B. Lee, a storehouse was established for the benefit of the poor. It was stocked with goods produced on a variety of stake projects or donated by Church members.

A Churchwide Effort

The General Authorities gave encouragement, counsel, and support to efforts by local Church units to meet the Depression emergency.

FIRST PRESIDENCY INSTRUCTIONS

An especially important document in the history of the Church's welfare program was a circular letter issued by the First Presidency in July 1933. President J. Reuben Clark Jr. had a significant role in formulating the letter's instructions, which not only set forth basic governing principles, but for the first time outlined specific welfare activities and practices that were to be implemented Churchwide. "Reported conditions in the state and nation suggest that a considerable burden may rest upon our Church relief activities in the near future. While it seems our people may properly look, as heretofore, for relief assistance from governmental and perhaps other sources," the Presidency acknowledged, "it cannot now be certainly foretold either what or how fully sufficient this assistance will be." The Church had a particular responsibility to care for those who had faithfully paid their tithes and offerings before losing their jobs. The First Presidency believed that the regular Church organization, "if properly coordinated by the bishops and presidents of stakes," would be capable of meeting the emergency. Nevertheless, the Presidency cautioned: "Our faithful Church members are independent, self-respecting, and self-reliant; they do not desire charity. Our able-bodied members must not, except as a last resort, be put under the embarrassment of accepting something for nothing." Church leaders were, therefore, encouraged to arrange for recipients to render some kind of service as compensation for the help they received.

Local leaders were assured that the Church stood "ready to assist the wards in this relief work to the utmost of its ability," but the First Presidency reminded them that the plan's success depended on "a most generous, free giving by the people of all materials necessary for relief purposes." Individual wards were to be prepared to meet the needs not only of their own members but also to be ready to help other units that might require extra assistance.

The Presidency specifically called for a "detailed and exhaustive study of the actual condition of every ward." Careful yet prompt response by bishops and stake presidents was imperative so that plans for the coming winter might be completed in time.

The Presidency concluded its message by urging upon the members "the paramount necessity of living righteously, of avoiding extravagance, of cultivating habits of thrift, economy, and industry, of living strictly within their incomes, and of laying aside something, however small the amount may be, for the times of greater stress that may come to us. By no other course will our people place themselves in that position of helpful usefulness to the world which the Lord intends we shall take."[9] This important message anticipated many of the points that would be stressed when the Church more fully organized its welfare program three years later.

Ninety-five of the 104 stake presidents responded. Of these, only ten knew of members who needed direct relief and were not receiving it, and nine were aware of members receiving help who didn't need it. All but eleven presidents reported that they had coordinated efforts with governmental agencies in providing relief or employment to needy members.

HAROLD B. LEE'S CALL

A key turning point in developing the Church's welfare program was the meeting of the First Presidency on April 20, 1935, with President Harold B. Lee of the Pioneer Stake. Lee later acknowledged that he "was astounded to learn" that for years the Presidency had been considering the essence of the welfare plan, waiting for the time when "the faith of the Latter-day Saints was such that they were willing to follow the counsel of the men who lead and preside in this Church."[10] The Presidency informed

The General Welfare Committee in April 1936: (from left to right) Elders Harold B. Lee, Albert E. Bowen, Henry D. Moyle, Melvin J. Ballard, and John A. Widtsoe. The newly founded welfare program of the Church sought to help Saints achieve self-sufficiency, even during difficult economic times. (LDS Church Archives)

Harold B. Lee that he was to have a part in educating the people and introducing the new welfare program Churchwide. They would release him as stake president and wished him to resign from the city commission so he could give full time to this assignment. This important interview took place on a Saturday when Presidents Grant and McKay did not have other commitments so they could spend the entire morning with President Lee. "I had thought I was overstaying their hospitality," he later reflected, "but they were instructing, encouraging, and outlining what I was supposed to do."[11]

REO SPEED WAGON

A delivery truck outside the Bishop's Salt Lake Regional Storehouse during the Great Depression. Bishops' storehouses were established to make goods available to the needy. (LDS Church Archives)

The Church Security (Welfare) Committee in April 1938: (from left) Ted De Bry, J. Frank Ward, Mark Austin, Stringham A. Stevens, Campbell M. Brown, Harold B. Lee, J. Reuben Clark Jr., Heber J. Grant, David O. McKay, Melvin J. Ballard, John A. Widtsoe, Albert E. Bowen, Sylvester Q. Cannon, Henry D. Moyle, and Robert L. Judd. (LDS Church Archives)

At the conclusion of this meeting, Harold B. Lee drove his car up to the head of nearby City Creek Canyon and walked up into the trees where he could be alone.

> I prayed most earnestly. I had started out with the thought that there would have to be some new kind of organization set up to carry forward the Welfare Program. . . . My spiritual understanding was opened, and I was given a comprehension of the grandeur of the organization of the Church and the Kingdom of God, the likes of which I had never contemplated before. The significant truth which was impressed upon me was that there was no need for any new organization to do what the Presidency had counseled us to do. It was as though the Lord was saying: "All in the world that you have to do is to put to work the organization which I have already given."[12]

LAUNCHING THE WELFARE PROGRAM

On Monday afternoon, April 6, 1936, following the close of the final regular general conference session, a special priesthood meeting for stake presidencies and ward bishoprics convened in the Assembly Hall on Temple Square. The First Presidency reviewed the results of a survey taken the previous year, pointing out the distressing fact that nearly one-sixth of all Church members were being supported by public relief, and many of them were not being required to work for what they received. The Presidency emphasized that the Church should encourage "financial independence" among its members. For the time being Latter-day Saints employed on such government work projects as the Works Progress Administration should "retain their positions, being scrupulously careful to do an honest day's work for a day's pay." Church authorities estimated that approximately $842,000 would be required annually for the Church to assume responsibility for those unable to provide for themselves.

Nevertheless, the First Presidency concluded, "the curtailment of Federal aid which is now forecast, makes it imperative that the Church shall, so far as it is able, meet this emergency."

President David O. McKay read a lengthy document (which would be issued the following day as a circular letter of the First Presidency) setting forth basic principles and specific guidelines for the Church's new "security" program. An immediate goal was to provide sufficient food and clothing for all the needy in the Church by October 1, 1936. This was to be accomplished largely through the existing organization. "Ward teachers," who for decades had been assigned to visit the homes of all Church members monthly, were to work closely with the Relief Society in determining needs. While tithing in cash was still preferred, "tithing in kind" (commodities) could be paid. The Saints were also challenged to increase their per capita annual fast offerings to one dollar (the figure at the time was less than one-fourth that amount). Available funds were to be spent first for relief in the ward where they were donated. Surpluses, if any, could be shared with other wards within the stake and then with other stakes in the Church. The First Presidency's message concluded with the admonition that the program's success depended on the faithfulness of the Saints themselves.[13]

The First Presidency reaffirmed the Presiding Bishopric's prime responsibility in directing the welfare program. The Presidency appointed a Church Relief Committee to aid the Bishopric with the details of administration. Elder Melvin J. Ballard of the Council of the Twelve was named chairman of the committee and Harold B. Lee and Mark Austin as members. Their assignment was to motivate and coordinate the welfare activities of local Church units.

A new level of Church administration, the region, was created to coordinate the functioning of the welfare program. The original fourteen welfare regions were set up at a series of meetings beginning April 21, 1936, in Ogden, Utah, and continuing at other points in the western United States and Canada through May 8. Each region, consisting of four to sixteen stakes, was to have a storehouse where surpluses from its own stakes or from other regions could be exchanged.

During the month of May, Elder Ballard went to Washington, D.C., and told President Franklin D. Roosevelt about the Church's welfare plan. The President praised the Church's efforts, wishing that more organizations would do the same. He and Elder Ballard pledged mutual cooperation in overcoming problems of the Great Depression.[14]

Fundamental Principles Reemphasized

At the October 1936 general conference, the First Presidency reviewed the welfare program's accomplishments during the past six months. An immediate objective had been to provide for the estimated fifteen thousand Church members who were receiving government aid without having to work for it. The Presidency, however, reminded the Church that there had been a more fundamental objective: "Our primary purpose was to set up, insofar as it might be possible, a system under which the curse of idleness would be done away with, the evils of a dole abolished, and independence, industry, thrift and self-respect be once more established amongst our people. The aim of the Church is to help the people help themselves. Work is to be re-enthroned as the ruling principle of the lives of our Church membership."[15]

In a key general conference address in 1937, President J. Reuben Clark focused on the responsibilities of individuals and families. He exhorted: "Let us avoid debt as we would avoid a plague; where we are now in debt let us get out of debt; if not today, then tomorrow. Let us straitly and strictly live within our incomes, and save a little. Let every head of every household see to it that he has on hand enough food and clothing, and, where possible, fuel also, for at least a year ahead."[16]

While working on projects to provide for the needs of the poor may seem essentially temporal, President David O. McKay insisted that, "permeating all these acts, inspiring and sanctifying them, is the element of spirituality."[17]

The most comprehensive exposition of the philosophy underlying the welfare program was presented by President Clark in 1939 at a citizens conference in Estes Park, Colorado: "While . . . the first task of the Church Welfare Plan is to supply food, clothing and shelter," this would not be providing a cure, but "would be treating the symptoms and not the disease." Because the solution to these problems was so obvious, the temptation to broaden the program to "include them all has had to be constantly and consciously restrained. The general economic principle behind the Church Plan," President Clark explained, "is to build up, develop, and establish individual security which promotes and preserves religious free agency and civic freedom and liberty, as against the presently touted tendencies to set up an alleged mass security which destroys all three."

All able-bodied individuals, President Clark insisted, were "entitled to have the opportunity to earn and acquire the necessaries and the essential comforts of life, which embrace food, clothing, shelter, hospitalization, education, amusement and cultural activities, and above all opportunity for spiritual growth and joy." Yet, as everyone's needs are not the same, instead of handing out a standardized cash allotment to all, he said, "the Church Plan aims to give wisely in kind and amount . . . the exact help which each individual needs." President Clark was convinced that seeking absolute economic equality had generally meant "a leveling downward not upward."

President Clark further pointed out that only a handful of administrators at the general level received a modest salary, while some fourteen thousand supervisors at the regional or local levels served without any material compensation. In each congregation those activities were directed by the bishop, the "father of his ward"; the Relief Society, which performed a multitude of compassionate acts of service as "the Mother."

Deseret Industries was established in 1938 to provide jobs for the elderly, the disabled, and others who could not obtain employment. (LDS Church Archives)

Finally, President Clark insisted, the Church welfare program was not designed to set up any collectivism or to compete with private enterprise. "The Church does not aim to destroy but to promote individualism."[18]

Expansion of the Welfare Program

Statistics during the later 1930s reflect a quickening pace in providing relief for the economically distressed. Reported Church expenditures for welfare increased by more than one-third between 1935 and 1936. The output of welfare projects in the latter year included 37,661 bottles of fruit; 175,621 cans of fruit or vegetables; 134,425 pounds of fresh vegetables; 105,000 pounds of flour; 1,393 quilts; and 363,640 items of clothing. Fast offerings, a major source of cash within the welfare program, continued to receive emphasis. Consequently, there were substantial gains in both the number paying and in the size of the offerings. Furthermore, wards and stakes continued to acquire farms, canneries, and other projects to produce food, clothing, or other items required to help those in need.

The Co-operative Securities Corporation was created in 1937 to hold title to welfare program properties and to coordinate its finances. This corporation also made loans to individuals who could not borrow from banks or through other ordinary channels.

From the beginning, an objective of the welfare program had been to inculcate the virtues of productive work and self-reliance. Many Latter-day Saints who wanted to work, however, could not find jobs because of age or because of physical, mental, or emotional disabilities. Consequently, in 1938 Church leaders decided to launch a new program, which they named "Deseret Industries." The new venture was patterned after the Good Will Industries sponsored by a group of Protestant churches in southern California. Members donated clothing, furniture, appliances, newspapers, magazines, or other items they no longer needed. Employees sorted, cleaned, and repaired these materials, which could then be sold at low prices in the Deseret Industries' own retail stores. Proceeds from these sales paid the employees' wages and covered other operating expenses. The modest salary could be supplemented with help from the bishop's storehouse if necessary. The important thing was that these members were doing worthwhile work and had proven to themselves and to the world that they could earn their own way.

The Relief Society continued to play a vital role in helping families become self-reliant. With the encouragement of the First Presidency, the Relief Society in 1937 sponsored courses in such homemaking skills as sewing, baking, and food preserving. Individual instruction was provided in the home, and group classes convened at welfare program canning or sewing centers.

Welfare Program in Perspective

Even though the welfare program follows already well-known principles, Latter-day Saints often refer to it as an example of the Church's being guided by divine revelation. As early as 1933, President J. Reuben Clark testified that the idea of basing the welfare program on principles in the Doctrine and Covenants had been given to President Heber J. Grant by revelation.[19] "I have not talked to angels; I have not had a vision," President Grant was later quoted as saying. "We have been meeting morning after morning for months. . . . After we had evolved a plan I went especially in prayer to the Lord and prayed with all earnestness to know whether or not this plan met with his approval. In response there came over me, from the crown of my head to the soles of my feet such a sweet spirit and a burning within, that I knew God approved."[20]

Likewise, Harold B. Lee credited divine inspiration for his guidance in helping develop the welfare program. Furthermore, he regarded it as a fulfillment of a prophecy made by President Wilford Woodruff in 1894: "The day will come, as we have all been told, that we shall see the necessity of making our own shoes and our own clothing, and providing our own foodstuffs, and uniting together to carry out the purposes of the Lord."[21] Elder Lee also regarded as "the voice of the Lord" the First Presidency's directive to produce "all the things needed by those who would otherwise be unable to provide for themselves."[22]

Elder Harold B. Lee recalled that just a few months after the welfare plan had been introduced, "there was an upturn in business, so much that some were questioning the wisdom of this kind of activity, and why hadn't the Church done it before now?" Some stake presidents, for example, believed that reacquiring projects like the old tithing yard was not worthwhile. "There came to me," Elder Lee testified, "a distinct impression that was as real as though someone had spoken audibly. . . . There is no individual in the Church that knows the real purpose, for which the program then launched had been intended, but hardly before the Church has made sufficient preparation, that reason would be made manifest, and when it comes it will challenge every resource of the Church to meet it."[23]

Women at the Salt Lake Regional Canning Center in 1936. The Church welfare program provided employment, clothing, and food for the economically distressed. (LDS Church Archives)

As the welfare plan was being introduced, Elder Melvin J. Ballard was repeatedly asked, "Is this the beginning of the United Order?" He consistently

A woman buys food at a storehouse. As part of the expansive welfare plan, storehouses were established to provide food for the needy. (LDS Church Archives)

replied in the negative and added: "But I wouldn't be surprised if in this program the Lord were not giving the Church an examination to see how prepared we were for the United Order."[24] President Clark concurred: "We have all said that the Welfare Plan is not the United Order and was not intended to be. However, I should like to suggest to you that perhaps, after all, when the Welfare Plan gets thoroughly into operation—it is not so yet—we shall not be so very far from carrying out the great fundamentals of the United Order."[25]

Stands on Related Issues

Church leaders were quite hesitant to take stands on political issues that did not significantly impact living gospel standards. In 1936, for example, President J. Reuben Clark felt keenly that actions by U.S. President Franklin D. Roosevelt would undermine the divinely-inspired American Constitution. President Grant encouraged his counselor to voice his feelings in a *Deseret News* editorial but insisted that it be done anonymously, lest it be regarded an official Church position.[26] Even though President Grant shared some of Clark's concerns, he refrained from criticizing Roosevelt in his April 1937 general conference address. "In my heart of hearts I feel that President Roosevelt is unworthy of the support of the people," President Grant confided in his journal. "But I give credit to my brethren who believe that the Lord is behind him and that he has done a great and wonderful work in taking care of them in the right way."[27]

Russian Communism became a frequently discussed point of controversy following the 1917 Bolshevik Revolution, and on this matter the Church did take a stand. Throughout the United States, congregations of Catholics, Protestants, and Jews joined on Sunday, March 23, 1930, to protest religious intolerance in the Soviet Union. In Salt Lake City the First Presidency personally presided over and participated in a service held for that purpose in the Tabernacle. The official recognition of the Soviet Union by the United States government under President Franklin D. Roosevelt in November 1933 sparked considerable debate. During the Depression of the 1930s a few Latter-day Saints advocated communism as the means of solving the world's economic problems and of reestablishing the Law of Consecration or United Order. Consequently, in 1936 the First Presidency insisted that "Communism is not the United Order, and bears only the most superficial resemblance thereto; Communism is based upon intolerance and force, the United Order upon love and freedom of conscience and action." In contrast to Communism's confiscation of property, the United Order is based on "voluntary consecration and sacrifice. Communists cannot establish the United Order, nor will Communism bring it about," the Presidency asserted. "The United Order will be established by the Lord in His own due time and in accordance with the regular prescribed order of the Church."

*Welfare Square in Salt Lake City. (*Deseret News *photo)*

The First Presidency was particularly critical of Communism's proscribing "the religious life of the people living within its jurisdiction," reaching "its hand into the sanctity of the family circle itself, disrupting the normal relationship of parent and child. . . . Such interference would be contrary to the fundamental precepts of the Gospel and to the teachings and order of the Church."[28]

The growing labor movement during the 1930s provided a second social issue on which Church leaders took a stand. Widespread difficulties and even violence accompanied attempts by the Congress of Industrial Organizations (CIO) to apply collective bargaining to entire industries for the first time.

The Church's labor philosophy was influenced by the traditional pioneer virtues of industry, freedom, and self-reliance on one hand, and of cooperation and love and concern for one's fellows on the other. "We have never at any time advised our people that they should not join labor unions," President Heber J. Grant declared in 1934, "neither have we recommended that they should do so." Church leaders, however, clearly condemned one of the unions' weapons, the "closed shop" (requiring all workers at a given firm to be union members), as a violation of free agency. President Grant approved men banding together in labor unions to protect their rights as long as they did not infringe on the rights of others. He described the practice of using strikes or boycotts to protest a nonunion man being on the job as being "in direct opposition to the law of God."[29] David O. McKay, one of President Grant's counselors concurred, insisting that the "closed shop" denied the individual's "divine right to work" where, when, and for whatever wages he chooses.[30]

While the Church was taking steps to meet the temporal concerns of its members, it was not neglecting their spiritual needs. A variety of activities receiving attention during the 1930s helped the Saints to focus on eternal matters, thus helping them to transcend the worries of the Great Depression.

8

Transcending the Depression, 1928–1941

The second decade of Heber J. Grant's administration not only brought the formation of the Church's welfare plan but also witnessed a series of refinements in other programs and activities as Church leaders sought the optimum method of perfecting the Saints and sharing the gospel with the world.

The "Priesthood-Auxiliary Movement"

Efforts to enhance the effectiveness of Church programs by consolidating activities sponsored by the priesthood quorums and auxiliary organizations came to be known as the "Priesthood-Auxiliary Movement." There were two important guiding principles: the priesthood was to assume its proper place at the center and core of all Church activity, and Church programs were to be simplified and consolidated.

EMPHASIZING THE PRIESTHOOD'S ROLE

"The Priesthood is the very foundation upon which the Church is built," and "the framework that supports the structure," the Presiding Bishopric affirmed in 1928. "It is the most potent means of real service."[1] Official publications during this time made frequent reference to President Joseph F. Smith's 1906 prophecy of a time "when every council of the Priesthood . . . will understand its duty; will assume its own responsibility, will magnify its calling, and fill its place in the Church."[2] Church leaders asserted that "for over a hundred years the Lord

The Australian Mission basketball team drew large crowds as they competed against local teams and won respect for the Church in that land. Despite a decrease in the total number of missionaries during the Great Depression, those serving found innovative ways to share the gospel. (LDS Church Archives)

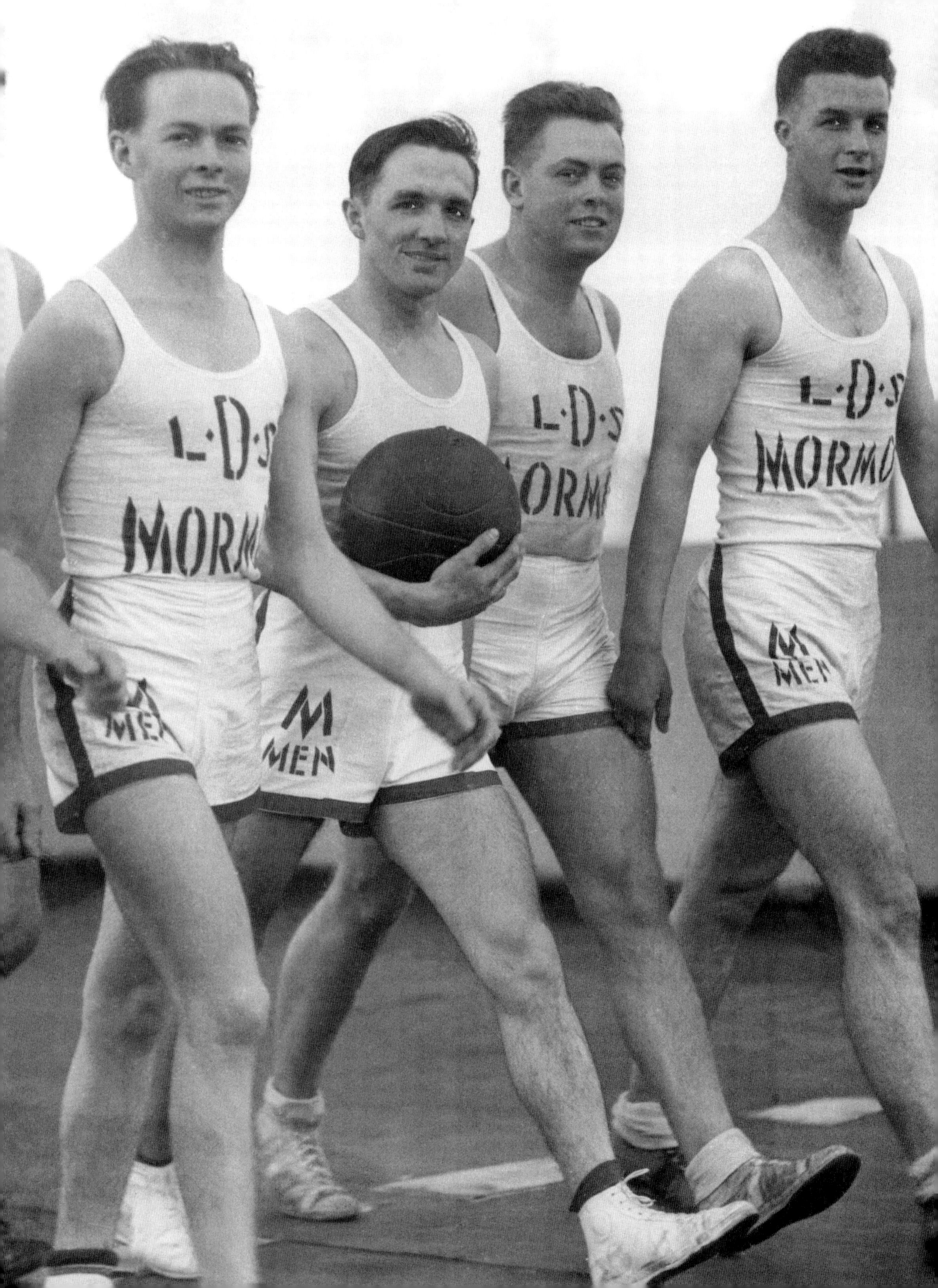
L·D·S
M
MEN

has had in his Church . . . a force for good; but until recently part of this force (the quorums of the Priesthood) has been left unutilized. . . . The clarion call for the present is to turn this potentiality into actuality."[3]

To this end in 1928, the Church issued *A Guide for Quorums of the Melchizedek Priesthood*. This manual, after treating the general nature and authority of the priesthood, placed its major emphasis on the purpose and function of priesthood quorums. The guide called for the organization of the following "standing committees" to carry out the work of the quorum: personal welfare (spiritual, intellectual, financial, and physical), class instruction, temple blessings and service, and social and athletic events. This committee system of administering quorums, though modified somewhat from time to time, has continued to the present.

The guide may well be regarded as the Church's first Melchizedek Priesthood handbook. Its material was quoted repeatedly and extensively in subsequent instructions, and it became the foundation for later handbooks. When Elder John A. Widtsoe compiled his widely read book *Priesthood and Church Government* a decade later, he drew heavily from the guide in his chapters dealing with the priesthood quorums.

SIMPLIFYING AND CONSOLIDATING ACTIVITIES

The priesthood and the auxiliaries typically planned their own programs without reference to what was being done by any other organization. Church leaders were concerned about the resulting frequent duplication in lessons and activities. Because all Church organizations served the same group of members, Elder Melvin J. Ballard asserted that "there must be one unified, simplified program. . . . No one organization in the Church can do everything for the entire group." Therefore, "There has been delegated to each organization its specific field."[4]

For example, in 1928 formal theological study, previously conducted in various organizations, became centered in the Sunday School, with lessons for adults prepared under the direction of the Council of the Twelve.[5] Changing the name "Parents' Class" to "Gospel Doctrine Class" reflected this course's heightened status as the official gospel study period for the adults of the Church.

In 1929 additional consolidations were made in two rather different areas: magazines for adults and programs for children. Both had been suggested as early as 1907 by the Committee on Adjustments.

Since 1889 the *Young Woman's Journal* had been the official periodical of the Young Ladies' Mutual Improvement Association. In 1897 the *Improvement Era* replaced the *Contributor* as the official publication of the Young Men's association. As the work of the two MIAs became more united, the idea of consolidating these two magazines gained popularity. At the 1929 June MIA conference, a "storybook wedding" dramatized the union of the two publications. The name *Improvement Era* was retained because it fit the two associations equally. The first of the combined

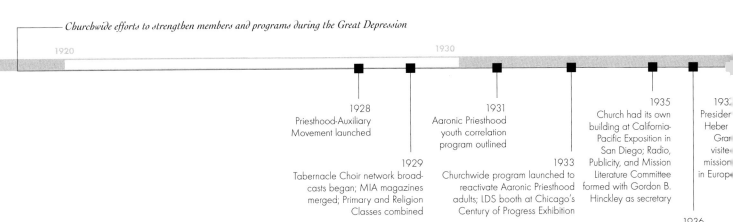

Churchwide efforts to strengthen members and programs during the Great Depression

1920

1930

1928
Priesthood-Auxiliary Movement launched

1929
Tabernacle Choir network broadcasts began; MIA magazines merged; Primary and Religion Classes combined

1931
Aaronic Priesthood youth correlation program outlined

1933
Churchwide program launched to reactivate Aaronic Priesthood adults; LDS booth at Chicago's Century of Progress Exhibition

1935
Church had its own building at California-Pacific Exposition in San Diego; Radio, Publicity, and Mission Literature Committee formed with Gordon B. Hinckley as secretary

1936
Welfare plan, stake missions, and youth award programs instituted; Church exhibit at Golden Gate International Exposition in San Francisco

193
Presider
Heber
Grar
visite
mission
in Europ

issues appeared in November 1929 in an enlarged and improved format.

During the opening decades of the twentieth century, both the Primary and the Religion Class organizations had existed side by side to serve Latter-day Saint children. On one afternoon each week, the Religion Class provided gospel instruction for the children while on a different afternoon the Primary featured activities. In 1929 these similar programs were combined, the Religion Class being absorbed into the Primary.[6]

THE "AARONIC PRIESTHOOD CORRELATION PLAN"

After extensive preparation, the "Aaronic Priesthood Correlation Plan" was introduced at a special meeting held April 4, 1931, in conjunction with general conference. Church leaders announced that the three programs for young men would be more fully coordinated. The Aaronic Priesthood quorums would teach duties, promote worthiness, and foster brotherhood. In contrast, the two auxiliaries involved with the young men were to become "aids to the priesthood." The Sunday School would focus it efforts on providing instruction in gospel principles and history. The Young Men's Mutual Improvement Association, as the "activity arm of the priesthood," would then provide a practical application of these principles to life. The overall objective of these integrated efforts was "to prepare young men for missionary activity, for other Church service, and for life."[7] These assignments did not represent a redefinition of roles, but rather a heightened correlation of existing organizations and activities. To this end, monthly correlation meetings brought leaders and teachers together at the ward and stake levels.[8]

A special survey revealed that despite these efforts, not all young men were yet involved significantly in Church activity. Through the Aaronic Priesthood Correlation Plan, steps were taken to reclaim these youth. The Presiding Bishopric announced a goal of having one million priesthood assignments performed during 1935, every boy performing at least one. The following year the Presiding Bishopric provided certificates of award for those quorums meeting specified minimum standards. When LeGrand Richards became Presiding Bishop in 1938, he gave even more emphasis to these Aaronic Priesthood programs and made even greater progress.

Reactivating Aaronic Priesthood Adults

During the 1920s and especially during the 1930s, Church members began moving from the Intermountain area to seek better economic opportunities. At the same time, more non-Mormons began moving into Latter-day Saint communities. This meant that an increasing number of Church members were living in non-Mormon environments. One result of this influence was a larger number of young men becoming inactive and growing to adulthood without receiving the Melchizedek Priesthood.

As early as 1911 the General Priesthood Committee considered what should be done for these men. At that time, there was a campaign to

1940 — 1950

1941
Assistants to the Twelve appointed

1940
First Presidency declared Church organizations exist to strengthen the home; formerly separate genealogy meetings became class in Sunday School

1938
LeGrand Richards, new Presiding Bishop, emphasized youth work

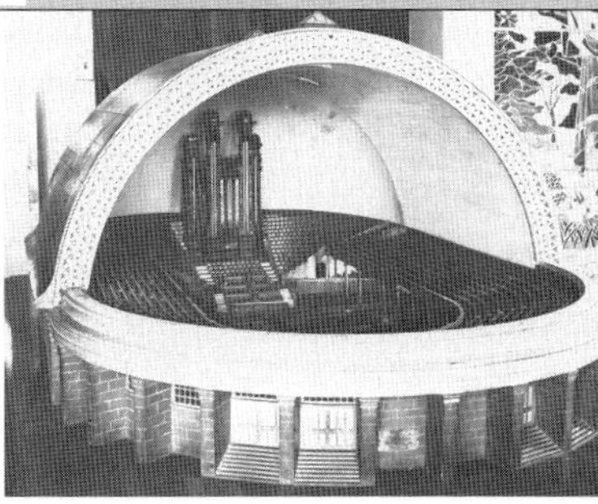

This scale model of the Salt Lake Tabernacle on display at Chicago's Century of Progress Exposition in 1933 helped tell the Church's story to visitors. (LDS Church Archives)

have everyone enrolled in his proper quorum. The committee wondered whether older men returning to activity should really associate with the younger boys in the deacons, teachers, or priests quorums. President Joseph F. Smith answered that question: "It is not a good idea to mix up the old men with bad habits with young boys. If they are not worthy to meet with their quorums," he instructed, "they should be labored with and that to get them to reform."[9]

In 1926 the Presiding Bishopric emphasized that these "overgrown members" of Aaronic Priesthood quorums should not be neglected, but invited to attend whatever priesthood class was closest to their age and interests.[10]

A. P. A. Glad, bishop of the Salt Lake Twenty-eighth Ward, pioneered the first successful program to help these older men. At first he invited "senior" members of the Aaronic Priesthood to attend the elders quorum, but he soon discovered these men did not feel at home. "The elders are so far advanced," the less-active men explained. "We would like to attend but feel out of place."

Through the Adult Aaronic Priesthood program, instituted in the 1930s, the Church reached out to reclaim those who had fallen into inactivity. This cartoon appeared on the cover of a guide for program leaders. (LDS Church Archives)

The bishop saw that these men needed a separate class of their own. He called a group of enthusiastic and devoted men to give their full attention to this program. The first class began meeting in September 1932. Group members were involved in planning their own activities; one of Bishop Glad's slogans was "We learn to do by doing."[11] After eight months of diligent effort, forty men had been brought into activity. M. Main Stauffer, a member of the original group, recalled how Bishop Glad's assistant "rousted" him out of bed to get him to attend the class. "I told him I'd go just to get rid of him," Stauffer admitted, but this began a pattern of regular Church activity, which led to his receiving the Melchizedek Priesthood. He went on to serve as high priests group leader, bishop, and high councilor.[12] Bishop Glad's work provided the pattern for the reactivation program introduced Churchwide during the fall of 1933.

Missionary Work During the Depression

While the Church was taking steps to reactivate some who were already members, it was also reaching out to those who had not yet heard the gospel. The Church continued to place emphasis on missionary work despite the problems caused by the Great Depression. Missionary service characterized the lives of the General Authorities who presided over the Church in the 1930s. Almost all had personally served as missionaries, many for periods far longer than the two years normally given by faithful Latter-day Saints. Elder David O. McKay had made a year-long around-the-world tour of the Church's missions in 1921. In addition, he and several other members of the Twelve had presided at different times over the European Mission. Almost all who served in the First Council of the Seventy had acted as mission presidents, either before or following their calls as General Authorities, some for prolonged periods of time. Charles A. Callis had presided over the Southern States Mission from 1908 until 1934, when he became a member of the Twelve. Rey L. Pratt of the First Council of the Seventy was president of the Mexican Mission from 1907 until his death in 1931. Samuel O. Bennion, who was called to the First Council of Seventy in 1933, presided over the Central States Mission and directed Church publishing activities in Independence, Missouri, from 1906 until 1935. Elder Joseph W. McMurrin, also a member of the First Council of the

Seventy, served fifteen years as a short-term or local missionary and nearly twenty-five years as a full-time missionary; he also presided over the California Mission for more than a decade, from 1919 to 1931. With such a background, these leaders enthusiastically gave impetus to the Church's missionary efforts.

The economic hardships of the early 1930s, however, curtailed many missionary activities and reduced the number of missionaries in the field. Because of the Depression, many families felt that they needed their sons to work at home and therefore could not afford a mission experience. Consequently, the number of missionaries entering the field fell sharply as the effects of the Depression spread throughout the country. During the 1920s between eight hundred and thirteen hundred accepted calls from the First Presidency to serve as missionaries annually; this represented from 13 to 20 percent of the total young men of missionary age. In 1932, on the other hand, only 399 were able to respond, about 5 percent of the potential. This shortage of missionaries was compounded by the early release of many because of economic difficulties at home.

Gordon B. Hinckley working as executive secretary of the Church's Radio, Publicity, and Mission Literature Committee. (Photo courtesy Hinckley family)

Mission presidents from all over the world reported that the work was being handicapped severely because of the lack of missionaries and urgently requested that more be sent. In France, for example, all but four branches had to be closed to missionary work; the scattered members were organized into a "branch at large" and could be contacted only by letter. The decision to begin proselyting in Italy was delayed, not because of possible religious opposition but because of a Depression-caused missionary shortage.[13] However, the consequences of this missionary shortage were not all negative.

To compensate for reduced numbers, the remaining missionaries were determined to work harder and more systematically in order to maintain productivity. Ideas on effective methods of contacting and teaching were incorporated into *The Missionary's Handbook*, published in 1937. In that same year, President LeGrand Richards of the Southern States Mission first issued "The Message of Mormonism," a booklet outlining twenty-four weekly presentations of basic gospel topics. Missionaries also employed innovative techniques to find interested persons to teach; a missionary chorus attracted favorable note in England and Ireland. Athletics were especially useful; a missionary basketball team made friends for the Church in Czechoslovakia; and in Germany four Elders were recruited as basketball referees for the 1936 Berlin Olympics. Lectures featuring colored slides of ancient America were particularly productive in making contacts. The Church Radio, Publicity, and Mission Literature Committee was organized in 1935 to supply materials for these illustrated lectures. With Gordon B. Hinckley (recently returned from a mission to Britain) as executive secretary, the committee directed the preparation of tracts and other mission literature and prepared scripts for special radio programs.

Another by-product of the Great Depression was a greater involvement of local members in missionary work. In California, the Saints had missionaries stay in their homes to help cut expenses. Alabama Saints traveled long distances to take investigators to district conferences. In many areas members provided referrals, enabling missionaries to phase out less-productive door-to-door tracting. The missionary corps around the world was expanded as local members donated several hours a week to work with the full-time missionaries or accepted special short-term mission calls. This growing involvement proved to be a blessing to both the members and the missionaries.

Church members became involved in missionary work in yet another way. In many areas, congregations had been led by missionaries rather than by local officers. But as the Great Depression cut the number of Elders, the Saints had to assume more responsibility for their own affairs. This not only freed the missionaries' time for proselyting, but it also enabled the local Saints to take greater pride in their own branches. The shortage of missionaries "has probably been a blessing in disguise," President Heber J. Grant concluded, "because it has forced us to make greater use of the local Saints."[14]

STAKE MISSIONS

The Depression decade also witnessed a new missionary thrust within the stakes. Stake missions were implemented Churchwide during the 1930s. As Latter-day Saints began to move into areas of predominantly non-Mormon population, such as California and the Pacific Northwest, and as non-Mormons began to move into the predominantly Mormon Intermountain region, many stake leaders began to organize efforts to preach the gospel to their new nonmember neighbors.

From the roof of the Deseret News Building, President Heber J. Grant utters the first words over KZN radio station, which the Church bought in 1924. Its name was later changed to KSL. (Front row, left to right) Nathan O. Fullmer, Elder George Albert Smith, Augusta Winters Grant, President Heber J. Grant, Salt Lake City Mayor C. Clarence Nelsen, and George J. Cannon. (Back row, left to right) President Anthony W. Ivins, H. C. Wilson, and B. F. Grant. (Photo courtesy Manuscripts Division, J. Willard Marriott Library, University of Utah)

In 1932 J. Golden Kimball, a member of the First Council of the Seventy, reported that hundreds had been converted to the Church as a result of local missionary efforts directed by stake presidents, notably in Los Angeles, Mesa, and Salt Lake City. Elder Kimball emphasized that all who held the office of Seventy had the particular duty of preaching the gospel and, therefore, admonished them to serve as stake missionaries. He wrote: "We know of no more promising field for missionary activity than right here at home where, who knows, precious souls are brought to us or we to them for the express purpose that they might hear the gospel sound."[15]

At the general conference in April 1936, Church leaders announced that supervision of these stake missions was being assigned to the First Council of the Seventy and that a mission was to be organized immediately in each stake. The Twelve and the Seventy anticipated that the new stake missionary work could "be made to rival in importance" the accomplishments of the full-time missionary work "for which the Church is so universally noted."[16]

Statistics for the first full year of operation of the expanded stake missionary program revealed its effectiveness. By the end of 1937, some 105 of the 118 stakes had organized missions. A total of 2,030 missionaries were instrumental in the baptism of 1,757 converts. In addition, 2,756 members of the Church had been brought back into activity. One ward reported that as a result of stake missionary efforts there had been a 50 percent increase in overall activity among its members.[17]

REACHING THE PUBLIC

During the Great Depression the Church employed a variety of methods to supplement the work being done by its increasingly scarce proselyting missionaries. The new medium of radio broadcasting emerged during the 1920s, and the Church was involved almost from the beginning. In 1924 the Church purchased radio station KZN, whose call letters were soon changed to the familiar KSL. The Tabernacle Choir began its weekly nationwide broadcasts in 1929. In its humble beginnings, the radio host had to climb a tall ladder to reach the single microphone hanging above the choir in order to announce the program. The series was planned for only three months, but favorable response from throughout the United States and from Europe prompted the network to continue the program indefinitely. During its

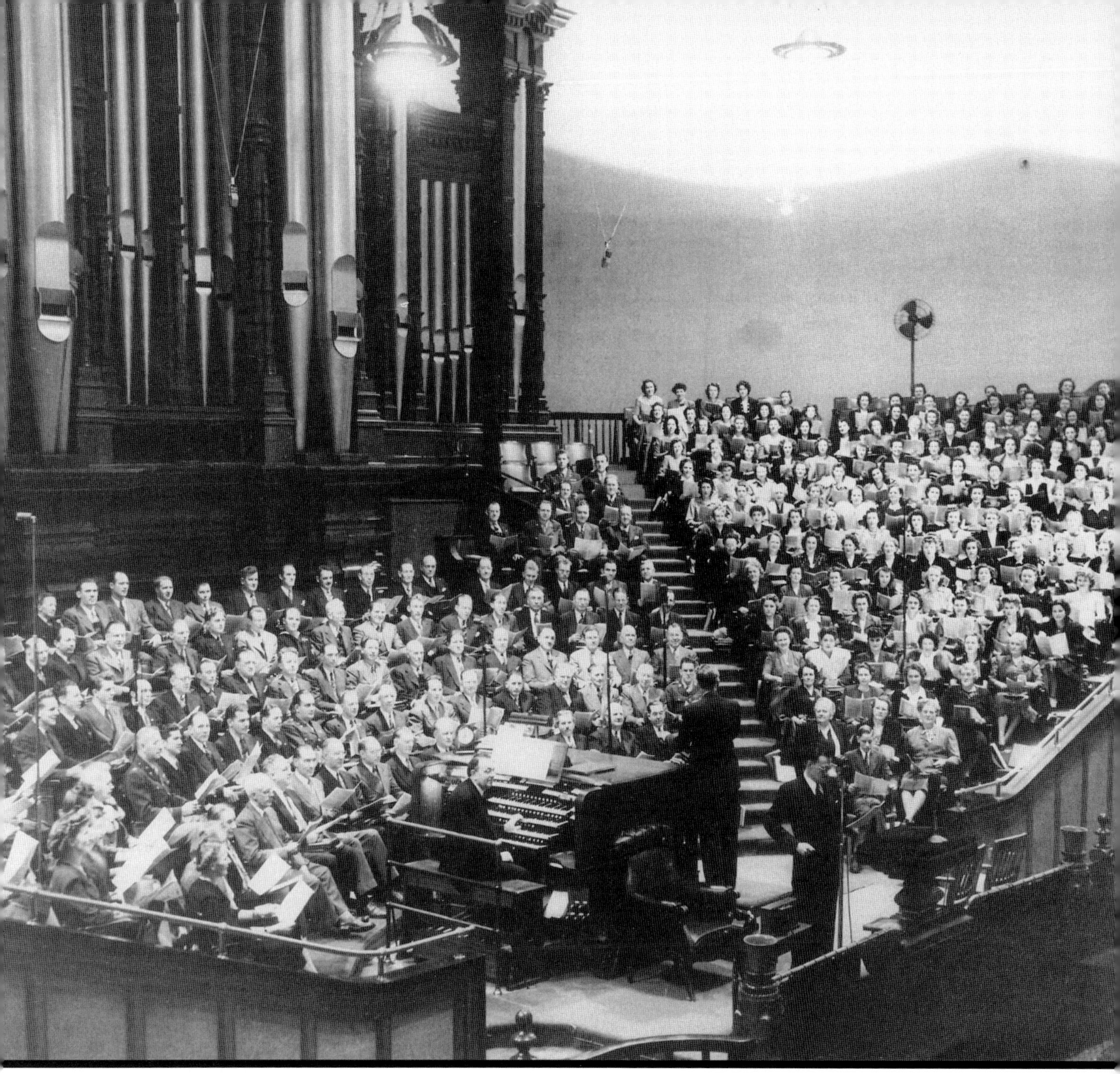

The Tabernacle Choir during a broadcast of "Music and the Spoken Word." The radio program would become the longest continuously running in the history of American network radio. (LDS Church Archives)

first three years the broadcasts were aired on Monday afternoons. An average of two hundred choir members donated their time without compensation, and Salt Lake area employers cooperated by giving singers time off. The choir program proved to be a very productive source of goodwill toward the Church. As the twentieth century drew to its close "Music and the Spoken Word" was widely heralded as the longest continuous program in the history of American network radio. Several other Latter-day Saint groups also originated radio programs of their own. Elders in the Eastern States Mission were especially successful in broadcasting their messages over the air. The Church showed an early interest in international shortwave radio, and a portion of general conference was broadcast to Europe via this medium on April 5, 1936.

Partly as a result of the Tabernacle Choir's increasing popularity, Temple Square continued to be an effective missionary tool. Many visitors went miles out of their way to be present for the weekly choir broadcasts or noon organ recitals. Temple Square attracted even more visitors than Yellowstone or other popular national parks in the area.

Exhibits at fairs were another means of sharing the Church's message with the world. An exhibit at the International Hygiene Exposition in 1930 at Dresden, Germany, featured the Mormon health code revealed in the Word of Wisdom. It attracted an average of five thousand visitors per day and resulted in the distribution of over 250,000 pieces of missionary literature. An estimated 2.3 million persons visited the Church's booth at the Chicago Century of Progress Exposition in 1933 and 1934. A changed attitude was reflected as Elder B. H. Roberts, who had been denied the opportunity to speak at Chicago's 1893 Columbian Exposition, was well received as he spoke at the Congress of Religions in conjunction with the Chicago exposition forty years later. At the California-Pacific International Exposition held in San Diego during 1935 and 1936, the Church for the first time erected its own exhibit building. The Golden Gate International Exposition was held on Treasure Island in San Francisco Bay in 1939 and 1940. Capitalizing on the Tabernacle Choir's popularity, the Church's pavilion was built in the form of a miniature Tabernacle with a fifty-seat auditorium in which missionaries could present illustrated lectures on the history and beliefs of the Church.

Church members pose before the fifty-seat replica of the Salt Lake Tabernacle at the 1939 Golden Gate International Exposition on Treasure Island in the San Francisco Bay. Gordon B. Hinckley, executive secretary of the Church Radio, Publicity, and Mission Literature Committee, stands third from the right. (Photo courtesy Hinckley family)

Beginning in 1937, the annual Hill Cumorah Pageant became one of the Church's most successful public relations ventures. Featuring a cast composed mostly of missionaries serving in the area, "America's Witness for Christ" was presented on three large stages constructed on the slopes of the hill. It depicted scenes from the Book of Mormon, culminating with the Savior's visit to the ancient inhabitants of America. Just a month before the first pageant was presented, Elder Harold I. Hansen, who had just received his bachelor's degree in drama, entered the Eastern States Mission. He was immediately assigned to help with the final preparations and rehearsals. He believed that his call to that mission at that time resulted from divine guidance. He would continue to be associated with the pageant for the next forty years, most of the time as its director.

Moves Toward Greater Correlation, 1939–1940

With the stimulation of Church activities during the 1930s came an increased financial burden as well as greater demands on the time and energy of the Saints. To lessen this load, the General Authorities undertook a new study of all Church programs with the goal of correlation and simplification where possible.

In January 1939 the First Presidency reaffirmed that the real reason for all Church organizations "is to instruct the people in the gospel, to lead them to a testimony of its truthfulness, to care for those in need, to carry on the work entrusted to us by the Lord, to promote culture among the people, and to encourage, foster, and secure among the people the living of righteous lives. . . . The work of the auxiliary organizations and of our educational institutions should be coordinated, unified, and standardized to avoid duplication and overlapping, and to provide the training which is required by the young people." The Presidency therefore appointed a Committee of Correlation and Coordination, headed by three members of the Twelve. The committee's assignment was "to define, to simplify, to intensify, and to correlate the work of each auxiliary and educational group in the Church."[18]

After a yearlong study by this committee, President J. Reuben Clark Jr., representing the First Presidency, convened a meeting of auxiliary executives on March 29, 1940. He emphatically declared that "the home is the basis of a righteous life, that no other instrumentality can take its place nor fulfill its essential functions, and that the utmost the Auxiliaries can do is to aid the home in its problems, giving special aid and succor where such is necessary." President Clark then outlined the specific role each organization was to play and announced the formation of the Church Union Board of the Auxiliaries to "coordinate, consolidate, eliminate, simplify and adjust the work of the auxiliary organizations."[19] A tangible step in this direction came that same year when the separate weekly genealogical meeting was discontinued and replaced by a genealogy class in Sunday School.[20]

In his presentation to the auxiliaries, President Clark had also proposed a further merging of existing Church magazines. One resulting action was the discontinuation of the *Utah Genealogical and Historical Magazine*, which had been published since 1910, and transferring its material to the *Improvement Era*.

Reaching Out to the Saints Abroad

As the Church continued to grow in various parts of the world, its members lived in increasingly diverse circumstances. Nowhere were challenges greater than in Germany.

THE CHURCH AND THE NAZIS

Ever since the National Socialists, or Nazis, had gained control in 1933, the Church and its members in Germany had to walk an increasingly sensitive line. Gestapo agents frequently observed Church meetings; and most branch and mission leaders were thoroughly interrogated by the police about Mormon doctrines, beliefs, and practices, and were warned not to concern themselves with political matters. Increasingly, Latter-day Saint meetings had to be canceled during Nazi rallies, and the Church-sponsored Boy Scout program was replaced by the Hitler Youth Movement. Copies of Elder James E. Talmage's popular doctrinal work *The Articles of Faith* were confiscated and burned because of frequent references to Israel and Zion. In one town, police ripped out of hymnbooks all pages referring to these topics.

These conditions caused feelings of uneasiness and concern, which led some members to quit coming to Church, lest the police cause trouble for them. These worries also increased interest in emigration. Nevertheless, The Church of Jesus Christ of Latter-day Saints was never officially persecuted, nor was it forced to cease functioning, as were some other small religious groups in Germany. This was partially due to the Saints' belief in the separation of Church and state and their emphasis on obeying the laws of the land.

West German missionaries and mission leaders in 1938. Conditions for the missionaries and German Saints were tense during the prewar years. (LDS Church Archives)

In fact, at least three Nazi actions actually benefitted the Church. When Mormon Elders were invited to coach the German basketball teams and to officiate at the 1936 Berlin Olympics, the Church received favorable publicity. When the police banned door-to-door tracting, missionaries were forced to develop a more efficient "friend-to-friend" referral system. The Nazis' emphasis on racial purity stimulated an interest in genealogy. Earlier government officials had often regarded the Mormons as an unpopular sect and so denied them access to vital records; now the Saints were honored as patriotic because of their genealogical research, even though it

Members of the Church in New Zealand in front of a traditional Maori building. Elder George Albert Smith's visit to this nation in 1938 and the leadership of Elder Matthew Cowley helped keep the Church aware of the Pacific Saints' needs. (LDS Church Archives)

was done for an entirely different purpose.[21] Nevertheless, the situation for the Church and its missionaries would become much more precarious during the later 1930s as Hitler launched his program of expansion.

VISITS TO OVERSEAS SAINTS

Church growth was reflected in two extended trips overseas taken by General Authorities. During a three-month tour in 1937, President Heber J. Grant and other Church leaders visited the Latter-day Saints in Belgium, Switzerland, Czechoslovakia, Germany, England, Holland, Denmark, Sweden, and Norway. Tears of joy streamed down the faces of hundreds of Church members as they fulfilled the hope of a lifetime—to personally hear the words of their living prophet and to shake his hand. Wherever he went, the President encouraged the Saints to stay where they were and build up the Church there.

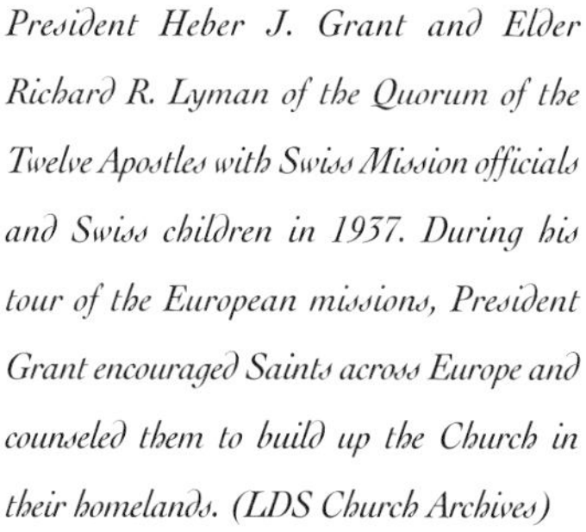

President Heber J. Grant and Elder Richard R. Lyman of the Quorum of the Twelve Apostles with Swiss Mission officials and Swiss children in 1937. During his tour of the European missions, President Grant encouraged Saints across Europe and counseled them to build up the Church in their homelands. (LDS Church Archives)

Large crowds at public meetings and extensive press coverage helped build goodwill for the Mormons in areas where they had generally been unknown or misunderstood. This was particularly true in Czechoslovakia, where a mission had opened only eight years earlier (the first time the gospel was taught in a Slavic language). Although by 1937 there were just over a hundred members in

Czechoslovakia, numerous high government officials received President Grant graciously as the leader of a noble, God-fearing people. Mission president Wallace F. Toronto reported that these government contacts, together with a special conference where President Grant spoke, resulted in a flood of publicity, which made the people "Mormon conscious" more than ever before. President Grant was given the privilege of speaking over Czech radio. Forty articles appeared in newspapers or magazines, all favorable to the Church. President Toronto concluded that "few people in Czechoslovakia failed to see a picture of the venerable leader of the Mormon people."[22]

President Heber J. Grant and other Church leaders mark the British Mission's centennial in 1937 at the River Ribble, site of the first baptisms in England. Shown here (front row, from left) are Ruth May Fox, George D. Pyper, J. Reuben Clark Jr., President Grant, Richard R. Lyman, and Hugh B. Brown. (Deseret News *photo*)

When President J. Reuben Clark joined President Grant to commemorate the British Mission's centennial, two members of the First Presidency were in Europe together for the first time. Other Church leaders in attendance included Elder Richard R. Lyman of the Council of the Twelve and president of the European Mission, the General Sunday School Superintendent, and the complete presidency of the Young Women's Mutual Improvement Association. Centennial observances commenced with two days of missionary meetings. On July 30, exactly 100 years from the day that the first convert was baptized in Great Britain, missionaries and members made a pilgrimage to historic LDS sites in nearby Preston. President Grant was the featured speaker at conference meetings that were filled to overflowing. He paid tribute to the more than 52,000 British converts who had emigrated and helped build up communities throughout the Intermountain West. Among the nine General Authorities born in Britain were President John Taylor, George Q. Cannon, James E. Talmage, and B. H. Roberts. Noted composers George Careless and Evan Stephens were also British immigrants.

Other Latter-day Saints had been under the jurisdiction of the European Mission, although they lived in areas too remote to have been included in President Grant's itinerary. In the 1930s, only ten members remained from the branches that had flourished in the Balkans prior to World War I. These Saints received only infrequent visits by representatives of the Czechoslovak mission or one of the other missions in Europe.[23] At that time the Palestine-Syrian Mission Elders proselyted principally among Armenians living in the Near East. In addition, a well-established mission carried on the work in South Africa. Latter-day Saint interest in the Holy Land continued. Apostle Orson Hyde's 1841 dedicatory prayer had been reconfirmed in later years by other ordained Apostles: George A. Smith (a counselor to Brigham Young) together with Lorenzo Snow and Albert Carrington in 1873; Francis M. Lyman in 1902; David O. McKay in 1921; and James E. Talmage in 1927. Once again, in 1933, Elder John A. Widtsoe, then serving as President of the European Mission, ascended the Mount of Olives at Jerusalem and blessed the land.[24]

In 1938, Elder George Albert Smith of the Council of the Twelve made a six-month visit to the Pacific missions, visiting Australia, New Zealand, Tonga, and Samoa. He was accompanied by Elder Rufus K. Hardy of the First Council of the Seventy who had formerly been the New Zealand Mission President. They were well received wherever they went. In Samoa the two were rowed ashore in a seventy-foot war canoe lavishly decorated with flowers. Upon landing, they were greeted by a crowd of two thousand Saints and were welcomed to the music of four brass bands. A group of two hundred Relief Society sisters, all dressed in white, led the procession to the mission home.[25] A high point was Elder Smith's participation in the Maori Saints' annual mission conference, or "hui tau." On this occasion, he installed a new mission president, Matthew Cowley (son of former Apostle Matthias Cowley), who would become noted for his many spiritual experiences among the Polynesian Saints. As President Grant had done in Europe the year before, Elder Smith not only strengthened Church members in the Pacific but also developed more favorable attitudes toward the Church through holding interviews with the press, speaking on the radio, and meeting with governmental officials.

The Saints in the Pacific told their visitors that they would appreciate greater personal contact with leaders from Church headquarters. Church members in Europe had expressed the same need. This, plus continued Church growth resulting in a multiplication of the number of stakes and missions around the world, placed an ever heavier administrative load on the shoulders of the General Authorities. Consequently, steps were taken to lighten their assignments and to provide more help.

President Heber J. Grant (sitting) and two of his counselors during the Depression years, David O. McKay (left) and J. Reuben Clark Jr. (LDS Church Archives)

Developments in Administration

GENERAL AUTHORITIES AND THE AUXILIARIES

For some years, leading women had served as the presidents of the Relief Society, Young Women's Mutual Improvement Association, and Primary, while General Authorities had served as the "superintendents" of the Sunday School and Young Men's Mutual Improvement Association. Wilford Woodruff, for example, was already serving as superintendent of the YMMIA when he became President of the Church in 1889, and he continued in both capacities. Upon President Woodruff's death in 1898, Lorenzo Snow was sustained in both of these offices. President Snow also became superintendent of the Sunday School following George Q. Cannon's death in 1901. When Joseph F. Smith became President of the Church later that year, he assumed the superintendency of both the YMMIA and the Sunday School.

Following President Smith's death in 1918, the decision was made to no longer have a President of the Church preside personally over these auxiliaries. Consequently, two members of the Twelve assumed this responsibility; Elders David O. McKay and George Albert Smith became superintendents of the Sunday School and YMMIA, respectively. When Elder McKay was called as Second Counselor in the First Presidency in October 1934, he was released from the Sunday School superintendency, and was succeeded by a non-General Authority.

Consistent with this new pattern, the First Presidency in January 1935 decided to release the superintendency of the YMMIA, all three of whom were Apostles. "It is now deemed advisable, indeed absolutely necessary, to relieve members of the Twelve of their duties not only as presiding officers, but also as members of the general boards," the Presidency affirmed, emphasizing that the General Authorities' well-being and the good of the Church "demand that this action be taken without further delay."[26]

Beginning in the mid-1930s one or more members of the Twelve were assigned as advisers to each of the auxiliary organizations. This pattern continued until the late 1970s when General Authorities would once again be called to form the presidencies of the Sunday School and the Young Men. They were not members of the Twelve, however, but were drawn from the recently expanded ranks of the Seventy.

ASSISTANTS TO THE TWELVE

As the number of stakes and missions grew, the administrative load carried by the General Authorities

Assistants to the Twelve were first appointed in 1941. Pictured here are four of the first five men called to this position: (from left) Marion G. Romney, Clifford E. Young, Thomas E. McKay, and Alma Sonne; not pictured is Nicholas G. Smith. (LDS Church Archives)

increased accordingly. At the close of 1900 there had been forty-three stakes; the one hundredth stake was organized in 1928, and by April 1941, there were 137. During the 1930s the Saints had increasingly moved to scattered areas, and new stakes had been organized in such distant centers as New York, Washington, Chicago, Seattle, and Honolulu. Not only did this mean there were a greater number of stake conferences for Apostles to conduct, but also the General Authorities had greater distances to travel. Some considered completing the First Quorum of Seventy to help meet the administrative need (at that time only the seven presidents were called as General Authorities). But, as President Spencer W. Kimball later pointed out, "The scope and demands of the work at that time did not justify the reconstitution of the First Quorum of the Seventy."[27] Hence, a decision was made to create a new and smaller group of General Authorities to help shoulder the load. At the April general conference in 1941 the First Presidency announced:

> In the past history of the Church, especially in President Brigham Young's time, it was found necessary for the First Presidency or the Twelve, or both, to call brethren, frequently designated as Counselors, to help carry on their assigned work in the Church.
>
> The rapid growth of the Church in recent times, the constantly increasing establishment of new Wards and Stakes, the ever widening geographical area covered by Wards and Stakes, the steadily pressing necessity for increasing our missions in numbers and efficiency that the Gospel may be brought to all men, the continual multiplying of Church interests and activities calling for more rigid and frequent observation, supervision and direction—all have built up an apostolic service of the greatest magnitude.
>
> The First Presidency and Twelve feel that to meet adequately their great responsibilities and to carry on efficiently this service for the Lord, they should have some help.
>
> Accordingly it has been decided to appoint Assistants to the Twelve, who shall be High Priests, who shall be set apart to act under the direction of the Twelve in the performance of such work as the First Presidency and the Twelve may place upon them.
>
> There will be no fixed number of these Assistants. Their number will be increased or otherwise from time to time as the necessity of carrying on the Lord's work seems to dictate to be wise.[28]

Initially five men were named Assistants to the Twelve, but as the administrative burden continued to increase, their number was enlarged.

Thus, the 1930s brought not only the Welfare Plan but the perfection of other programs to bless the Saints and to share the gospel more effectively. As the 1940s began, a new challenge faced the world which would again test the Saints' resilience and resourcefulness.

The Latter-day Saints and World War II

Most people hoped that World War I had been the "war to end all wars" and that it had "made the world safe for democracy." After two decades, however, it was obvious that war had not been eradicated from the earth. The world was still recovering from the Great Depression when World War II began in Europe. Under the leadership of Adolf Hitler and the Nazi Party, Germany sought to expand the "Third Reich" in quest of *Lebenstraum*, or "room in which to live." During these same years, Japan was pushing into China, Southeast Asia, and the Pacific, seeking new sources of raw materials and expanded markets for its industries. The United States did not become actively involved in the hostilities until the Japanese attack on the Pearl Harbor naval base in Hawaii on Sunday morning, December 7, 1941. The coming of war not only disrupted Church activities but altered the lives of most Latter-day Saints worldwide. These tragic circumstances led Latter-day Saints to ponder their attitudes about war and provided the occasion for the Church to expand its programs for members in military service.

Missionaries Evacuated to Safety

As tensions mounted in Europe, the General Authorities became increasingly concerned over the safety of Latter-day Saint missionaries serving there. In the autumn of 1937, Hitler announced his intention to expand Germany by annexing

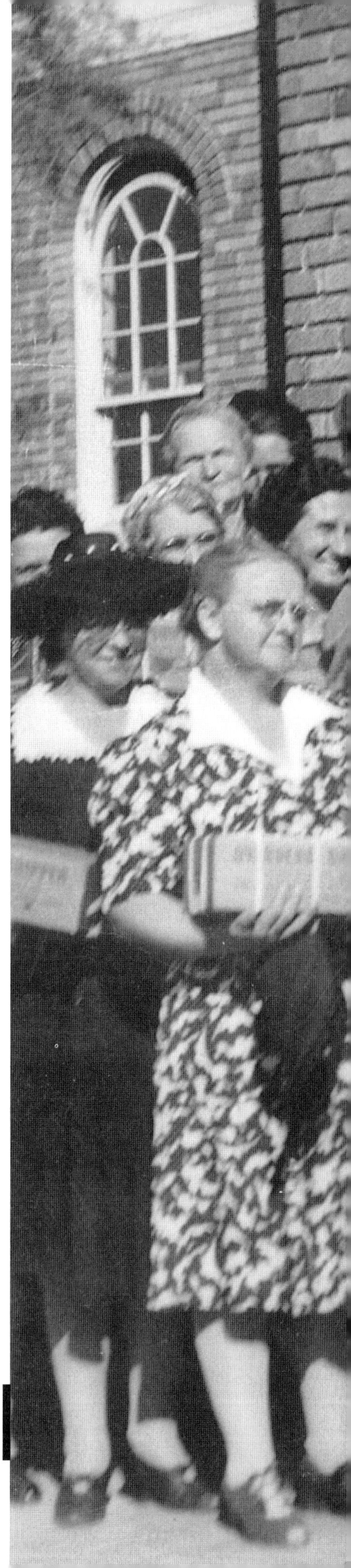

Downy, Idaho, Relief Society members in 1944 with care packages for family members serving in World War II. (Photo courtesy Jay Burrup)

Austria and the Sudetenland region of Czechoslovakia, areas both inhabited by large German-speaking populations. In March 1938 Germany carried out the *anschluss* or annexation of Austria. By September of that year, Hitler was accusing the Czechs of persecuting the German minority in that country and asserted the right to intervene in their behalf. As troops were massed on both sides of the German-Czech border, war seemed inevitable. On September 14, the First Presidency ordered the evacuation of all missionaries from Germany and Czechoslovakia. However, at a meeting with Hitler in Munich held at the end of that month, Britain and France capitulated to Hitler's annexation of the Sudetenland on the condition that he commit no further aggression. Thus, at least temporarily, war was averted, and the First Presidency permitted the evacuated missionaries to return to their fields of labor. This brief evacuation had a sobering effect on the missionaries, causing them "to rededicate their efforts with greater fervor than ever to the work of the Lord" and to feel that "Germany was the most wonderful place in the world to work, and that we must not let any time pass without making the most of it."[1]

The outbreak of World War II in 1939 would put young LDS servicemen and members from around the world in the midst of the world's most destructive military conflict to date.

However, yielding to Hitler's demands at Munich did not sustain peace for long. By the spring of 1939, German troops occupied not only the Sudetenland, but all of Czechoslovakia. Then, echoing his charges against Czechoslovakia during the previous year, Hitler began accusing Poland of mistreating the large German population in the Polish Corridor. To strengthen his position, Hitler signed a military pact with Benito Mussolini of Italy, creating the Rome-Berlin Axis.

In the midst of these tensions, Elder Joseph Fielding Smith of the Council of the Twelve received the assignment to tour the missions in Europe and to conduct the annual mission presidents' conference there. Meanwhile, in August 1939 Germany and Russia were concluding a nonaggression treaty and a secret pact to partition Poland, thus clearing the way for a new German offensive. As these tensions mounted in Europe, President J. Reuben Clark's diplomatic background proved to be valuable to the First Presidency. Through his contacts at the State Department, he was able to keep Church leaders apprised of developments in Europe on an almost hour-by-hour basis. Finally, on Thursday, August 24, the First Presidency ordered the evacuation of missionaries from Germany and Czechoslovakia and directed Elder Joseph Fielding Smith, who was still in Europe, to take charge of this operation.

Major events in the Church related to World War II

1930 1940 1950

1939
Missionaries evacuated from Europe as World War II breaks out

1940
Hugh B. Brown appointed as servicemen's coordinator; missionaries evacuated from the South Pacific

1941
Attack on Pearl Harbor brought U.S. into war, Dec. 7

1942
Church meetings curtailed prior to restrictions on travel; First Presidency statement on war and military service

1945
End of World War II

Group of LDS servicemen in the Admiralty Islands during World War II. (LDS Church Archives)

In this evacuation, particularly from western Germany, participants were convinced they received divine assistance. Because of the time difference between Germany and Utah, the First Presidency's telegram was not received until Friday morning, August 25. Elder Smith and Mission President M. Douglas Wood were in Hanover to conduct a conference when they received the word, so they immediately returned to mission headquarters at Frankfurt. By that afternoon they had sent telegrams to all missionaries, directing them to leave at once for Holland. On Saturday morning, however, the Dutch closed their borders to almost all foreigners, fearing that the influx of thousands of refugees would deplete the already short food supply. At the same time, bulletins broadcast on German radio warned that by Sunday night all railroads would be placed at the disposal of the military and that no further schedules could be guaranteed for civilian travel.

German missionaries pose by an anti-Jewish display before the outbreak of World War II. Conditions in Nazi Germany were tense for missionaries and Church members, and in 1939 the missionaries were evacuated as World War II broke out. (LDS Church Archives)

The closing of the Netherlands border posed a significant challenge to President Wood and his missionaries. Knowing that they could take no more than ten marks (about $2.50) out of Germany, most of the missionaries had used their excess funds to purchase cameras or other goods that they could take with them. When they discovered that they could not enter Holland, they did not have enough money to buy tickets to Copenhagen, Denmark, the alternate evacuation point. Several groups of missionaries were therefore stranded at the Netherlands border.

In Frankfurt President Wood gave Norman G. Seibold, a missionary and a former football player from Idaho, a very special assignment: "Elder, we have 31 missionaries lost somewhere between here and the Dutch border. It will be your mission to find them and see that they get out."[2] The mission president instructed him to follow his impressions, because there was no way of knowing exactly where the Elders were. After four hours on a crowded train, Elder Seibold arrived at Cologne. "I rode the entire distance from Frankfurt to Cologne standing up," he recalled, "the trains were so crowded. It was almost impossible to get off the train at Cologne because of the crowds."[3]

"Cologne was not his destination," President Wood explained, "but he felt impressed to get off the train there."[4] The huge station was crowded with thousands of people trying to reach their destinations. Elder Seibold continued: "I had no idea where the brethren would be, so I hunted through the station for anyone that looked like a missionary. I jumped up on a baggage cart and whistled 'Do What Is Right,' a favorite mission hymn. I couldn't whistle nor sing, but I did the best I could. We picked up about eight missionaries there."

As he rode along on the train he was impressed to remain on board at some towns, but at others he was impressed to get off and whistle. Elder Seibold explained: "I had the feeling to stop at the station in a small town. . . . I had a premonition to go out of the station, which seemed silly to me at the time. I went inside a restaurant. As surely as someone had taken me by the hand, I was guided there. I found two missionaries who were happy to see me. They had spent their last dime for a soft drink."[5]

Having arrived in Copenhagen by Monday, August 28, President Wood learned that fourteen of his thirty-one missing missionaries had entered Holland safely. That afternoon he received a telegram from Elder Seibold stating that the remaining seventeen would arrive in Denmark that evening.[6]

While missionaries from western Germany were struggling to reach Denmark, quite a different drama was unfolding in Czechoslovakia. On July 10, two Elders had been arrested for exchanging money illegally. The next day two more were also arrested when they happened to come looking for their mission associates at the time the gestapo was searching the latter's apartment. All four were put in the gestapo's Pankrac Prison, where political prisoners were held. For the next six weeks Mission President Wallace Toronto worked persistently for the Elders' release. This was not achieved until August 23, just before the Czech Mission received the First Presidency's directive to evacuate. Most of the missionaries, as well as Sister Toronto and her children, left promptly, but President Toronto remained behind to help the Elders who had been in prison recover their passports and other possessions. As Hitler's armies were massing for their invasion of Poland, all communications with Czechoslovakia were cut off. Sister Toronto recalled: "Naturally, I was very upset over the whole thing and expressed my concern and worry to President Joseph Fielding Smith. . . . Seeing that I was very worried and getting more upset by the minute, President Smith came over to me, put his protecting arm around my shoulders and said, 'Sister Toronto, this war will not start until Brother Toronto and his missionaries arrive in this land of Denmark.' "[7]

President Wallace F. Toronto, president of the Czechoslovak Mission (second from left), with Apostle Richard R. Lyman and two missionaries in front of the Swiss-German mission home in 1937. President Toronto was instrumental in the safe evacuation of all of the missionaries from the Czechoslovak Mission, just hours before the outbreak of World War II. (LDS Church Archives)

In Czechoslovakia President Toronto and the remaining four missionaries were able to complete their business by Thursday, August 31. Just before leaving, however, one of the missionaries was arrested and once again sent to Pankrac Prison. Following quick action by President Toronto and American diplomatic representatives, it was learned that there had been a case of mistaken identity: the missionary had the same name as a man sought by the Germans as a British spy. The Elder was promptly released. By midnight, the group boarded a special train sent to evacuate the British legation—the last train to leave Czechoslovakia. They passed through Berlin early Friday morning, September 1, and that afternoon caught the last ferry to cross from Germany to Denmark.[8] This was the very day that the Germans commenced their invasion of Poland, the event generally regarded as the beginning of World War II. Thus Elder Joseph Fielding Smith's prophetic promise to Sister Toronto was fulfilled.

In Salt Lake City, the First Presidency continued to monitor the mounting war crisis and soon ordered the evacuation of all missionaries from Europe. Finding passage back to America presented a monumental problem. Franklin J. Murdock, the Netherlands Mission president, recalled: "As I got close to the Holland America Line office I noticed a great crowd of people around the front door. I thought to myself, 'Oh, how am I going to get through that crowd of people?' A voice came to me just as clear as if you and I were talking. It said, 'Telephone.' " President Murdock went directly to a pay phone and called the general manager, with whom he had done business on other occasions. This official told him to come to the back door, where he was admitted.

President Murdock stated, "I need ninety spaces on your first ship going to the United States."

"You don't realize what you are asking," the manager replied. "I'm sorry; our ships are booked up until February." Just then he was called away from the office for a few minutes. While he was gone, the mission president did some urgent praying. When the manager returned, he unexpectedly said: "How did you know we were going to charter a new boat? You can have the first ninety spaces on it." Although President Murdock did not have any money with him, he was able to book the space simply by signing the name of the Church.[9]

Most missionaries, however, were not fortunate enough to secure space on passenger liners. Most crossed the Atlantic on cargo ships with makeshift accommodations for two to three hundred passengers each. Typically, the ships' holds were filled with bunks, with only a curtain separating the men's and women's dormitories. President J. Reuben Clark regarded the successful evacuation as truly miraculous: "The entire group was evacuated from Europe in three months, at a time when tens of thousands of Americans were besieging the ticket offices of the great steamship companies for passage, and the Elders had no reservations. Every time a group was ready to embark there was available the necessary space, even though efforts to reserve space a few hours before had failed. . . . Truly the blessings of the Lord attended this great enterprise."[10]

In 1940 more areas of the world were drawn into the rapidly expanding war. By June the Low Countries and France had fallen to the Germans, and Britain was preparing to fight for its life. This crisis made the overseas colonies of these countries more vulnerable to attack. In September 1940 Japan signed a ten-year mutual assistance treaty with Germany and Italy and began occupying French Indochina. These developments provided the background for the First Presidency's decisions the following month to withdraw all Latter-day Saint missionaries from the South Pacific and South Africa. Unlike the situation in Europe, communications between these areas and Church headquarters in America were not cut off, and mission presidents were permitted to remain in their areas. Missionaries were not evacuated from South America, but after 1941 no new missionaries were sent to that continent, and by 1943 none remained there. Thus, by that time proselyting by regular full-time missionaries was limited to North America and Hawaii, although even in these areas the number of missionaries was drastically reduced as more and more young men were drafted into military service.

The Saints Who Were Left Behind

When the missionaries were withdrawn, Saints were left on their own, often in isolated circumstances. Many personally witnessed the death and destruction brought by war. Even beyond the actual combat zone the preoccupation with war was demoralizing and detracted from interest in spiritual things. Another problem faced the Saints in the occupied countries: while some felt that the wisest course was to collaborate with the Nazis, others were convinced that their patriotic duty was to resist the German occupation. These Saints were left to make such difficult choices without guidance from the General Authorities and mission leaders. Evacuated missionaries were encouraged to write letters of faith and

Undated photograph of the Aalborg Branch choir in Denmark. Because of the evacuation of the missionaries, branches in Europe had to rely more heavily on their own strengths during the war. (LDS Church Archives)

hope to members where they had served, and the mission presidents were given a special assignment to keep in touch through correspondence with the local leaders whom they had left in charge. Unfortunately, the war disrupted the mails, and even from neutral Switzerland no letters were received for a period of two years.

Although there were some isolated exceptions, the Saints were able to buck the demoralizing tide, and their faithful adherence to Church doctrines and procedures was actually strengthened during the war. In several areas the contribution of tithes and fast offerings, as well as attendance at Church meetings, increased. In Switzerland local missionaries gave two evenings per week and succeeded in baptizing more converts than the full-time missionaries had done just before the outbreak of the war. Much credit is due the local Saints who assumed responsibilities as the missionaries from America were withdrawn. During prewar years, mission presidents had actively prepared the Saints for such an eventuality. Time and again during his 1937 visit to Europe, President Heber J. Grant had urged the Saints to assume their own responsibilities and not to lean so much on the Elders from America. Max Zimmer, who assumed responsibility for the Swiss Mission during the war, was a good example of these capable local leaders. He conducted regular training programs for local priesthood and auxiliary leaders and distributed current Church periodicals to them.

Of course the greatest suffering was experienced by Saints in the areas of actual fighting, and local leaders felt they were often inspired as they carried out their responsibilities amid these trying conditions. For example, Hamburg was bombed 104 times during a ten-day period in 1943. During Church meetings a member of each branch presidency would monitor the radio for information about possible air raids. On one Sunday, Branch President Herbert Baarz in Hamburg had not heard anything about a raid, but he felt inspired to close the meeting abruptly and to have the congregation go immediately to the nearest shelter, a ten-minute walk. Branch members had no sooner reached the shelter than bombs hit the area near the meetinghouse.[11]

When regular meeting places were destroyed, the Saints continued to hold services in their homes. But in some areas, 95 percent of the homes were destroyed. Local leaders launched a variety of self-help programs. Mission leaders directed that food, clothing, and household supplies be stockpiled at branch meeting places. All contributed to a fund with which the Relief Society purchased material to patch or remodel old clothing or to sew new garments. Members in Hamburg participated in the *Loeffelspende* or "spoon contribution," bringing a spoonful of flour or sugar to each Church meeting. Although one spoonful might have seemed insignificant, when "multiplied by 200 [it] was sufficient to bake a cake for a young couple for their wedding, or to give to a mother who was expecting or nursing a baby."[12]

Impact on North American Saints

While the Saints in North America did not suffer in the way that their counterparts in Europe did, the war still had a substantial impact on Church members and programs. As World War II began, shipyards, aircraft plants, and other defense industries created many new jobs along the West Coast. These economic opportunities lured many Mormons from the Intermountain area to the Pacific Coast. This continued the pattern—established during the 1920s and accelerated during the Depression of the 1930s—of young people leaving the Intermountain area in search of improved employment opportunities.

This population drain might have been even larger had the war not brought unaccustomed prosperity to Intermountain-area agriculture. Additionally, the establishment of defense industries such as the Geneva Steel plant near Provo created new jobs in Utah and surrounding areas. Many who had left the Intermountain area during earlier decades wanted to return and establish their permanent homes in a predominantly Latter-day Saint environment. These improved economic conditions made it possible for them to do so.

These war-simulated population shifts created several challenges for the Church. Mormon youth were among those seeking employment in defense industries. Near the end of the war, more than half of the priests in the Aaronic Priesthood, most of whom were young men of high school and college age, were living away from home. The General Authorities encouraged local Church leaders to take a special interest in these youth who were deprived of the stabilizing influence of home and family.[13]

At the same time, the coming of new industries to predominantly Mormon areas resulted in a sudden population influx. While some longtime Intermountain residents were concerned about the introduction of such a large "outside element," Church leaders encouraged the Saints to fellowship the newcomers and to share the gospel with them. This created a fertile field for the stake missions, which had been established just a few years before.

Wartime conditions affected programs sponsored by the Church in still other ways. In January 1942, just a month after the United States entered World War II, the First Presidency suspended all stake leadership meetings for the duration of the war. "This action," the Presidency stressed, "places increased responsibility upon the ward and branch auxiliary organizations to see that their work not only does not suffer, but is increased in intensity, improved in quality, and in general made more effective" in the lives of those who more than ever before needed spiritual support.[14] Auxiliary general boards kept in touch and gave direction by mail, and the home was increasingly stressed as the key to preserving faith among the youth. The First Presidency also limited attendance at general conferences to specifically invited priesthood leaders. At the same time, the Tabernacle was closed to the public and the weekly choir broadcasts were made without audiences present.

Women socialize and prepare beans for canning at a World War II "victory garden." Elder Harold B. Lee felt that, prior to the war, the Lord had inspired Church leaders' instruction for members to produce and store food as preparation for wartime needs and challenges. (Used by permission, Utah State Historical Society, all rights reserved)

Observations of the Relief Society's 1942 centennial had to be postponed and the annual Hill Cumorah Pageant was cancelled for the duration of the war.

Thus, when United States President Franklin D. Roosevelt, on April 27, 1942, spoke of the need to control wages and prices, to ration, and to increase taxes, Latter-day Saint Church leaders had already taken steps to adapt programs to these conditions.

Elder Harold B. Lee was convinced that the timing of the Church's precautions was the result of revelation. He pointed out that the January 1942 restrictions on auxiliary meetings and travel "happened from eight months to nearly a year before the tire and gas rationing took place" and concluded "that here again was the voice of the Lord to this people, trying to prepare them for the conservation program that within a year was forced upon them. No one at that time could surely foresee that the countries that had been producing certain essential commodities were to be overrun and we thereby be forced into a shortage."[15] Furthermore, Elder Lee was convinced that Church leaders were inspired when, beginning in 1937, they counseled the Saints to produce and store a year's supply of food. He believed that this helped prepare Church members for rationing and scarcity and anticipated the government's emphasis on "victory gardens."

Church activities were hampered in yet other ways. As building supplies were diverted to military use, construction of meetinghouses and even of the Idaho Falls Temple came to a halt. Perhaps no Church activity felt the impact of war more than did the missionary program. In 1942 the Church agreed not to call young men of draft age on missions. Hence the number of missionaries serving plummeted. While 1,257 new full-time missionaries had been called in 1941, only 261 were called two years later. Before the war, five-sixths of all missionaries were young men holding the offices of elder or seventy; by 1945, most new missionaries were women or high priests. Members living in mission fields again assumed more responsibilities, just as they had done when the number of missionaries dropped during the Great Depression a decade earlier. Throughout North America these Saints accepted

THROW YOUR SCRAP INTO THE
WAR BONDS
EVERYBODY
EVERY PAY DAY
10%
SALT LAKE ZONE

The state of Utah and members of the Church demonstrated great patriotism on the front lines and at home. (Used by permission, Utah State Historical Society, all rights reserved)

calls as local part-time missionaries and assumed greater roles in district or branch organizations.

The Church sponsored special wartime programs and in other ways encouraged its members to patriotically support the war effort. The first Sunday in 1942 was designated as a special day of fasting and prayer. As they had done during World War I, the General Authorities again commended the Saints for their generous contributions to the Red Cross and other charitable funds. Women in the Relief Society put together first-aid kits for home use and prepared bandages and other supplies for the Red Cross. During the winter of 1942–43 the Church's twelve- and thirteen-year-old Beehive Girls donated 228,000 hours, collecting scrap metal, fats, and other needed materials, making scrapbooks or baking cookies for soldiers, and tending children for mothers working in defense industries. A special "Honor Bee" award was offered for such service. Then in 1943, Mutual Improvement Association youth in the United States and Canada raised more than three million dollars to purchase fifty-five badly needed rescue boats to save the lives of downed airmen.

The Saints' Attitudes on War

As war engulfed the world, Latter-day Saints again had to examine their feelings relative to the appropriateness of resorting to arms. They were guided by the Book of Mormon's teachings, which denounced offensive wars but condoned fighting "even to the shedding of blood if it were necessary" in defense of home, country, freedom, or religion (see Alma 43:45–47; 48:14). Still, in 1833, when the Saints were being driven from Missouri, a revelation had directed them to "renounce war and proclaim peace" (D&C 98:16).

As World War II approached, Latter-day Saints in the United States, along with the majority of their fellow citizens, continued to cling to a hope for peace. Speaking in general conference only a month after Hitler's 1939 invasion of Poland, President J. Reuben Clark, emphatically declared that "nothing is more unrighteous, more unholy, more un-Godly than man-declared mass slaughter of his fellowman for an unrighteous cause."[16] President Clark specifically opposed American intervention: "This is one of those questions which can be settled only by the parties themselves by themselves."[17] President Heber J. Grant concurred: "I pray with all the earnestness of my heart that our country may not get into war."[18]

In their annual Christmas message issued less than a week after the attack on Pearl Harbor, the First Presidency insisted that only through living the gospel of Jesus Christ would enduring peace come to the world. Echoing the counsel given by President Joseph F. Smith at the outbreak of World War I, the Presidency now exhorted members in the armed forces to keep "cruelty, hate, and murder" out of their hearts even during battle.[19]

These points were all incorporated in the First Presidency's official statement read at the April 1942 general conference just four months after the attack on Pearl Harbor. This declaration represented the most comprehensive and authoritative review of the Church's attitude on war, and it was widely distributed in pamphlet form. "Hate can have no place in the souls of the righteous," the Presidency declared, emphasizing the Savior's injunction to love one another.

Nevertheless, the Presidency explained that members of the Church were also members of "the body politic," and urged "members fully to render that loyalty to their country and to free institutions which the loftiest patriotism calls for." Therefore, the Presidency continued, "the members of the Church have always felt under obligation to come to the defense of their country when a call to arms was made." During World War I, the Saints had served "on both sides of the conflict. Likewise in the present war, righteous men of the Church in both camps have died, some with great heroism, for their own country's sake. . . . The Church has been benefitted by their service and sacrifice."

Nevertheless, we have not forgotten that on Sinai God commanded, 'Thou shalt not kill.' " Addressing this delicate situation, the First Presidency explained that, if in the course of combat, servicemen "shall take the lives of those who fight against them, that will not make of them murderers, nor subject them to the penalty that God has prescribed for those who kill. . . . For it would be a cruel God that would punish His children as moral sinners for acts done by them as the innocent instrumentalities of a sovereign whom He had told them to obey and whose will they were powerless to resist.

". . . This Church is a worldwide Church. . . . On each side they believe they are fighting for home, and country, and freedom. On each side, our brethren pray to the same God, in the same name, for victory." The Presidency conceded "both sides cannot be wholly right; perhaps neither is without wrong."

In conclusion the First Presidency exhorted those in military service to "live clean, keep the commandments of the Lord, pray to Him constantly to preserve you in truth and righteousness, live as you pray, and then whatever betides you the Lord will be with you and nothing will happen to you that will not be to the honor and glory of God and to your salvation and exaltation. . . . Then, when the conflict is over and you return to your homes, having lived the righteous life, how great will be your happiness—whether you be of the victors or of the vanquished—that you have lived as the Lord commanded."[20]

Latter-day Saints in Military Service

Heeding the counsel of their Church leaders, Latter-day Saints responded when calls came for military service. By the war's end, the number in uniform approached one hundred thousand, or in other words, about one out of every ten Church members.

Even though LDS servicemen's groups were organized during the Spanish-American War and Elder B. H. Roberts served as a chaplain during World War I, the most complete development of the Church's programs for servicemen came during World War II.

In 1940, over a year before the United States entered the war, the Church appointed Hugh B. Brown, a former stake president (and future General Authority), to serve as servicemen's coordinator. Having attained the rank of major in the Canadian army during World War I, he was able to capitalize on this title in making contact with military authorities. Brown traveled extensively, meeting with LDS servicemen, giving them encouragement, and receiving from them recommendations concerning what the Church could do. His warm personality and deep spirituality made him particularly well suited for this assignment.

A Church Servicemen's Committee was organized in October 1942, with Elder Harold B. Lee, a new member of the Twelve, as chairman. The committee worked with United States military officials to secure the appointments of Latter-day Saint chaplains. Achieving this aim posed a formidable challenge. Army and Navy officials were reluctant to appoint chaplains who did not meet the usual requirements of a professional clergyman. The Army Chief of Chaplains, however, remembered favorably how a local Mormon bishop had cared for the spiritual well-being of the servicemen in his area. Through the committee's efforts, military officials gradually approved the appointment of additional LDS chaplains, and by the end of World War II the number peaked at forty.[21]

Certainly forty chaplains were not enough to give religious leadership to the thousands of Latter-day Saints scattered throughout the widely separated theaters of war. As early as the Spanish-American War the Mutual Improvement Association had sponsored servicemen's groups. During the course of World War II this program was revived under the direction of the Servicemen's Committee, and approximately a thousand group leaders served. Once set apart by Church authorities, these group leaders could officiate anywhere their services might be needed. Each received a certificate identifying him as "an Elder in the Church" and as "an authorized Group Leader of the Mutual Improvement Association . . . empowered, after first obtaining permission of the proper military authorities, to conduct study classes and other worshipping assemblies."[22]

The Church sponsored several other measures to benefit members in the service. Servicemen's "homes" were opened in Salt Lake City and California. For those away from home, "budget cards" became "passports" to the social and recreational activities offered by the Church. Members entering military service received pocket-size copies of the Book of Mormon and *Principles of the Gospel.* A miniature version of the *Church Section* carried messages of inspiration, reports of servicemen's activities, and important announcements.

Latter-day Saint servicemen set an outstanding example of faith and devotion. Military officials frequently reported astonishment at the initiative and ability of the Mormon soldiers to conduct their own religious worship without the need for professional clergymen. On Saipan a group of LDS Marines who had no place to meet set to work building their own chapel. German LDS soldiers during the occupation of Norway shared their rations with needy Saints in that land. Similarly, LDS American soldiers helped German Saints to rebuild as the war drew to a close. Always eager to share the gospel, Church members took advantage of opportunities even under wartime conditions. Numerous conversions resulted from the worthy example of Mormon "buddies." While in a German prison camp, a Dutch member shared the gospel with a fellow POW who later became the first stake president in their native country. Eldin Ricks, an LDS chaplain, presented a copy of the Book of Mormon to Pope Pius XII at the Vatican.

Elder Ezra Taft Benson lamented the wartime drop in the number of full-time missionaries, but added: "I cannot help feeling that we are probably doing more total missionary work today than we have ever done in the history of the Church" because nearly one hundred thousand LDS servicemen are also "doing effective missionary work." He mentioned that a group of men in uniform approached him and enthusiastically declared, "Brother Benson, it is just like being on another mission. Conditions are different, but we have opportunities to preach the gospel, and we are taking advantage of it."[23] Latter-day Saint servicemen were even responsible for introducing the gospel into new areas of the

A member from Bradford, England, with four unidentified German prisoners of war who attended branch meetings, circa 1945. Several prisoners were reported to have been baptized by LDS servicemen. Although the war brought a significant drop in full-time missionaries, servicemen found ways to spread the gospel message. (LDS Church Archives)

world. For example, they provided the Church's first contact with the Philippine Islands.[24]

Latter-day Saint servicemen, like many of other faiths, often saw divine protection in the preservation of their lives amid the terrors of combat. For example, Melden J. Smith told how his life was spared when a copy of the *Improvement Era* in his shirt pocket retarded a machine gun bullet.[25] A widely recounted incident involved two U.S. marines who were seriously wounded during the invasion of Kwajalein early in 1944. A war correspondent described how the less-severely wounded marine, a Latter-day Saint, refused attention until his buddy was helped and then pronounced a blessing on him: "In the name of Jesus Christ, and by virtue of the Holy Priesthood which I hold, I command you to remain alive until the necessary help can be obtained to secure the preservation of your life." His life was saved, and his recovery was the "wonder of the medical unit."[26] To testify of the power of the priesthood, President George Albert Smith on several occasions read the United Press account of this story, dateline Honolulu, February 8, 1944.

Of course, the lives of many LDS servicemen were not spared. Why some were saved, even miraculously, and others were not, is difficult or impossible to know. The Servicemen's Committee reported that a total of 5,714 Latter-day Saints were killed, wounded, or missing in action. Speaking at general conference in 1942, Elder Harold B. Lee offered one possible justification for the death of faithful Latter-day Saint servicemen: "It is my conviction that the present devastating scourge of war in which hundreds of thousands are being slain, many of whom are no more responsible for the causes of the war than are our own boys, is making necessary an increase of missionary activity in the spirit world and that many of our boys who bear the Holy Priesthood and are worthy to do so will be called to that missionary service after they have departed this life."[27]

The need for military forces continued even after the close of World War II in 1945. The spread of the "Cold War" meant that a large number of Latter-day Saints would always be serving in the armed forces, and the Church would continue its interest in them. Programs developed for servicemen during World War II would continue to play a key role, and they would be supplemented by several important new activities. The Church conducted annual conferences for servicemen beginning in 1953. Often attended by more than a thousand, these gatherings would become the largest "retreats" conducted among American military personnel. These conferences featured leadership workshops, recreational activities, and addresses by General Authorities, and were generally climaxed by inspirational testimony meetings. A further boost came in 1968 when the first servicemen's stake was organized in Germany. During these years, the General Authorities continued to reaffirm their commitment to giving the growing number of members entering the military service encouragement and help similar to that given to departing missionaries. Latter-day Saints who served in the military during these postwar years would also be instrumental in opening doors for the gospel in new parts of the world even as their predecessors had done during World War II.

10

George Albert Smith and Recovery from War

President Heber J. Grant died on May 14, 1945, one week after Germany's surrender in Europe, and just three months before Japan's surrender would bring World War II to a close. His funeral was held in the Salt Lake Tabernacle, which was opened to the public for the first time in over three years, and the building was filled to overflowing. His successor, George Albert Smith, would face the challenging task of leading the Saints during an era when the world needed to overcome hate and begin to rebuild following the end of the war. President Smith's experience and character suited him well for this task.

George Albert Smith's Earlier Life

George Albert Smith was born in Salt Lake City in 1870. When he was thirteen years old, his patriarchal blessing suggested the direction his life would take, promising that he would "become a mighty Apostle in the Church and kingdom of God upon the earth," and "A mighty prophet in the midst of the sons of Zion."[1]

On May 25, 1892, he married his childhood sweetheart, Lucy Emily Woodruff, the granddaughter of President Wilford Woodruff. Only a month later, the new husband departed for a two-year mission in the southern states. On at least two occasions he was convinced that his life was spared through divine intervention—once when a hostile mob fired shots into the house where he was sleeping, and again when he was warned

George Albert Smith was an avid proponent of Scouting, serving on the national executive committee and receiving the silver buffalo, the highest award presented by the Boy Scouts of America. (Used by permission, Utah State Historical Society, all rights reserved)

on a dark night to stop just short of the edge of a high precipice.[2] After Elder Smith had been in the field only a few months, Mission President J. Golden Kimball called him to be his secretary, often leaving him in charge of mission affairs.

Just nine years later, George Albert Smith was called to the apostleship. Because of a particularly busy day at his office, he had not been able to attend the session of general conference where his call was announced. As he came home that afternoon, a woman congratulated him enthusiastically. He was at a loss to know what she was talking about. She told him he had been sustained that afternoon as a new member of the Council of the Twelve Apostles. With characteristic modesty he insisted that she must certainly be mistaken, as he knew nothing at all about it. Flustered, she went back to the Tabernacle to verify what had happened and soon returned to assure him that she had not heard wrong. That evening he confided to his journal: "I was completely dumbfounded and I could hardly believe it possible at this time . . . that I might become an apostle. I didn't feel capable or worthy but if it pleases the Lord I will try to do my full duty."[3]

Elder Smith became the fourth generation in his family to serve as a General Authority; he would also become the fourth generation to serve in the First Presidency. His great-grandfather, John Smith was an uncle and assistant counselor to the Prophet Joseph Smith and later became Patriarch to the Church. His grandfather, George A. Smith, had been an Apostle and a counselor to Brigham Young. His

George Albert Smith (right) at age sixteen. (LDS Church Archives)

father, John Henry Smith, was a member of the Twelve at the time of George Albert's call. These two served together in the Quorum until 1910, when John Henry was called into the First Presidency. This was the only time that a father and a son had served simultaneously in the Council of the Twelve.

Throughout his life George Albert Smith was plagued with poor health. A few years after his call to the apostleship, he was convalescing from an especially serious illness when he had a dream in which he saw his grandfather, after whom he had been named.

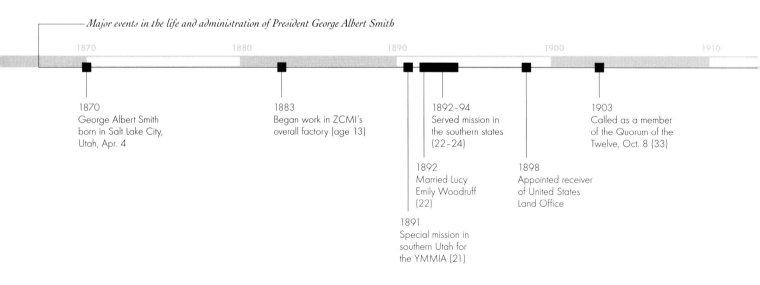

Major events in the life and administration of President George Albert Smith

1870 1880 1890 1900 1910

1870
George Albert Smith born in Salt Lake City, Utah, Apr. 4

1883
Began work in ZCMI's overall factory (age 13)

1891
Special mission in southern Utah for the YMMIA (21)

1892
Married Lucy Emily Woodruff (22)

1892–94
Served mission in the southern states (22–24)

1898
Appointed receiver of United States Land Office

1903
Called as a member of the Quorum of the Twelve, Oct. 8 (33)

He looked at me very earnestly and said:

"I would like to know what you have done with my name."

Everything I had ever done passed before me as though it were a flying picture on a screen. . . . I smiled and looked at my grandfather and said:

"I have never done anything with your name of which you need be ashamed."

He stepped forward and took me in his arms, and as he did so, I became conscious again of my earthly surroundings.[4]

From 1919 to 1921 George Albert Smith presided over the European Mission. In the aftermath of World War I, food was scarce in Europe, and so several countries refused to admit any foreigners. As Elder Smith negotiated with these governments to obtain permission for missionaries to enter their borders, he gained experience that would be valuable as he faced similar circumstances following the close of World War II.

Upon his return home, Elder George Albert Smith was called to preside over the Young Men's Mutual Improvement Association. This service continued until 1935, when the First Presidency released all members of the Twelve from auxiliary boards. His interest in the youth was long-standing. At the age of twenty-one he had served four months as a special MIA missionary in southwestern Utah, working to stimulate activity among the young men there. From the earliest days of the Boy Scout movement, Elder Smith had been an avid booster. He became an active local Scout council member and was proud to wear his Scouter's uniform. In 1932 he was elected to the national executive committee of the Boy Scouts of America. Two years later Elder Smith received the Silver Buffalo, the highest award presented by the national Boy Scout organization in recognition of outstanding service. This concern for young people would aid President Smith as he counseled returning servicemen about meeting their challenges following the close of World War II.

George Albert Smith was actively interested in preserving and marking historic sites. In 1930 he founded the Utah Pioneer Trails and Landmarks Association, and he served as its president until his death. He supervised the erection of more than one hundred substantial markers at historic sites throughout the western United States. Elder Smith linked these activities with his concern for youth. As superintendent of the YMMIA he involved Latter-day Saint young people in numerous projects to suitably mark points of local interest. He saw this as a way to help the youth identify and better appreciate their heritage. Appropriately, he would be serving as President of the Church at the time of the pioneer centennial celebration in 1947.

A Christlike love for others was perhaps the outstanding quality George Albert Smith would bring to his calling as President of the Church. Years earlier Elder Smith had formulated a creed to guide his life:

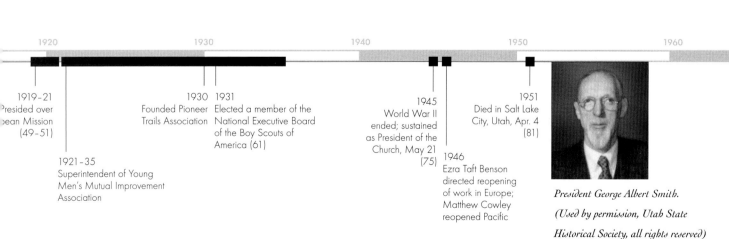

1920 1930 1940 1950 1960

1919–21
resided over
ean Mission
(49–51)

1921–35
Superintendent of Young Men's Mutual Improvement Association

1930
Founded Pioneer Trails Association

1931
Elected a member of the National Executive Board of the Boy Scouts of America (61)

1945
World War II ended; sustained as President of the Church, May 21 (75)

1946
Ezra Taft Benson directed reopening of work in Europe; Matthew Cowley reopened Pacific

1951
Died in Salt Lake City, Utah, Apr. 4 (81)

President George Albert Smith. (Used by permission, Utah State Historical Society, all rights reserved)

George Albert Smith, around the time of his marriage to Lucy Emily Woodruff. (Deseret News *photo)*

I would be a friend to the friendless and find joy in ministering to the needs of the poor. I would visit the sick and afflicted and inspire in them a desire for faith to be healed. I would teach the truth to the understanding and blessing of all mankind. I would seek out the erring one and try to win him back to a righteous and a happy life. I would not seek to force people to live up to my ideals but rather love them into doing the thing that is right. I would live with the masses and help to solve their problems that their earth life may be happy. I would avoid the publicity of high positions and discourage the flattery of thoughtless friends. I would not knowingly wound the feeling of any, not even one who may have wronged me, but would seek to do him good and make him my friend. I would overcome the tendency to selfishness and jealousy and rejoice in the successes of all the children of my Heavenly Father. I would not be an enemy to any living soul. Knowing that the Redeemer of mankind has offered to the world the only plan that will fully develop us and make us really happy here and hereafter I feel it not only a duty but a blessed privilege to disseminate this truth.[5]

His biographer would later say of Elder Smith, "You can put this creed in the past tense and it epitomizes his life—this is what he has actually done."[6] His capacity to love would prove invaluable to George Albert Smith as he assumed the Presidency of the Church at the very time when the world was turning its attention from war to a quest for lasting peace. The Council of the Twelve Apostles and the Patriarch of the Church, meeting in an upper room of the Salt Lake Temple on May 21, 1945, sustained George Albert Smith as the new President of The Church of Jesus Christ of Latter-day Saints.

The Close of World War II

The formal end to World War II came on August 14, 1945, when Japan accepted the Allies' terms for surrender. Even before the war had ended, machinery was set in motion to create a new international organization designed to prevent future conflict. In 1945 at a special conference in San Francisco, the charter for the United Nations was adopted. In contrast to the heated and prolonged debates over the League of Nations following World War I, the United States Senate approved participation in the new UN swiftly and almost unanimously. The Church did not take an official stand either for or against the new international body. Even though President J. Reuben Clark feared that membership in such a body would compromise the nation's sovereignty, there was none of the active campaigning against the United Nations by prominent Latter-day Saints that there had been against the League of Nations a quarter century earlier.[7] Nevertheless, Church leaders reminded the Saints that the only hope for enduring peace was the world's acceptance of and adherence to the principles of the gospel of Jesus Christ.

Within a few months of the war's end, thousands of Latter-day Saints were discharged from military service. This was the joyous time eagerly anticipated by relatives and sweethearts, and of course by the servicemen themselves, when "Johnny would come marching home." Nevertheless, the return to civilian life was not free from perils, and the Church took steps to help its members make this transition. The General Authorities encouraged bishops to interview returning servicemen promptly and to see that they received callings to Church service. Priesthood quorums sponsored welcome-home parties and assisted with finding employment. The Mutual Improvement Association played a key role in fellowshipping veterans through athletic and social activities.

A pressing need was for the Church to reestablish contact with the European Saints, with whom there had been no contact for as many as six years. Hundreds of Saints had been left homeless as cities were destroyed, especially in Germany and Holland. An acute shortage of food compounded the suffering immediately after the war.

Latter-day Saint servicemen brought the first help to the suffering members. One American soldier later described his contact with Dutch Saints:

> I attended Sunday School in the Apeldoorn branch. With me I brought what food we were able to save from our army rations. After Sunday School we held a "banquet" for the thirty-five members who were present.
>
> "Dear Lord," prayed Brother Dodenbier, "forgive us for holding a feast on thy holy day, but the need is great."
>
> After a song of rejoicing, each person was served one small meat or cheese sandwich, two raisin pancakes, a cup of cocoa. For the children there was the added treat of a small piece of chocolate, the first candy many of them had ever tasted. They were children of the occupation, born during the darkest years of their country's history. The "banquet" was received with an appreciation unknown to us who have never suffered for want of food.
>
> "It has come in answer to our prayers," concluded the branch president.[8]

These contacts strengthened the faith of the needy Saints as well as of the servicemen providing succor.

Summarizing the impact of Mormon men in the military, Elder Ezra Taft Benson later wrote from Europe: "The willing service and clean, exemplary lives of the many L.D.S. servicemen, who have been among the peoples of Europe, have left a splendid impression over here."[9]

Hugh B. Brown, president of the British Mission, was the first Church official to visit the European continent following the close of the war. On July 20, 1945, only two months after the formal end of hostilities in Europe, President Brown flew to Paris. There, in the large ballroom of an exclusive hotel, he conducted a meeting that was attended by some 350 servicemen and local Saints. He then continued by train to Switzerland for a hectic series of meetings. At Lausanne, not a member was absent even though the meeting was held during normal working hours. Elder Brown wrote: "The sheer joy of these humble folk at seeing someone from 'Zion' again made me realize how really lonely they had been during the isolation of the war years."[10]

As early as the fall of 1945 the Church sent relief supplies to Europe. These were addressed to branch presidents or other responsible individuals. The supplies had to be sent through regular mail, which meant that only small packages were accepted and

Hugh B. Brown, the Church servicemen's coordinator and a former major in the Canadian army, addresses Church servicemen in Paris in 1945. (Deseret News *photo*)

President George Albert Smith confers with U.S. president Harry S. Truman about shipping food and clothing to the suffering peoples of Europe in the wake of World War II. (LDS Church Archives)

that the cost was almost prohibitive. By January 1946 the Church had shipped some thirteen thousand of these packages, besides many more mailed by individuals. In the meantime the Church was seeking means of shipping larger quantities. This would require the special cooperation of government officials. Consequently, President George Albert Smith together with Elders John A. Widtsoe and David O. McKay went to Washington, D.C., where they spent considerable time conferring with ambassadors and other officials of foreign nations. On November 3, President Smith and his party had a twenty-minute interview with President Harry S. Truman at the White House. President George Albert Smith later recalled:

> When I called on him, he received me very graciously—I had met him before—and I said: "I have just come to ascertain from you, Mr. President, what your attitude will be if the Latter-day Saints are prepared to ship food and clothing and bedding to Europe."
>
> He smiled and looked at me, and said: "Well, what do you want to ship it over there for? Their money isn't any good."
>
> I said: "We don't want their money." He looked at me and asked: "You don't mean you are going to give it to them?"
>
> I said: "Of course, we would give it to them. They are our brothers and sisters and are in distress. God has blessed us with a surplus, and we will be glad to send it if we can have the cooperation of the government."
>
> He said: "You are on the right track," and added, "we will be glad to help you in any way we can."[11]

Elder Benson's Mission to Europe

On January 14, 1946, the First Presidency announced the calling of Elder Ezra Taft Benson, one of the newest of the Twelve Apostles, to preside over the European Mission.[12] His extensive experience with national agricultural cooperatives, including international travel and extensive government contacts, prepared him well for this assignment. Elder Benson would reopen the missions in Europe, "attend to the spiritual affairs of the Saints," and "make available food, clothing, and bedding for the members of the Church in these distressed areas."[13]

In Elder Benson's letter of appointment, the First Presidency declared: "Your influence [will] be felt for good by all you come in contact with, and . . . you and they [will] be made to feel that there is a power and spirit accompanying you not of man."[14] Events of succeeding months would amply demonstrate the prophetic nature of this promise.

Elder Benson was accompanied by Frederick W. Babbel, who had served in the Swiss-German Mission just before the outbreak of World War II. They left Salt Lake City on January 29, 1946. From the beginning of their mission they frequently referred to a scriptural promise that they believed was fulfilled in their behalf: "And they shall go forth and none shall stay them, for I the Lord have commanded them" (D&C 1:5). Elder Benson recalled: "Barriers have melted away. Problems that seemed impossible to solve have been solved, and the work in large measure has been accomplished through the blessings of the Lord. I remember well our first inquiry as to the time we could set sail, either by plane or boat. We were told it would take three months, that all bookings were filled for that period. Yet within twenty-one days from the time our appointment was announced, we landed at Hurn Airport sixty miles south of London." Within two days, despite an "acute housing shortage," headquarters were established at an ideal spot in London.[15]

Elder Ezra Taft Benson became the first nonmilitary American permitted to travel throughout all four occupied zones of Germany. His travels were often characterized by an amazing series of events enabling him to meet his demanding schedule. He and his associates accepted these circumstances as manifestations of divine intervention. Typical were his experiences as he traveled with Howard C. Badger, an LDS military chaplain, from Paris to the Hague. Railway officials in Paris advised him that there would be a day's delay because Holland could be entered only through its eastern border rather than via a more direct route. Elder Benson recounted:

> We were almost resigned to taking the service they recommended. It was then that I noticed a train on one of the tracks preparing to leave. "Where is that train headed?" I asked the stationmaster. "Antwerp, Belgium," he answered. I told him we would take that train and he assured me that we would lose an extra day because all connections between Antwerp and Holland had been cut off as a result of the war.
>
> But I felt impressed to board that train in spite of his protestations. . . .
>
> When we arrived at Antwerp, the stationmaster was very upset and advised us that we would have to back-track somewhat and lose an extra day. Again I saw another train getting ready to leave and inquired where it was going. We were advised that this was a local shuttle-service which stopped at the Dutch border where the large bridge across the Maas River still lay in ruins. I felt impressed that we should board that train in spite of the stationmaster's protests.
>
> When we reached the Maas River, we all had to pile out. As we stood picking up our luggage, we noticed an American army truck approaching us. Brother Badger flagged it down and, upon learning that there was a pontoon bridge nearby, he persuaded them to take us into Holland. When we arrived at the first little village on the Dutch side, we were pleasantly surprised to find this local shuttle-service waiting to take us into The Hague.[16]

One of Elder Benson's early visits was to Karlsruhe, a key German city on the Rhine River. Upon inquiring where the Latter-day Saints might be meeting, the group was directed to an area of almost totally demolished buildings. Elder Babbel wrote, "Parking our car near massive heaps of twisted steel and concrete, we climbed over several large piles of rubble and threaded our way between the naked

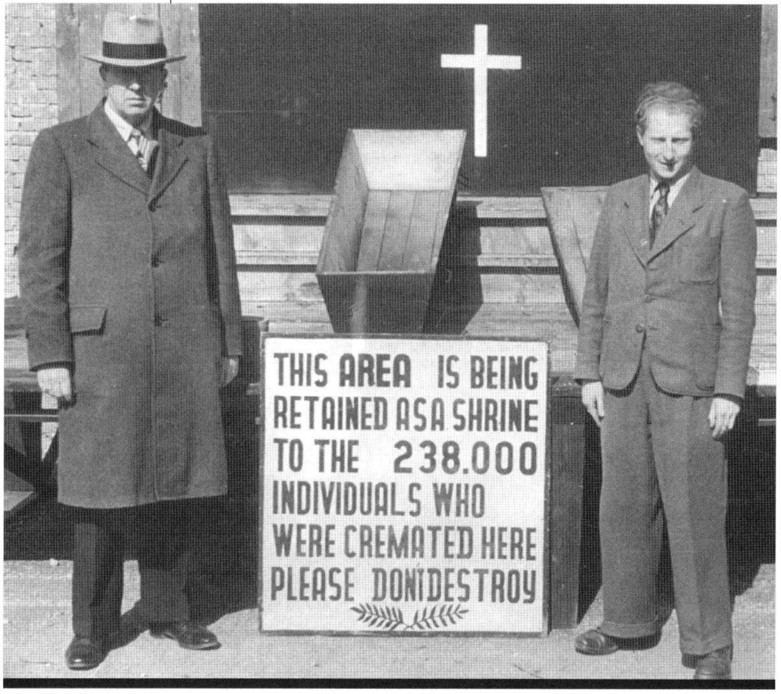

Elder Ezra Taft Benson with a former prisoner at Dachau, a World War II concentration camp in Germany. (LDS Church Archives)

blasted walls in the general direction which had been pointed out to us. As we viewed the desolation on all sides of us, our task seemed hopeless. Then we heard the distant strains of 'Come, Come Ye Saints' being sung in German. We were overjoyed. No strains of music were ever more welcome!" They found 260 Saints waiting for them in a badly damaged building. Brother Babbel recalled that he had never "seen President Benson so deeply and visibly moved as on that occasion."[17] Elder Benson later described these feelings:

> The Saints had been in session for some two hours waiting for us, hoping that we would come because the word had reached them that we might be there for the conference. And then for the first time in my life I saw almost an entire audience in tears as we walked up onto the platform, and they realized that at last, after six or seven long years, representatives from Zion, as they put it, had finally come back to them. Then as the meeting closed, prolonged at their request, they insisted we go to the door and shake hands with each one of them as he left the bombed-out building. And we noted that many of them, after they had passed through the line went back and came through the second and third time, so happy were they to grasp our hands. As I looked into their upturned faces, pale, thin, many of these Saints dressed in rags, some of them barefooted, I could see the light of faith in their eyes as they bore testimony to the divinity of this great latter-day work, and expressed their gratitude for the blessings of the Lord.
>
> That is what a testimony does.[18]

Food and clothing were desperately needed throughout war-torn Europe. "Starvation is very near to many of our people," Elder Benson lamented, "and all the help we can give them will not come too soon."[19] This posed a substantial challenge to the Church's decade-old welfare program. Its prompt and efficient response attracted extensive favorable comment both nationally and internationally.

By March 1946, Elder Benson had made necessary arrangements with government and military authorities in Europe to have relief supplies sent. To supplement commodities already in storage, the Church launched drives for used clothing and other goods. President George Albert Smith took the lead in demonstrating love and concern for the suffering Saints in Europe. He donated at least two suits fresh from the cleaners and several shirts still in their wrappings from the laundry. During a visit to Welfare Square to inspect the results of these clothing drives, he took off his own topcoat and laid it on one of the piles of clothing being prepared for shipment to Europe. Despite the protestations of his associates, the weather being quite cold, he insisted on returning to the office without his coat.[20]

*Elder Ezra Taft Benson (right) and Max Zimmer inspect Church welfare supplies sent to Europe by the Saints in America. (*Improvement Era *photo)*

In Europe, Elder Benson reported that military and other officials were amazed at the speed with which the shipments arrived from the Church in America. European Church leaders wept for joy and gratitude when they visited the storehouses where the welfare goods had been received. Elder Benson wrote: "I wish you could have seen the clothes as they had them neatly arranged on the floors and in cabinets at the mission home and witnessed the expressions of gratitude, both facial and by word of mouth, from the mission presidency and other Saints."[21] Many wept openly as they examined clothing or ran their fingers through sacks of grain.

Not all Church assistance came from America, however. Europeans also found ways to help one another. During the closing months of the war, Saints in the East German Mission began gathering clothing, hiding it in safe places and sharing it cooperatively. The mission president compared the German members to the early Latter-day Saints who were driven closer together by the difficulties they suffered.[22] When President Benson instructed the Dutch Saints to grow potatoes to meet their own welfare needs, permission was secured from the government to plant them in the median strip of a major highway. At the end of the growing season, the Saints harvested sixty-six tons of potatoes—plenty to meet their needs. Mission President Cornelius Zappey issued a challenging proposal to the Saints. He acknowledged the bitter feelings that had existed towards the Germans, but announced: "Those people are now much worse off than you are and we are asking you to send your entire potato harvest to the German saints. Will you do it?"[23] The Saints responded. Incredulous government officials exclaimed in bewilderment, "We ourselves are starving and here you want to send food to our former enemies."[24]

On the other hand, Denmark suffered less during the war than most other European countries. The Danish Saints regarded their more fortunate circumstances as the fulfillment of Elder Joseph Fielding Smith's prophetic promise made at the outbreak of the war—that because Denmark had opened its doors to the missionaries being evacuated from Germany and Czechoslovakia when other countries were closing their borders her people would be spared much of the atrocities of war. Although Denmark was occupied by the Germans, it did not suffer the bombings and other destruction nearly to the extent as did its neighbors.

Poland was one of the hardest-hit countries during the war. Elder Benson felt a sense of urgency to visit the scattered Saints in what had been East Prussia but was now Polish territory. Repeated visits to the Polish embassy in London, however, failed to secure the needed visas to Warsaw. Elder Babbel later described what happened as they pondered their predicament: "After a few moments of soul-searching reflection, during which neither one of us broke the silence, [President Benson] said quietly but firmly, 'Let me pray about it.' Some two or three hours after President Benson had retired to his room to pray, he stood in my doorway and said with a smile on his face, 'Pack your bags. We are leaving for Poland in the morning!' At first I could scarcely believe my eyes. He stood there enveloped in a beautiful glow of radiant light."[25]

After flying to Berlin, Elder Benson there obtained the necessary clearances for his party to go to Poland, even though he had been told that the Polish Military Mission in Berlin had no authority to provide it.

Upon arriving in Poland, Elder Benson's party drove to a small town where a German branch of the Church had been located. Elder Babbel recalled:

> Not a sign of life was upon the streets as we entered the little village of Zelbak. . . . Proceeding to the further end of the village we spied the branch chapel—the only Church-owned chapel in all of what was formerly Germany—and upon alighting from our vehicle we asked the only woman in sight if this was the Mormon chapel and where we might find the branch president.
>
> We had spotted the woman hiding behind a large tree. Her expression was one of fear as we stopped, but upon learning who we were she greeted us with tears of gratitude and joy. . . .
>
> Within minutes the cry went from house to house, "The brethren are here! The brethren are here!" Soon we found ourselves surrounded by about fifty of the happiest people we had ever seen.
>
> Having seen our strange jeep approaching with what they feared to be Russian or Polish soldiers, they had abandoned the street as if by magic. Likewise, when they learned of our true identity and mission, the village became alive with joyous women and children—women and children, because only two of our former twenty-nine priesthood holders remained.

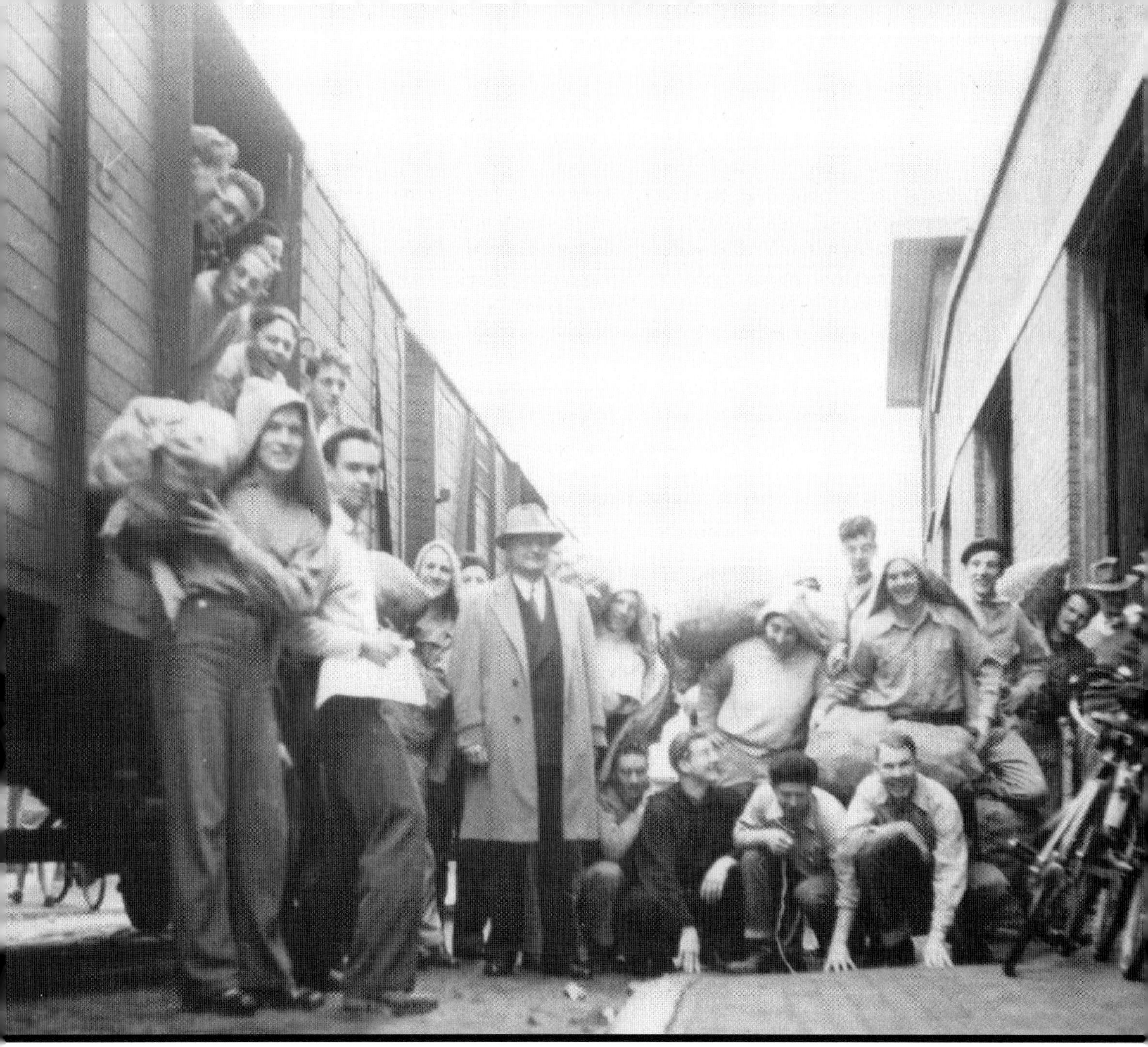

A sign of reconciliation and charity, Dutch members donate the produce of their potato farm to the impoverished Saints in Germany. (LDS Church Archives)

That morning in fast and testimony meeting over one hundred saints had assembled together to bear their testimonies and to petition Almighty God in song, in fasting and prayer, to be merciful to them and let the leaders again come to visit them. Our sudden and unheralded arrival, after almost complete isolation from Church and mission headquarters since early 1943, was the long-awaited answer, so wonderful they could scarcely believe their good fortune.[26]

Although the European Saints were eager to resume accustomed Church activities, substantial obstacles had to be overcome. Many branches could not be fully reorganized because so many of their priesthood leaders had been lost during the war. Furthermore, as meetinghouses and homes had been destroyed, the Saints lost not only material possessions but items of spiritual importance as well. In some branches not even copies of the scriptures remained. Nevertheless, Elder Benson found their faith to be stronger than ever before. Throughout the war-ravaged countries he saw the faithful Saints, without any material possessions, but with great courage. This greatly contrasted the general despair he witnessed all around them.[27]

In addition to reestablishing contact in areas where the Church had functioned before the outbreak of war, Elder Benson was also instrumental in extending regular missionary work to Finland. Prior to World War II there had been only infrequent contacts by missionaries from the Swedish Mission with the few scattered Swedish-speaking Saints living in Finland. In 1946, however, Elder Benson directed that regular proselyting be inaugurated in Finland, and then on July 15, on a beautiful hill near Larsmo, he dedicated and blessed Finland that it might be receptive to the gospel. The following day, a surprising 245 persons attended a meeting in Helsinki and manifested a genuine interest in the Latter-day Saints' message.[28] A separate Finnish Mission would be organized the following year.

Elder Benson returned home in December 1946, having traveled more than sixty thousand miles during his ten-month assignment in Europe. Some ninety-two carloads of welfare supplies, about two thousand tons, had been received and largely distributed. By this time, newly called presidents were directing the work in the missions of Europe. All the prewar missions were functioning again. But, where military regulations wouldn't permit American missionaries, local missionaries were serving full-time missions and doing a commendable work.[29]

By the spring of 1947 Church leaders had not yet been able to find a Finnish-speaking member with sufficient experience to serve as president of the new Finland Mission. While returning home from Washington, D.C., Elder and Sister Benson got off their train in Indianapolis to purchase a newspaper. When they returned, they were shocked to see their train leaving the station with all their belongings on board. With the help of a friend, Elder Benson arranged a flight to Chicago to meet their train. He telephoned the president of the Chicago Stake, asking to have someone meet them at the airport. They were picked up by Henry A. Matis, a member of the stake presidency. When Matis expressed a particular interest in Finland, Elder Benson learned that he had been born of Finnish parents and could speak the language with some fluency. The Apostle had found the man for whom he had been seeking, and Elder Matis was soon called as the first president of the Finnish Mission.[30]

A district presidents' conference in Berlin, circa 1946. By the end of Elder Ezra Taft Benson's mission to Europe, all prewar missions had been reopened and the Church was fully functioning again. (LDS Church Archives)

Foundations for Growth in Other Areas

Reopening missionary work in the Pacific was less complicated than in Europe. Although missionaries had been withdrawn, except from Hawaii, mission presidents had been able to remain at their posts. Furthermore, areas served by these missions were never in actual combat zones (except Pearl Harbor). Therefore, following the end of hostilities missionaries could easily be reassigned.

Members and missionaries in Takaroa, Tahiti, in 1948. The Church was able to quickly reopen missionary work in most of the South Pacific missions after the close of World War II. (LDS Church Archives)

A different situation existed in Japan. The Latter-day Saint mission there had been closed in 1924, long before the outbreak of World War II. By 1945 only about fifty members remained in the "Land of the Rising Sun." Latter-day Saint servicemen among the American occupation forces made an important contribution to the future of the Church in Japan. Many were anxious to bless the Japanese people with the spirit and message of the gospel. When three Mormon soldiers were offered a cup of tea in a curio shop in the village of Narumi, they declined and took the opportunity to explain the Church's teachings concerning the sanctity of the body. This led to further gospel conversations, and on July 7, 1946, the shop's proprietor, Tatsui Sato, and his family became the first postwar converts baptized in Japan. The young serviceman who baptized Mrs. Sato was Boyd K. Packer, a future member of the Council of the Twelve.[31] Other convert baptisms followed, and thus foundations were laid for the eventual reopening of the Japanese Mission.

The appointment of Elder Matthew Cowley to be president of the Pacific Mission was announced by the First Presidency on December 7, 1946. He had presided over the New Zealand Mission for eight years, including the period during World War II. He had been called to the Council of the Twelve almost immediately after being released from his mission assignment. During his three years presiding over the Pacific Mission, he would travel widely and have many remarkable experiences. On one occasion, for example, he blessed fifty people. On another day he gave blessings to seventy-six, many getting in line as early as 5:00 A.M. "This seemed the usual thing," Elder Cowley noted in his journal. "And they are made well, such is their faith. I know that when I lay my hand upon their heads that they are made whole," he testified.

"It is not my faith. I just have faith in their faith."[32] Elder Cowley's humble spirituality, his great love for the peoples of the Pacific, and his enthusiastic leadership helped provide the impetus for postwar Church growth throughout the area.

In 1947 the First Presidency called Edward L. Clissold, who had served in Japan as part of the Allied occupation forces, to return and open the mission there. Upon his arrival in Tokyo, he found the climate far more conducive for successful missionary work than in former decades. In the wake of war's devastation, there was a spiritual void that needed to be filled.

Two of President Clissold's most urgent tasks were to get the Japanese Mission formally registered and to find a suitable mission home. Fortunately his earlier experience with the occupation authorities provided him key contacts with Japanese government officials and others. Still, several weeks of diligent searching, persistent contacting, and frequent fasting and prayer were required before these objectives could be achieved. Finding a home was not easy because so many buildings had been destroyed by the war. Finally a partially bombed residence was found in a good location near many embassies, across the street from a beautiful park, and only five minutes from downtown Tokyo. On June 26, 1948, the first five missionaries arrived. All were former servicemen, come to share the gospel with the nation that so recently had been their enemy. About a year later Elder Matthew Cowley came to Japan and dedicated the home, praying that the Lord's work might progress and that temples might be erected in this land. Thirty years later, this home would be torn down to make way for the Tokyo Temple, the first of these sacred structures in the Orient.

Boyd K. Packer, serving in the U.S. Air Force, participates in the first Japanese baptisms following the close of World War II. (Photo courtesy President Boyd K. Packer)

The Church continued to gain strength in areas of North America where the Saints had been attracted outside the Intermountain region during the war. This was reflected in the creation of several new stakes along the Pacific Coast. In 1947 the formation of the Florida and South Carolina stakes, the first in the South, evidenced progress in that area.

Elder Matthew Cowley, president of the Pacific Mission during the postwar years, had a special love for the Polynesian peoples. He is shown here with local residents.

Some important developments in Latin America anticipated the great growth that would soon occur there. In 1936, a large group of members in Mexico, responding to the growing spirit of nationalism in their country, had demanded a mission president of their own blood and had become disaffected from the regular Church organization. Arwell L. Pierce, who became president of the Mexican Mission in 1942, devoted his effort to bringing these people back into full harmony with the Church. He repeatedly demonstrated genuine love for them and a spirit of helpfulness as he held out the goal of eventually having a stake in Mexico under local leadership and urged the Saints to unite in working toward that objective. The climax came at a special mission conference in 1946, attended by George Albert Smith, the first Church President ever to visit Mexico. He radiated his Christlike love as he stressed the need for harmony and unity. Former differences were overcome. The fifteen hundred attending the conference were eager to show their love and respect for the prophet and thronged around him. Though ill, President Smith graciously received their attention, further cementing the spirit of unity which would be vital for future progress.[33] The following year, missionary work was expanded from Mexico to Central America. At the same time, growth in South America was evidenced by the 1947 formation of the new Uruguayan Mission.

The Church passed a significant milestone in 1947 as its membership reached the one million mark. President George Albert Smith's administration not only witnessed a growth in numbers and geographical expansion, but also a significant period of revitalization and refinement for the Church's varied programs and activities.

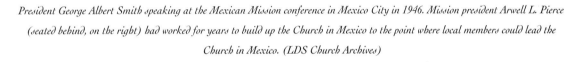

President George Albert Smith speaking at the Mexican Mission conference in Mexico City in 1946. Mission president Arwell L. Pierce (seated behind, on the right) had worked for years to build up the Church in Mexico to the point where local members could lead the Church in Mexico. (LDS Church Archives)

II

Postwar Resurgence

The Salt Lake Tabernacle was opened to the public on August 13, 1945, for the first time in nearly four years. Audiences were again able to enjoy daily organ recitals and attend weekly choir broadcasts. The first general conference without wartime restrictions on travel and attendance convened that October. These changes typified the shift from wartime to peace and the beginning of an era when Church activities revived and expanded. They also provided the occasion for reevaluating and refining Church programs.

Revival and Expansion of Church Programs

Missionary work and the construction of Church buildings were undoubtedly the activities most hampered by wartime restrictions. With the ending of hostilities, however, these and other activities not only revived but also expanded in order to better meet the needs of the Saints.

The number of missionaries after the war reached a new peak of 2,244 in 1946; by 1950, some 5,156 were serving. As had been the case before the war, most missionaries again were young elders. As their number exploded, new proselyting outlines were developed along with other measures to assure the missionaries' effectiveness.

As the number of missionaries increased, the administrative load of mission presidents expanded correspondingly. Unlike ward bishops, stake presidents, or most other executives in the

Mutual Improvement Association youth dance in a Church-sponsored dance festival. Such activities gave youth opportunities to socialize and make friends in wholesome environments. (Deseret News *photo)*

Church who enjoyed the assistance of two counselors, mission presidents served alone despite their responsibilities for missionaries and members. Therefore in 1947 the General Authorities directed mission presidents to call two counselors, typically one drawn from local Melchizedek Priesthood bearers to work with districts and branches, and the other from the missionaries to supervise proselyting. Elder Spencer W. Kimball later affirmed that the decision to appoint counselors was a revelation to the Presidency of the Church.[1]

While mission organization was being strengthened and proselyting missionaries were refining their methods, the Church was also taking advantage of other means to share its message with the world. With the end of wartime gasoline rationing and the consequent upsurge in travel, Temple Square was reestablished as an important missionary tool. In 1948 the number of visitors topped one million for the first time. In that same year the annual Hill Cumorah Pageant, "America's Witness for Christ," resumed. The Church's first major involvement in motion picture production also came during these postwar years. Because they were impressed with teaching and training films produced by the Walt Disney Studios as part of the war effort, Church leaders became interested in using motion pictures as a teaching medium. Church films appearing during the later 1940s focused on historic sites, Temple Square, and the welfare program. Likewise, as television developed during the postwar years, the Church was quick to make use of it. In October 1949 a general conference was telecast for the first time.[2]

Cast members of the Hill Cumorah Pageant performing a scene from "America's Witness for Christ." This and other Church programs and activities flourished in the years following World War II. (LDS Church Archives)

With the return of peace, Latter-day Saints looked forward to the construction of meetinghouses and other much needed facilities. As materials became available, the Church embarked on an ambitious chapel-building program. By 1949 some two hundred local meetinghouses had been completed, and the total reached nine hundred only three years later. As early as the mid-1950s, more than half of all Latter-day Saint buildings in use had been constructed since the close of World War II. Expenditures for these building projects accounted for more than half of the appropriations from general Church funds during these years.

Major events following the close of World War II

1930 1940 1950

1945
Idaho Falls Temple, delayed in construction by war, dedicated

1946
Spencer W. Kimball named head of Indian committee

1947
Pioneer centennial; Church membership reaches one million

1949
General conference telecasts began

1950
LDS Girls Program taken over by YWMIA; Indian Student Placement Program implemented Churchwide

The Idaho Falls Temple. (Photo courtesy Darrel Chamberlain)

The need for new buildings was particularly acute at Brigham Young University as it experienced a sudden expansion of its student body following the close of World War II. BYU's prewar enrollment had stood at just less than 3,000 students; but as more and more young men responded to calls into military service, the student body shrank to a wartime low of only 1,155 during the 1943–44 school year. As the conflict ended and veterans began pouring back onto the campus, the school's enrollment soared to 5,082 for the 1946–47 year and continued to grow. Over 2,200 veterans enrolled as freshmen during the 1946 fall quarter. Thus almost overnight Brigham Young University was transformed from a dormant wartime campus dominated by "coeds" into a bustling campus on which men outnumbered women for the first time. To meet the resulting housing shortage, BYU purchased twenty-six barracks from the Army as temporary buildings to accommodate two hundred married students and three hundred single veterans.

George Fudge, who pioneered genealogical microfilming in Britain, later managed the Genealogical Department of the Church. (Used by permission, Utah State Historical Society, all rights reserved)

The Church's administration building in Salt Lake City was remodeled during 1948 and 1949. The central light well was filled in to create more office space. As a result, all the General Authorities' offices were under one roof for the first time.

In 1937 President Heber J. Grant had announced plans to build a temple in Idaho Falls, Idaho, and construction got under way two years later. The work moved forward, and on October 19, 1941, the capstone was laid. From the outside the structure appeared to be completed. But less than two months later, the attack on Pearl Harbor propelled the United States into war, and as strategic building materials suddenly became scarce, the temple's completion had to be postponed. Finally, by mid-1945 the temple was completed and ready for dedication. In his dedicatory prayer President George Albert Smith expressed gratitude for the cessation of war and for the coming of peace. He prayed that the peoples of the world might be inclined to live the gospel of Jesus Christ, thereby making the peace permanent and hastening the time of the Lord's coming.

The General Authorities encouraged and gave greater direction to the Saints' temple and genealogical activity. Elder Joseph Fielding Smith, a member of the Quorum of the Twelve and president of the Genealogical Society, was called in 1945 to become president of the Salt Lake Temple and to give general supervision to the work of all of the Church's temples.

One of the society's most valuable services was the microfilming of vital records from many countries. This made records widely available to genealogical researchers. The project had commenced during the late 1930s but was interrupted with the coming of World War II. It was resumed even before the war ended. In March 1945 the Church began microfilming 365 English parish registers that had been sent to Salt Lake City for this purpose. During 1947 Archibald F. Bennett, secretary of the Genealogical Society, spent four months in Europe conferring with government and religious officials. He was successful in obtaining permission for the society to microfilm records in England, Scotland, Wales, Denmark, Norway, Sweden, Holland, Germany, Finland, Switzerland, northern Italy, and France. George Fudge, who many years later would become director of the Genealogical Society, was called to inaugurate the work of microfilming records in England. At first he had only a used camera with no light meter, and he had to work alone. Nevertheless, within three months nearly a quarter of a million pages had been filmed. Only occasionally did Church representatives encounter anti-Mormon opposition from local churchmen. In the wake of war most archivists were eager to cooperate with the microfilmers in order to ensure that a copy might be preserved in case the original records were destroyed. Furthermore, the society presented each

Elder Spencer W. Kimball of the Twelve (center) and Elder Bruce R. McConkie of the Seventy (third from right) inspect the first microfilmed records in Mexico with local officials and other Church leaders, in 1952. Following World War II the Church's microfilming efforts had expanded into Mexico and many European countries. (LDS Church Archives)

library or church with a copy of the material microfilmed, allowing the public to have access to this information without having to handle the already fragile originals. By early 1950 twenty-two full-time microfilmers were at work in the United States and in several European countries. Prior to the war some 3,340 records had been microfilmed and cataloged. By 1950 this total reached 24,579.[3]

Postwar social trends placed stress on the family and caused Church leaders to give added attention to the home. The close of World War II brought a sharp increase in the number of marriages, followed by what demographers have called the postwar baby boom. Hence, there were probably more new families and new parents than at any previous time in the Church's history. Unfortunately, the divorce rate in the United States almost doubled from 1940 to 1945. Elder Richard L. Evans considered this highest divorce rate in history one of the appalling "costs of war" and acknowledged that it was a subject very much on Church leaders' minds.[4] Under the direction of the General Authorities, various Church organizations in 1946 inaugurated programs to strengthen families and to specifically promote a regular "family hour."

The same wartime conditions that undermined family stability also posed significant challenges for the youth. The General Authorities had repeatedly instructed local Church leaders to look out for the welfare of these young people. The Granite Stake in Salt Lake City had developed a method of checking on and encouraging the activity of young women, similar to the Presiding Bishopric's program for young men bearing the Aaronic Priesthood. In 1944 the Twelve recommended that all stakes adopt this program for girls. In order to avoid unnecessary duplication of effort, responsibility for the LDS Girls Program was formally assumed by the Young Women's Mutual Improvement Association in 1950. Under the leadership of the Young Men's and Young Women's MIAs, new age-group and activity programs were sponsored for the youth. As a result, active Latter-day Saint young people regularly spent time participating in dramatic, cultural, recreational, social, and athletic activities. Road shows, dance festivals, speech competitions, and Churchwide softball and basketball tournaments attracted widespread attention and praise. Involvement in such activities helped the Church's youth retain their religious faith at a time when others had become restless in their search for new values and beliefs.

A sacrament meeting, circa 1953. In 1946 the First Presidency directed that there should be complete silence while members partake of the sacrament instead of soft music played, as had been the tradition. (LDS Church Archives)

In this spirit of refining Church activities and programs to more adequately meet the needs of the Saints, the General Authorities also made adjustments in the sacrament meeting, the Church's basic weekly worship service. Over the years the practice had developed of having soft instrumental or even vocal music during the passing of the sacrament. In 1946, however, the First Presidency specified that there should be absolute quiet during this time, that nothing should distract the Saints from reflecting on the Atonement of Jesus Christ and on the sacred covenants they had made with Him.[5] The Church certainly was not opposed to music as such. To the contrary, during these postwar years Church leaders encouraged special courses of instruction for Church musicians. A new edition of the Latter-day Saint hymnal was prepared. Publication of *Recreational Songs* and *The Children Sing* in 1949 and 1951, respectively, represented an important new expansion of Latter-day Saint music literature.

The Church was also taking steps to enhance the temporal welfare of its members. For some time the Church had operated a few hospitals in the Intermountain area, and during the years immediately following World War II it took steps to strengthen this system. Hospitals in Salt Lake City and Ogden underwent major renovation and expansion. The Church also cooperated with rural communities in Utah, Idaho, and Wyoming to open and operate several smaller hospitals. Then, in 1949, ground was broken for the new Primary Children's Hospital in Salt Lake City. This 1.25-million-dollar facility would provide badly needed health care to children of all religions and races—free of charge to families unable to pay.

After moving into its new building, which was dedicated in 1952, the Primary Children's Hospital developed into one of America's leading pediatric facilities. (LDS Church Archives)

The Day of the Lamanites

Latter-day Saints have always had an interest in the American Indians and related groups, whom they identify generally as descendants of the Book of Mormon peoples. The scriptures describe great blessings for these "Lamanites" (see 2 Nephi 30:3–6; D&C 49:24) and have charged the Saints to assist. As a result, the Church since its beginning has sponsored missions and other programs to benefit the Lamanites. The 1940s brought a significant expansion of these activities, and many Church members became more involved in working with the Lamanites.

Modern missionary work among the North American Indians dates from 1936, when the First Presidency directed the Snowflake Stake in northeastern Arizona to open formal missionary work among the Navajo and other tribes. Soon other stakes became involved.

*President George Albert Smith shows the Book of Mormon to two Navajos, Many Turquoise (left) and Manuelito Begay. President Smith took a personal interest in expanding missionary work among the American Indians and other Lamanites. (*Improvement Era *photo)*

Missionary work among the Indians received a significant boost in November 1942. George Jumbo, a Navajo Latter-day Saint, had gone to Salt Lake City for back surgery. Before returning home, his wife, Mary, expressed the desire to meet President Heber J. Grant. Arrangements were made. "Mary stood before him in her beautiful Navajo costume and eloquently pleaded that missionaries be sent to her people. President Grant, eyes filled with tears, turned to Elder George Albert Smith and said, 'The time has arrived for the preaching of the gospel to the Lamanites of the Southwest,' " and directed the Apostle to give more attention to this matter.[6] Early the following year the Navajo-Zuni Mission was organized. The work soon spread beyond these tribes, reaching Indians throughout the United States and Canada. Very successful missionary work among other Lamanite groups, particularly in Latin America and Polynesia, would also take place in the second half of the twentieth century.

While these American Indian missionary programs were moving forward, another group of Lamanites was being blessed in a different way. Most Latin American Saints did not fully understand the temple ceremonies as presented in English, so in 1945 the temple endowment was presented in Spanish—its first presentation in a language other than English. In November of that year, about two hundred Spanish-speaking Saints gathered at the temple in Mesa, Arizona, for a weeklong "Lamanite conference" where, among other things, they would receive the temple blessings in their native language. Many of the Saints attending made substantial sacrifices to travel the long distances to the temple, from as far away as Mexico City; some even gave up their jobs. At the opening session of the conference, President David O. McKay congratulated those who had gathered.[7] Most came from small branches, often meeting in dingy facilities. Uniting together, they discovered that the Church was much larger. During succeeding years the Lamanite conference and Spanish-speaking temple sessions at Mesa became eagerly anticipated events.

President George Albert Smith over the years had manifested a special interest in the Lamanites, and soon after becoming President of the Church he called Spencer W. Kimball, who had lived among the American Indians; Matthew Cowley, whose service among the Polynesians is well

*An Indian youth reads a bedtime story to young friends. The Indian Student Placement Program made it possible for Indian students to live with Latter-day Saint families where they could have access to better educational programs. (*Deseret News *photo)*

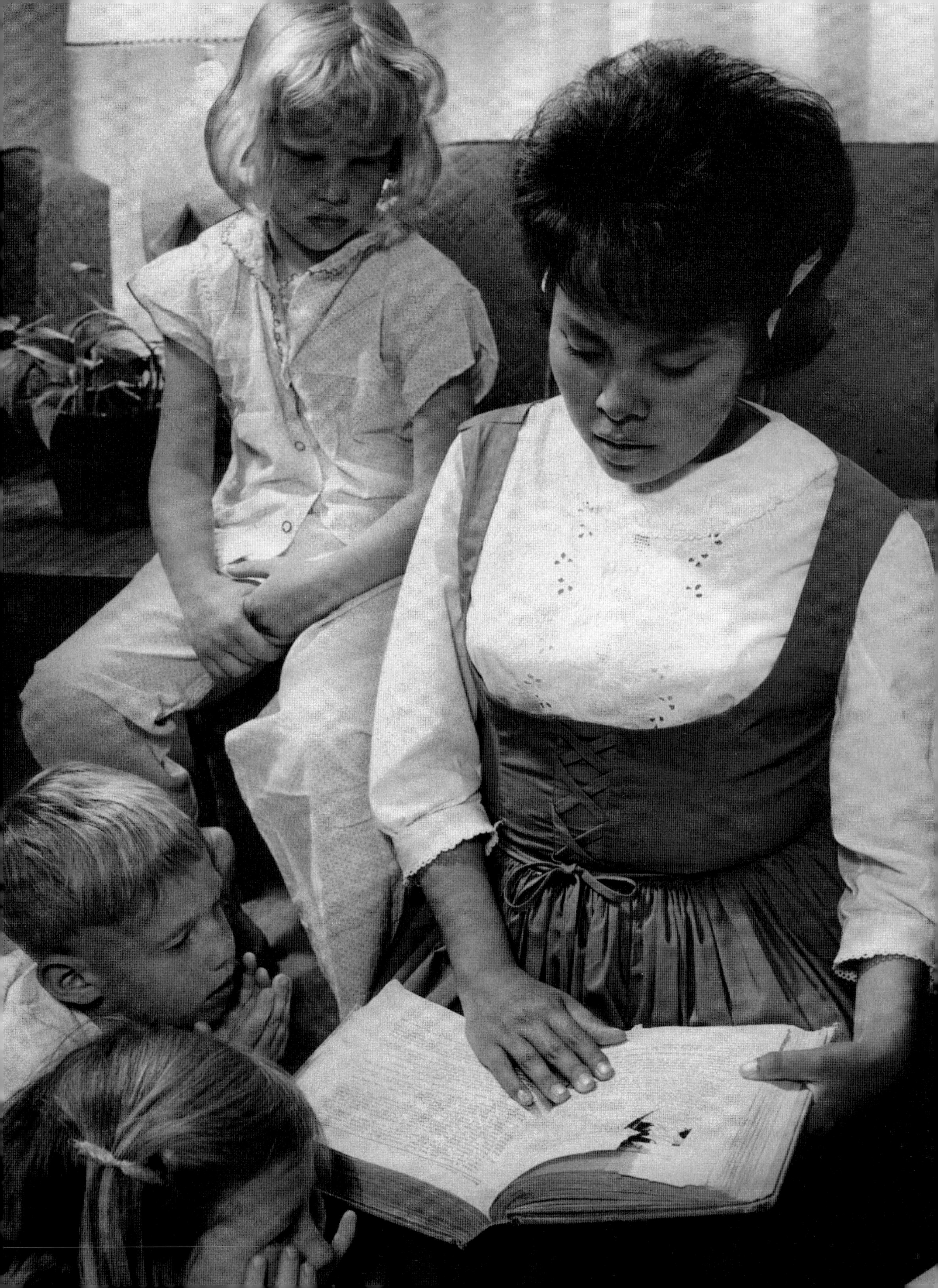

known; and Antoine R. Ivins, who had been reared in Mexico to give special attention and leadership to these people. "I do not know when I began to love the children of Lehi," Elder Kimball reflected. "It may have come from my patriarchal blessing which was given to me . . . when I was nine years of age. One line of the blessing reads: 'You will

Elder Spencer W. Kimball (standing at left) with instructors and students at a school near Blanding, Arizona. Elder Kimball and Native American members of the Church felt a mutual love and respect for one another. (Deseret News *photo)*

preach the gospel to many people, but more especially to the Lamanites. . . .' And now, forty-two years after the promise, President George Albert Smith called me to this mission, and my blessing was fulfilled." Elder Kimball testified, "a great thrill came to me such as I have had few times in my life."[8]

While touring the Mexican Mission in 1947, Elder Kimball envisioned a glorious future for the Lamanites, which he related at the Lamanite conference in Mesa during November of that year. Some thirty years later, as President of the Church, he would conduct an area conference at Mexico City. As he addressed the large audience, he again told them of his 1947 vision, which he could see well on its way to fulfillment. "In my dream I no longer saw you the servant of other people, but I saw you as the employer." He also envisioned them as businesspeople and professionals, as heads of government. "As good legislators and good Latter-day Saints you were able to make the best laws for your brothers and sisters." He also saw them influencing others for good through artistic and literary creations. "I saw the Church growing in rapid strides and I saw wards and stakes organized. I saw stakes by the hundreds. I saw a temple."[9]

Education was one of the Lamanites' most critical needs. The postwar years brought the development of Latter-day Saint schools in Polynesia and later in Latin America. Two programs, which had their beginnings during the later 1940s, would be of particular benefit to American Indians.

Golden R. Buchanan was a member of the Sevier Stake presidency in central Utah. During the autumn of 1947 he had occasion to observe the deplorable condition of some Navajo workers in the area. Speaking at a stake conference he admonished the Saints to take better care of their Lamanite brethren. Shortly afterwards a member from a neighboring town came to President Buchanan and told him of a teenage Indian girl named Helen John who did not want to return to the reservation with her family but was determined to remain and go to school. "If you'll let me pitch my tent out back of your house," she pleaded to her Latter-day Saint employers, "I promise I won't be any bother to you. I'll take care of myself, but I would like to live where I can go to school with your girls."

President Buchanan was impressed with the idea. "If a program of this sort were undertaken by the Church," he envisioned, "literally hundreds of Indian children would have the privilege of living in LDS homes where they not only could be taught in school but they could be taught the principles of the gospel."[10] He outlined his ideas in a letter to Elder Spencer W. Kimball. The Apostle did not respond by mail but chose to drive directly to Richfield and personally invite the Buchanans to take Helen into their home. Several other Indian youth were placed in homes in the area. Some of the Saints had to overcome prejudices that stemmed from the era of Indian wars in pioneer times. From these beginnings the Indian Student Placement Program grew and became an official Church-sponsored program in the 1950s. Eventually as many as five thousand students were placed in Latter-day Saint homes, especially throughout the western United States and Canada. Many of the Indian students achieved marked success in school and became leaders among their people.[11]

By the 1970s, public education had improved on the reservations, allowing an increasing number of Indian youth to remain at home while going to school. Still, the placement program would represent the key to success for hundreds of other Indian students.

Another special education program designed particularly for Lamanites was the Indian Seminary. When a military hospital near Brigham City, Utah, was converted in 1949 into the Intermountain Indian School, local Church authorities took steps to provide seminary classes for the Latter-day Saint Indian youths attending the school. Boyd K. Packer, a member of one of the local stake high councils and future member of the Council of the Twelve, played a key role in developing the program and served as the first teacher. In 1949 the Church bought property adjacent to the school's entrance and later erected a seminary building there. Gradually, the need for similar programs at other government Indian schools had become apparent, and in 1955 Indian Seminaries were officially inaugurated as a distinct program of the Church's educational system. Within a few years, more than ten thousand Indian students, from kindergarten through the twelfth grade, were being served. Some Indian Seminary classes met daily as did other seminaries, but most were allowed to provide instruction to the Indian students only once a week.

In later years, Brigham Young University inaugurated specialized programs for Indian students on campus and helped train teachers and other professionals interested in working with Indians. BYU also sponsored a special institute to conduct research and service projects aimed at improving the standard of living on numerous Indian reservations.

"The Days of '47"

In the midst of the postwar revival of Church activities, the celebration of the pioneer centennial in 1947 focused the Saints' attention on their heritage. President George Albert Smith, who seventeen years earlier had become founding president of the Utah Pioneer Trails and Landmarks Association, was now appointed chairman of the committee to plan appropriate observances for the centennial of the pioneers' arrival in the Salt Lake Valley. Few Church leaders, if any, excelled President Smith's zeal in commemorating the achievements of the past. It was fitting, therefore, that he should be serving as President of the Church at the time of the pioneer centennial. At the April 1947 general conference almost all speakers paid tribute to the faith and courage of the early pioneers and reflected on the Saints' accomplishments during the intervening century. During the spring and summer, dozens of musical performances, art exhibits, sporting events, and dramatic productions marked the occasion. The pageant, "Message of the Ages," which had been popular during the 1930 centennial, was again staged in the Salt Lake Tabernacle. Some 1,400 persons were involved in the production, and a total of 135,000

Automobiles made to look like covered wagons attract attention during the Salt Lake City parade that concluded a reenactment of the pioneer trek, part of Utah's 1947 centennial celebration. (LDS Church Archives)

As part of the centennial celebration of the pioneers' arrival in the Salt Lake Valley, President George Albert Smith dedicated the "This Is the Place" monument in July 1947. (LDS Church Archives)

witnessed the twenty-five performances from May 5 to June 5. A musical production, "Promised Valley," was presented in the University of Utah stadium from July 21 through August 10 with more than 85,000 people attending. Featuring the original music of Crawford Gates, this production depicted the frustrations and dedication of the early pioneers. It was presented throughout the Church by local MIA groups, and in later years it became a popular annual attraction in Salt Lake City during the summer tourist season.

A feeling of goodwill accompanied the centennial celebrations. During July the nation's governors held their annual meeting in Salt Lake City. President George Albert Smith hosted the group, and the friendship manifested by these leaders was a far cry from the persecutions of a century earlier. Members of the Sons of Utah Pioneers reenacted the original pioneer trek, following the 1846–47 route from Nauvoo, Illinois, to the Salt Lake Valley. Each of their seventy-two vehicles was outfitted with a wagon box, a canvas cover, and plywood oxen to give the appearance of a covered wagon. The "trekkers" presented programs and were well received in each of the towns where they stopped along the way.

The centennial celebration climaxed on July 24, exactly one hundred years from the day Brigham Young and the pioneers entered the Salt Lake Valley. A gigantic "Days of '47" parade included numerous floats honoring these early founders. On this day the United States Post Office issued a commemorative stamp in memory of the pioneers. The highlight of the celebration was the unveiling of the sixty-foot-high "This Is the Place" monument near the mouth of Emigration Canyon. The monument featured fifteen separate sculptures honoring the early settlers in the Great Basin. It was located near the spot where Brigham Young had gazed out over the valley, recognized it as the Saints' resting place shown him in vision, and declared, "This is the right place, drive on." The monument was dedicated by President George Albert Smith.

Reflecting on the significance of the pioneer centennial, the First Presidency declared: "As that small group of pioneers looked upon what appeared to be a sterile desert, so today the Church faces a world lying in moral lethargy and spiritual decline." The Presidency compared the physical dangers faced by the pioneers with the temptations confronting the Church, particularly the youth, in the twentieth century and charged the Saints to be prepared to meet these challenges as their forebears had done.[12]

The Saints' continuing interest in their heritage was reflected in efforts during and following World War II to acquire additional sites of historic importance to the Church. In 1944 the Church began purchasing land at Adam-ondi-Ahman in northern Missouri. Not only was this the site of a small Mormon settlement in the late 1830s, but Latter-day Saints also identified this as the place where Adam met his posterity just before his death, where Book of Mormon Nephites had erected an altar, and where a great priesthood conference will convene just before Christ's Second Coming.[13] In 1946 and 1949 nearly two hundred acres were purchased at Harmony, Pennsylvania, including the banks of the Susquehanna River where John the Baptist had restored the Aaronic Priesthood in 1829. These purchases were made on behalf of the Church by Wilford C. Wood, who had taken great personal interest in researching, identifying, and acquiring historical sites. President Smith also took a personal interest in acquiring and suitably marking these sites.

George Albert Smith had been afflicted with poor health throughout his life. On April 4, 1951, just three months after the midpoint of the twentieth century, he died peacefully following a prolonged illness. It was his eighty-first birthday. Countless individuals paid tribute to the departed leader. Almost all made specific reference to President Smith's great capacity to love his fellowmen. His second counselor, President David O. McKay, affirmed that George Albert Smith had "lived as nearly as it is humanly possible for a man to live a Christ-like life. He found that the answer to the yearning of the human heart for fullness lies in living outside oneself by love."[14] President Smith's emphasis on love had heightened the Saints' spirit of unity. Under his leadership there had been a revival, refinement, and resurgence in Church activity and growth. In these and other ways he had helped lay the foundations for the unprecedented growth during the following decades.

David O. McKay and His Administration

David O. McKay holds the distinction of having lived longer than has any other President of the Church. His life extended from the days of Brigham Young to the space age. The two decades in which he presided over the Church were an era of unprecedented growth and expansion.

David O. McKay's Earlier Life

David O. McKay was born on September 8, 1873, in Huntsville, a small agricultural community in northern Utah. His father and mother were converts who had immigrated from Scotland and Wales, respectively. The wholesome home environment they created had a profound influence on young David's life, and throughout his life he frequently referred to their worthy examples.

"My home life from babyhood to the present time has been the greatest factor in giving me moral and spiritual standards, and in shaping the courses of my life," he recalled. "Sincerity, courtesy, consistency in word and deed, unselfishness are dominant virtues exemplified in the lives of my parents and others in the two homes that have proved a safeguard and guidance."[1]

David was only seven years old when his father was called to return as a missionary to Great Britain. The two oldest girls in the family had recently died from serious illnesses, and David's mother was now expecting another child. Under these trying circumstances David's father felt that he shouldn't leave his wife

President David O. McKay on a favorite horse, Sonny Boy, in 1957. (LDS Church Archives)

and considered asking for a postponement. "Of course you must accept," David's mother insisted; "you need not worry about me. David O. [the eldest son] and I will manage things nicely!"[2] During his father's absence, young David learned how to assume responsibility and how to work. As "man of the house," he rapidly matured beyond his years.

During the summer of 1887, John Smith, the Patriarch of the Church, visited the McKays' rural community in order to give patriarchal blessings to the faithful Saints. As he blessed thirteen-year-old David, Patriarch Smith clearly anticipated the vast contributions this young man would one day make in the Lord's work: "Thou art in thy youth and need instruction, therefore I say unto thee, be taught of thy parents the way of life and salvation, that at an early day you may be prepared for a responsible position, for the eye of the Lord is upon thee. . . . The Lord has a work for thee to do, in which thou shalt see much of the world, assist in gathering scattered Israel and also labor in the ministry. It shall be thy lot to sit in council with thy brethren and preside among the people and exhort the Saints to faithfulness."[3]

David O. McKay as a young child on his father's lap. When David was only seven years old his father served a mission in Great Britain, making David the "man of the house." (Deseret News *photo*)

David's quest for spiritual development began early. He later recalled how as a teenager he prayed fervently for a sure testimony: "I had in mind that there would be some manifestation, that I should receive some transformation that would leave me without doubt." But, as shall be seen, the desired answer would come only after several more years of seeking.[4]

David O. McKay had a well-rounded college experience. Besides attending to his studies, he played the piano for dances, was left guard on the University of Utah's first football team, courted his sweetheart, and graduated as president and valedictorian of his class.

David had planned to go to work immediately in order to finance the education of other family members, but shortly before graduating he received a mission call to the British Isles. Even though this represented a financial sacrifice for his family, he accepted the call. After being in Scotland for a short time, he was discouraged and homesick. Then one day in Stirling he noticed an inscription on an unfinished building: "Whate'er thou art, act well thy part." He accepted this message "as if it came from One in whose service

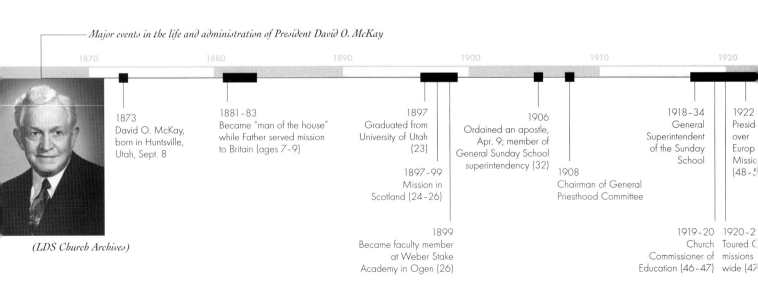

Major events in the life and administration of President David O. McKay

1870 1880 1890 1900 1910 1920

(LDS Church Archives)

1873 David O. McKay, born in Huntsville, Utah, Sept. 8

1881-83 Became "man of the house" while Father served mission to Britain (ages 7-9)

1897 Graduated from University of Utah (23)

1897-99 Mission in Scotland (24-26)

1899 Became faculty member at Weber Stake Academy in Ogen (26)

1906 Ordained an apostle, Apr. 9; member of General Sunday School superintendency (32)

1908 Chairman of General Priesthood Committee

1918-34 General Superintendent of the Sunday School

1919-20 Church Commissioner of Education (46-47)

1920-2 Toured C missions wide (47

1922 Presid over Europ Missic (48-5

we were engaged," and he resolved to act well his part as a Latter-day Saint missionary.[5]

David O. McKay's missionary experience brought great spiritual growth that laid the foundation for his lifetime of service. During a very spiritual conference session in Scotland, an unusual feeling of harmony and faith prevailed. One Elder's declaration that there were angels in the room was confirmed by James L. McMurrin, a counselor in the mission presidency. President McMurrin then prophesied the future of several of the missionaries who were present, including that of David O. McKay, who later wrote: "His words made an indelible impression upon me: . . . 'Let me say to you, Brother David, Satan hath desired you that he may sift you as wheat, but God is mindful of you.' Then he added, 'If you will keep the faith, you will yet sit in the leading councils of the Church.' I knew that the answer to my boyish prayer had come."[6]

David O. McKay as a missionary in Scotland. (Used by permission, Utah State Historical Society, all rights reserved)

On January 2, 1901, David O. McKay married his college sweetheart, Emma Ray Riggs, their sealing being the first performed in the Salt Lake Temple in the twentieth century. He accepted a teaching position at the Church's Weber Stake Academy in Ogden. His service as a teacher confirmed his love of reading the scriptures and the works of Shakespeare, Robert Burns, and other literary masters, whom he would quote in sermons throughout his life. At the same time he was called to the Weber Stake Sunday School superintendency, where his inspired initiative developed patterns of teaching that would "find their way into all the Sunday Schools of the Church and which resulted in revolutionizing the teaching throughout the entire organization."[7]

In April 1906 David O. McKay was called to the Council of the Twelve, at the age of thirty-two. In October of the same year, he became assistant to the General Sunday School superintendent, Church President Joseph F. Smith. When President Smith died in 1918 Elder McKay succeeded him as superintendent and the following year also became the Commissioner of Education for Church Schools. In these roles he stimulated the improvement of teaching throughout the Church. During these same years, he profoundly influenced the development of Church programs in his capacity as chairman of the General Priesthood Committee and of several other committees appointed to better correlate the programs of various Church organizations.

David O. McKay's yearlong tour of the Church's missions in 1921 gave him a worldwide perspective. Early in this tour, Elder McKay and Hugh J. Cannon, his traveling companion, felt they were guided to a secluded cypress grove within the

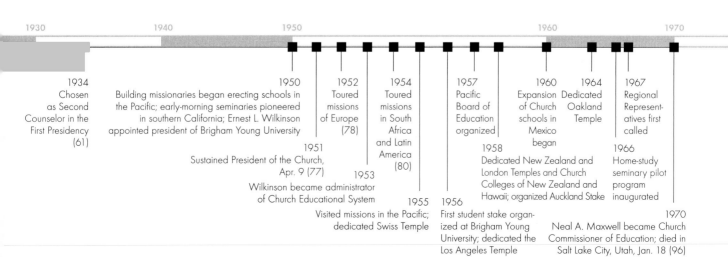

1930 1940 1950 1960 1970

1934 Chosen as Second Counselor in the First Presidency (61)

1950 Building missionaries began erecting schools in the Pacific; early-morning seminaries pioneered in southern California; Ernest L. Wilkinson appointed president of Brigham Young University

1951 Sustained President of the Church, Apr. 9 (77)

1952 Toured missions of Europe (78)

1953 Wilkinson became administrator of Church Educational System

1954 Toured missions in South Africa and Latin America (80)

1955 Visited missions in the Pacific; dedicated Swiss Temple

1956 First student stake organized at Brigham Young University; dedicated the Los Angeles Temple

1957 Pacific Board of Education organized

1958 Dedicated New Zealand and London Temples and Church Colleges of New Zealand and Hawaii; organized Auckland Stake

1960 Expansion of Church schools in Mexico began

1964 Dedicated Oakland Temple

1966 Home-study seminary pilot program inaugurated

1967 Regional Representatives first called

1970 Neal A. Maxwell became Church Commissioner of Education; died in Salt Lake City, Utah, Jan. 18 (96)

"Forbidden City" at Peking (Beijing), China. There, away from the noisy throngs, Elder McKay blessed the land and its people that famine and superstition might be removed, that the government might become stable, and that missionaries might come who can "comprehend the Chinese nature, so that in the souls of this people an appreciation of the glorious gospel might be awakened."[8]

Elders David O. McKay and Hugh J. Cannon (middle, back row) with members in Hawaii on their world tour in 1921. Their travels would take them to the Pacific, Asia, and Europe. (LDS Church Archives)

In Hawaii Elders McKay and Cannon enjoyed some remarkable spiritual experiences. During a prayer, they were made aware of the presence and blessing of Joseph F. Smith and George Q. Cannon (the father of Hugh J. Cannon), who had introduced the gospel to the Islands seventy years earlier. On another occasion, Elder McKay was impressed to get off a lookout ledge just before it crumbled into the molten lava Kilauea Volcano crater.[9] They visited a small missionary-conducted elementary school in the town of Laie where the Hawaii Temple had been dedicated about a year and a half earlier. As Elder McKay witnessed a flag-raising ceremony in which students representing several races participated, he felt impressed that Laie would become an educational as well as spiritual center for the peoples of the Pacific.

One of the last stops in their three-week visit to the Samoan Mission was at the small mountain town of Sauniatu, which had been colonized by the Latter-day Saints. Elder McKay was the first Apostle these people had ever seen. As the final meeting closed, the Saints formed a line to shake hands with the special visitors. They began singing a beautiful Samoan farewell hymn, but their sobbing soon interrupted their singing. After being fondly embraced by the Saints, Elder McKay and his party rode off on horseback. But after going only a short distance, they were prompted to turn back. As they reached the point where the Saints were gathered, Elder McKay dismounted and pronounced a beautiful apostolic blessing on the Samoan Islands and people. After he had ridden away again, the Saints recorded the words of the prayer and marked the spot with a pile of stones. A year later they erected a permanent stone monument to commemorate this inspiring moment.[10]

At a meeting in New Zealand, Elder McKay "faced an audience that had assembled with unusual expectations." In other meetings he had spoken through a translator, but on this occasion he longed to speak directly to the people. He informed Brother Stuart Meha, who stood at his side ready to translate, that he would speak without a sentence-by-sentence translation. After Elder McKay had spoken for about forty minutes, Brother Meha gave a synopsis in Maori. Several times, however, he was corrected by his Maori listeners—who did not know English but who had understood Elder McKay's words by the gift of tongues.[11]

In the Holy Land, Elder McKay received instructions by telegram to meet J. Wilford Booth to tour the Armenian Mission. Booth had served a mission among those people, and without his knowledge of the area the tour would have been impossible. Elders McKay and Cannon had no idea where to meet Booth, but as they were preparing to leave Jerusalem, Elder McKay felt impressed to travel by train rather than by car. After waiting a few minutes on the railway platform at Haifa, the Apostle was tapped him on the shoulder by another traveler, who asked, "Isn't this Brother McKay?" The stranger turned out to be Brother Booth. They were astonished to have found one another at just the right time. "As we recounted to each other our experiences," Elder McKay reflected, "we had no doubt that our coming together was the result of divine interposition."[12]

Before returning home, Elders McKay and Cannon visited the Church's missions in western Europe. By the time they returned to Utah on Christmas Eve of 1921, they had traveled more than twice the circumference of the globe. These experiences gave Elder McKay a vision of the Church's challenges and opportunities internationally—perspective which would be invaluable to him in later years as he presided over rapid Church growth worldwide.

Elder McKay's missionary expertise was further enhanced as he presided over the European Mission from 1923 to 1925. Using the motto "Every Member a Missionary," he encouraged the European Saints to share the gospel with their neighbors. This slogan would become a well-known emphasis of President McKay's teachings during the 1960s.

An even more important assignment came to Elder McKay in 1934 when he was called to fill a vacancy in the First Presidency of the Church. During the next seventeen years he would serve as the Second Counselor to Presidents Heber J. Grant and George Albert Smith. He carried the responsibility for missionary work and many other Church programs. He served in the First Presidency during the Great Depression of the 1930s and during World War II and its aftermath in the 1940s.

President McKay's Teachings

President George Albert Smith died on Wednesday, April 4, 1951, just two days before the scheduled opening of general conference. The Saturday sessions of conference were canceled so President Smith's funeral could be held. The conference had been scheduled to conclude on Sunday, but a special "solemn assembly" session convened on Monday, April 9, at which David O. McKay was sustained as the ninth President of the Church. As he accepted this high and holy office, President McKay sounded a theme which would be central to his teachings: "No one can preside over this Church without first being in tune with the head of the Church, our Lord and Savior, Jesus Christ. He is our head. This is his Church. Without his divine guidance and constant inspiration, we cannot succeed. With his guidance, with his inspiration, we cannot fail."[13]

President McKay taught that, in order to live on this loftier plane, the Saints must overcome worldliness and their carnal nature. The world and individuals, he believed, needed "to be saved . . . from the dominating influence of animal instincts, of passions, of appetites."[14]

To this end, he insisted that the development of spirituality should be a top priority: "Spirituality is the highest acquisition of the soul, the divine in man; 'the supreme, crowning gift that makes him king of all created things.' It is the consciousness of victory over self and of communion with the infinite. It is spirituality alone which really gives one the best in life."[15]

This emphasis on spirituality characterized President McKay's life. During his 1921 world tour, he witnessed a spectacular sunset while aboard his ship in Apia Harbor, Samoa. As beautiful and glorious as this was, he realized that it did not stir his emotions as much as did pure and worthy lives of God's children. These thoughts became the setting for a profound spiritual experience. As he slept that night, he dreamed of "a great concourse of people" approaching a beautiful city.

> Instantly my attention seemed centered upon their Leader, and though I could see only the profile of his features and his body, I recognized him at once as my Savior! The tint and radiance of his countenance were glorious to behold! There was a peace about him which seemed sublime—it was divine!
>
> The city, I understood, was his. It was the City Eternal; and the people following him were to abide there in peace and eternal happiness.
>
> But who were they?
>
> As if the Savior read my thoughts, he answered by pointing to a semicircle that then appeared above them, and on which were written in gold the words: "These Are They Who Have Overcome The World—Who Have Truly Been Born Again!"[16]

Home and family were other major emphases in President David O. McKay's teachings. He taught

President David O. McKay giving an address in 1953. President McKay's counsel to the Saints included guidance on such topics as spirituality and the importance of the home. (Deseret News *photo*)

that the home was the most important place for Latter-day Saints to manifest the noble attributes of character which grow out of increased spirituality. He urged husbands and wives to treat each other with loving courtesy and respect, and parents to teach their children through precept and proper example. The loving relationship between David O. and Emma Ray Riggs McKay became for the Saints a model of ideal family life. President McKay adopted the declaration, "No other success can compensate for failure in the home," which quickly became one of the Church's most widely quoted mottos during the second half of the twentieth century.[17]

President of a Worldwide Church

The two decades of President David O. McKay's administration was a period of unprecedented growth. From 1951–1970 the Church population nearly tripled, growing from approximately 1.1 to 2.9 million members. Taking into account those who had died during this period, it is probable that as many as two-thirds of all Church members living at the beginning of 1970 had known no other President than David O. McKay. When he took office in 1951 the Oahu Stake in Hawaii was the only one outside of North America. President McKay would direct the formation of the first South Pacific, European, and Latin American stakes. His personal background suited him well to give leadership during this era of expansion. His mission to Scotland, his 1921 world tour, his service as president of the European Mission, and his responsibility for missionary work as a counselor in the First Presidency all made him personally aware of the Church's worldwide responsibilities and opportunities. President McKay's commitment to gaining a broad understanding of the world around him made it easier for him to relate to the wide spectrum of leaders he would contact in the interest of spreading the gospel.

The First Presidency, 1951–59; (from left to right) Stephen L Richards, President David O. McKay, and J. Reuben Clark Jr. (Used by permission, Utah State Historical Society, all rights reserved)

As President McKay's administration opened, however, certain forces threatened to halt Church growth. In the previous two years, international tensions had led to the closing of Latter-day Saint missions in the Near East and in Czechoslovakia. Also, the 1949 Communist takeover in China and the 1950 outbreak of the Korean War led to the temporary closing of the Chinese Mission in Hong Kong. The impact of the Korean War was not limited to the Far East, however. As the United States assumed a major share in the United Nations peacekeeping force, young men were again being drafted into military service. As had been the case during World War II ten years earlier, the number of elders available for missionary service was cut drastically. In contrast to the 3,015 called by the First Presidency in 1950, only 872 received mission calls in 1952. To make up for the loss in the number of young Elders, the General Authorities called upon the stake seventies quorums throughout the Church to provide one thousand additional missionaries. This would represent a significant sacrifice because typical seventies were older than the elders and most were married and already established in their careers. Nevertheless, seventies regarded missionary service as their special responsibility and opportunity, so they responded to the call from their Church leaders. Hence, many of the missionaries serving during the early 1950s were young married men who had left their wives, families, and jobs behind. With the end of the Korean War in 1953 the Church was able to resume calling more of its younger single men as missionaries. Despite continuing tensions incident to the "Cold War," conditions during the remainder of President McKay's administration were more favorable for Church growth in most parts of the free world.

David O. McKay traveled more than any other Church President before him. In 1952 he visited the missions in Britain and on the European continent.

The following year he returned to Europe to dedicate temple sites in Switzerland and England. In 1954 he stopped briefly in London on the first leg of a thirty-seven-thousand-mile tour that took him to South Africa and Latin America. On this trip he became the first General Authority ever to visit South Africa (a mission he had not visited in 1921) and the first President of the Church ever to travel to South America. Then, in 1955, he journeyed throughout the South Pacific, returning to places where he had enjoyed sacred experiences some thirty-four years earlier. While on this trip he announced plans to construct a temple in New Zealand, the first in the Southern Hemisphere.

The Swiss Temple, about the time of its dedication in 1955. This was the first temple outside the United States and Canada. (Deseret News *photo*)

A few months later he traveled to Europe for the fourth time in four years, this time to dedicate the Swiss Temple. The Tabernacle Choir, which participated in the dedication, was then on a concert tour of Europe. Their Berlin concert was almost canceled because of visa problems, the city being located more than a hundred miles behind the Iron Curtain. Elder Ezra Taft Benson, then serving as Secretary of Agriculture in the Eisenhower cabinet, contacted the Russian ambassador in Washington and permission was granted for the choir to travel by train to Berlin. As the visitors entered the *bahnhof* (railway station), they were greeted by a small choir of German Saints singing beloved Church hymns. As they sang the spirited anthem "Let the Mountains Shout for Joy," members of the Tabernacle Choir joined in. As each choir tearfully sang in its own language, Saints from two nations were welded into one by the power of music and the Spirit of God.

In 1958 he returned to the Pacific to dedicate the New Zealand Temple. While there he also organized the Auckland Stake, the first outside of North America or Hawaii. Later that same year he returned to Europe to dedicate the London Temple.

Everywhere President McKay went he was greeted with love and respect. He was the first living prophet most of the scattered Saints had ever seen in person. At airport after airport they welcomed him with tear-filled eyes and choked voices as they sang the familiar strains of the hymn, "We Thank Thee, O God, for a Prophet."

President McKay often witnessed divine blessings and guidance as he traveled. In 1955, for example, his flight was delayed because of warnings that a hurricane was headed toward Fiji, the next stop. By the time they reached the area, however, they were able to land safely. Officials in Fiji were puzzled to see how the hurricane "had suddenly reversed its course" at the very time of President McKay's arrival. Heavy tropical rains continued, delaying the McKays' departure from Fiji. Until he unexpectedly met two Elders on the street, President McKay was not aware that Latter-day Saint missionaries had begun working in the area only three months earlier. He immediately arranged to meet with the small group of Latter-day Saints living in Suva. They met at the home of C. G. Smith, who, on his own, had kept the little flock of Saints together for many years. As Brother Smith welcomed God's prophet to his home and to their meeting "he broke down and wept tears of joy and thanksgiving." The congregation with tears in their eyes sang "We Thank Thee, O God, for a Prophet," "every word as if it were a prayer." President McKay remarked that "this was a significant meeting." Not aware that there were members in Fiji, he had planned to go directly to Tonga. He compared this occasion to the meeting at Philippi where the Apostle Paul and his associates had started the first European branch of the primitive Church. He also reported that he had stopped at Fiji in 1921, "but decided that the time was not ripe for the preaching of the gospel to the people of that country" at that time. He declared that circumstances had now caused them to remain so that they might "commence the building up of the Kingdom of God" in Fiji. "Surely," he concluded, "God has had a hand in changing our schedule so that we can be with you members of the Church."[18]

President McKay's travels were a source of inspiration to more than just those scattered Saints he visited. The *Church News* carried day-by-day accounts of his experiences, which were followed with great interest. Even those in the strong central areas of the Church found their faith strengthened as they read about the feelings of faith and gratitude manifested by their fellow Saints in far-flung countries.

Educational Expansion

By the 1930s the Church's educational program had assumed the basic form that would characterize it during subsequent decades of the twentieth century. Henceforth, growth, especially following World War II, would be the major feature of its history. Enrollment in the Church's various educational programs increased approximately fivefold while David O. McKay presided over the Church.

David O. McKay's background and personal commitment to education suited him well as he gave leadership during this era of phenomenal growth. At only twenty years of age he had become the principal of the district school in his hometown of Huntsville, Utah. He then completed a three-year teacher-education course at the University of Utah, thus becoming the first President of the Church to hold a college degree. After serving as a teacher and principal at the Church's Weber Stake Academy, he became superintendent of the Church's entire educational system.

Few individuals had greater impact on Church education during President McKay's administration than did Ernest L. Wilkinson. He was an attorney in Washington, D.C., at the time of his appointment as president of Brigham Young University in 1950. Three years later he was also named administrator of the Unified Church School System (later renamed the Church Educational System) including schools, seminaries, and institutes of religion worldwide. In these capacities he would give dynamic and powerful direction to the entire Church educational program during the next two decades.

CHURCH SCHOOLS IN THE UNITED STATES

Brigham Young University was not alone in facing the pressures caused by the surging enrollments following the close of World War II. Ricks College, the Church's two-year school in southeastern Idaho, also was affected by the postwar expansion. In 1948 the Church Board of Education approved Ricks's becoming a four-year school. Not only did this provide additional educational opportunities for Church members, but it also allowed the school to accommodate persons seeking to comply with a 1947 Idaho law requiring four years of college training for a public school teaching certificate. By 1954, however, postwar pressures had lessened and the board decided to return Ricks to its former status, suggesting that it could make a greater contribution as "a first class junior college than by continuing as a relatively small four-year college."[19] This also fit into the plan of Wilkinson and his associates to center the Church's educational system around a single university (BYU) supported by other schools.[20]

During the postwar decades, Brigham Young University grew to become one of the largest privately owned institutions of higher education in the United States. (Photo courtesy Mark Philbrick, BYU)

At the time of Ernest L. Wilkinson's appointment as president of Brigham Young University, he sought the First Presidency's support to make BYU "the greatest educational institution in the world."[21] For the next two decades Wilkinson labored energetically to see this hope realized. A well-trained lawyer,

Wilkinson argued persuasively and successfully before the board that Brigham Young University needed to expand significantly in order to more effectively meet the educational needs of the Saints. Under his leadership and with the board's backing, BYU launched an unprecedented building program. Major academic buildings were constructed; the capacity of on-campus student housing was tripled; and other facilities, including a motion picture studio, a student center, and a new stadium, were also added. During the years 1951 to 1971 the estimated value of BYU's campus, including buildings and equipment, soared from just over six million dollars to well over one hundred million.[22] President Wilkinson took steps to see that academic progress kept pace with physical growth. He actively recruited faculty members with doctor's degrees from prestigious universities. In 1960 BYU offered its own doctorates for the first time. In that same year it also launched the Honors Program, allowing serious students to enjoy contact in small classes with the university's most outstanding faculty members.

The religious activity of students was a source of concern for Church leaders. In some wards adjacent to college campuses, students tended to crowd out local members. At the same time, there were other students who did not affiliate with any Church unit when away from home. As early as 1947 two special branches were formed at Brigham Young University to meet the needs of married and single students, respectively. At first these units were considered experimental, but they soon demonstrated their success by setting the highest attendance records in the East Provo Stake. As enrollment mushroomed, the first complete student stake in the Church was organized at BYU in 1956. This made a unique and significant contribution to BYU's lifestyle and to the students' personal development.

Soon, student wards and stakes were organized on campuses wherever numbers were sufficient. Typically a faculty member or a person from the community would be the bishop, but students would fill most other positions. Thus they gained experience as quorum or auxiliary leaders, teachers, clerks, and so on. Mature students even had the opportunity to serve as counselors in the bishopric or as members of the stake high council. In contrast to the campuses of most major universities, which were almost deserted on Sundays except for a handful attending chapel services, at Brigham Young University and Ricks College the buildings where the student wards met were as crowded on Sunday as during the week. As President Wilkinson reflected on his two decades of leadership at BYU, he declared that the organization of the student stakes and wards was "the most satisfying accomplishment during the time I have been here."[23]

PART-TIME RELIGIOUS EDUCATION

While the foregoing developments were occurring on the campuses of the Church's schools, significant progress was also being made in its programs of part-time religious education. Seminaries and institutes were spreading throughout the United States and around the world to meet the needs of high school and college students.

Adaptations in the seminary program made possible the rapid growth in the number of high school students enrolled. Originally all seminaries were "released-time." In predominantly Latter-day Saint communities of Utah and adjoining areas, a seminary building was erected near the high school and students were released during the regular school day to take a seminary class as one of their electives. As Latter-day Saints spread beyond the Intermountain states, they increasingly lived in areas where such an arrangement was not possible. Therefore early-morning and home-study programs were developed to meet their needs.

Early-morning seminary classes had been inaugurated in Salt Lake City and Pocatello, Idaho, in 1929; the program in Pocatello was discontinued after only one year. As early as 1941 the institute director in southern California reported that there were five high schools in the Los Angeles area alone having more than one hundred Latter-day Saint students each, and that there were several others approaching that number. However, wartime restrictions precluded any new programs at that time. In 1950 the eleven Los Angeles-area stake presidents, chaired by Howard W. Hunter of the Pasadena Stake, unanimously urged that a seminary program be started at once.

Formidable obstacles had to be overcome. Most classes would have to serve more than one high school. Differences in schedules from one school to another meant that the only possible time for seminary was before school. Classes would have to begin at 7:00 A.M. or earlier. Almost no chapels were located within walking distance of the high schools, so car pools or other transportation would need to be arranged. In September 1950, six pilot classes were inaugurated; their success led to the addition of seven more classes that same school year. Despite the difficulties of time and distance, the 461 southern California seminary students had an average attendance of 88 percent that first year. Three years later there were fifty-nine classes achieving an average attendance of 92 percent. This record was a tribute to the devotion of students and their parents who were willing to get up as early as five-thirty in order to attend or help their children attend a religion class before school. In coming years, early-morning classes would make seminary instruction available to Latter-day Saint students in many parts of the world, especially in centers of Church population in the United States and Canada beyond the Intermountain area.[24]

The first home-study programs were started as pilot projects in the Midwest during the 1966–67 school year. These were developed where there were not enough students within a reasonable distance to make a daily class possible. The young people would study their seminary lessons at home during the week and then meet with others in their branch to go over this material with a volunteer teacher as part of their regular meetings on Sunday. About once every month students from several branches would gather at a central location for a "Super Saturday," featuring more in-depth instruction from a professional seminary coordinator during the morning and recreational activities conducted by the MIA in the afternoon. These home-study programs made seminary instruction available to Latter-day Saints no matter where they lived throughout the world. A similar home-study institute course for college students was inaugurated in 1972.[25]

DEVELOPMENTS ABROAD

The worldwide growth of the Church brought a corresponding overseas expansion in the educational system during the years of President David O. McKay's administration. In the Pacific and in Latin America, two areas of particularly rapid Church growth, public education was not widely available, and Church leaders were concerned that a substantial portion of the Saints did not have the opportunity for even an elementary education. In these areas, therefore, the Church returned to the practice of the pioneers—establishing schools to teach the basics of secular education along with religious instruction.

The Church College of Hawaii in Laie, Hawaii. (LDS Church Archives)

During the early twentieth century several of the Pacific missions had conducted schools, generally small, for the benefit of Latter-day Saint children. An outstanding example was the Maori Agricultural College in New Zealand. Full-time missionaries were called as teachers in these schools. Church growth following the close of World War II heightened the need for these schools to be expanded. During the early 1950s the Church opened the Liahona College in Tonga, the Pesega and Mapusaga high schools in Samoa, the Church College of New Zealand near Hamilton, and several elementary schools in these same countries. Even though two of these schools were called colleges, they included work only through the high school level. Buildings for these schools were constructed through the "building missionary" program that had its beginning at this time in the South Pacific.

The Church College of Hawaii (CCH), a four-year institution of higher education at Laie, opened in 1955. The school came to serve about a thousand students, most coming from the Pacific Islands. Emphasis was on teacher education, thus making it possible for many Polynesian young people to return

The Polynesian Cultural Center near completion. Dedicated in 1963 near the campus of the Church College of Hawaii (later BYU—Hawaii), the center celebrated the varied traditions of Pacific cultures. (Deseret News *photo)*

to their homelands and become faculty members in the Church schools there. In 1958 President David O. McKay dedicated a complex of fine new buildings on the CCH campus. A thirty-three-foot mosaic on the facade of the administration building depicted the flag-raising ceremony that had prompted Elder McKay to prophesy some thirty-seven years earlier that Laie would one day become the educational center for the Saints in the Pacific. In 1963 the Church opened the Polynesian Cultural Center adjacent to the college campus. It not only helped to preserve and share the unique cultures of several Pacific peoples, but it also became a very popular tourist attraction which created goodwill for the Church and provided meaningful employment for a large number of CCH Polynesian students. In 1974 the Church College of Hawaii became the Hawaii Campus of Brigham Young University, emphasizing subjects that could be taught more advantageously in the Pacific setting than on BYU's main Provo campus.

At first the Church's schools in the Pacific were operated under the supervision of the respective missions where they were located. By 1957, however, the system had grown to the point that the First Presidency formed a separate Pacific Board of Education to give direction to these schools as a group. Called as chairman of the board was Wendell B. Mendenhall, who was also head of the Church's building program in the Pacific. Under the board's leadership, the transition from missionary teachers to a professionally trained faculty accelerated, the process virtually completed by 1959.[26]

The expansion of the Church's educational program in Latin America also came during these same years. There had been only one school there, the Juarez Academy in the Mormon colonies, dating from the turn of the century. Beginning in 1960, however, with the encouragement of President David O. McKay, a system of some forty elementary and secondary schools was established to meet the educational needs of Saints in various parts of Mexico. Over two thousand students, many at the college level, attended the Church's school *Benemerito de las Americas* near Mexico City. Here again, emphasis was on teacher preparation. As in the Pacific, these schools made a significant contribution to Latter-day Saint activity as a whole, a sizable number of local Church leaders having graduated from them. The Church also operated a few schools in Chile and Peru.

Church Commissioner of Education, Neal A. Maxwell. (LDS Church Archives)

An especially important contribution was made by the Church's literacy program. In some developing areas, people were being called as leaders and teachers who did not even know how to read or write. Under the direction of Brigham Young University, a simple plan was developed to teach these basic skills. In Bolivia, for example, members received fifteen hours of one-to-one instruction teaching them to read Spanish. Having completed this course, an additional four hours of training prepared these people to teach others. In this way hundreds of Latter-day Saints were enabled for the first time to read the scriptures as well as handbooks, lesson manuals, and other Church literature. Not only were many able to obtain better employment, but their self-esteem received a substantial boost. One branch president commented that before he had learned to read, opportunities had been like a closed book for him; now his life was rich and full like an open book.

GUIDELINES FOR THE FUTURE

With the growth of the Church's schools and other educational programs, it became necessary in 1964 to divide the administrative responsibility. Ernest L. Wilkinson continued as president of Brigham Young University, while Dr. Harvey L. Taylor became "chancellor" of the remainder of the Church educational programs. By June 1970 (five months after President McKay's death), the General Authorities felt the need to have a more thorough unification of the entire system under one leader. Dr. Neal A. Maxwell, the executive vice president of the University of Utah (and future member of the Council of the Twelve), was appointed commissioner of the Church Educational System.

Commissioner Maxwell outlined the major objectives of the Church's efforts in education:

1. "Literacy and basic education are gospel needs. . . . Education is often not only the key to the individual member's economic future, but also to his opportunities for self-realization, for full Church service and for contributing to the world around him—spiritually, politically, culturally and socially." To meet these needs, the Church was operating seventy-five elementary and seven secondary schools in ten countries of Latin America and the Pacific with a combined enrollment of 15,200.

2. "Church programs will not duplicate otherwise available opportunities especially in higher education." The Church did choose to operate four college-level institutions, but of the 200,000 members then enrolled in higher education, only 32,000 were at these schools.

3. "Ultimately, all high school and college-age Latter-day Saints should have access to weekday religious education, in tandem with secular education." The Church's part-time programs enrolled by far the largest number of students, 50,000 in institutes and 140,000 in seminaries.[27]

In conclusion, Commissioner Maxwell anticipated that Church Education in conjunction with priesthood and auxiliary programs could help individual Latter-day Saints strengthen their testimonies and become more effective Church and community leaders.

Education was only one branch of Church activity that experienced significant development during the administration of President David O. McKay. During an era of unprecedented worldwide growth, programs involving missionary work, public relations, temporal resources, correlation of Church organizations, the home and family, and temples all took on increasing importance.

Growth into a Worldwide Church

*T*he gospel of Jesus Christ is intended to bless all the peoples of the earth. Hence worldwide growth was essential to the Church's accomplishing its mission and was also the fulfillment of prophecy. The Old Testament prophet Daniel declared that in the latter days the Lord would set up a kingdom which would roll forth and fill the earth (see Daniel 2:26–45). Latter-day Saints believe they have a divine commission to pray for and strive to accomplish what Daniel foresaw (see D&C 65:2, 5). To achieve this, the Church must not only be numerically strong, but its members must be geographically distributed around the world.

Patterns of Growth

The growth of The Church of Jesus Christ of Latter-day Saints in this era has not fit usual patterns. Normally, as an organization grows larger, its rate of increase drops off. This is because the ratio of truly committed members declines and the group approaches the ceiling of its potential population. The Church, by contrast, is not only growing, but is doing so at an increasingly higher rate. Between 1920 and 1950, the Church grew approximately 28 percent every ten years. During the next three decades, however, the rate was twice as high, around 57 percent.

The source of Latter-day Saint growth also departs from the norm. According to one sociologist of religion, growth in new

King Bhumibol Adulyadej of Thailand receiving a copy of the Book of Mormon from Thailand Mission president Harvey D. Brown. (LDS Church Archives)

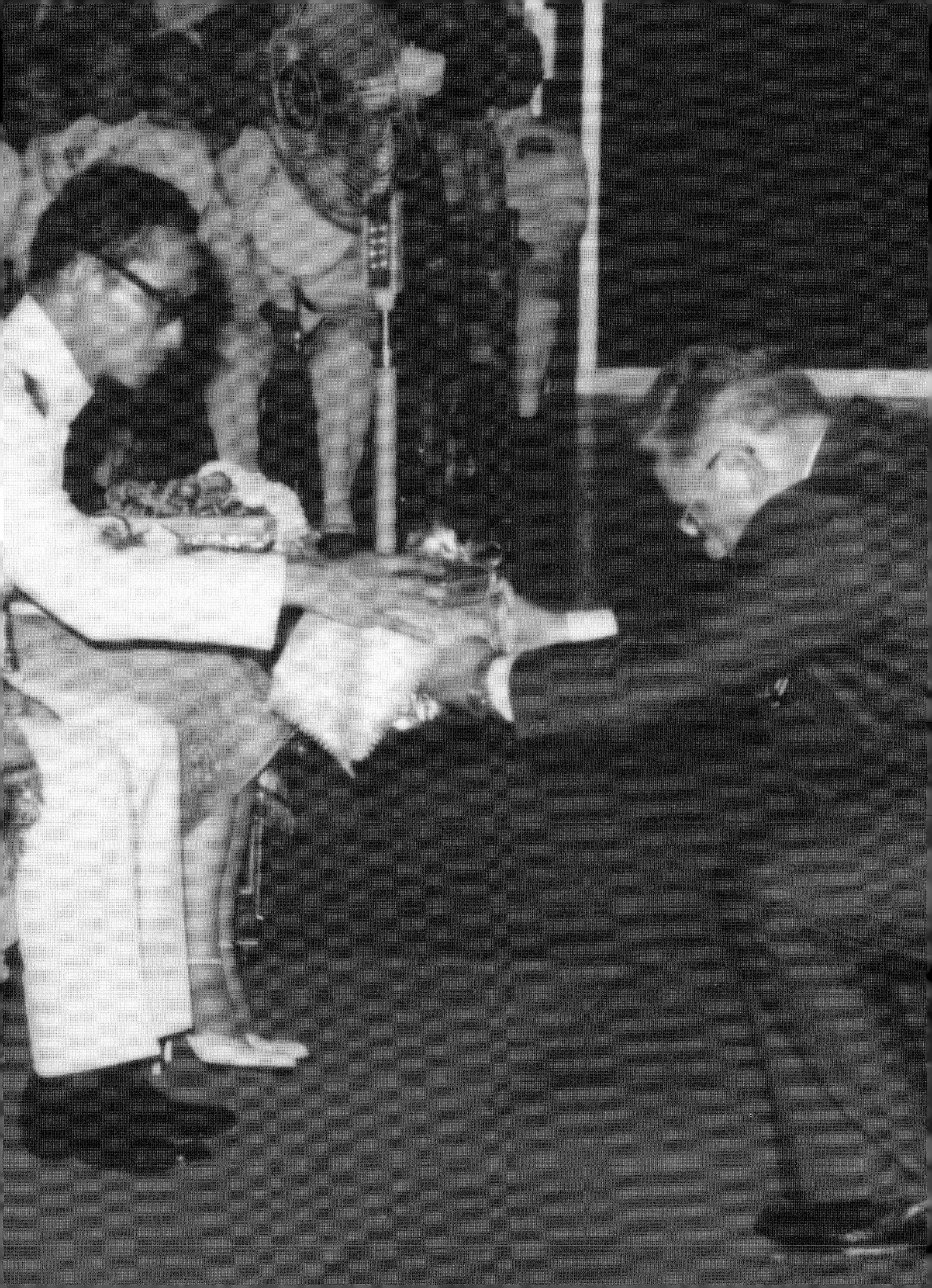

and relatively small religious groups typically comes from converts who bring added vitality. Larger bodies or denominations, on the other hand, tend to grow primarily through natural increase—children being born to members. The Mormons have avoided this denominational "stagnation."[1] Even though The Church of Jesus Christ of Latter-day Saints would become one of the half dozen largest faith groups in the United States during the later twentieth century, approximately three-fourths of its increase would come through convert baptisms.

Missionary Earl Underwood stands with a Guatemalan family by a baptismal font in 1960. (LDS Church Archives)

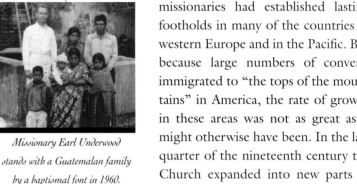

Not only did the Church grow larger during this period, but its members became more widely distributed around the world. This geographical diffusion was due to increased missionary success and to Church leaders' urging the Saints to remain in their own lands and to build up the kingdom there.

This same counsel would be given throughout the twentieth century. At the Mexico City area conference in 1972, for example, Elder Bruce R. McConkie explained: "The gathering of Israel consists of joining the true Church" and that "any person, therefore, who has accepted the restored gospel, and who now seeks to worship the Lord, in his own tongue, and among his own people, and with the Saints of his own nation has complied with the law of gathering and is entitled to all the blessings promised the Saints in these last days." Therefore, "The place of gathering for the Mexican Saints is in Mexico; the place of gathering for the Guatemalan Saints is in Guatemala; the place of gathering for the Brazilian Saints is in Brazil; and so it goes throughout the length and breadth of the whole earth. Japan is for the Japanese; Korea is for the Koreans; Australia is for the Australians; every nation is the gathering place for its own people."[2]

Historically, Latter-day Saint growth began in some lands much earlier than in others. By the 1850s missionaries had established lasting footholds in many of the countries of western Europe and in the Pacific. But because large numbers of converts immigrated to "the tops of the mountains" in America, the rate of growth in these areas was not as great as it might otherwise have been. In the last quarter of the nineteenth century the Church expanded into new parts of North America, into Mexico, and into other parts of the South Pacific.

As has been seen, a new era of growth followed the close of World War I. Many Saints in the Intermountain area began an exodus, particularly to southern California, in pursuit of improved economic opportunity. Elder David O. McKay's yearlong inspection tour of the Church's far-flung missions in 1921 gave him a heightened worldwide vision. A door was opened to the gospel in South America when German immigrant Saints in Argentina actively shared the gospel with their neighbors. During the 1930s, preaching also began among German immigrants in Brazil, but as World War II approached,

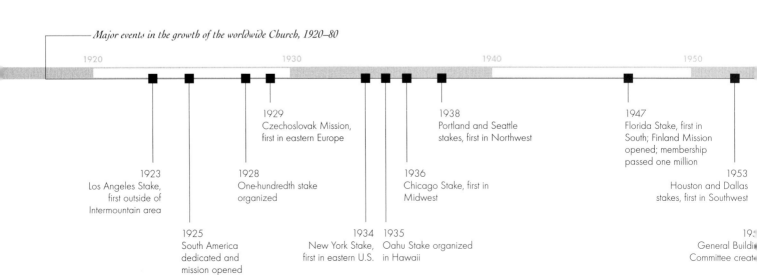

Major events in the growth of the worldwide Church, 1920–80

1920 — 1930 — 1940 — 1950

1923 Los Angeles Stake, first outside of Intermountain area

1925 South America dedicated and mission opened

1928 One-hundredth stake organized

1929 Czechoslovak Mission, first in eastern Europe

1934 New York Stake, first in eastern U.S.

1935 Oahu Stake organized in Hawaii

1936 Chicago Stake, first in Midwest

1938 Portland and Seattle stakes, first in Northwest

1947 Florida Stake, first in South; Finland Mission opened; membership passed one million

1953 Houston and Dallas stakes, first in Southwest

19[illegible] General Buildi[illegible] Committee creat[illegible]

Brazil's restrictions on the use of German in public meetings led the missionaries to give more attention to the Portuguese-speaking majority. The interwar years also brought the opening of missionary work in Czechoslovakia in eastern Europe.

The impact of World War II on Church growth was both positive and negative. The Saints in Europe demonstrated faith and devotion as they withstood the intense suffering brought by the conflict; never before had such a large number of Church members lived within an active war zone. As the missionary force was greatly reduced, Latter-day Saints around the world assumed more responsibility for local Church activity and gained experience that would prove valuable in the years of rapid growth that would follow. Further, Latter-day Saint servicemen carried the gospel to new areas, particularly to southern Europe and eastern Asia. Also, hundreds of Latter-day Saints moved to communities along the U.S. Pacific Coast to work in defense industries during the war. These areas, together with predominantly "Lamanite" Central America and western South America, became important new mission fields during the second half of the twentieth century.

The establishment of new stakes provides a better measure of Church progress than does a mere increase in membership. The prophet Isaiah, seeing the latter-day glory of Zion, wrote figuratively about her preparation for rejoicing: "Enlarge the place of thy tent, and let them stretch forth the curtains of thine habitations: spare not, lengthen thy cords, and *strengthen thy stakes*" (Isaiah 54:2; emphasis added). Latter-day revelations identify "stakes" as sources of spiritual strength and refuge (see D&C 82:14; 115:5–6; 133:9). In contrast to a mission district, which generally must *receive* strength and leadership *from* the Church, a stake is able to *give* strength and stability *to* the Church, just as stakes support a tent. Thus, "stakehood" is the ideal for which every mission district prepares. Stakes cannot be organized unless there are local leaders trained and experienced in operating the full programs of the Church. Hence, the formation of new stakes and the consequent increased percentage of Church members living in them is a measure of maturity and development. One of the greatest barriers to this progress is the lack of the Melchizedek Priesthood bearers required to provide the necessary leadership.

The growth and maturity of the Church in this era is well illustrated by the creation of new stakes in diverse parts of the world. The Church's one hundredth stake was organized in 1928, and the five hundredth stake was formed in 1970 on the very day President David O. McKay died. Until the later 1950s, all these stakes were located in North America or Hawaii. With the advent of jet travel, however, President McKay decided that organizing stakes in distant lands was now feasible.[3] The first "overseas stake" was organized at Auckland, New Zealand, in 1958. In 1960 the first European stake was organized at Manchester, England; and the next year, the first non–English-speaking stake was formed in Holland, and the first Latin American stake was created in Mexico City. The first stakes in Asia and Africa were organized in 1970.

Another evidence of mature growth in this period was the erection of temples. During the 1950s the Church's largest temple was at Los Angeles, and the first

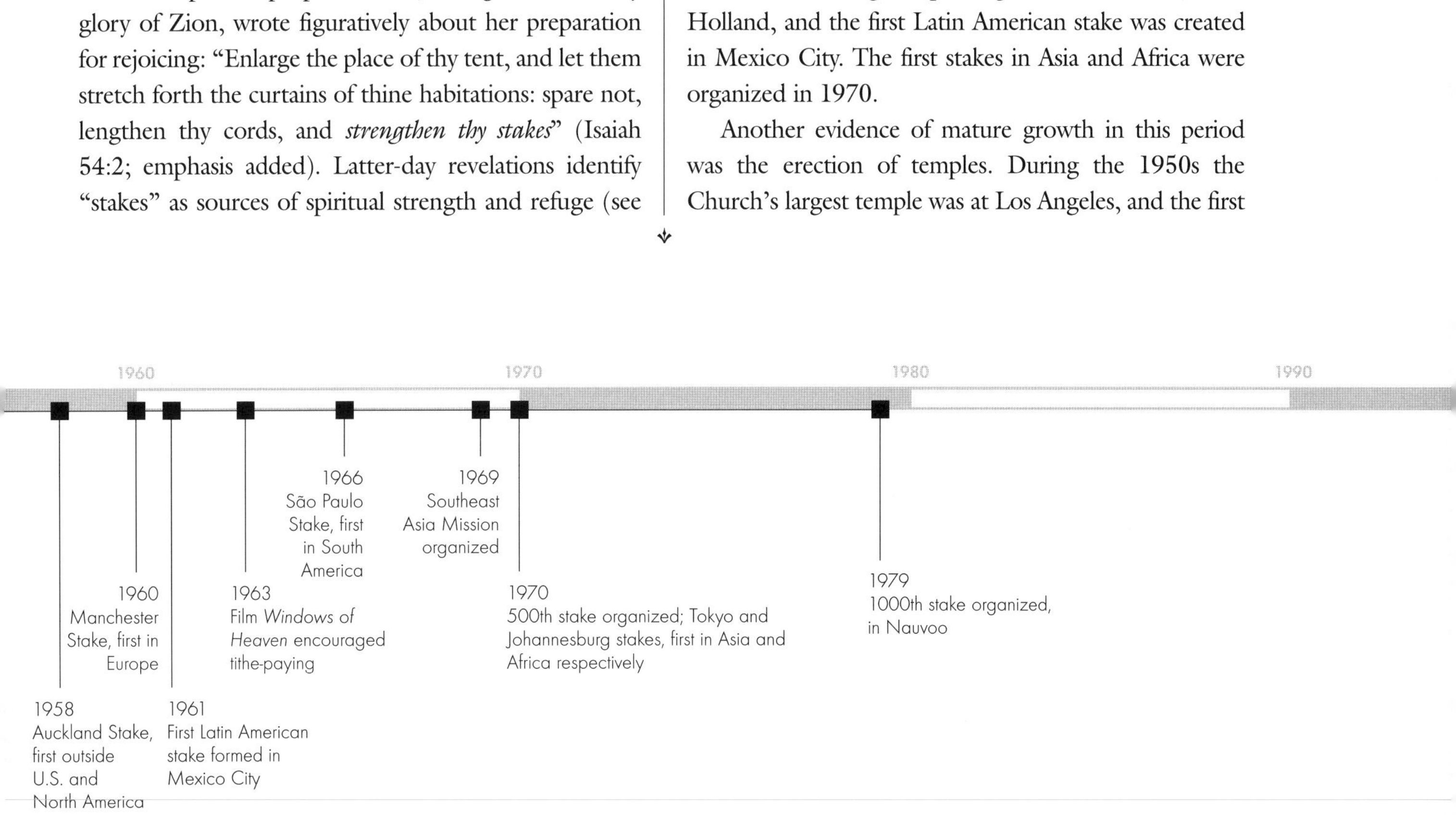
1960
1970
1980
1990
1966
São Paulo Stake, first in South America
1969
Southeast Asia Mission organized
1960
Manchester Stake, first in Europe
1963
Film *Windows of Heaven* encouraged tithe-paying
1970
500th stake organized; Tokyo and Johannesburg stakes, first in Asia and Africa respectively
1979
1000th stake organized, in Nauvoo
1958
Auckland Stake, first outside U.S. and North America
1961
First Latin American stake formed in Mexico City

A local priesthood leadership conference in Samoa in 1972. Samoa was the first country to be completely covered by stakes. (LDS Church Archives)

overseas temples were dedicated in Switzerland, New Zealand, and England.

Yet another evidence of the Church's growing international strength was the appointment of General Authorities from areas outside of Anglo-America. Since 1975 these Church leaders have been called from such diverse areas as the Netherlands, Germany, England, Japan, and Argentina.

Perhaps the greatest benefit of Church growth in this era was evident in the lives of the scattered Saints. Elder Gordon B. Hinckley declared: "It is my judgement that the work today is on a more stable basis in Europe than it has ever been. We have stakes of Zion. We have strong missions. We have capable local leaders. . . . We have mission presidents coming out of those lands, and missionaries who are working among their own people as well as going to other lands to serve. . . . This is most encouraging."[4]

While the Church was growing rapidly in some parts of the world, formidable barriers still remained in others. The postwar spread of communism closed large sections of the world to the gospel. Furthermore, local laws made other countries inaccessible. Nevertheless, the spread of the gospel was beginning to overcome even these obstacles. An ever-increasing number of faithful Latter-day Saints were living in almost every nation of the earth as a result of government, military, or business assignments.

Although the Church's growth in this period had been phenomenal, still Church leaders saw ample room and a pressing need for much more expansion. During the 1970s Church membership would pass the four million mark, but the estimated world population was about four billion. Hence, only one in a thousand was being blessed by the gospel of Jesus Christ and the program of the restored Church. Furthermore, there were large areas of the earth where the gospel had not yet been introduced—the Communist bloc, much of Africa, the Islamic nations, and most parts of Asia.

The Church in Many Lands

As the Church increasingly became a worldwide movement, Church programs had to be flexible enough to take into account the unique customs and environments of Latter-day Saints in many nations.

Saints in different parts of the world faced and continue to face unique challenges and circumstances. Europeans, for instance, enjoyed a rich, centuries-long cultural heritage. However, in many parts of Europe prosperity had contributed to religious indifference. High taxes and other economic pressures made having more than one or two children a real sacrifice and required many mothers to be employed outside of the home. Lax moral standards and liberal laws on pornography as well as customs contrary to the Word of Wisdom all provide challenges for local Latter-day Saints. Additionally, because so many diverse languages were spoken by peoples living in relatively close proximity to one another, Church conferences, temple sessions, and other activities generally needed to be multilingual.

The Saints in Latin America face yet a different set of challenges. Perhaps nowhere else in the world is a single religion so pervasively reflected throughout the culture—place names, holidays, individuals' given names, and so on. Hence, conversion to the restored gospel represents a major cultural change to the convert. Revolutions in Mexico during the mid-nineteenth century brought greater religious freedom, helping to set the stage for the gospel's introduction there. Another series of revolutions in the early twentieth century, however, lead to the martyrdom of two Latter-day Saints near Mexico City. Another challenge had been anti-U.S. feelings in some areas which hindered missionaries' receiving needed visas. Such difficulties generally strengthened the faith and resourcefulness of the Saints. Church members in Latin America, especially in Mexico, Central America, and western South America, regard themselves as being among the descendants of the Nephites and Lamanites described in the Book of Mormon and hence as heirs to the great promises contained in that volume.

A Boy Scout-Beehive dance at a youth conference in Tutuila, Samoa, in 1958. The Church made great strides in the South Pacific in the years following World War II. (LDS Church Archives)

As the Church expanded into the South Pacific it found the Polynesians to be a warm and loving people. Their spirituality was evidenced by remarkable healings and inspiring manifestations of other spiritual gifts. Traditions described how their forbears sailed in primitive crafts thousands of miles from the Americas to the islands of the South Pacific. Latter-day Saints in Polynesia therefore identify themselves with the peoples of the Book of Mormon. Families are important to the Polynesians, as reflected by elaborate genealogies memorized and recited orally or intricately carved in wood. For these and other reasons the Church experienced phenomenal growth in the South Pacific.

In 1974 Samoa became the first country in the world to be completely covered by stakes. Nevertheless, life in this "tropical paradise" was not always easy. In some areas dependence on a single crop often provided only a meager living. At times LDS missionaries had faced opposition from governments influenced by Europe-based missionary societies. Transportation was a practical challenge for Church leaders who needed to visit local units on separate islands.

Missionaries carrying the gospel to East Asia felt as though they were entering a different world. Christianity was not the dominant religion. Not even the familiar alphabet was used, so languages seemed strange and terrifying to missionaries. Despite these cultural differences, the gospel has took root in several of the nations in this region, and the Church would later begin to experience rapid growth there. Latter-day Saint emphasis on the importance of families struck a responsive chord in the hearts of many whose families for generations have revered their ancestors.

Other Challenges Posed by Worldwide Growth

As the Church grew, effort was made to meet the challenges inherent in providing the blessings of the gospel and the Church effectively to the Saints in all parts of the world. Careful distinction needed to be made between the gospel of Jesus Christ and peculiar traits of western American culture.

Worldwide growth greatly affected the planning of Church programs. No longer could activities be planned for a single and mostly homogeneous group in western America. Church writers had to keep in mind an international audience with a variety of social, intellectual, physical, and spiritual needs. More flexibility had to be built into manuals and handbooks. This in turn placed added responsibility on local leaders to suit the implementation of Church programs to meet their specific needs.

TRANSLATION AND DISTRIBUTION OF CHURCH LITERATURE

Not only did Church literature and programs need to be related to people in varying cultures, but they also had to be made available in an ever growing number of languages. During the Church's first century almost all translation was done by the staffs of various overseas mission offices. It was not until 1939 that Eduardo Balderas became the first full-time translator assigned work at Church headquarters in Salt Lake City. Just after World War II he was joined by a few others who were brought to Salt Lake City from several European missions. Translation of materials continued to be done in Salt Lake City until the responsibility for translation was transferred to translation centers around the world.

In 1963 the distribution of supplies by various Church organizations was consolidated. Then in

Undated picture of traditionally dressed Church members in the Japanese Mission. (LDS Church Archives)

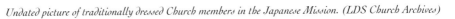

1965 the Presiding Bishopric was given responsibility for the translation of Church literature, and in the following year these two operations were brought together in one department. "It is my conviction," Presiding Bishop Victor L. Brown testified, "that the Lord has touched the hearts and the lives of men and women in many lands who have been preparing for such a work, and then he has led us to them." The original charge was to see that Spanish-speaking members receive lesson manuals and other materials "at the same time they were received by the members of the Church in the center stakes."[5] This assignment was soon expanded to include Portuguese and other European languages. The Polynesian languages of the South Pacific were added at a later date. Officials estimated that twelve thousand pages had to be translated yearly into each language.[6]

Bishop Brown explained that translation posed a very demanding challenge and required extensive preparation. Even though specific English words may not exist in some other languages, translation still needed to be accomplished with a "minimum of distortion." The translator had to understand the context and author's intended meaning. One Relief Society lesson, for example, contained a recipe calling for "Chicken of the Sea," a popular American brand of tuna. "The translator checked her encyclopedia and other reference books. She checked the library and university. Finally, in desperation, she translated 'Chicken of the Sea' as 'hen of the ocean.' "

The "Unified Magazine" was first published in March 1967 in nine languages. (Photo courtesy LDS Church)

Bishop Brown also testified that translators often recognized divine assistance in their exacting task. Even though poetry and music was especially difficult, a sister who was translating *The Children Sing* "could not write fast enough to keep up with the flow of words as they came to her."[7]

By 1970 shipping materials from Church headquarters to destinations all over the world became too costly. Furthermore, there were some countries that did not permit materials to be imported from the United States. To lessen these difficulties, the Church developed a worldwide organization with publishing plants and distribution centers in such places as Manchester, England; Frankfurt, Germany; Mexico City, Mexico; São Paulo, Brazil; Aukland, New Zealand; and Tokyo, Japan; as well as the center in Salt Lake City. These international facilities enabled the Church to avoid the usual delays and expense of long-distance shipping, as well as eliminating the problem of sending imported materials through customs.

A high-quality monthly magazine has been another important means of instructing and inspiring Church members throughout the world. Over the years, most missions had developed publications of their own. However, when Elder Howard W. Hunter of the Council of the Twelve was supervising the European Mission in 1966 he became concerned with the great amount of time expended by mission presidents and their staffs in producing mission magazines which varied widely in quality and content. To remedy these problems, Elder Hunter proposed centralizing and coordinating these efforts.[8]

Material for the new "Unified Magazine" was selected from the Church's basic English-language publications. The English manuscript, together with necessary graphics, was sent from Church headquarters to the area centers for translation and publication. Space was provided in the magazine for news and other features of local interest. The magazine first appeared in nine European languages in 1967. For a time, the unified magazine retained such traditional names as *La Liahona* (Spanish), *Der Stern* (German), and *L'Etoile* (French). By the year 2000 the magazine would appear in forty-two languages, all under the name *Liahona*.

Providing a full range of Church curriculum materials placed members speaking various languages on more of an equal footing than ever before. Members in Europe were pleased to point out that they actually commenced new courses of study before members in

Salt Lake City because of the difference in time. The great expansion of non-English stakes has come since the Church enlarged its translation program. Because the Lord indicated that "every man shall hear the fulness of the gospel in his own tongue, and in his own language" (D&C 90:11), those involved in Church translation feel that their service is a literal fulfillment of prophecy.

"Building missionaries" constructing the São Jose dos Campos meetinghouse in Brazil. (LDS Church Archives)

MEETING THE NEED FOR CHURCH BUILDINGS

During the later twentieth century the number of congregations worldwide was increasing by several hundred each year. Even if an average of two wards or branches shared each meetinghouse, approximately one new building every day was needed just to keep up with the new congregations being created. In addition, more specialized buildings for educational, welfare, genealogical, and administrative activities were required.

The need for additional buildings was particularly acute during the era of rapid Church growth following World War II. In 1965, for example, there were 2,219 Church buildings in existence; of these, 2,034 were chapels. At the same time, 556 new chapels, or more than 27 percent of those then in existence, were under construction. In 1964 more than 60 percent of all Church buildings then in service had been constructed during the previous decade.[9]

The Hyde Park Chapel in London, England, in 1961. To keep pace with its escalating membership, the Church embarked on an extensive building program that erected an average of one building every day. (LDS Church Archives)

A unique program resulted when the Church encountered a labor shortage while erecting schools in the South Pacific. Beginning in 1950 the Church resolved the problem by calling young men as "building missionaries" to donate their labor for two years. They learned necessary skills as they worked under the direction of experienced builders, most of whom had been called on special missions from the United States or Canada. Not only were the needed buildings completed, but the young men gained self-confidence as they learned a valuable trade.[10] During the early 1960s this program spread to other parts of the world, especially to Europe and Latin America. As economic conditions changed, however, the need for this type of service declined, and by the 1970s most Church buildings were once again being constructed by regularly contracted workmen.

To coordinate the Church's widespread building program, a General Building Committee was called in 1955. This group considered local needs and circumstances as it recommended new building projects for approval. Members of the Building Committee also worked with local architects in finalizing plans and in supervising and inspecting construction.

Throughout the years, the architecture of Latter-day Saint buildings had been influenced by a variety of factors both inside and outside the Church. General architectural trends as well as individual architects left their mark. Because many early Church members came from the northeastern United States, Mormon architecture for over a century reflected the style of the New England Colonial meetinghouse.

Probably the most important influence on chapel design was the expansion of Church programs. In pioneer times Mormon chapels were simple meeting halls that accommodated a variety of community activities. By the turn of the century, they typically included a chapel or assembly room, a few smaller rooms for instruction or other purposes, and perhaps an "amusement hall" in the basement. The development in the Church's cultural and recreational programs called for a larger "cultural hall" to accommodate dances as well as basketball games; a well-equipped stage was needed for

Kim, Ho Jik (back row, middle), a pioneer for the Church in Korea, with a wedding party in 1957. District President Kim married the couple, the first Saints to be wedded in Korea. (LDS Church Archives, photo by Elder John K. Carmack)

dramatic presentations. The multiplication of priesthood and auxiliary organization age groupings necessitated a larger number of classrooms. Over the years specialized rooms have been provided for children's worship, seminary, the Boy Scout program, and Relief Society.

The need for economy had been another concern. During the Great Depression of the 1930s, Church leaders repeatedly counseled against unnecessary extravagance. The appeal of the simpler "contemporary" design was due in part to its comparatively low cost of construction. Experience in designing and erecting hundreds of chapels enabled the Building Committee to develop a series of standardized plans that incorporated the most desirable features and were engineered to minimize construction costs. By the 1960s, "expandable chapels" were designed to be built one phase at a time, thus reducing the initial cost and more fairly distributing the total expense among all members of a growing congregation.

FINANCIAL CHALLENGES

Even though the Church's mission is essentially spiritual, material needs must be provided for. The Church's worldwide growth, especially during the years following World War II, required that increasing attention be given to these matters. This rapid growth came at a time when construction costs were escalating. This compounded the financial burden placed on the Church and its members.

To meet the Church's needs, leaders reemphasized tithing—"the Lord's law of revenue." In 1963 the Church produced a new film, *The Windows of Heaven*, to emphasize the importance of tithe-paying by depicting President Lorenzo Snow's miraculous experience in St. George. At the special general conference session where this film was first shown, President Henry D. Moyle, a counselor in the First Presidency, called on the Church to double the amount of tithing being paid because more funds were needed to take advantage of new technologies in sharing the gospel. "We're not going to leave the President of the Church in the position where he has to say 'no' to any opportunity the Lord presents us, to continue to establish His Church and kingdom here upon this earth. . . . And what was done in the days of President Snow can be accomplished today. So far as I am concerned," President Moyle admonished, "it is just as urgent for us to meet this problem. And I tell you my brethren that the plans that are being forecast for the future are nothing short of phenomenal, and I know with all my heart and soul just as sure as I know the gospel is true that the Lord will not be pleased if we do not make these funds available."[11]

There were other challenges that the Church faced during these years. The sheer growth in the number of stakes and missions placed an increasingly heavy administrative load on the Church's leadership. More conferences needed to be conducted. More local leaders needed to be called and trained. Thus, it is apparent that the Church's organization and programs had to be flexible enough to respond to the varied challenges of international growth. Just as revelation through living prophets led the Saints in meeting the challenges of the past, so also did divine guidance help meet the challenges of growth into a worldwide church.

14

Sharing the Gospel

The phenomenal growth and expansion of the Church after Word War II came in large part from the efforts of a strengthened full-time missonary force, as well as from refined proselyting methods. Likewise, the opening or reopening of missionary work in many parts of the world soon after the war allowed Saints to follow the Savior's injunction to His ancient Apostles: "Go ye into all the world, and preach the gospel to every creature" (Mark 16:15).

From the beginning, Latter-day Saints have been a missionary-minded people, eager to share the blessings of the restored gospel. Their commitment to missionary work has been strengthened by such latter-day exhortations as: "Now behold, a marvelous work is about to come forth among the children of men. . . . For behold the field is white already to harvest; and lo, he that thrusteth in his sickle with his might, the same layeth up in store that he perisheth not, but bringeth salvation to his soul" (D&C 4:1, 4), and such promises as: "And if it so be that you should labor all your days in crying repentance unto this people, and bring, save it be one soul unto me, how great shall be your joy with him in the kingdom of my Father!" (D&C 18:15).

This great work has been done primarily by thousands of young Church members who volunteer for missionary service. Approximately three-fourths of the force have been young men about nineteen years of age. Most of the others are either

In the years following World War II, improved proselyting methods and an increased number of missionaries helped the Church share the gospel message. (Copyright Intellectual Reserve, all rights reserved)

RAILROAD
CROSSING

young women or older couples who have reached retirement age. Although missionary service certainly provides a broadening experience, most have been willing to give approximately two years of their lives and to pay their own expenses for another reason—to share the gospel which they believed has the power to change the lives of men and women for the better.

Proselyting Methods

Building on past innovations, the Church sought ways in the postwar years to make the missionaries' labors more effective and efficient. During the Church's first century, missionaries frequently held meetings in public halls or on street corners to reach large groups with their message. Door-to-door "tracting" was another popular technique. Here the object was to leave a religious tract at every home, hoping for a possible discussion later if individuals had any questions from their reading. Often weeks would go by without any apparent results from the missionaries' efforts.

Elder LeGrand Richards in 1966. After serving as president of the Southern States Mission, he left each missionary with a copy of an proselyting outline entitled The Message of Mormonism. *This work gained popularity and was later expanded and renamed* A Marvelous Work and a Wonder. *(*Deseret News *photo)*

Several twentieth-century mission presidents compiled materials to help missionaries be more effective in their work. One early example was "On Tracting," (1928), in which Elder B. H. Roberts of the First Council of the Seventy, President of the Eastern States Mission, gave suggestions on contacting people at the door. Further instructions were given by Elder John A. Widtsoe of the Council of the Twelve, president of the European Mission, in "The Successful Missionary." The content of all these publications was incorporated into *The Missionary's Handbook*, which appeared in 1937.

Another publication released that same year was destined to have a long-lasting impact on Latter-day Saint missionary work. As LeGrand Richards, a future Presiding Bishop and member of the Council of the Twelve, concluded his presidency of the Southern States Mission, he left with each missionary a copy of *The Message of Mormonism*. This outline was prepared to assist the missionaries in their study and presentations of the gospel in a systematic and logical manner. In twenty-four weekly lessons President Richards showed how basic doctrines of the restored gospel were taught in the Bible but could not be understood fully without latter-day revelation. During the next several years many other missions adopted this plan. Repeated requests for copies eventually led Elder Richards to enlarge his material and to publish it in book form, under the title *A Marvelous Work and a Wonder*. This would become one of the

Significant developments in missionary training and proselyting methods, 1920–78

1920 1930 1940 1950

1925
Missionary home in Salt Lake City began providing instruction

1929
Tabernacle Choir inaugurated weekly network broadcast

1936
Shortwave radio beamed First Presidency's message to Europe

1937
Missionary Handbook and LeGrand Richards's proselyting outline published

1947
Richard L. Anderson developed improved proselyting methods in Northwestern States Mission

1952
First official proselyting outline published by the Church

most popular Latter-day Saint doctrinal works of the twentieth century.

Following the close of World War II the Church's full-time missionary force soared from an average of 477 in 1945 to 2,244 a year later. This meant that there were many new missionaries in the field who lacked experience and who could profit from some help and direction. Without question the most widely circulated postwar proselyting outline was that prepared by Richard L. Anderson, a young Elder who arrived in the Northwestern States Mission in the fall of 1946.

As a young missionary serving in the Northwestern States Mission during the later 1940s, Elder Richard L. Anderson pioneered improved proselyting methods. (Photo courtesy Richard L. Anderson)

Elder Anderson built on a teaching program he had worked out as a stake missionary while in the military service. Under this program, rather than merely handing out tracts at the door, missionaries would try to be invited inside the homes in order to present their message. Placing copies of the Book of Mormon was another important goal. Fifteen doctrinal discussions were arranged in a logical sequence to lead investigators to conversion. These discussions stressed a careful study of the scriptures and the bearing of testimony. Elder Anderson gained some key ideas from earlier successful missionaries. As these methods were adopted throughout the mission, the results were apparent. The number of converts per missionary climbed from 1.87 in 1946 to 5.72 in 1949. In this latter year, the Northwestern States Mission baptized 1,001 converts, thus becoming the first mission during the twentieth century to exceed one thousand baptisms during a single year.

The first proselyting plan published officially by the Church for use in all missions worldwide appeared in 1952. *A Systematic Program for Teaching the Gospel* condensed the missionaries' presentation into only six discussions. The plan's preface explained: "Experience has shown that it is not always necessary to take people through an extended series of lessons before they become converted to the Church. Agreement may be gained on . . . fundamental doctrines in a relatively short time through a logical presentation of gospel principles, fortified by scripture, together with reading, convincing testimony, and sincere prayer."[1]

In 1961 Church leaders convened the first worldwide seminar for mission presidents. Under the leadership of the General Authorities, the mission presidents pooled their experience in refining proselyting methods. The result was a new missionary plan, *A Uniform System for Teaching Investigators.* Using President David O. McKay's slogan of "Every Member a Missionary," emphasis was placed on the Saints' role in finding and fellowshipping potential

1960 — 1970 — 1980 — 1990

1961
Worldwide mission presidents seminar; missonary language training inaugurated at BYU

1964
Church pavilion opened at New York World's Fair

1978
All missionaries began receiving instruction at Missionary Training Center near BYU

57
urch Information
rvice established

converts. Church members were admonished to lead exemplary lives that would win the respect of others and open the way for gospel discussions. For some time the referral system, in which the Saints gave names of interested friends to the missionaries, had proved successful. Now the Saints were encouraged to invite nonmembers into their homes for "group meetings" to hear the missionaries' message. This method proved even more successful and had at least two important advantages. First, missionaries could use their time more efficiently. One mission president reported that in contrast to the tracting method, in which missionaries had spent 90 percent of their time searching for contacts and only 10 percent teaching, the cooperation of Church members enabled the missionaries to spend 90 percent of their time actually teaching the gospel and only 10 percent searching. Second, the same families who first introduced nonmembers to the missionaries could also fellowship these friends as they became converted to the gospel, helping them make the transition from one way of life to another and often from one circle of friends to another. Subsequent proselyting plans would build on the same principles developed during these decades.

Missionary Preparation

Following World War I, as young people came to Salt Lake City to be endowed in the temple and set apart as missionaries, President Heber J. Grant and his counselors recognized the need to provide a suitable place for them to stay, where the environment would be conducive to reading the scriptures and other appropriate learning activities. In 1924 the First Presidency approved a "Church Missionary Home and Preparatory Training School." Homes on State Street just north of the Beehive House were purchased, and the first group of missionaries entered March 4, 1925.

Before leaving for their respective fields, the missionaries spent a week at the Missionary Home receiving instructions on Church programs and points of doctrine, being trained in etiquette and other practical skills, and hearing messages of inspiration from General Authorities.[2] Over the years, other facilities have been provided, and the instructional program has been refined to provide the best possible orientation for outgoing missionaries.

Junius F. Wells is shown here addressing a group of missionaries. Beginning in 1925 the Salt Lake Missionary Home provided orientation for outgoing missionaries. (LDS Church Archives)

A further step in missionary preparation was taken in 1961. Elders and Sisters were experiencing lengthy delays in obtaining visas to enter Argentina and Mexico. A special language training program was set up for them at Brigham Young University to take advantage of this waiting period.

The aim was "to place a missionary in the field ready to speak the language," explained Ernest J. Wilkins, the program's first director.[3] The daily schedule was full of intensive instruction emphasizing conversation. The "Live Your Language" program encouraged the missionaries to speak only in the tongue they were learning.

In addition to language instruction, there was opportunity to practice the missionary discussions with native speakers posing as contacts. Furthermore, the elders and sisters adhered to standards of missionary dress and conduct, and so were able to develop proper habits and attitudes even before reaching the field.

Because of its success, the program was organized as a formal mission in 1963, and all going to Spanish- or Portuguese-speaking countries were first sent to BYU for training. In 1964 German was added to the program, and more than a dozen other languages have followed since.

The Language Training Mission (LTM) was expanded in 1969 to include instruction in Dutch and the Scandinavian languages at Ricks College, and training in the languages of the Pacific and Asia at the Church College of Hawaii. Four years later, however, Church leaders announced that all of these activities were to be consolidated at BYU and ground was broken for a $15-million complex near the Provo campus.

In 1967 these elders were assigned to open the missionary work in Venezuela. (Photo courtesy Stephen Edmunds)

Beginning in 1976 all missionaries called to non-English missions reported directly to the LTM rather than first receiving training at the Missionary Home in Salt Lake City. Then in 1978 all full-time missionaries began to receive their complete training at the Provo facility rather than in Salt Lake City. Those going to English-speaking missions received four weeks of training in missionary discussions and procedures. Those assigned to non–English-speaking missions continued to receive eight weeks of instruction in their language as well as in missionary matters. In 1978, the name Language Training Mission was changed to Missionary Training Center to reflect its broadened function.[4]

Architect's rendering of the Missionary Training Center in Provo, Utah. (Photo courtesy BYU Physical Plant Dept.)

Meanwhile, missionary orientation centers were established at scattered locations around the world. They served missionaries called from lands far removed from the United States. The first of these opened in São Paulo, Brazil, in 1977. With the opening of the temple there missionaries were able to receive the blessing and instructions of the endowment, and their orientation period was extended from three days to one week.

Public Relations

To supplement the personal contacts by proselyting missionaries, the Church employed a variety of other methods, including the mass media, to present its message to the world. Visitors' centers and broadcasting have played an important part in improving the public's understanding of the Church and its people during the twentieth century, especially in the latter half.

BUREAUS OF INFORMATION OR VISITORS' CENTERS

The Church's system of visitors' centers had its beginning at the dawning of the twentieth century with the opening of the "Bureau of Information" on Temple Square in 1902. As the volume of travel increased during the years following World War II, the annual number of visitors to Temple Square soared past the million mark. Only Yellowstone National Park attracted more visitors in the Intermountain West. During the 1960s and 1970s the Church built two new commodious structures on Temple Square, each equipped to effectively teach various facets of the gospel message and programs.

In the light of this success, the Church continued its program of opening visitors' centers at other historic sites. Likewise, because of the positive response to the Hill Cumorah Pageant, additional pageants at other locations were created to share the gospel with the public.

The restoration of the old Mormon city of Nauvoo began during the 1960s. This ambitious project was patterned after the very successful restoration of the colonial city of Williamsburg in Virginia. The objective was to depict interesting facets of Nauvoo life in the 1840s when it was one of the largest cities in the state of Illinois; but more important, the site would communicate the faith of the Saints who sacrificed to build the city only to leave it in the face of religious persecution.

The Church had also found opportunities to share the gospel message with the public at fairs and expositions. As had been the case with exhibits at several major fairs during the 1930s, the Church again enjoyed success during the New York World's Fair during 1964 and 1965. More than three million people visited the Mormon pavilion, a half-sized replica of the Salt Lake Temple's familiar triple-towered east facade. For the first time, the Church used a copy of Bertel Thorvaldsen's famous statue, *The Christus* to bear testimony of the Savior. A new BYU Motion Picture Studio film, entitled "Man's Search for Happiness," depicted the Latter-day Saint concept of life before, during, and following mortality. Experience gained at the New York fair enabled the Church to transform its bureaus of information, renamed "visitors' centers," into more effective tools for teaching the gospel. At Joseph Smith's birthplace in Vermont, for example, guides had formerly stressed details like the exact location of the family home relative to a nearby township boundary line. Now they emphasized Joseph Smith's prophetic calling in restoring the gospel of Jesus Christ.

RADIO AND TELEVISION

As radio broadcasting began to develop in the 1920s, the Church was quick to use this new medium as an aid in declaring the gospel message to the world. As early as 1922 President Heber J. Grant delivered a message by radio, and two years later sessions of general conference were broadcast. The weekly nationwide broadcasts of the Salt Lake Tabernacle Choir began in 1929. Richard L. Evans (not yet a General Authority) joined the program the following year; for over four decades his well-known "sermonettes" made many friends for the Church.[5] In addition to these activities in Salt Lake City, members and missionaries around the world prepared special programs for presentation on local stations.

As television was perfected during the years immediately following World War II, the Church did not delay in making use of this new means of communication. General conference sessions were carried by closed-circuit TV from the Tabernacle to other buildings on Temple Square as early as April 1948, and in October of the following year the conference was broadcast by television for the first time. Television coverage of conference was extended to California by the late 1950s, and in 1962 sessions were carried from coast to coast for the first time. The Church paid the cost of getting the conference broadcast to the local stations, many of which in turn donated air time as a public service. Because of these innovations speakers at general conference had to prepare addresses not only for the congregation of a few thousand in the Tabernacle, but rather for a potential audience of many millions.

Beginning in 1952 the general priesthood session of conference was transmitted by closed-circuit direct-wire audio to an increasing number of selected stake centers and other Church buildings. Soon, well over a thousand separate groups of priesthood bearers throughout the United States and Canada as well as in Australia, New Zealand, and several other countries could simultaneously participate in this meeting.

Church leaders early on became interested in international broadcasting. At the April 1936 general conference, the three members of the First Presidency beamed a message to Europe via shortwave radio. In 1962 international conference broadcasts were inaugurated, in English to Europe and Africa and in Spanish to Latin America. Later, however, emphasis would shift to providing general conference and other Church programs for broadcast on standard local radio stations around the world. The perfection of communications satellites during the 1970s made it possible to relay radio or television programs to distant points on the earth for local broadcast. By 1980, the Church was equipping selected stake centers with their own satellite-receiving antennas, making it possible for the Saints

The Church's half-sized replica of the east facade of the Salt Lake Temple was a popular exhibit at the New York World's Fair in 1964–65. More than three million people visited the Mormon pavilion. (Deseret News *photo*)

gathered there to see and hear conference proceedings and other broadcasts from Church headquarters.

Over the years, the Church developed various materials to be used by the media. Beginning in 1935, the Radio, Publicity, and Mission Literature Committee distributed radio programs, filmstrips, and literature needed both in and out of the Church. Similarly, the Church Information Service, created in 1957, maintained a photo library, coordinated publicity for special events such as conferences or temple dedications, prepared feature articles on Church activities that interested the public most about Mormons, and provided posters, displays, and other help for local open houses.

A hosting service was also created to entertain important visitors to Church headquarters, including government or business officials, heads of other churches, artists, and entertainers. These groups were taken to such points of interest as Temple Square and Welfare Square. These visitors often appreciated being entertained in individual Latter-day Saint homes as well as attending Church services in local wards.[6]

By 1980, many stake centers were equipped with satellite dishes for receiving broadcasts from Church headquarters. (Photo courtesy Don Thorpe)

The Church's Popular Image

As has been seen, the public's attitude about the Church, its programs, and its members, has exerted a powerful influence on the course of Latter-day Saint history. Popular misunderstandings during the Church's early decades led to intense persecution and suffering. During the second half of the nineteenth century, the relative isolation of the Latter-day Saints in the Rocky Mountains made misunderstanding and misrepresentation even more likely. Articles published in nationally circulated periodicals reflected this predominantly negative image during this period. Joseph Smith was portrayed as an ignorant farm boy, and the religion he founded was branded as an "imposture." Of all Latter-day Saint doctrine and practices, plural marriage was the most widely condemned in the press. Furthermore, nationalistic writers regarded Mormon convert immigrants as "ignorant foreigners," and described what they called the ecclesiastical "hierarchy" as a "menace" to the rest of the country.

Following President Wilford Woodruff's 1890 Manifesto, which officially announced the suspension of plural marriage, Mormonism cooled as a controversial issue. The periodical press began to recognize in the Mormon people some of the virtues then being advocated by the American populist movement—industry, thrift, temperance, self-reliance, and so forth. Significantly, it was during this decade that Utah finally became a state.

However, during the Progressive Era, the agitation surrounding the elections of Elders B. H. Roberts and Reed Smoot to the United States Congress reversed these good feelings and sparked a revival of earlier anti-Mormon sentiments in the national press.

After Reed Smoot was finally given his Senate seat in 1907, Mormonism again declined as a controversial issue. With the coming of World War I, the American public tended to forget old charges. The Mormon Church and people amply demonstrated their loyalty during the war crisis. In the following decade Latter-day Saints began moving away from the traditional centers of Mormon population, seeking greater economic opportunities. As the Saints thus entered the mainstream of American life, the

The Mormon Tabernacle Choir on the Ed Sullivan Show *in 1958. The well-respected choir did much to increase public interest in the Church.* (Deseret News *photo)*

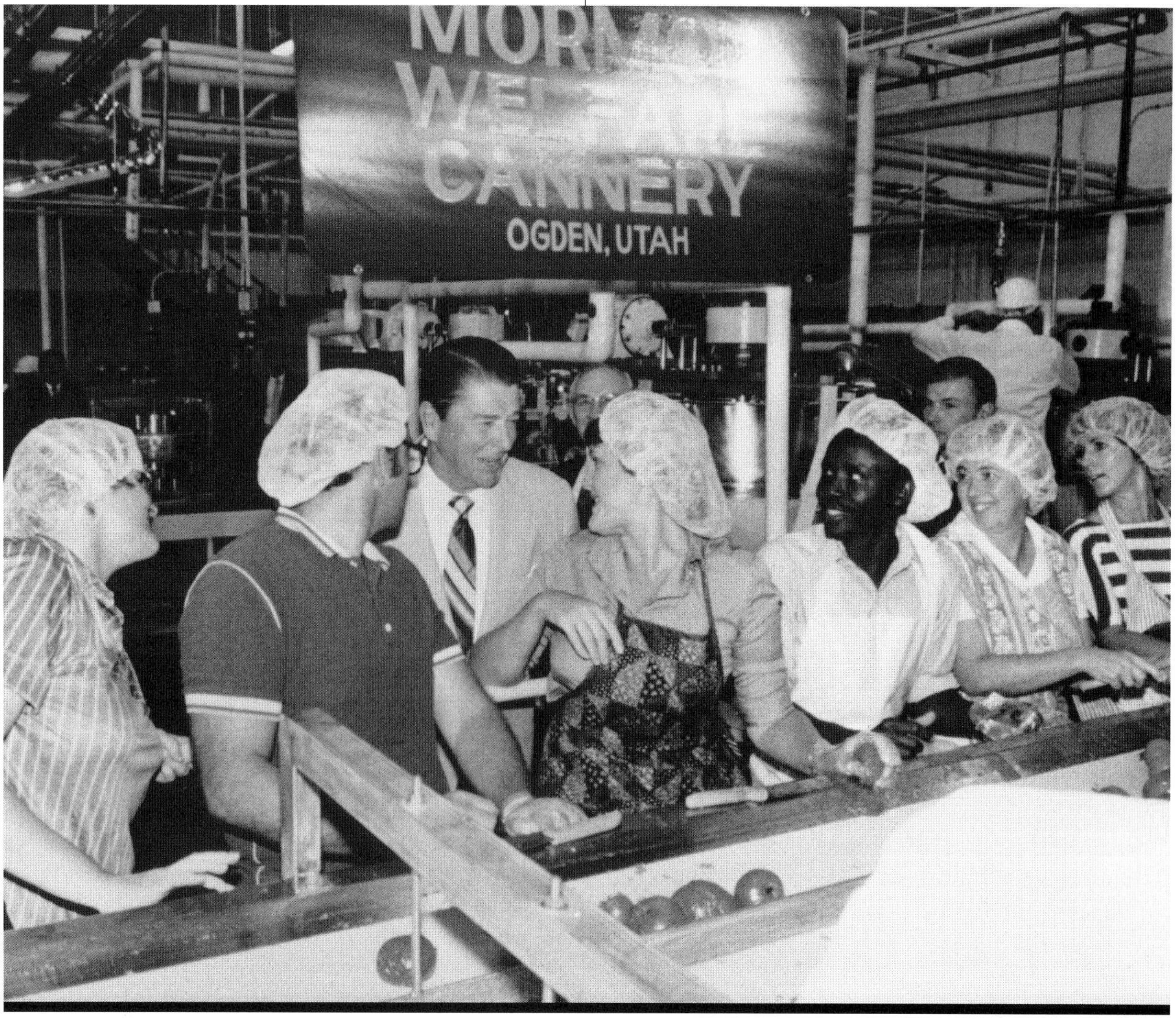

U.S. president Ronald Reagan at the Ogden Area Welfare Service Center in 1982. Since its inception, the welfare program has received much acclaim from national press as well as civic leaders. (LDS Church Archives)

nation began to exhibit a more sympathetic understanding.

During the 1930s, two new features were seen in the popular image which have been characteristic ever since. First, the Church's image became predominantly positive. Second, there was more media interest in the Church social programs than in its theology. This change reflected America's growing interest in the "social gospel."

In 1936 the successes of the welfare program attracted widespread admiration. During the next two years the titles of four-fifths of all magazine articles treating Mormonism made specific reference to this new Church security program. Observers praised the Church for taking positive steps to satisfy the temporal as well as the spiritual needs of its members. This praise was especially pronounced when Mormon welfare assistance was the most prompt and effective relief at the time of several major disasters. Magazine articles also reflected an interest in other Church programs, especially its cultural and recreational activities and its excellent program for the youth.

During the second half of the twentieth century, more and more Latter-day Saints were achieving prominence in government service, in professional circles, and in a variety of other fields. These individuals had a very positive influence on the public's attitude. While praising them for their achievements, the press almost always explicitly identified them as Mormons. The virtues of their religion were often described as contributing to their personal success. For example, articles about golfer Johnny Miller or the Osmond family often discussed the Word of Wisdom as well as the gospel's emphasis on family solidarity.

There were at least two negative themes in the press's treatment of Mormonism during this time—the Church's position on women's issues and its practice of not granting the priesthood to blacks. During the emphasis on civil rights in the 1960s, there were related violent demonstrations against BYU athletic teams. Nevertheless, the popular attitude continued to be largely positive. Significantly, a large number of converts first became interested in the restored gospel because of favorable publicity about the Tabernacle Choir, prominent Latter-day Saints, or Church programs. Along with the key roles being played by the Church public relations organization and proselyting missionaries, the examples set by individual Latter-day Saints everywhere must be acknowledged as one of the most important factors in bringing others to a knowledge of the gospel of Jesus Christ.

Priesthood Correlation and Emphasis on the Family

During the era of rapid international growth following World War II, the General Authorities felt an urgent need to assure that Church programs were effectively fulfilling their mission to perfect the Saints (see Ephesians 4:11–12). Because each organization planned its own program and was anxious to do all possible to bless those it served, some unnecessary duplication of activities inevitably resulted. At the same time, other key areas were not receiving enough emphasis. For this reason Church leaders during the twentieth century repeatedly gave attention to these concerns and made adjustments in Church activities and programs as needed.

Correlation Principles Defined

The most thorough of these correlation efforts began in 1960 when the First Presidency directed the Priesthood Committee of the Twelve under Elder Harold B. Lee to conduct "an exhaustive, prayerful study" of all programs in the light of the Church's ultimate objectives, "so that the Church might reap the maximum harvest" from the devotion and knowledge of members serving in the various organizations.[1]

Elder Lee and his committee recognized that more was needed than simply ensuring that all gospel topics were being treated adequately in the Church's curriculum. They realized that an organization was needed at Church headquarters to bring about the desired correlation of programs and activities.

The Church correlation efforts begun in the early 1960s brought a renewed emphasis on the centrality of the family in the gospel plan.

Elder Lee announced the results of the study at the fall general conference in 1961 and stressed basic principles that would guide what came to be known as "Priesthood Correlation." He cited Paul's comparison of the Church to a perfectly functioning body (see 1 Corinthians 12:14–28). He then explained that a similar passage in latter-day scripture had served as the text for his committee's work: "Let every man stand in his own office, and labor in his own calling; and let not the head say unto the feet it hath no need of the feet; for without the feet how shall the body be able to stand? Also the body hath need of every member, that all may be edified together, that the system may be kept perfect" (D&C 84:109–10).

Elder Harold B. Lee. (LDS Church Archives)

Elder Lee concluded that "each organization was to have its specific function, and it was not to usurp the field of the other, which would be like the eye saying to the hand, 'I have no need of thee.'" In this way the Church would "perform as a perfectly organized human body, with every member functioning as it was intended."

Elder Lee cited another fundamental principle which the First Presidency had set forth in connection with the 1940 correlation effort: "The home was the basis of a righteous life and . . . no other instrumentality can take its place nor fulfil its essential functions and . . . the utmost the auxiliaries can do is to aid the home in its problems, giving special aid and succor where such is necessary."[2]

Thus, as Elder Lee later defined it: "Correlation means merely to place the priesthood of God where the Lord said it was to be—as the center and core of the Church and kingdom of God—and to see that the Latter-day Saint homes also have their place in the divine plan of saving souls."[3]

Elder Lee announced that the First Presidency and Quorum of the Twelve wanted "more co-ordination and correlation" among the activities of the priesthood, auxiliaries, and educational system which should result in a "consolidation and simplification" of curricula, publications, meetings, and even buildings.[4] This would be accomplished step by step in coming decades.

Plan and Organization for Correlation

As he made his announcement, Elder Lee explained, "The function of the all-Church coordinating council is to formulate policy which will govern the planning, the writing, co-ordination, and implementation of the entire Church curriculum." This group included four members of the Twelve plus the executives of the auxiliaries and other Church organizations.

Three age-group committees, representing children, youth, and adults, were to "plan, provide,

Significant events in priesthood correlation, 1960–80

1960
First Presidency directed Priesthood Committee to make exhaustive study of all Church courses and activities

1961
Announcement of organization to plan and prepare programs for children, youth, and adults under direction of the priesthood

1962
Curriculum for children, youths and adults outlined

1963
Priesthood committees established to give direction to home teaching, missionary, genealogical, and welfare activities

1964
Above four functions placed under local priesthood quorum leaders; home teaching implemented; ward priesthood executive committees and correlation councils formed

1965
Family home evening manuals published; priesthood and auxiliary lessons specifically designed to strengthen parents

1967
Unified dates established for starting church programs and age groupings standardized

197
Aaronic Priesthoo and YMMIA leadershi consolidate

write, and co-ordinate curricula and activities" for their respective age groups.[5]

Were the Church compared to a perfectly functioning human body, suggested Elder Gordon B. Hinckley, these correlation committees "might be likened to the nervous system whose responsibility is to keep the various aspects of the great teaching program of the Church operating harmoniously together."[6]

Elder Lee explained that the auxiliary organizations would continue to implement the programs but that they would now be developed by the correlation committees, thus eliminating unnecessary duplication.[7]

In April 1963, four committees were added to this organization with the mission of giving leadership to four key priesthood programs: home teaching and home evening, genealogy and temple work, missionary work, and welfare.

Specific aspects of this organizational structure changed from time to time, but the principles remained the same. During the early 1970s, for example, the responsibility for developing instructional materials for all age groups was assigned to a single Curriculum Department. In 1975 Correlation became a distinct department with major responsibilities of reviewing all written materials for doctrinal accuracy and of evaluating the effectiveness of Church programs and activities. The Correlation Department thus exercised a type of judicial function, seeing that the policies and programs approved by the First Presidency and the Twelve were being carried out as intended for the maximum benefit of the Saints.

Correlation at the Local Level

Although significant strides had been taken in coordinating the planning of programs at the all-Church level, more still needed to be done at the ward and stake levels in implementing these activities. Teachers in one organization often did not have the occasion to coordinate lessons and activities with those teaching the same age group in other organizations. In fact, the age groupings in some cases varied from one organization to another.

To implement the desired correlation, a priesthood executive committee and a ward correlation council were established at the ward level in 1964. The priesthood executive committee consisted of the bishopric and priesthood quorum leaders; their weekly meeting enabled them to give correlated direction to all ward activities. The monthly ward council meeting included the above leaders plus auxiliary and other organization executives; here they could correlate schedules and activities and, most important of all, discuss how the ward's programs could best meet the specific needs of individual members or families. Similar organizations were implemented at the stake level three years later.

A key step in implementing priesthood correlation at the local level was the beginning of home teaching in 1964. Prior to this time, several Church organizations were involved in contacting families in their homes. Under the direct supervision of the

1980

971
ll magazines for adults, youth,
nd children, respectively, merged
nder the priesthood; responsibility
r producing all instructional
aterials consolidated into
ngle department

1974
Seventies quorums' and stake missions' leadership combined

1975
Separate Correlation Department responsible for reviewing and evaluating curriculum and activities

1980
Ward meetings consolidated

bishopric, "ward teachers" had been assigned to visit ward families, each month presenting a message published for use throughout the Church. Melchizedek Priesthood quorums were likewise responsible for making regular contacts with their members. A given family might also receive visits from auxiliary teachers interested in enlisting family members in their respective activities. All these contacts were now consolidated or at least coordinated through the home teachers. Home teaching thus provided a channel for two-way communication between the home and the priesthood and ward leaders, making the various programs and activities of the Church available to the family.[8]

A 1964 handbook described this "pipeline" of presiding authority, emphasizing, "All priesthood activities should properly recognize and be funneled through this line of authority," and that auxiliaries and others, when "not officially in this line of authority, should . . . sustain priesthood and Church activity."[9]

Strengthening the Family

Emphasis on the home and family was a major feature in the teachings and leadership of President David O. McKay. "No other success can compensate for failure in the home," he declared. "The poorest shack in which love prevails over a united family is of greater value to God and future humanity than any other riches. In such a home God can work miracles and will work miracles."[10] As the priesthood correlation program unfolded, Church leaders focused on the home as the most effective place for teaching and applying gospel principles. Strong homes, they believed, would provide the surest defense against the temptations of modern life. In the face of these increasing challenges, the General Authorities took steps to strengthen the family in its vital role.

TEACHING THE GOSPEL IN THE HOME

The scriptures in all ages have affirmed that parents have the primary responsibility to teach their

Priesthood Line of Authority

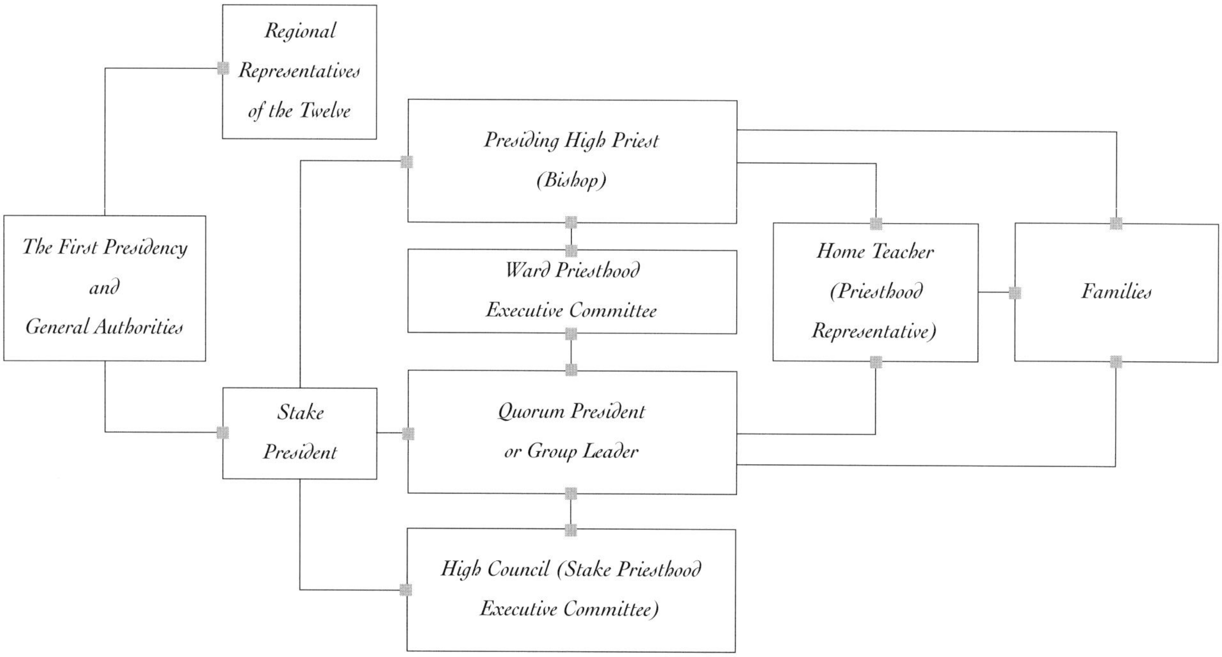

children. An Old Testament proverb admonished: "Train up a child in the way he should go: and when he is old, he will not depart from it" (Proverbs 22:6). In his great concluding discourse, King Benjamin counseled the Nephites that those who were truly converted would not permit their children to "transgress the laws of God, and fight and quarrel one with another, and serve the devil," but rather they would "teach them to walk in the ways of truth and soberness . . . [and] to love one another, and to serve one another" (Mosiah 4:14–15). Latter-day revelations have commanded parents to bring up their children "in light and truth" (D&C 93:40) and to teach them "to pray, and to walk uprightly before the Lord" (D&C 68:28) warning that if they fail to do so, "the sin [will] be on the heads of the parents" (D&C 68:25). Twentieth-century prophets have echoed this same message. For example, President Heber J. Grant cautioned: "I have heard men and women say that they were going to let their sons and daughters grow to maturity before they sought to teach them the principles of the gospel, that they were not going to cram the gospel down them in their childhood, before they were able to comprehend it. . . . I may know that the gospel is true, and so may my wife; but I want to tell you that our children will not know that the gospel is true, unless they study it and gain a testimony for themselves. Parents are deceiving themselves in imagining that their children will be born with a knowledge of the gospel."[11]

President David O. McKay further explained that "the character of the child is formed largely during the first twelve years of his life. It is estimated that in that period the child spends sixteen times as many waking hours in the home as in school and more than a hundred times as many hours in the home as in the Church." He concluded, "Every child is, to a great degree, what he is because of the ever constant influence of home environment and the careful or neglectful training of parents."[12]

Later, President Harold B. Lee would admonish: "Keep your home ties strong. . . . As I have repeated it many times . . . 'the greatest of the Lord's work you brethren will ever do as fathers will be within the walls of your own home.' "[13]

Latter-day prophets have also promised divine assistance to parents who faithfully accept this sacred obligation. President Wilford Woodruff declared: "Our children should not be neglected; they should receive a proper education in both spiritual and temporal things. That is the best legacy any parents can leave to their children. We should teach them to pray, and instil into their minds while young every correct principle. Ninety-nine out of every hundred children who are taught by their parents the principles of honesty and integrity, truth and virtue, will observe them through life."[14]

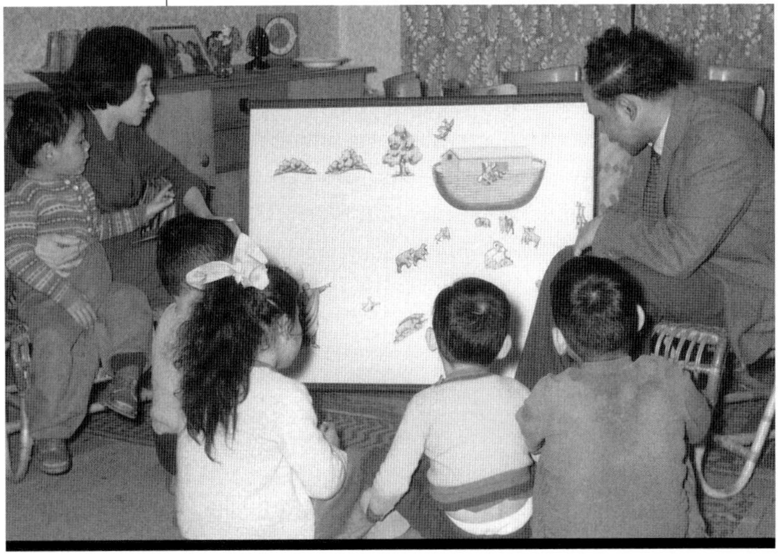

The children of the Horstmanhoff family in Delft, Holland, enjoy a flannelboard story during a family home evening. (LDS Church Archives)

President Joseph F. Smith likewise promised: "Not one child in a hundred would go astray, if the home environment, example and training, were in harmony with the truth in the gospel of Christ, as revealed and taught to the Latter-day Saints."[15]

FAMILY HOME EVENING

Although the Church's family home evening program flowered during the 1960s, its seeds were planted much earlier. Frequently cited was the First Presidency's 1915 admonition that parents conduct a weekly "Home Evening" to teach the gospel to their children and become more familiar with family needs. Especially meaningful were the promises that the First Presidency had made at the conclusion of that message: "If the Saints obey this counsel, we promise that great blessings will result. Love at home and obedience to parents will increase. Faith will be developed in the hearts of the youth of Israel, and they will gain power to combat the evil influence and temptations which beset them."[16]

For the next fifty years, home evenings were promoted primarily by local Church leaders and to some extent by the auxiliaries. From time to time the General Authorities reminded the Saints of their responsibility and blessing in conducting these family gatherings. In 1936 the First Presidency commended these local activities: "In this day when socials, parties, dinners, business interests, etc., all tend to lead away from home associations," the Presidency declared, "the adoption of a Home Evening is highly advisable."[17] Then, in the midst of the strains on family life which accompanied the close of World War II, Church leaders launched another effort to revive family home evening. In a 1946 circular letter, the Quorum of the Twelve reviewed previous home evening programs beginning with the First Presidency's 1915 instructions and then announced the appointment of a special committee composed of General Authorities and auxiliary representatives to plan home-centered activities. Ward teachers taught families the importance of regular gatherings. The Sunday School demonstrated how this could be done. Through the *Children's Friend* the Primary offered suggestions every month. The Relief Society published a pamphlet entitled "The Family Hour," which was distributed by visiting teachers. It was not until 1965, however, that the Church launched an ongoing promotion of family home evening, including the publication of lesson manuals distributed to every family.

Elder Harold B. Lee announced this new emphasis at the general conference in October 1964 and declared that the following year would see "some definite steps taken to strengthen the hands of the parents in carrying out these great God-given admonitions in placing stress upon the teaching of the gospel in the home."[18] The first step was to provide a manual containing weekly lessons to be taught in the home. Throughout the year, the various Church organizations published suggestions for home activities. The Relief Society provided specific help for mothers, and the priesthood quorums provided training for fathers. All was correlated into a single effort entitled "Teaching and Living the Gospel in the Home." Elder Lee testified that this new program had come as a result of inspiration given through President David O. McKay: "My mind has been filled with the realization that in 1964 and the year just preceding, we have been receiving as pertinent and important divine direction as has ever been given to the Church in any similar period in its history."[19] He then concluded: "I say to you Latter-day Saint mothers and fathers, if you will rise to the responsibility of teaching your children in the home, . . . the day will soon be dawning when the whole world will come to our doors and will say, 'Show us your way that we may walk in your path.' "[20] (See Micah 4:1–2.)

In the preface to the first family home evening manual, President David O. McKay declared that "the problems of these difficult times cannot better be solved in any other place, by any other agency, by any other means, than by love and righteousness, and precept and example, and devotion to duty in the home."[21]

A later manual contained this promise: "Families who prayerfully prepare and constantly hold their weekly Home Evenings, and who work together during the week to apply the lessons in their lives, will be blessed. There will be better feelings between husband and wife, between parents and children, and among children. In such homes the Spirit of the Lord will be made manifest."[22]

Encouraged by such promises, Latter-day Saint parents around the world took steps to teach their children. Whether the family home evenings were taking place in a New York City apartment, a Navajo hogan, or a Polynesian thatched house, certain common elements were usually present: Family members took turns in conducting the program, offering prayers, leading the singing, and presenting the lesson. Families often combined these elements of their home evenings with special recreational activities and almost always with refreshments. In 1971 Church leaders announced that Monday evening was being designated as the time for these family gatherings and that no other Church activities were to be scheduled on that night.[23]

FAMILY-RELATED CURRENT ISSUES

The revival of family home evening coincided with and helped defend against a general disintegration of many traditional social institutions and values and a growing disregard for moral standards. These trends were in marked contrast to the Latter-day Saints' continuing emphasis on the sanctity of the home and of family relationships.

In 1966 the First Presidency lamented the growing flood of pornography, stating that "its detrimental effect upon standards of morality is becoming so serious that all thoughtful people must unite to combat it. . . . We are unalterably opposed to sexual immorality and to all manner of obscenity. We proclaim in the strongest terms possible against the evil and wicked designs of men who would betray virtuous manhood and womanhood, enticing them to thoughts and actions leading to vice, the lowering of standards of clean living, and the breaking up of the home."

The First Presidency therefore called on government officials "to do all in their power to curb this pernicious evil" and called on the Latter-day Saints and others "to join in a concerted movement to fight pornography wherever it may be found."[24]

In many areas Church members responded by mounting campaigns to protest indecency or other forms of pornography in their communities. Some picketed theaters which were showing pornographic motion pictures, while others gathered signatures on petitions requiring higher moral standards for material shown on television.

The growing number of divorces was another concern to Church leaders. In the United States during 1925, there were 1.5 divorces per thousand people annually. By 1965 the divorce rate had risen to 2.5; during the next decade it almost doubled, rising to 4.9 in 1975, and it has continued to climb. The growing number of divorces was even a source of concern in predominantly Latter-day Saint areas. In Salt Lake County, for example, half as many divorces as marriages were being recorded. It was in this setting that President David O. McKay spoke out against this family-destroying trend. In the April 1969 general conference he declared: "Christ's ideal pertaining to marriage is the unbroken home, and conditions that cause divorce are violations of his divine teachings. Except in cases of infidelity or other extreme conditions, the Church frowns upon divorce. . . . A man who has entered into sacred covenants in the house of the Lord to remain true to the marriage vow is a traitor to that covenant if he separates himself from his wife and family just because he has permitted himself to become infatuated with a pretty face and comely form of some young girl who flattered him with a smile."[25]

Birth control was yet another issue. By the 1960s a variety of contraceptive devices and especially the "pill" were gaining popularity. These were used by both unmarried and married couples to avoid unwanted pregnancies. Thus the use of contraceptive devices not only encouraged sexual immorality but also threatened one of the basic functions of the family. During the two decades between 1955 and 1975, the annual number of births per thousand in the United States dropped from twenty-five to only fifteen. In 1969 the First Presidency wrote: "We seriously regret that there should exist a sentiment or feeling among any members of the Church to curtail the birth of their children. We have been commanded to multiply and replenish the earth that we may have joy and rejoicing in our posterity. . . . However," the Presidency counseled, "men must be considerate of their wives who bear the greater responsibility not only of bearing children, but of caring for them." In making these decisions, "Married couples should seek inspiration and wisdom from the Lord."[26]

Some Further Accomplishments of Priesthood Correlation

During the later 1960s the General Authorities continued the process of refining, correlating, and even consolidating Church activities. These later developments built on the foundations of priesthood correlation laid in the earlier years of that decade.

First issue of the Ensign, *1971.*
(Photo courtesy LDS Church)

An important improvement came in 1967 with the adoption of a uniform Church year. Previously, some organizations had commenced their lesson work at the beginning of the local school year, while others operated on a calendar year basis. Now all priesthood and auxiliary organizations would begin and finish their courses of instruction at the same time. Furthermore, the age groupings were standardized from one organization to another. All this facilitated more cooperation among those serving a given group of members and a greater coordination of curriculum materials and of the Church's programs in general.

First issue of the New Era, *1971.*
(Photo courtesy LDS Church)

Other refinements brought together similar activities formerly conducted by separate organizations. In many wards, for example, each auxiliary had maintained its own collection of teaching aids. Beginning in 1967 a single "meetinghouse library" was established to serve all Church organizations meeting in that particular building. Over the years several of the auxiliaries had developed teacher-training programs to enhance this most vital aspect of their work. Beginning in 1970, one teacher development director was called in each ward to coordinate these efforts. This director was responsible for teaching a basic course in instructional methodology as often as necessary to meet the needs of new and existing teachers in all Church organizations. Each organization then presented follow-up "in-service" instruction tailored to its specific programs and needs as part of its regular ward and stake leadership or preparation meetings.

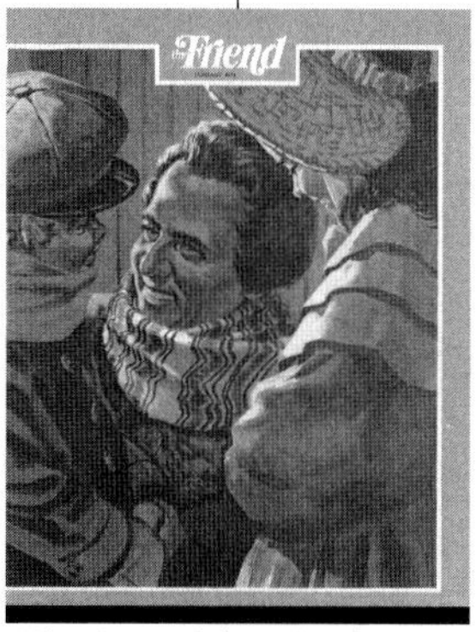

First issue of the Friend, *1971.*
(Photo courtesy LDS Church)

The various auxiliary organizations published their own magazines throughout most of the twentieth century. Beginning in 1971, however, three new magazines—the *Friend* for children, the *New Era* for youth, and the *Ensign* for adults—were published under the direct supervision of the General Authorities. Material in these magazines supported all Church programs serving their respective age groups. At the ward level, this eliminated the need for several persons to represent the different Church publications; a single magazine director now was called to promote the regular use of all three Church magazines.

The Church's program for the youth underwent both expansion and restructuring. As part of the increased emphasis on missionary work during the early 1960s, "youth missionary committees" had been created in many parts of the Church. These committees brought young people together to motivate and coordinate their efforts in sharing the gospel with their peers. Many ward bishops recognized in these gatherings a golden opportunity to enlist the youth themselves in planning and promoting the Church's youth programs. General Church leaders also recognized the value of involving the youth, and in 1967 they directed that these "bishop's youth councils" meet monthly in each ward.[27] A major reorganization came when the formerly separate Aaronic Priesthood and the Young Men's Mutual Improvement Association programs were merged in 1970. Rather than have one group of leaders teach the boys during priesthood meetings and another group conduct weeknight activities for them, the quorum advisers became the ward Young Men's presidency, responsible for both instruction and activity. The number of women required to staff the Young Women's program was similarly reduced. From their beginnings in the nineteenth century, the Young Men's and Young Women's Mutual Improvement Associations had conducted educational, cultural, social, and recreational programs for all Church members twelve years of age and above. A major redefinition came in 1974 when Church leaders transferred responsibility for adult programs to Melchizedek Priesthood quorums and the Relief Society. This left Young Men and Young Women leaders free to concentrate on the unique needs of the youth.[28]

All these adjustments helped define responsibilities, eliminate unnecessary duplication, and assure that Church programs were blessing the Saints as individuals and families. Elder Thomas S. Monson regarded priesthood correlation as the Lord's inspired battle plan:

We can take strength from the example of Gideon. You will remember how Gideon and his army faced the overwhelming strength of forces vastly superior in equipment and in number. . . . The outcome of that mighty battle is recorded in one short sentence: "And they stood every man in his place . . ." (Judges 7:21), and the victory was won.

Today, we are encamped against the greatest array of sin, vice, and evil ever assembled before our eyes. Such formidable enemies may cause lesser hearts to shrink or shun the fight. But the battle plan whereby we fight to save the souls of men is not our own. It was provided to our leader, even President David O. McKay, by the inspiration and revelation of the Lord. Yes, I speak of that plan which will bring us victory, even the Correlation Program of the Church. And as we do battle against him who would thwart the purposes of God and degrade and destroy mankind, I pray that each of us will stand in his or her appointed place, that the battle for the souls of men will indeed be won.[29]

Joseph Fielding Smith, Harold B. Lee, and the Early 1970s

The brief administrations of Joseph Fielding Smith and Harold B. Lee as Presidents of the Church during the early 1970s represented in each case the capstone of long and significant service to the Church. Each set a record for presiding for a shorter period than any of his predecessors—Joseph Fielding Smith serving as President of the Church for two and a half years, and Harold B. Lee for only a year and a half. They are considered together in this chapter, not just because their administrations were so brief, but because most of the significant developments of this period can be attributed to the leadership of both these men. These years saw not only a continuation of the key developments of earlier decades, but also witnessed the defining of policies and new patterns of activity that would become increasingly important in later years.

Two Latter-day Prophets

JOSEPH FIELDING SMITH

The son of the sixth President of the Church, Joseph Fielding Smith was born in Salt Lake City in 1876, just one year before the death of President Brigham Young. While other boys occupied their time hunting, fishing, or playing ball, young Joseph Fielding was more interested in reading. He had read the Book of Mormon twice before he reached ten years of age. He often carried a pocket edition of the New Testament which

President Joseph Fielding Smith (center) and his counselors, Harold B. Lee (left) and N. Eldon Tanner. (Deseret News *photo)*

he could read in every available spare minute, and he began early to commit favorite scriptural passages to memory. Many years later he concluded that he had "received more pleasure and greater satisfaction out of the study of the scriptures, and reading of the Lord Jesus Christ, and of the Prophet Joseph Smith, and the work that has been accomplished for the salvation of men, than from anything else in all the world."[1] Joseph Fielding Smith inherited these interests from his father, after whom he was named. (To avoid confusion, the father is generally referred to as Joseph F. Smith and the son as Joseph Fielding Smith.) Only four years after Joseph Fielding was born, his father was called as a counselor to President John Taylor. Joseph F. Smith had personally experienced the exodus from Nauvoo following his father Hyrum's martyrdom and had participated in the colonization of the Great Basin; he passed on to his son a keen interest in the history of the Church. Joseph F. Smith was also a clear and powerful expounder of gospel doctrines, a quality for which his son would also be known. Young Joseph Fielding Smith found in his father's library many of the volumes from which he learned so much.

Apostle Joseph Fielding Smith and his father, President Joseph F. Smith, in 1914. (LDS Church Archives)

When Joseph Fielding was twenty years old, he received a patriarchal blessing from his uncle, John Smith, the Patriarch to the Church and the half brother of his father. This blessing foreshadowed key activities and qualities of Joseph Fielding Smith's later life: "It is thy privilege to live to a good old age and the will of the Lord that you should become a mighty man in Israel. . . . It shall be thy duty to sit in counsel with thy brethren and to preside among the people. It shall be thy duty also to travel much at home and abroad, by land and water, laboring in the ministry, and I say unto thee, hold up thy head, lift up thy voice without fear or favor as the Spirit of the Lord shall direct."[2]

In 1899 Joseph Fielding Smith commenced a two-year mission to England. Upon his return he served as a home missionary, as a member of his stake high council, and as a member of the Young Men's Mutual Improvement Association general board. He accepted employment as a clerk in the Church historian's office, where he would make a substantial contribution during succeeding decades.

In 1910 he was ordained an Apostle by his father, President Joseph F. Smith. In that same year he became secretary of the Genealogical Society of Utah, serving in various administrative capacities and eventually as president of that organization until 1963. He launched the *Utah Genealogical and*

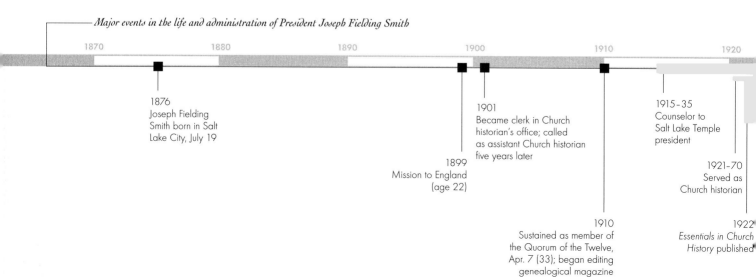

Major events in the life and administration of President Joseph Fielding Smith

1870 · 1880 · 1890 · 1900 · 1910 · 1920

1876
Joseph Fielding Smith born in Salt Lake City, July 19

1899
Mission to England (age 22)

1901
Became clerk in Church historian's office; called as assistant Church historian five years later

1910
Sustained as member of the Quorum of the Twelve, Apr. 7 (33); began editing genealogical magazine

1915–35
Counselor to Salt Lake Temple president

1921–70
Served as Church historian

1922
Essentials in Church History published

President Joseph Fielding Smith's doctrinal and historical writings constitute a significant part of his legacy to the Church. (Copyright Intellectual Reserve, all rights reserved)

Historical Magazine, helped direct the formation of the Temple Records Index Bureau and the creation of the family group sheets that were used widely throughout the Church for many years, and directed the inauguration of the society's widespread microfilming program. During much of this time he also served in the presidency of the Salt Lake Temple. Family history and temple work were major themes in his sermons and writings.

Elder Smith was sustained as Church historian and recorder in 1921, a position in which he would serve until he was sustained as President of the Church a half century later. Under his direction, report forms were standardized, countless ward and stake histories were collected and cataloged, and other significant steps were taken to preserve the history of the Church. Soon after becoming Church historian, he published *Essentials in Church History*, which would be the most widely read, single-volume LDS history for many years to come. This work reflected his philosophy that history should record virtuous events and at the same time help us profit from the mistakes of the past. Nevertheless, he believed history must be accurate.[3]

Despite his many pressing ecclesiastical duties, Elder Joseph Fielding Smith was a prolific author. In *The Way to Perfection*, published in 1931, he placed human history in the context of scriptural doctrines, emphasizing developments in early dispensations as well as prophesied latter-day events. An especially significant and widely cited volume which he compiled was *Teachings of the Prophet Joseph Smith*. First published in 1938, it contained chronologically arranged extracts from doctrinal sermons and writings of the Church's founder. Elder Smith's own teachings were compiled and published in the three-volume set, *Doctrines of Salvation*, from 1954 to 1956. In all, Joseph Fielding Smith's writings filled twenty-five volumes.

These writings and sermons often cast him in the role as a defender of the faith against false notions, a role foreseen in his patriarchal blessing. To him, a proper understanding of the scriptures was essential. As he forcefully expounded revealed gospel truths, he gained a public reputation of being stern and unyielding. Those who were close to him, especially his family, saw a different side of his personality. After

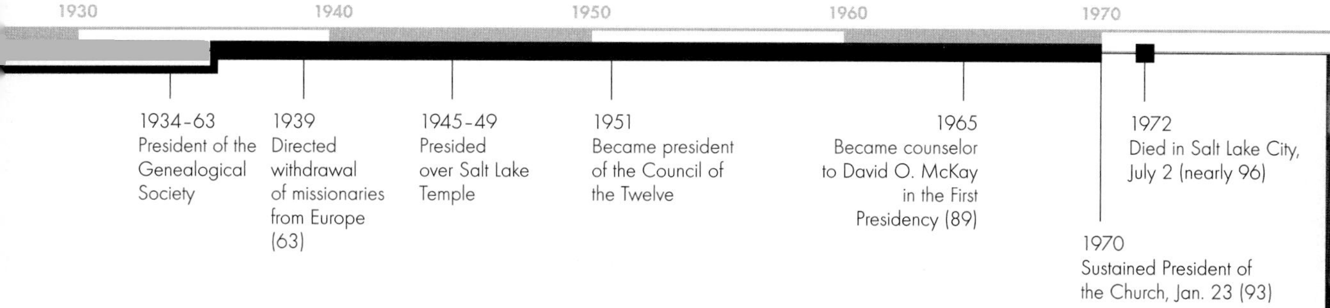
1930
1940
1950
1960
1970
1980
1934–63 President of the Genealogical Society
1939 Directed withdrawal of missionaries from Europe (63)
1945–49 Presided over Salt Lake Temple
1951 Became president of the Council of the Twelve
1965 Became counselor to David O. McKay in the First Presidency (89)
1970 Sustained President of the Church, Jan. 23 (93)
1972 Died in Salt Lake City, July 2 (nearly 96)

President Joseph Fielding Smith, tenth President of the Church. (LDS Church Archives)

President Joseph Fielding Smith and a young friend, circa 1970. A great scholar and defender of the faith, President Smith also had an intimate side, which included a love for children. (LDS Church Archives)

twenty-four years of marriage, his wife Ethel said: "I have often thought when he is gone people will say, 'He is a very good man, sincere, orthodox, etc.' They will speak of him as the public knows him; but the man they have in mind is very different from the man I know. The man I know is a kind, loving husband and father whose greatest ambition in life is to make his family happy, entirely forgetful of self in his efforts to do this. . . . The man I know is most gentle, and if he feels that he has been unjust to anyone the distance is never too far for him to go and, with loving words or kind deeds, erase the hurt."[4]

The First Presidency, from 1970–72: (from left) Harold B. Lee, President Joseph Fielding Smith, and N. Eldon Tanner. (LDS Church Archives)

As he assumed the leadership of the Church in 1970, President Joseph Fielding Smith affirmed that the Latter-day Saints "join with men of good will in all churches in expressing love and concern for the temporal and spiritual well-being of all our Father's children."[5] These thoughts reflected the spirit of Joseph Fielding Smith's presidency. He assumed the reigns of leadership at the age of ninety-three, the greatest age at which any Church President had entered that office. Many Church members expected this to be a period of waiting, until a younger man might again provide dynamic leadership. This expectation proved to be wrong. With the help of his two able counselors, Presidents Harold B. Lee and N. Eldon Tanner, President Smith directed the implementation of a variety of improvements in Church activities and programs. He traveled widely, conducting conferences, dedicating buildings, and in other ways strengthening the Church and its members. One reason he was able to follow such a demanding schedule was that he enjoyed his work. On one sunny afternoon his sister found him busy in his office. She chided him for working too hard, citing the examples of several former Church leaders who had always taken naps in the afternoon. "Yes," quipped President Smith, "and look where they are now."[6] After serving for two and a half years, President Joseph Fielding Smith died peacefully just two weeks before his ninety-sixth birthday.

Harold B. Lee around age 5 (left) with his brother. Working on the family farm at a young age taught Harold important practical and spiritual lessons. (Deseret News photo)

HAROLD B. LEE

Following President Smith's death, Harold B. Lee was sustained as the eleventh President of the Church. Like his predecessor, President Lee had already made significant contributions that had a far-reaching impact on the Church and its programs.

Growing up on a farm in southeastern Idaho taught Harold B. Lee many valuable character traits and provided experience from which he could draw in his later life. "We began to do 'chores' shortly after daybreak so we could 'start' with the day's work by sunup. When the day's work was finished, we had yet to do our evening 'chores,' usually by the aid of a lantern."[7] While gaining an appreciation for hard work, he learned an even more important lesson as a boy. One day he had the urge to explore an old broken-down shed, but he heard a voice warning: "Harold, don't go over there." He looked around to see who was speaking but could see no one. "Then I realized that someone that I could not see was warning me not to go over there," Elder Lee later recalled. "I learned early that there are those beyond our sight that could talk to us."[8]

After attending the Church-operated Oneida Stake Academy, Harold B. Lee qualified as a teacher at the Albion State Normal School. He began his teaching career at age seventeen in the small, rural, one-room Silver Star School. A year later he became principal of the district school, some of whose students were older than he was. Harold's interests were varied. While in school he played basketball and participated in debates. He also played the trombone and piano in dance bands in and around his community.

The Silver Star School, where Harold B. Lee taught at age seventeen. (LDS Church Archives)

After serving in the Western States Mission, Harold B. Lee moved to Salt Lake City, where he completed his college education by attending summer sessions at the University of Utah and by taking extension and correspondence courses. He successively became principal of two schools and then district manager of a library supplies company. In 1932 he was appointed to be a member of the Salt Lake City Commission with responsibility for streets and public properties.

The activities and contributions for which Harold B. Lee is remembered, however, center around a different effort in his life-the relief of those in need. In 1930 he became president of the Pioneer Stake at the age of thirty-one. He presided during the Great Depression, and the members of his stake, located on the less-affluent west side of Salt Lake City, were particularly hard hit. Under Harold B. Lee's leadership, the stake developed a series of innovative projects to produce and preserve needed food and other supplies for the destitute. President Lee was also concerned about the social and recreational needs of stake members. Using materials from a demolished business building, the stake constructed a gymnasium and then set up a stakewide budget to provide wholesome Church-sponsored activities for all, regardless of their financial status. Because of this background the First Presidency in 1935 appointed Harold B. Lee to develop the Churchwide welfare plan announced the following year. During the next several years he traveled extensively throughout North America, counseling with local leaders concerning the implementation of the welfare program. Thus, he was already widely known and respected when he received his next significant calling.

On April 6, 1941, Harold B. Lee was sustained a member of the Council of the Twelve Apostles. Soon

Major events in the life and administration of President Harold B. Lee

1870 1880 1890 1900 1910 1920

1899
Harold B. Lee born in Clifton, Idaho, Mar. 28

1916
Began teaching school (age 17); became principal the following year

1920
Called to Western States Mission

1923-
School principal Salt Lake C

President Harold B. Lee, eleventh President of the Church. (LDS Church Archives)

afterwards, Elder Stephen L Richards, chairman of the Church's radio committee, invited the new Apostle to speak on the Resurrection as part of the Church's Easter broadcast the following week. Elder Richards reminded him, "You understand now, of course, that as a member of the Council of the Twelve, you are to be one of the special witnesses of the life and mission of the Savior and of that great event."[9] Elder Lee found a secluded room in the Church Office Building where he could prepare for this assignment. As he reviewed the Gospel's account of the Savior's life he was overwhelmed "to realize what a call into the Council of the Twelve meant. I discovered that something was happening to me," he recounted. "I was not just reading a story; it seemed actually as though I was living the events; and I was reading them with a reality the like of which I had never before experienced. And when, on the Sunday night following, after I had delivered my brief talk and then declared, simply, 'As one of the humblest among you, I, too, know that these things are true, that Jesus died and was resurrected for the sins of the world,' I was speaking from a full heart, because I had come to know that week, with a certainty which I never before had known."[10]

Visits to stake conferences, tours of missions, and assignments to advise auxiliary organizations all broadened Elder Lee's experience. As World War II broke out, he was called as the first chairman of the Church's Servicemen's Committee. Elder Lee was particularly responsive to the challenges and needs of the younger members of the Church. In 1945 he gave a series of radio addresses that were subsequently published as a book, *Youth and the Church.* A revised version of this volume, *Decisions for Successful Living*, appeared in 1973. By 1960, Elder Harold B. Lee had become chairman of the General Priesthood Committee of the Twelve. It was in that year that the First Presidency directed him and his committee to conduct an exhaustive review of the Church's programs and curriculum. The result of this study was the Priesthood Correlation effort of

Elder Harold B. Lee (middle), chairman of the Church's Servicemen's Committee, poses with military officials in front of a chapel in Pusan, Korea, in 1954. (LDS Church Archives)

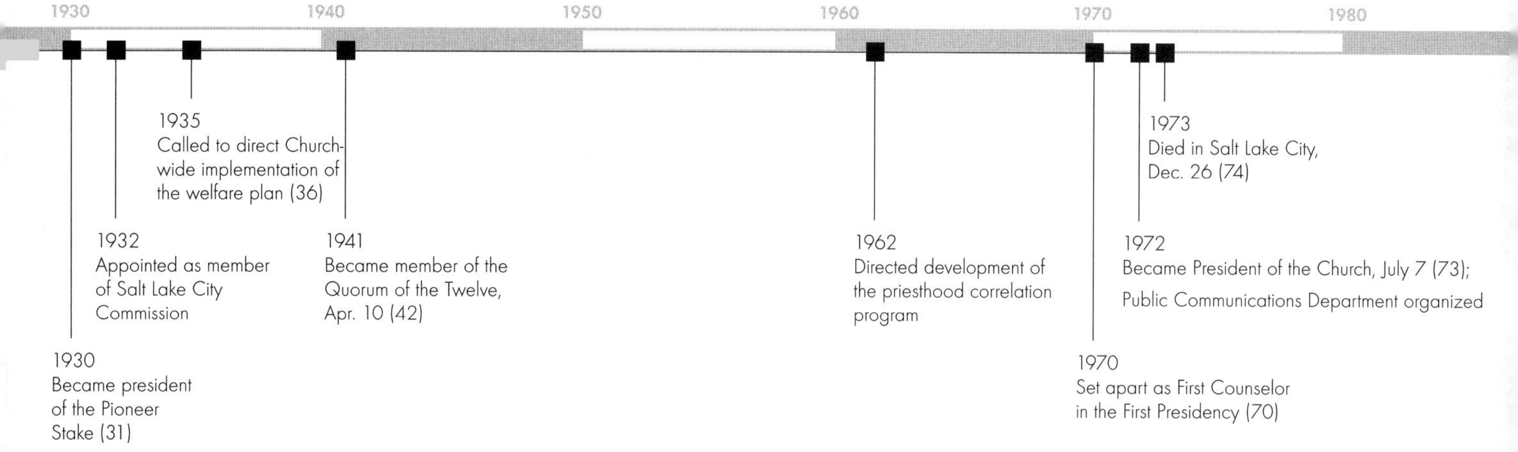
1930
1940
1950
1960
1970
1980
1935
Called to direct Church-wide implementation of the welfare plan (36)
1932
Appointed as member of Salt Lake City Commission
1930
Became president of the Pioneer Stake (31)
1941
Became member of the Quorum of the Twelve, Apr. 10 (42)
1962
Directed development of the priesthood correlation program
1973
Died in Salt Lake City, Dec. 26 (74)
1972
Became President of the Church, July 7 (73);
Public Communications Department organized
1970
Set apart as First Counselor in the First Presidency (70)

the 1960s. In the priesthood session of several successive general conferences Elder Lee introduced and explained such significant developments as ward correlation councils and priesthood executive committees, home teaching, and family home evenings.

Dramatic personal experiences sensitized Elder Lee to the needs of others. During the Great Depression Elder Lee learned empathy as he shared the suffering of those over whom he presided in the Pioneer Stake. Then, during the 1960s, he experienced deep sorrow of his own when his wife and then one of his two daughters died. Reflecting on these tragic experiences, Elder Lee drew strength from comparing his challenges to those of the Prophet Joseph Smith: "At times it seemed as though I too was like a rough stone rolling down from a high mountainside, being buffeted and polished, I suppose, by experiences, that I too might overcome and become a polished shaft in the quiver of the Almighty."[11]

That for which Elder Lee was being prepared became obvious when President Joseph Fielding Smith passed away on July 2, 1972, and Elder Lee assumed the leadership of the Church. At the press conference where his calling was announced, he declared that the Church's greatest challenge was to keep up with the worldwide growth in its membership. President Lee insisted on this occasion, "The safety of the church lies in the members keeping the commandments. There is nothing more important that I could say. As they keep the commandments, blessings will come."[12] President Harold B. Lee would lead the Church for only a year and a half before his unexpected death on December 26, 1973. Though brief, his administration continued the important trends that had been inaugurated by his predecessors.

*President Harold B. Lee and President Spencer W. Kimball at an area conference in Munich, Germany, in 1973. (*Deseret News *photo)*

Keeping in Touch with the Saints Abroad

During the administrations of Presidents Joseph Fielding Smith and Harold B. Lee the Church took steps to improve communications with its worldwide membership. Area conferences became an important link in this communication. The first of these conferences convened in Manchester, England, in August 1971. One purpose for initiating these conferences was to bring the leadership closer to those who were not able to attend the general conferences at Church headquarters. The three-day conference included a leadership meeting, seminars and activities for the youth, and special meetings for priesthood bearers and for women. The general sessions were attended by crowds ranging from twelve thousand to fourteen thousand Saints, about one-fifth of the Church's total membership in Britain. Addressing this vast throng, President Joseph Fielding Smith asserted: "We are members of a world church. . . . The day is long since past when informed people think of us as a peculiar group in the tops of the Rocky Mountains in America. . . . But now we are coming of age as a church and as a people."[13]

The 1971 area conference provided an unprecedented opportunity for the British Saints to have personal contact with a large group of General Authorities and to be blessed by their personal spiritual guidance. Similar area conferences were held

*A priesthood session at the first area conference, held in Manchester, England. Area conferences helped link the General Authorities with the Saints worldwide. (*Deseret News *photo)*

during succeeding years in Mexico (1972), Germany (1973), and Sweden (1974). In 1975, four such conferences were held, two in South America and two in East Asia. These area conferences became an increasingly important tie between the General Authorities and the growing worldwide Church membership.

By the early 1970s there were a few thousand isolated Latter-day Saints living in parts of the world where there were no organized stakes or missions. The International Mission, organized in 1972, was designed to reach out to these scattered Saints. Presided over by a General Authority and headquartered in Salt Lake City, this unit served these isolated members by facilitating interviews for priesthood advancement, issuing temple recommends, and receiving tithes. It also put newcomers to a given area in touch with other Saints living nearby.

Refining and Consolidating Church Activities

The principles of priesthood correlation, enunciated so clearly during the 1960s, continued to guide the development of Church activities during the following decade. Some changes during this period involved abandoning long-standing names of Church programs. After ninety-nine years, the title "Deseret Sunday School Union" was discontinued. This title had been descriptive of how the central organization was originally formed through the union of separate local Sunday Schools in pioneer times, but this meaning became less significant during an era of worldwide growth.[14] In 1971, the name was changed to the "Sunday School of The Church of Jesus Christ of Latter-day Saints." Other traditional names discontinued during these years included "Trail Builders" (nine- to eleven-year-old boys in Primary), "M-Men" and "Gleaners" (young single adults), and even the name "Mutual Improvement Association." The newer names were generally simpler, more descriptive, and less provincial than their predecessors. However, the shift from "Senior Aaronic" to "Prospective Elder" represented a basic change in the Church's approach to these Saints. The former title seemed to reflect a man's past failure to advance beyond the lesser priesthood, while the new name reflected the hope for future progress. Giving the elders quorum responsibility for reactivating these men placed them in the mainstream of priesthood activity and associations. Recently returned missionaries, usually found in the elders quorums, could employ the same skills they had used in teaching investigators in the mission field to benefit their less-active brethren.[15]

President Joseph Fielding Smith's interest in gospel scholarship was reflected in another refinement of Church activity. Up to that time, a variety of manuals had been prepared for the Gospel Doctrine class in Sunday School; but beginning in 1972 the standard works themselves became the sole text. The Old Testament, the New Testament, the Book of Mormon, and the Doctrine and Covenants were studied in rotation, two years (and later only one year) being spent on each. The Pearl of Great Price was studied in conjunction with relevant sections of the other works. Latter-day Saints took scripture study more seriously than ever before. Not only did they read the week's assignment for the Gospel Doctrine class, but the scriptures were cited more frequently in sermons and other instructions, and an increasing number of Saints could be seen with their copies of the standard works open during meetings. Church leaders anticipated a spiritual resurgence as a result of the Saints' added contact with the word of God.

Under the leadership of Presidents Smith and Lee, the momentum in temple activity continued to build. In 1972 the Provo and Ogden temples were dedicated. These immediately became the most productive temples in terms of the number of ordinances performed. Construction of the Washington D.C. Temple, one of the largest ever built by the Church, was commenced. The thorough remodeling of five existing temples was also announced. The level of ordinances performed soared to new heights, and a new system of submitting names promoted a resurgence in genealogical activity.

Consolidating Church Administration

The four years during which Joseph Fielding Smith and Harold B. Lee presided saw the Church grow from 2.8 to 3.3 million members. New and innovative methods of sharing the gospel enhanced this growth. Over six million people visited the Church's pavilion at "Expo '70" in Osaka, Japan. This made the Church's programs and teachings more widely known than ever before in Japan and other countries of eastern Asia. In 1972 the Church opened a visitors' center in San Diego at the terminus of the Mormon Battalion's epic nineteenth-century march and also opened a special public relations office in New York City. The following year a complex of restored buildings was dedicated in Nauvoo, and Japanese-language tours were inaugurated at the Hawaii Temple visitors' center.

The rapid growth of the Church around the world during the 1950s and 1960s placed mounting responsibilities on the General Authorities. There were more stake conferences to attend, and more local leaders to call, train, and supervise. One step taken during the early 1970s was to increase the number of the Assistants to the Twelve; this group of General Authorities grew from eleven to eighteen in 1974. Church leaders also adopted the policy of delegating whatever responsibilities they could to others who were not General Authorities. One example was Neal A. Maxwell's appointment as commissioner of the Church's educational system in 1970.

As the Church's administrative structure expanded to meet these growing needs, the First Presidency carefully considered the best way to organize it. They employed two outside nationally-known business consulting firms to make in-depth studies, the findings of which became the basis for some important reorganizations at Church headquarters.

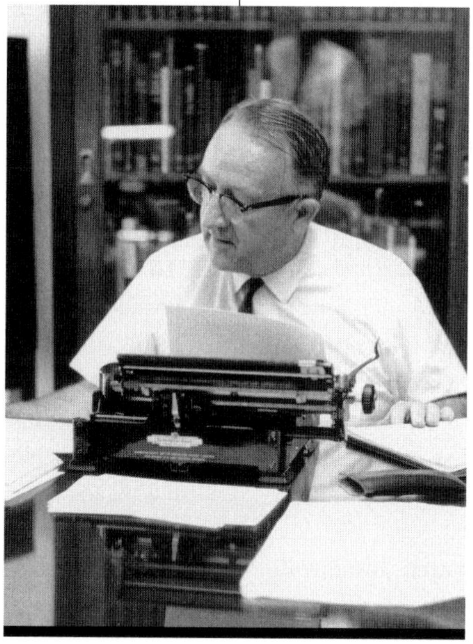

Leonard J. Arrington served as Church historian from 1972 to 1982. In this responsibility and later as head of the Joseph Fielding Smith Church Institute at BYU, Arrington wrote extensively on Church and Utah history to both Mormon and non-Mormon audiences. (Used by permission, Utah State Historical Society, all rights reserved)

The reports pointed out that the General Authorities, particularly the Twelve, were carrying extensive responsibility for dozens of Church agencies or programs. They recommended that these activities be grouped into several large departments, and that responsibility for day-to-day operations be delegated to full-time executive directors. In 1972, therefore, under the supervision of the General Authorities, the new Internal Communications Department brought together the preparation, publication, and distribution of magazines, lesson manuals, and instructional materials intended for use within the Church. (Many of these responsibilities were later transferred to the Presiding Bishopric's office.) During that same year, the External Communications Department (later renamed Public Communications) coordinated the Church's visitors' centers, broadcasting, and other public relations activities. In 1972 the Building Committee and the Real Estate and Maintenance departments were merged, forming the Physical Facilities Department under the supervision of the Presiding Bishopric. Similarly, in 1973 the Church's Welfare, Social Services, and Health programs became part of the new Welfare Services Department. The new Historical Department in 1972 also resulted from this consolidation movement, combining the collection of Church records with the responsibility to research and publish historical information. This latter function, under the leadership of noted historian Leonard J. Arrington, was transferred a few years later to Brigham Young University as the Joseph Fielding Smith Church Institute.

Completed in 1972, the twenty-eight-story Church Office Building provided much needed facilities at the headquarters of a growing worldwide Church. (Deseret News *photo)*

At about this same time, Lee S. Bickmore, an active Church member who was chairman of the board and chief executive officer of Nabisco, was named special consultant to the First Presidency for business operations, finances, building, communications, and other related activities.[16]

A tangible consolidation of Church administration came with the construction of the Church's $31-million twenty-eight-story office building in Salt Lake City. When this facility was occupied in 1972, departments that had been located in a dozen different buildings in the area were housed under a single roof for the first time. This not only contributed to the Church's efficiency of operation but also enhanced a feeling of unity-each agency seeing itself more clearly as an integral part of the total Church program.

Another major construction project grew out of the need for a new meetinghouse in New York City. Real estate costs prohibited the construction of a traditional chapel. Therefore, in conjunction with other investors, the Church erected a thirty-six story office and apartment tower at Lincoln Center to make the project economically feasible. A four-story wing with its own entrance housed a stake center, facilities for three wards, a visitors' center, mission offices, and a family history center. Construction began in 1973 and the building was dedicated two years later.[17]

Responding to New Needs

The postwar decades had witnessed a general disintegration of institutions and traditions that in earlier years had brought stability and security. Crime rates increased. Growing numbers of divorces were breaking up families. A larger proportion of the population was living in urban rather than rural environments. Large cities typically were impersonal and were characterized by a hectic lifestyle, which placed added emotional strain on the individual. In contrast to farming communities, where the family was central to economic survival, cities presented an extensive array of attractions pulling individuals away from the family. Even though the gospel offered a defense against these social ills, Latter-day Saints were not totally immune.

President Harold B. Lee was concerned about these problems, so he stressed the need of blessing each member with the programs of the Church. He emphasized that the Church and its programs were designed to strengthen and bless the members, that the programs were a means to this end rather than being the end in themselves. Paraphrasing Mark 2:27, President Lee asserted that "man was not made for the Church: but the Church was made for man."[18] This concern for meeting the needs of each member was reflected in the Church's efforts to help the Saints cope with the new challenges they were facing.

The Doctrine and Covenants instructed the Saints to "remember in all things the poor and the needy, the sick and the afflicted" (D&C 52:40). The traditional welfare program had aided "the poor and the needy," and now more attention would also be given to "the sick and the afflicted." Some of the twentieth century's greatest challenges lay in the areas of physical and emotional health. To meet these challenges, the Church established its health and social services programs.

Health Services

The importance of physical and emotional health is affirmed by the scriptures (see 1 Corinthians 3:16–17; D&C 89). Healing is one of the gifts of the

Spirit, and many of the Lord's miracles were of this nature. Over the years, Church programs and teachings have focused on the physical well-being of Latter-day Saints.

In 1882, with the help of a dollar-a-month contribution by Relief Society and MIA members, the Deseret Hospital provided the first nurses' training and maternity care in the Intermountain area. Unfortunately, after only eight years of operation, this critical institution was forced to close because of financial problems. Salt Lake City's new LDS Hospital opened in 1905. Over the years, the hospital's facilities and equipment were enlarged and modernized, and its staff became noted in such areas as heart surgery.[19]

Other Church-sponsored hospitals were opened in Utah, southeast Idaho, and southwest Wyoming, bringing the total to fifteen. In 1962 an administrator was appointed to provide central coordination for the system; in 1970, under the direction of President Joseph Fielding Smith, a health services commissioner was named to head a legally distinct corporation under the leadership of the Presiding Bishopric.

The early 1970s, however, witnessed a new worldwide emphasis in the Church's health program. Church leaders outlined the fundamental objectives and the basic procedures for this expanding program. "Health services for worthy members in need have primarily been provided in the United States. There are, however, challenges facing the entire Church today that relate to the health of a worldwide membership. The purpose of priesthood correlation of health services is to assist priesthood leaders and, through them, Church members to meet these challenges successfully."[20]

A health service missionary blesses Guatemalan Saints and friends by teaching principles of nutrition, sanitation, and first aid. (Ensign *photo)*

In accordance with these concerns, the Church in 1971 called its first "health missionaries." These missionaries performed traditional proselyting duties and provided special medical instruction. Their first task was to identify the greatest medical needs of both Church members and nonmembers in an area. They then developed programs to be implemented through existing local Church organizations to meet these needs.

Most programs sponsored by government agencies or other religious groups featured clinics for the curing of illness; doctors worked long hours doing "a lot for a few [but] nothing for many." In contrast to this pattern, LDS health missionaries emphasized prevention of illness. By enlisting Church members to help in teaching basic health principles and sanitation, the missionaries were able to reach thousands. The Church sent its health missionaries into parts of the world where the need was greatest. By the end of the program's second year, two hundred health missionaries were serving, but many more were needed.[21] In later years they received a wider variety of assignments and were called "welfare services missionaries" or "missionaries with special assignments."

This new direction in the Church's health activities was also reflected in the First Presidency's 1974 decision to transfer the operation of the hospitals in Utah, Idaho, and Wyoming from the Church to an independent corporation and to "divert the full efforts of the Health Services of the church to the health needs of the worldwide church membership." The First Presidency's announcement pointed out that operating these hospitals was not "central to the mission of the church," and that it was "difficult to justify provision of curative services in a single, affluent, geographical locality" when the needs around the world were so great. An independent and self-perpetuating corporation, Intermountain Health Care, was established to own and operate these hospitals.[22]

Social Services

Over the years, the Church had established three special programs to meet specific twentieth-century social challenges. The Relief Society Social Welfare Department, established in 1919, served as an adoption agency and provided foster homes for disadvantaged children. The Indian Student Placement Program under the chairmanship of Elder Spencer W. Kimball had extended the advantages of attending good schools and living in a wholesome LDS family environment to thousands of Lamanite youth since the mid-1950s. Under Elder Thomas S. Monson's direction, the "youth guidance" program worked to prevent problems and to make foster care or day camps available to youth in need. Licensed, professional social workers were required by law in all three of these programs. In 1969 they were unified to form the new Social Services Department.[23]

From this beginning the program expanded to provide a wide variety of services. Young people with severe social or emotional problems received, together with their parents, short-term professional counseling. Foster care was provided in extreme cases to youth when their home environment was such that a wholesome family relationship was not possible. The goal was to have them return home as soon as problems were resolved. Summer day camps provided helpful experiences in coping with social situations for disturbed children between the ages of eight and fourteen. Indian student placement also continued to be provided through the Social Services Department. Special foster homes aided unwed parents in the process of repentance, encouraging them to marry where appropriate. The Church's adoption agency helped create families for barren couples and found Latter-day Saint homes for children. Services to Church members in prison and their families included counseling and rehabilitation, and special home evenings were arranged for the inmates. In helping members with drug or alcohol problems, Church social services coordinated with public agencies and provided instruction for local Church leaders.[24]

Concerning the necessity of this help, President Harold B. Lee declared that the social services program "seeks to respond to many problems that beset our members in an affluent society, and it will no doubt increase in its importance, because so many of the problems which this cluster of agencies deals with are symptomatic of our time. Members may need counseling more than clothing." President Lee noted that they "should feel no more hesitancy in asking for help of this kind" than they would for financial assistance.[25]

In areas where Church membership was more concentrated, particularly in the western United States and Canada, the Church established social service agencies. These employed professionally trained and licensed personnel and operated in accordance with government regulations.[26] In areas where members were too scattered to support such an arrangement, Church leaders worked with local professional counselors who could provide help consistent with gospel standards.

While priesthood leaders typically dealt with the kind of social or emotional problems that they felt could be remedied by a demonstration of warmth, firmness, and love; state and local laws usually required that professionally trained and licensed social workers conduct such services as adoptions, foster care arrangements, and counseling with severe types of social-emotional disturbance. To carry on these services and to meet legal requirements, the Church in 1973 organized a separate Social Services Corporation.[27]

MEETING OTHER NEEDS

Over the years, the Church had published literature in braille or in audio form for blind Latter-day Saints. In the 1970s the concern for the unique needs of the blind as well as Saints with other disabilities continued and even expanded. Bishops received instructions on how to involve members with disabilities more fully in Church activities.

Sighted companions were invited to help blind teachers prepare their lessons. Home teachers helped members confined to wheelchairs get to church. Young people learned sign language in order to interpret services for deaf friends. The number of special branches for the deaf expanded throughout the United States. A conference in 1972 considered ways to better meet the needs of deaf Latter-day Saints. The Church produced a film to teach how priesthood ordinances can be performed without the

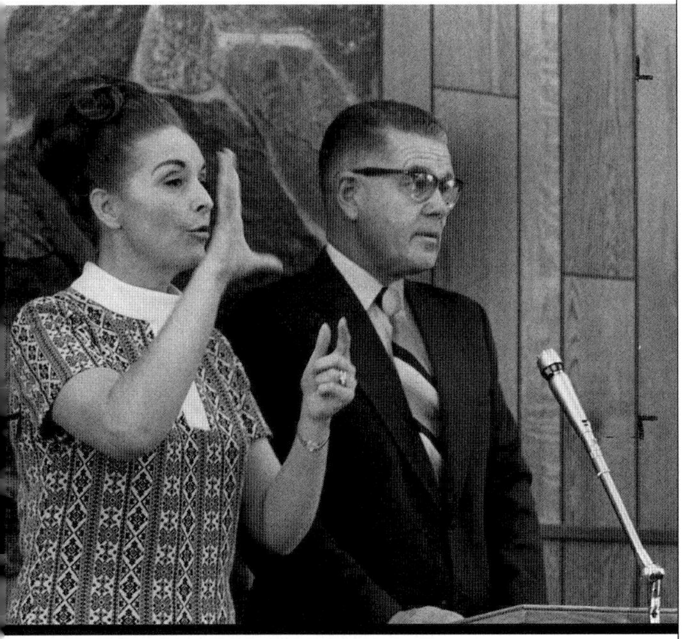

Madelaine Burton translates in sign language for President Clifford U. Gee as a new ward is formed in 1971. Providing such services for the deaf was part of the Church's efforts to meet members' special needs. (Deseret News *photo)*

use of speech. Additionally, a new dictionary was compiled in order to standardize signs used to interpret unique gospel or Church-related terms to the deaf.[28]

The early 1970s were an era of growing minority awareness in the United States. Ethnic groups became increasingly proud of their unique heritages. The Church took steps to meet the special needs of these groups. In 1970 the name of the Indian Committee was changed to "Committee for Lamanites and Other Cultures" to reflect a broader scope. The committee considered how gospel principles could be related more effectively to individuals from various cultures. It also sought to identify and help preserve unique traits such as art, literature, and traditions from each culture that might benefit Church members as a whole.[29]

In 1972 President Harold B. Lee and his counselors instructed local priesthood leaders to assume the responsibility for meeting the needs of minority groups residing within their boundaries. Special attention was to be given to those not speaking the language of the majority. As a result, translation facilities, special classes taught in the minority language, and even separate branches or wards were provided as needed. Still, the basic goal was to involve minority members as fully as possible in the mainstream of Church activity.

Another group with special needs was the single adults. While in 1900 only 1 percent of Church members over twenty-five years of age were divorced, this proportion grew more than fivefold by 1975, dramatically increasing the number of single adults. Traditional couple-oriented activities did not adequately meet the needs of single, widowed, or divorced members. President Harold B. Lee expressed a special concern for these people and encouraged the Church to develop programs to meet their special needs.[30] An outgrowth of this concern was the creation of the new Young Special Interest program for singles twenty-six through forty years of age, and the revitalization of Special Interest activities for older single Latter-day Saints.

The formation of social, health, and related programs in the twentieth century illustrated how, under inspired direction, the Church was able to respond to new needs as they arose.

17

Spencer W. Kimball and His Dynamic Administration

Because of Elder Spencer W. Kimball's former battles with health problems, some Latter-day Saints conjectured that his administration would be even shorter than the previous two, and that it would bring little in the way of new developments or progress. Those who entertained such ideas were in for a great surprise: few periods in Church history have witnessed more significant developments than did the administration of President Spencer W. Kimball.

Earlier Life

Although he was born in Salt Lake City, Spencer W. Kimball spent his formative years in the Gila Valley of southeastern Arizona. His life was not easy, but it was full of character-building experiences. These trials included suffering from a facial paralysis for several months as a boy and losing his mother when he was only eleven years old.

Following his return from the Central States Mission, Spencer married Camilla Eyring, who was teaching school in the area. He soon became a community leader as he entered banking, real estate, and related enterprises. Church responsibilities came to him early. These he accepted willingly, and through them he enriched the lives of many. When he was only twenty-three years of age his father, Andrew Kimball, president of the St. Joseph Stake, called Spencer to be the stake clerk. At that time, the position was very demanding because stake clerks were required to handle many financial and reporting matters later taken over by the Presiding Bishopric. A few years later

Spencer W. Kimball, twelfth President of the Church. (Deseret News *photo)*

Spencer W. Kimball about the time of his mission. (Deseret News *photo)*

Andrew Kimball died, and the new stake president called Spencer to be one of his counselors.

For over ten years, Spencer served as a counselor in the stake presidency and continued as stake clerk because no qualified replacement could be found. Finally, the stake president decided to release Spencer as a counselor and retain him as the clerk. Although he would lose some of the responsibility and honor to which he had become accustomed as a member of the stake presidency, Spencer felt good about the change, as it didn't matter to him where he served. "I'd like to serve wherever I am called," he affirmed.[1] When the stake was divided a few years later, Spencer became president of the new Mount Graham Stake. He was serving in this capacity when his call to the apostleship came in 1943. Despite his excellent preparation, Spencer W. Kimball felt unprepared for this high call. In his first general conference address, Elder Kimball described the period of soul-searching through which he had just passed:

> As I came home at noon, my boy was answering the telephone and he said, "Daddy, Salt Lake City is calling."
>
> I had had many calls from Salt Lake City. They hadn't ever worried me like this one. I knew that I had no unfinished business in Salt Lake City, and the thought came over me quickly, "You're going to be called to an important position." Then I hurriedly swept it from my mind, because it seemed so unworthy and so presumptuous, and I had convinced myself that such a thing was impossible by the time that I heard President Clark's voice a thousand miles away saying: "Spencer, this is Brother Clark speaking. The brethren have just called you to fill one of the vacancies in the Quorum of the Twelve Apostles."
>
> Like a bolt of lightning it came. I did a great deal of thinking in the brief moments that I was on the wire. There were quite a number of things said about disposing of my business, moving to headquarters, and other things to be expected of me. I couldn't repeat them all, my mind seemed to be traveling many paths all at once—I was dazed, almost numb with the shock; a picture of my life spread out before me. . . .
>
> I sensed immediately my inability and limitations and I cried back, "Not me, Brother Clark! You can't mean that!" I was virtually speechless. My heart pounded fiercely.[2]

During the next several weeks Spencer went to all those with whom he had had business dealings, wanting to be sure before he embarked on his new calling that everything was right between him and

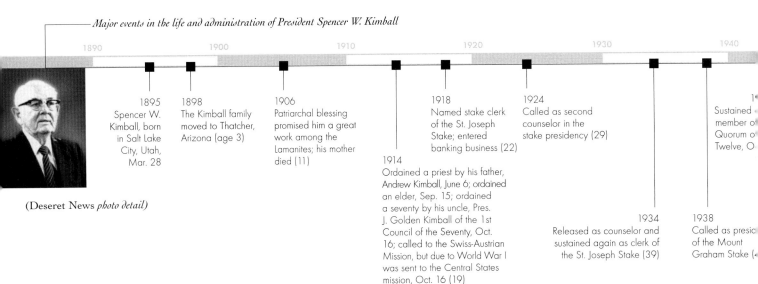

Major events in the life and administration of President Spencer W. Kimball

1890 1900 1910 1920 1930 1940

(Deseret News *photo detail)*

1895 Spencer W. Kimball, born in Salt Lake City, Utah, Mar. 28

1898 The Kimball family moved to Thatcher, Arizona (age 3)

1906 Patriarchal blessing promised him a great work among the Lamanites; his mother died (11)

1914 Ordained a priest by his father, Andrew Kimball, June 6; ordained an elder, Sep. 15; ordained a seventy by his uncle, Pres. J. Golden Kimball of the 1st Council of the Seventy, Oct. 16; called to the Swiss-Austrian Mission, but due to World War I was sent to the Central States mission, Oct. 16 (19)

1918 Named stake clerk of the St. Joseph Stake; entered banking business (22)

1924 Called as second counselor in the stake presidency (29)

1934 Released as counselor and sustained again as clerk of the St. Joseph Stake (39)

1938 Called as presic of the Mount Graham Stake (4

1 Sustained member o Quorum o Twelve, O

them. This was also a period of spiritual preparation. "I remember reading that Jacob wrestled all night, 'until the breaking of the day,' for a blessing; and I want to tell you that for eighty-five nights I have gone through that experience, wrestling for a blessing. Eighty-five times, the breaking of the day has found me on my knees praying to the Lord to help me and strengthen me and make me equal to this great responsibility that has come to me."[3]

On one occasion during this period, Elder Kimball went fasting to the top of a high mountain in order to be alone. "There was one great desire, to get a testimony of my calling, to know that it was not human and inspired by ulterior motives, kindly as they might be. How I prayed! How I suffered! How I wept! How I struggled!" After several hours of pleading, the desired answer came. "My tears were dry, my soul was at peace. A calm feeling of assurance came over me, doubt and questionings subdued. It was as though a great burden had been lifted. . . . I felt nearer my Lord than ever at any time in my life."[4]

Spencer W. Kimball (left) and his companion L. M. Hawkes as missionaries in St. Louis in 1915. (Deseret News *photo)*

He was sustained as a member of the Twelve at the October 1943 general conference. Soon, with his background in banking, Elder Kimball became an important member of the committees that determined how the funds of the Church should be spent. Perhaps the assignment that was closest to his heart, however, was his appointment as chairman of the Church's Indian Committee. Elder Kimball regarded this calling as a fulfillment of his patriarchal blessing.

Serious health problems plagued Elder Kimball during his adult years. Following his call to the Twelve, he suffered a series of heart attacks. Then in 1951 he lost his voice, but it was remarkably restored through a blessing by three General Authority colleagues. Six years later, however, throat cancer was diagnosed, and the doctors recommended that Elder Kimball's vocal cords be removed in order to save his life. He feared that the operation might rob him of his voice altogether, and that it might prevent him from fulfilling his calling as an Apostle. "Shall I ever preach again?" he agonized. Following much prayer and fasting, Elder Kimball underwent the operation, which proved to be less radical than his doctors had originally thought necessary. Nevertheless, Elder Kimball continued to worry: "Shall I ever return to [full] activity with the loss of my vocal cord and my weak, poor voice? Will the Brethren give me service? Will my gruff fringe voice be an affront to the people?"[5]

A long period of recuperation and readjustment followed. Elder Boyd K. Packer, a colleague in the Quorum of the Twelve, later recalled: "The [old] voice was all but gone, but a new one took its place. A quiet, persuasive, mellow voice, an acquired voice, an appealing voice, a voice that is loved by the Latter-day Saints."[6]

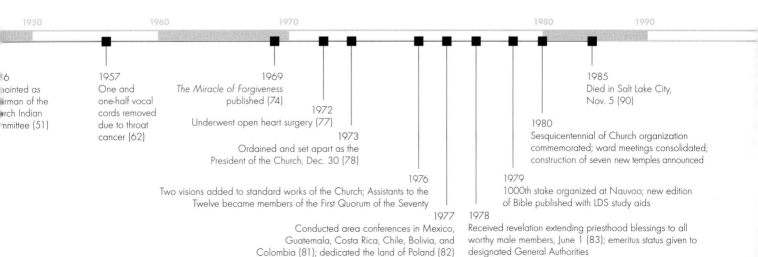

1950 1960 1970 1980 1990

6
ointed as
irman of the
rch Indian
mmittee (51)

1957
One and one-half vocal cords removed due to throat cancer (62)

1969
The Miracle of Forgiveness published (74)

1972
Underwent open heart surgery (77)

1973
Ordained and set apart as the President of the Church, Dec. 30 (78)

1976
Two visions added to standard works of the Church; Assistants to the Twelve became members of the First Quorum of the Seventy

1977
Conducted area conferences in Mexico, Guatemala, Costa Rica, Chile, Bolivia, and Colombia (81); dedicated the land of Poland (82)

1978
Received revelation extending priesthood blessings to all worthy male members, June 1 (83); emeritus status given to designated General Authorities

1979
1000th stake organized at Nauvoo; new edition of Bible published with LDS study aids

1980
Sesquicentennial of Church organization commemorated; ward meetings consolidated; construction of seven new temples announced

1985
Died in Salt Lake City, Nov. 5 (90)

In 1972, when earlier heart ailments flared up again, Elder Kimball underwent a particularly complicated open-heart operation. With the faith of many and through the outstanding skill of a devoted Latter-day Saint surgeon, Dr. Russell M. Nelson (a future member of the Twelve), Elder Kimball's life was spared again.

These difficulties did not stop him from setting an example of hard work in his calling. A plaque on his desk proclaimed the motto "DO IT."[7] He lived by these words. Sixteen- to eighteen-hour workdays were not uncommon. Many times while traveling to conferences he would have his portable typewriter in his lap, papers spread out on the seat beside him, so he could take advantage of every minute to answer the many letters he had received.

His personal character and all these experiences helped prepare Spencer W. Kimball to meet the challenge of giving leadership to the worldwide Church.

Following the unexpected death of President Harold B. Lee the day after Christmas in 1973, Spencer W. Kimball became the twelfth President of the Church. "We will, in large measure," he humbly announced, "carry forward the same program, which we have helped in a small way to make."[8] President Kimball later said: "I anticipate no major changes."[9] Despite this modest declaration, President Kimball's administration would be noted for numerous and significant innovations.

The First Presidency and President of the Quorum of the Twelve speak to the press about their hopes for the future as they assume Church leadership in December 1973. Pictured are (from left) N. Eldon Tanner, Spencer W. Kimball, Marion G. Romney, and Ezra Taft Benson.

President Kimball's Challenge to "Lengthen Our Stride"

As President Kimball's administration began, Church membership exceeded 3.3 million, having doubled in the previous fourteen years. One of his first presidential addresses was at the regional representatives' seminar just prior to the April 1974 general conference. Elder W. Grant Bangerter of the Seventy, who was a regional representative at the time, recalled that many at the seminar looked back to the powerful leadership of President Harold B. Lee and were lamenting that "things would not be the same." These apprehensions, however, were quickly dispelled as President Kimball masterfully unfolded his vision of how the gospel should be taken to the world. "He had not spoken very long," Elder Bangerter recounted, "when a new awareness seemed suddenly to fall on the congregation. We became alert to an astonishing spiritual presence, and we realized that we were listening to something unusual, powerful, different from any of our previous meetings. . . . It was as if he were drawing back the curtains which covered the purpose of the Almighty and inviting us to view with him the destiny of the gospel and the vision of its ministry."[10]

President Kimball began, "It seems to me that the Lord chose his words when he said [the gospel must go to] 'every nation,' 'every land,' 'uttermost bounds of the earth,' 'every tongue,' 'every people,' 'every soul,' 'all the world,' 'many lands.'

"Surely there is significance in these words. . . .

"I believe the Lord can do anything he sets his mind to do.

"But I can see no good reason why the Lord would open doors that we are not prepared to enter. Why should he break down the Iron Curtain or the Bamboo Curtain or any other curtain if we are still unprepared to enter?"

Speaking of his recent visits to the Far East and Latin America, President Kimball continued to describe his vision. He saw "a great movement when there would be thousands of local men prepared and anxious and strong to go abroad . . . in great numbers qualifying themselves for missionary service within their own country and then finally in other lands until the army of the Lord's missionaries would cover the earth as the waters cover the mighty deep. . . .

"My brethren, I wonder if we are doing all we can," the president challenged. "Are we complacent in our approach to teaching all the world? We have been proselyting now 144 years. Are we prepared to lengthen our stride? To enlarge our vision?"[11]

*David M. Kennedy, a former businessman, U.S. Secretary of the Treasury, and ambassador at large, was appointed by President Spencer W. Kimball to be a special consultant on diplomatic affairs. His efforts helped the Church gain legal recognition in Poland in 1977. (*Deseret News *photo)*

When President Kimball concluded his address, having spoken for over forty-five minutes, President Ezra Taft Benson echoed the feelings of all present as he declared with an emotion-filled voice: "Truly, there is a prophet in Israel."[12]

In order to promote this worldwide expansion of the gospel, President Kimball called David M. Kennedy to be a special consultant on diplomatic affairs. Kennedy, who had served in a stake presidency in Chicago, had ample background for his significant new assignment. He had been chairman of the board and chief executive officer of one of the United States banks most heavily engaged in international business. He had also served as Secretary of the Treasury and as ambassador at large for the United States. In succeeding years he played a key role working with governments of many nations in order to resolve problems that had hindered the Church's activities there.[13] He was instrumental in arranging for mature couples to serve as "special representatives" of the Church in countries where traditional missionary work was not yet possible. An outstanding achievement in 1977 was the granting of legal status and the official recognition of the Church in Poland. This came as the result of efforts by local Latter-day Saints and through several visits by Kennedy to Polish government officials. This, in turn, opened the way for a visit by President Kimball to Warsaw where he "dedicated the land of Poland and blessed its people that the work of the Lord might go forth."[14] Just three years later, the Solidarity Labor movement successfully defeated Communist candidates in national elections—the event often regarded as the catalyst that led to the fall of Soviet Communism in Eastern Europe.

Similar negotiations with the government of Israel led to the Church's developing the five-acre Orson Hyde Memorial Garden on the western slope of the Mount of Olives, overlooking the old city of Jerusalem.[15] The 1979 dedicatory services for the garden were seen in Utah via the recently developed satellite relay.

Bolstering this continued worldwide expansion, President Kimball gave emphasis to the importance of every young man being worthy and prepared to serve a mission. The development of the

President Spencer W. Kimball (center), his wife, and their traveling companions are accompanied by Minister Kazimierz Kakol (next to President Kimball) and other Polish officials during an August 1977 visit to dedicate the land of Poland for the preaching of the gospel. (Photo courtesy Kimball family)

Converts in Nigeria line up for baptism in 1978. Soon after President Kimball's revelation on the priesthood, missionary work was opened in West Africa and other regions of Africa. (Deseret News *photo)*

Missionary Training Center in Provo and similar orientation facilities throughout the world helped prepare this growing missionary force.

Student performing groups from Brigham Young University became another effective means of building goodwill for the Church. In 1978 the Young Ambassadors presented their music and dance variety shows in Poland and the Soviet Union. Before their tour the performers spent several weeks studying the cultures and languages of the peoples they would visit. They learned enough to announce their numbers in the local language and to greet members of the audience individually following the performances. They were eager to communicate the spirit of the gospel by setting a good example and by radiating a feeling of heartfelt love. In both countries the performers were well received and were permitted to tape an extended program for later release on nationwide television. The following year another group of Young Ambassadors toured mainland China. Here again their performances were highly appreciated, whether by the working people at impromptu performances in factories or by those able to attend presentations in the most prestigious concert halls of the country.[16]

The 1978 Revelation on Priesthood

Few events have had a greater impact on the worldwide spread of the Church than has the 1978 revelation received through President Kimball extending the priesthood to worthy males of all races. This change came many years after the demonstrations of the 1960s had ceased. Over a period of several months in early 1978 the General Authorities had discussed this topic at length in their regular temple meetings. In addition, President Kimball frequently went to the temple, especially on Saturdays and Sundays when he could be there alone to plead for guidance. "I wanted to be sure," he later reflected.[17]

Then, on June 1, 1978, nearly all the General Authorities gathered, fasting, for their regular monthly meeting in the temple. After this three-hour session, which brought inspiration and enlightenment, President Kimball invited his counselors and the Twelve to remain while the other General Authorities were excused. When the First Presidency and the Twelve were alone, he again brought up the possibility of conferring the priesthood on worthy brethren of all races. He expressed the hope that there might be a clear answer received one way or the other. "At this point," Elder Bruce R. McConkie recalled, "President Kimball asked the brethren if any of them desired to express their feelings and views as to the matter in hand. We all did so, freely and fluently and at considerable length, each person stating his views and manifesting the feelings of his heart. There was a marvelous outpouring of unity, oneness, and agreement in the council."[18] After a two-hour discussion, President Kimball asked the group to unite in formal prayer and modestly suggested that he act as voice. He recalled:

> I told the Lord if it wasn't right, if He didn't want this change to come in the Church that I would be true to it all the rest of my life, and I'd fight the world . . . if that's what He wanted. . . . I had a great deal to fight, of course, myself largely, because I had grown up with this thought that Negroes should not have the priesthood and I was prepared to go all the rest of my life till my death and fight for it and defend it as it was. But this revelation and assurance came to me so clearly that there was no question about it.[19]

Elder McConkie described what happened: "It was during this prayer that the revelation came. The Spirit of the Lord rested mightily upon us all; we felt something akin to what happened on the day of Pentecost and at the dedication of the Kirtland Temple. From the midst of eternity, the voice of God, conveyed by the power of the Spirit, spoke to his prophet. . . . And we all heard the same voice, received the same message, and became personal witnesses that the word received was the mind and will and voice of the Lord."[20]

Reflecting on this experience, President Spencer W. Kimball and President Ezra Taft Benson concurred that neither of them "had ever experienced anything of such spiritual magnitude and power as was poured out upon the Presidency and the Twelve that day in the upper room in the house of the Lord."[21]

Joseph Freeman Jr., the first black man to receive the priesthood following President Kimball's 1978 revelation, with his family after being sealed for eternity in the Salt Lake Temple. (Photo by Eldon K. Linschoten)

The impact of this revelation was far-reaching. Faithful black Latter-day Saints rejoiced as they received long-hoped-for ordinations to the priesthood, mission calls, calls to serve in bishoprics or stake presidencies, and, of course, the eternal blessings of the temple. In November 1978, just five months after the revelation came, the First Presidency called two experienced couples to open missionary work in the Black African nations of Nigeria and Ghana. Soon thereafter, missionary work was also expanded into the Caribbean region.

Spencer W. Kimball's Voice of Warning

During his years as an Apostle, Elder Kimball's discourses, famous for their vivid imagery, captured the Saints' attention. In these poetic expressions he usually stressed one of two themes—the importance of personal purity, and the Saints' opportunity and obligation to work with the Lamanites. In one sermon, he described how a small parasitic plant had killed a large, beautiful tree. "How like the mistletoe is immorality. The killer plant starts with a sticky, sweet berry. Once rooted, it sticks and grows—a leaf, a branch, a plant. It never starts mature and full grown. It is always transplanted an infant."[22]

On another occasion he counseled: "Sinful habits may be compared to a river which flows slowly and placidly at first, then gains speed as it nears the falls over the precipice. . . . In the stream of sin, it is relatively easy to repent at first, but as the sin becomes more and more entrenched the overcoming becomes increasingly difficult. If one ignores the roar of the falls below, he is doomed; if he will not listen to the warnings given him, he is sucked into the swift current to destruction."[23]

Elder Kimball likewise used a graphic comparison to teach Church members their responsibility to assist the Lamanites: "A sail plane furnishes thrills and exhilarating experience to pilots in the great empty sky. . . . But there is one thing the glider lacks. It has no engine; it cannot lift itself into the sky. An airplane tows it aloft some two or three thousand feet and the tow line is cut loose and the glider is then free to soar and to bank and to rise and to descend. The sail plane is like the Lamanite; the tow plane, like the gospel and the Church; the tow line, like the programs of the Church. . . . The Lamanite must have initial help—a power beyond himself. The Church and its people can give this lift."[24]

When the mantle of the Church's presidency fell upon Spencer W. Kimball, his speaking style shifted noticeably. Whereas previously he would devote an entire talk to developing a single theme, as prophet he felt the responsibility to raise a warning voice on a variety of concerns. He sounded a clear trumpet call, giving the Saints the guidance and direction they so badly needed in the face of worldly pressures. His keynote addresses at the first two general conferences after he became President of the Church each raised the warning voice on a wide range of topics. For example, he reaffirmed the Saints' political responsibilities to elect wise leaders and to obey constitutional law and cautioned the Saints against allowing political differences to sow the seeds of disunity. He challenged the Saints to clean up and repair their homes and farms. He urged them to plant gardens, store food, and avoid waste. He also reminded

*President Spencer W. Kimball meets with United States president Gerald Ford in 1976. President Kimball frequently spoke out against societal trends that undermined families and individuals. (*Deseret News *photo)*

them of the virtues of work, industry, and thrift. At the same time, he urged the Saints to avoid worldliness and to keep the Sabbath holy, refraining from shopping on that day. He decried the growing incidence of taking the Lord's name in vain. "Profanity is the effort of a feeble brain to express itself forcibly," President Kimball quipped.[25] He counseled against the use of playing cards. He reminded the Saints of their long-standing belief in the Word of Wisdom and declared that "the Church has consistently opposed the improper and harmful use of drugs or similar substances under circumstances which would result in addiction, physical or mental impairment or in lowering moral standards." He also warned the Saints to have nothing to do with apostate polygamy cults.

Many of President Kimball's teachings centered on the family. He declared that all people should marry if they can and then become parents. President Kimball also counseled that owning one's own home and avoiding debt bring stability to the family. He was concerned about forces that broke families apart.

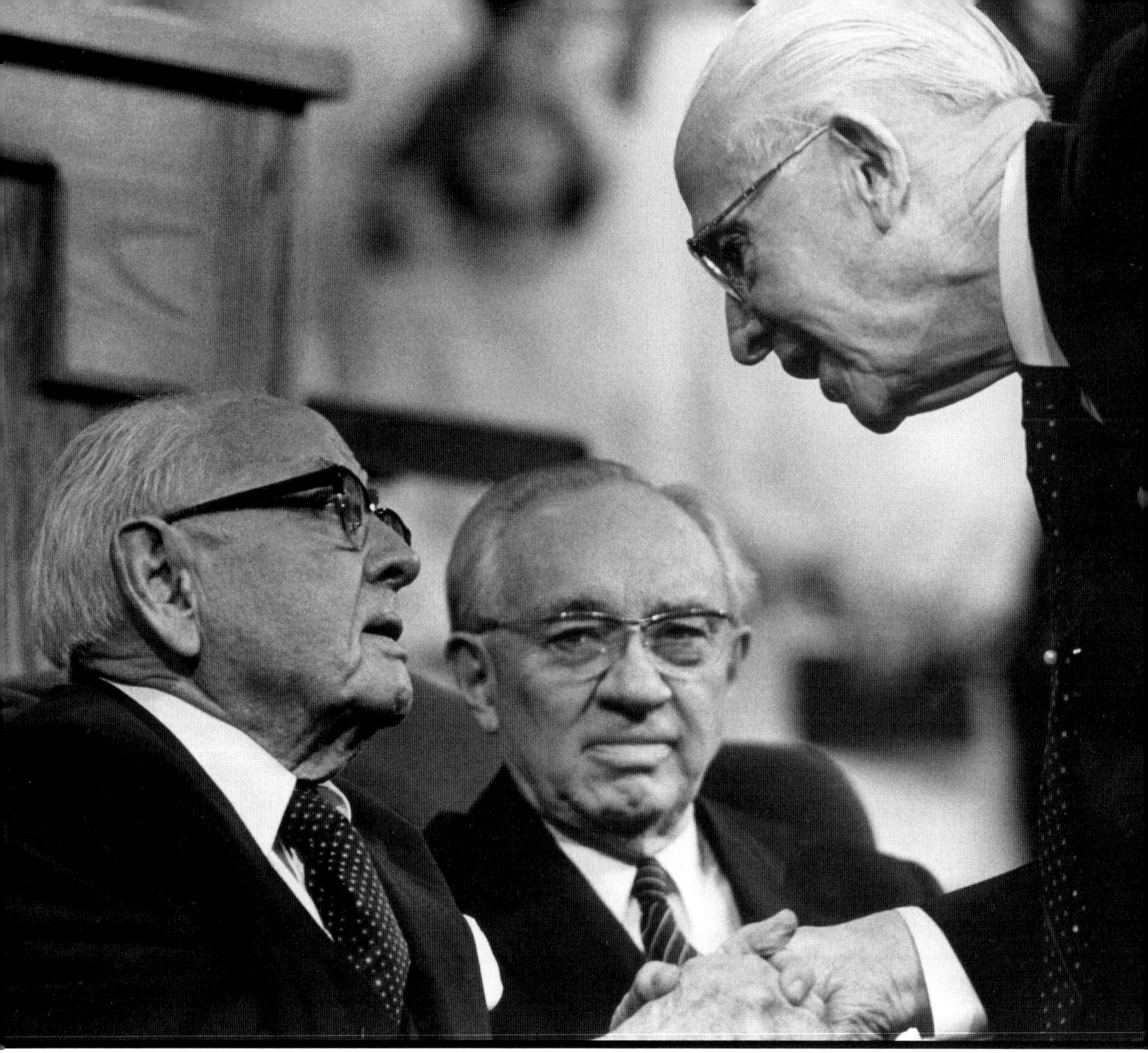

President Spencer W. Kimball with two future Presidents of the Church. (Deseret News *photo)*

"Every divorce is the result of selfishness on the part of one or the other or both parties to a marriage contract."[26] President Kimball noted that in the mid-1970s 24 percent of the Saints were marrying out of the Church and that on the average only one in seven of these nonmember spouses was ever baptized. Although 46 percent of Saints married in the temple, one in ten of even these marriages ended in divorce. He was appalled at the number of children who had to grow up without the essential benefit of having both parents in the home. President Kimball taught that the Lord planned for both parents to rear their children. He warned any who would deprive a child of a parent that there would be inevitable consequences stemming from such a decision.[27]

Abortion was a related concern. During the 1970s the rate of abortions soared. The United States government noted that by 1977, there were 568 abortions performed for every 1,000 live births.[28] In 1973 the First Presidency declared: "The church opposes abortion and counsels its members not to submit to or perform an abortion except in the rare cases where, in the opinion of competent medical counsel, the life or good health of the mother is seriously endangered or where the pregnancy was caused by rape and produces serious emotional trauma in the mother. Even then it should be done only after counseling with the local presiding priesthood authority and after receiving divine confirmation through prayer. Abortion must be considered one of the most revolting and sinful practices in this day, when we are witnessing the frightening evidence of permissiveness leading to sexual immorality."[29]

Another threat to the traditional family came with the increased prominence of homosexuality, especially during the 1970s. While in earlier years this practice had been prohibited by civil laws as well as by the scriptures, it increasingly came to be described simply as an "alternative lifestyle" that should be legalized. As early as 1973, Church leaders branded homosexuality "as sin in the same degree as adultery and fornication."[30] Seven years later, in a "Special Message to All Latter-day Saints," President Kimball denounced the various forms of immorality then so widely prevalent. Concerning homosexuality he warned: "Contrary to the belief and statement of many people, this sin, like fornication, is overcomable and forgivable, but again, only upon a deep and abiding repentance, which means total abandonment and complete transformation of thought and act."[31]

President Kimball also spoke out against "unisex" attempts to blur the distinction between masculine and feminine, the practice of couples living together without marriage, and the performing of vasectomies as a means to limit the birth of children.

Under President Kimball's leadership, the Church, responded to issues raised by the women's movement, which gained prominence and momentum during the 1970s. Few family-related issues generated more discussion both in and out of the Church than did the proposed "Equal Rights Amendment" (ERA) to the United States Constitution. Proposed by Congress in 1972, the amendment provided that "equality of rights under the law shall not be denied or abridged by the United States or by any State on account of sex." On the surface this provision appeared commendable and at first attracted widespread support. A more careful analysis, however, raised several concerns. Individual Church officers began voicing these concerns, but at the same time other groups of members organized to promote the ERA. In 1976 the First Presidency issued an official statement opposing passage of the proposed amendment. After praising the good work being done by the Relief Society, citing that Utah women received the vote fifty years before it was awarded nationally, and reaffirming the Church's commitment to women's rights, the First Presidency insisted that the proposed amendment was not the best way to correct the injustices to women. "While the motives of its supporters may be praiseworthy, ERA as a blanket attempt to help women could indeed bring them far more restraints and repressions. . . . We recognize men and women as equally important before the Lord, but with differences biologically, emotionally, and in other ways. ERA, we believe, does not recognize these differences."[32]

In 1980 the Church circulated with its magazines a special pamphlet detailing reasons for opposing the amendment. It pointed out that having an honest difference of opinion with Church authorities on such an issue did not constitute apostasy, but warned that trying to impose one's views on others, publicly criticizing the Church's leaders and policies, and seeking to create division could lead to a person's becoming "imbued with the spirit of apostasy" and being found "fighting against God and the authority which He had placed here to govern His Church."[33]

Although the Equal Rights Amendment was not ratified by the 1982 deadline, Church leaders anticipated that threats to the family would not cease. They therefore continued to encourage the Saints to strengthen family relationships as a protection against the challenges that lay ahead.

During the national debate, Church leaders became more aware of the pressures facing Latter-day Saint women as more and more attention was focused on the role of women in society. Articles in national magazines increasingly extolled women who

The rate of temple building accelerated greatly during the administration of President Spencer W. Kimball. He is pictured here with officials at the Tokyo Temple. (Deseret News *photo)*

found fulfillment in business or professional careers and portrayed traditional roles in the home as demeaning drudgery.

In 1978, the Church inaugurated annual meetings for women, preceding the fall general conferences. Like the priesthood meetings for men, these special sessions originated in the Salt Lake Tabernacle and were carried by closed circuit to hundreds of meetinghouses throughout the United States and in other countries. Speaking at the first of these meetings, President Spencer W. Kimball observed: "Much is said about the drudgery and confinement of the woman's role. This is not so. There is divinity in each new life, challenge in raising each child. Marriage is a partnership. . . . Mothers have a sacred role as partners with God." He challenged the women to be full and contributing partners with their husbands in marriage. He urged women to have programs of self-improvement, to reach for new levels of achievement and self-fulfillment. "Let there be no question in your mind about your value as an individual." He also encouraged them to seek spiritual attainment: "We want our sisters to be scholars of the scriptures as well as our men."[34] Because many women would face the challenge of earning a living for themselves or for their families, Church leaders encouraged them to qualify themselves for this role through education, without losing sight of their primary role as mothers in the home.

President Kimball commemorates the sesquicentennial of the founding of the Church in 1980 by having his conference address broadcasted from Fayette, New York, where the Church was founded. (Deseret News *photo)*

Changes in the Standard Works

The standard works of the Church underwent significant development in at least two ways under President Kimball's leadership. First, three new items were added to the scriptural canon—the first additions to the standard works in nearly three-quarters of a century. Two of these additions, which became sections 137 and 138 of the Doctrine and Covenants, shed light on temple work for the dead. At the time these were added, there were only sixteen temples in operation. Within the next quarter century, this number would increase sevenfold. The third new item to be added was the official announcement of President Kimball's 1978 revelation on the priesthood. Reflecting on these additions to the scriptures, Elder McConkie said: "Nothing is better known or more greatly appreciated than the fact that the canon of scripture is not now and never will be full. God speaks and his people hear. His words and his works are without end; they never close."[35]

The issuing of new editions constituted the second major scripture-related development of President Kimball's administration. In 1979, a new edition of the King James Bible appeared. Although the biblical text itself was not changed, this new edition featured an improved footnote system, references to related passages in the other standard works, quotations from Joseph Smith's "New Translation" or inspired revision of the Bible, more meaningful chapter headings, a 598-page topical guide and concordance, and a 194-page dictionary section, that reflected unique understandings available through latter-day revelation. Two years later a new edition of the Book of Mormon, the Doctrine and Covenants, and the Pearl of Great Price "triple combination" became a companion to the new edition of the Bible. It contained many of the same improvements. Elder Boyd K. Packer regarded these improvements as extremely important: "With the passing of years, these scriptures will produce successive generations of faithful Christians who know the Lord Jesus Christ and are disposed to obey His will. . . . They will develop a gospel scholarship beyond that which their forebears could achieve. . . . As the generations roll on, this will be regarded, in the perspective of history, as the crowning achievement in the administration of President Spencer W. Kimball."[36]

Activity Patterns Reshaped

President Kimball's administration also witnessed a significant reshaping of Latter-day Saint activity patterns. For decades priesthood meetings and Sunday School had been held during the morning on Sundays, and sacrament meetings had been held during the afternoon or evening. Relief Society meetings for women, Primary activities for children, and instruction and activities for youth had taken place during the week. All these basic ward meetings were streamlined so they could be consolidated into a single three-hour block on Sunday. With this new "consolidated" meeting schedule, such long-standing traditions as the Sunday School's half-hour opening exercises were discontinued. The Junior Sunday School was amalgamated into the Primary Association as part of this 1980 consolidation. Only a youth activity night, monthly Relief Society homemaking meetings, and occasional activities for children would continue during the week.

This step was taken at a time when a worldwide energy shortage had caused travel and heating costs to soar. This change, however, was not just an economizing measure. The consolidation enabled families to spend more time together for scripture study and other activities in the home and at the same time permitted the Saints to participate more in community affairs.[37] With this move, the Church again demonstrated its commitment to strengthening families, which had been one of the prime objectives of priesthood correlation during the 1960s.

This simplification of activities, in turn, paved the way for more compact chapel designs. A "new generation of meetinghouses" was announced in 1981. The use of movable partitions brought greater flexibility in meeting the needs for classrooms of varying sizes. Having a portable rather than a fixed stage not only saved room but also facilitated special musical and theater-in-the-round productions. Such innovations reduced the size of a typical ward meetinghouse from nineteen thousand to fourteen thousand square feet.[38]

Also, temple building accelerated under President Kimball's leadership. Previous to his presidency, no more than three temples had been under construction at any one time. Announcements of new temples by President Kimball, however, pushed the total number of temples being planned or under construction to twenty-two in 1982.

This increase in temple building was accompanied by a new direction in the Saints' genealogical responsibility. Here, again, modern technology had its impact. Using computers, the name extraction program, introduced in 1978, made the gathering of names much more efficient. President Kimball declared that he felt "the same sense of urgency about temple work for the dead" as he did about "missionary work for the living."[39]

Thus President Spencer W. Kimball came to be respected as a powerful leader who provided specific and timely counsel on the major questions and challenges facing the Saints. This leadership together with the far-reaching innovations during his administration made this an especially exciting and significant period of progress for the Church in the twentieth century.

18

Administering the Worldwide Church

The Church's accelerated worldwide expansion presented challenges as well as opportunities. The mushrooming number of stakes and missions around the globe placed an increasingly heavy administrative load on the General Authorities. The Church, however, took significant steps to meet this administrative challenge, especially under the leadership of President Spencer W. Kimball.

In 1967 Elder Harold B. Lee spoke of the challenges arising from the Church's rate of growth and the need to prepare for the prophesied "hastening of the Lord's work." He pointed out that the Church required its first seventy years to reach a quarter of a million members, but that during the 1960s a like number was added every two or three years. (In the early 1980s, that number was being added every year, and by the end of the century the annual increase reached a third of a million). Elder Lee cited examples of rapid increases in various sections of the world and concluded, saying, "We have no choice but to think regionally." He referred to research by Dr. Howard Nielsen of Brigham Young University indicating that by the year 2000 the Church should have in excess of ten million members. "By 1985," Elder Lee continued, "depending on our effectiveness and external events, we should have 1,000 stakes." (The thousandth stake was actually organized six years ahead of that projection). The General Authorities would need to appoint some two hundred new stake presidents each year, conduct five stake

Members at an area conference in Mexico in 1977 raise their arms in a sustaining vote. Begun in 1971, area conferences gave General Authorities an opportunity to keep in touch with the Saints across the world. (Deseret News *photo*)

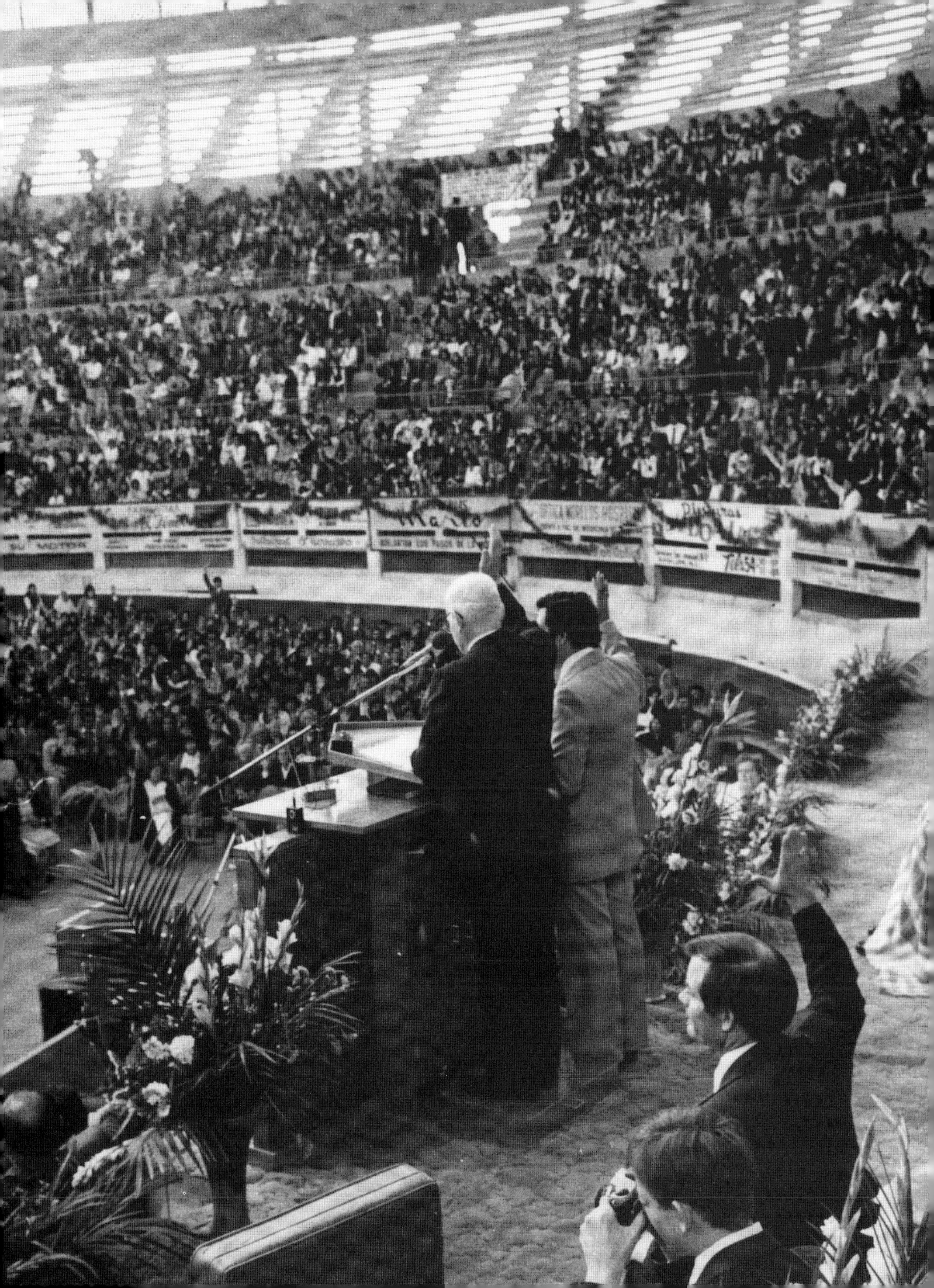

reorganizations each weekend, and clear fifty to sixty names for the office of bishop each week.[1] The fact that these milestones were actually reached sooner than had been predicted underscores the challenges this growth brought. Developments in the structure of the General Authorities of the Church during President Kimball's administration would help alleviate some of these challenges.

The General Authorities

No study of the Church's progress in this era would be complete without a consideration of the General Authorities. The "Brethren" have always played a special role in directing Latter-day Saint affairs. Not only did they possess the usual qualifications of organizational executives, but all were accepted as divinely called and inspired leaders. Although the basic structure of the Church's hierarchy was defined by revelations through the Prophet Joseph Smith during the early 1830s, there have been significant developments in later years, including the twentieth century.

THE FIRST PRESIDENCY AND THE TWELVE APOSTLES

Just as the Savior called three of the Apostles to preside over his Church in New Testament times (see Matthew 17:1–3), so also in the present era a revelation on Church goverment given in 1835 specified that "three Presiding High Priests" would constitute the First Presidency of the restored Church (see D&C 107:22).

Although the principles governing the selection of a new President of the Church were clarified just before the turn of the century, the Twelve still sought confirming inspiration each time they approached the selection of a new President. For example, Elder Bruce R. McConkie described the temple meeting following President Harold B. Lee's unexpected death in 1973: "Each member of the Council in turn, specifically and pointedly, expressed himself to the effect that now was the time to reorganize the First Presidency of the Church, that there should not be further delay. . . . Each one in turn expressed himself that President Spencer W. Kimball [the senior Apostle and President of the Twelve] was the man whom the Lord wanted to preside over the Church; there was no question whatever about that. There was total and complete unity and harmony."

After a full discussion, Elder Ezra Taft Benson, the next in seniority, formally moved that Spencer W. Kimball be sustained as the next President of the Church, and this was unanimously approved. President Kimball then chose his counselors and Elder Benson was sustained as the new President of the Twelve. "And then all those present placed their hands upon the head of President Kimball, and he was ordained and set apart, with President Benson being mouth, to serve as President of the Church and as the prophet, seer, and revelator for this time and this season."[2]

Although the basic structure of the First Presidency normally consists of the President and two counselors, special circumstances had sometimes resulted in this group being enlarged. Joseph Smith and Brigham Young, for example, had additional

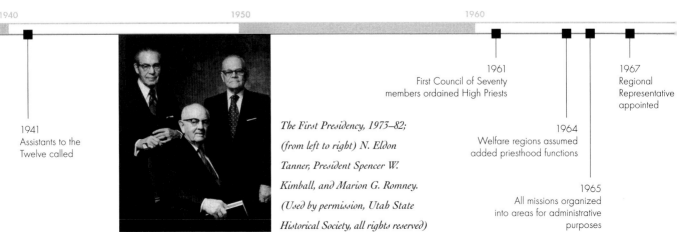

Significant developments in Church leadership and organization, 1940–97

1940 — 1950 — 1960

1941
Assistants to the Twelve called

The First Presidency, 1973–82; (from left to right) N. Eldon Tanner, President Spencer W. Kimball, and Marion G. Romney. (Used by permission, Utah State Historical Society, all rights reserved)

1961
First Council of Seventy members ordained High Priests

1964
Welfare regions assumed added priesthood functions

1965
All missions organized into areas for administrative purposes

1967
Regional Representative appointed

counselors during portions of their administrations. This pattern was not repeated for almost a century. In 1961 President David O. McKay called Elder Hugh B. Brown as an additional counselor; and when President J. Reuben Clark died a few months later, Elder Brown filled the vacancy as a regular counselor in the First Presidency. Then in 1965 President McKay called Elders Joseph Fielding Smith and Thorpe B. Isaacson, and in 1968 Elder Alvin R. Dyer, as additional counselors. They were released from this calling upon President McKay's death in 1970. No other additional counselors were appointed until 1981, when President Spencer W. Kimball named Elder Gordon B. Hinckley to this position. President Hinckley occupied this position only briefly, however, becoming Second Counselor the following year.

A quartet of Apostles: (from left) Elders Mark E. Peterson, Matthew Cowley, Spencer W. Kimball, and Ezra Taft Benson with Harold B. Lee as accompanist. (LDS Church Archives)

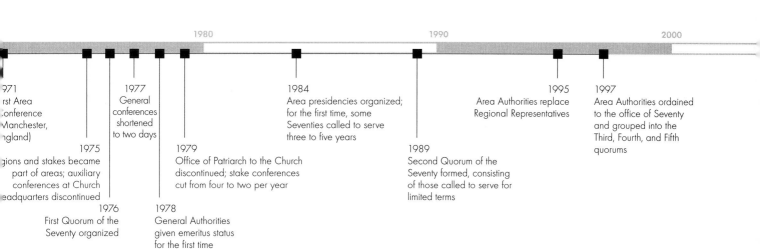

Latter-day revelation identified the Apostles as "special witnesses of the name of Christ in all the world" (D&C 107:23). Hence, the Twelve had played a key role in the Church's worldwide missionary effort. The Twelve or "Traveling Presiding High Council," were also to constitute an administrative body next in authority to the First Presidency and were responsible to "build up the church, and regulate all the affairs of the same in all nations" (D&C 107:33). Latter-day Saints sustain the members of the First Presidency and Quorum of the Twelve as "prophets, seers, and revelators." In 1960, Elder Spencer W. Kimball described the spirit and business of the meetings of the First Presidency and Quorum of the Twelve: "When in a Thursday temple meeting, after prayer and fasting, important decisions are made, new missions and new stakes are created, new patterns and policies initiated, the news is taken for granted and possibly thought of as mere human calculations. But to those who sit in the intimate circles and hear the prayers of the prophet and the testimony of the man of God; to those who see the astuteness of his deliberations and the sagacity of his decisions and pronouncements, to them he is verily a prophet. To hear him conclude important new developments with such solemn expressions as 'the Lord is pleased'; 'that move is right'; 'our Heavenly Father has spoken,' is to know positively."[3] Held on the first of each month, the meeting was expanded to include all of the General Authorities.

1980 — 1990 — 2000

971
rst Area
;onference
Manchester,
ngland)

1975
gions and stakes became part of areas; auxiliary conferences at Church eadquarters discontinued

1976
First Quorum of the Seventy organized

1977
General conferences shortened to two days

1978
General Authorities given emeritus status for the first time

1979
Office of Patriarch to the Church discontinued; stake conferences cut from four to two per year

1984
Area presidencies organized; for the first time, some Seventies called to serve three to five years

1989
Second Quorum of the Seventy formed, consisting of those called to serve for limited terms

1995
Area Authorities replace Regional Representatives

1997
Area Authorities ordained to the office of Seventy and grouped into the Third, Fourth, and Fifth quorums

Elders Yoshihiko Kikuchi (left), R. Enzio Busche, and Hugh W. Pinnock, new members of the First Quorum of the Seventy in 1977. The calling of Elder Kikuchi, a native of Japan, Elder Busche, of Germany, and other Seventies not of Anglo-American descent witnessed the growing strength of the international Church. (Deseret News *photo, by Gerald W. Silver)*

QUORUMS OF THE SEVENTY

The 1835 revelation on Church government assigned almost identical duties to the Seventy as were assigned to the Twelve (see D&C 107:23–26, 33–34). The Seventy, who were to be "especial witnesses" were organized to play a key role in assisting the Twelve to build up and regulate the Church worldwide.

The original quorum of the seventy was created in 1835. Only its seven presidents, which came to be known as the "First Council of the Seventy," were recognized as General Authorities. Eventually, there were hundreds of seventies quorums organized throughout the stakes under the general supervision of the First Council.

As the number of stakes and missions expanded during the 1930s, some Church leaders mentioned the possibility of forming a complete First Quorum of Seventies composed of General Authorities in order to assume part of the growing administrative load. Nevertheless, as President Spencer W. Kimball later explained: "The scope and demands of the work at that time did not justify the reconstitution of the First Quorum of Seventy."[4] Consequently, in 1941 five high priests were called to serve as "Assistants to the Twelve" with responsibilities similar to those envisioned in the revelation for the First Quorum of the Seventy.[5] Over the years as the Church continued to grow, the number of these assistants was enlarged as need dictated.

Responsibilities of the First Council of the Seventy were also increased. In 1961 President David O. McKay explained, "Under the direction of the Twelve Apostles, the First Council of Seventy go to all parts of the world to set in order the affairs of the Church. That means ordaining high priests, setting apart presidents of stakes, high councilmen, setting apart president[s] of high priests quorums, etc., and doing other things necessary for the advancement of the work." Therefore he announced that they were being ordained high priests so that there could be no question as to their authority to perform these duties.[6] Still, the practice was continued, at least temporarily, of only calling brethren into the First Council who were serving as seventies at the time.

Meanwhile, the number of Assistants to the Twelve continued to grow, reaching twenty-three by 1975. In that year President Spencer W. Kimball announced that the time had come to begin organizing a complete First Quorum of the Seventy. This would require at least thirty-six members, or a simple majority of a complete quorum of seventy. As a step toward this goal, three new General Authorities were added to the "First Quorum."[7] All three were seventies at the time of their call. In April 1976 four more were added, three being high priests and one an elder at the time; they were to have the same authority as Assistants to the Twelve. In October of that year, four more were called into the First Quorum of the Seventy. Including the twenty-one Assistants to the Twelve (two had died), the Seven Presidents of the Seventy, and the eleven additional members recently called to that quorum, the total had reached thirty-nine.

At the October 1976 conference, President Kimball announced that all the Assistants to the Twelve were being called "into the First Quorum of Seventy," thus surpassing the minimum required to form this quorum. "With this move the three governing quorums of the Church defined by the revelations—The First Presidency, the Quorum of the Twelve, and the First Quorum of Seventy—have been set in their places as revealed by the Lord. This will make it possible to handle efficiently the heavy workload and to prepare for the increasing expansion and acceleration of the work."[8]

After 1976, new members continued to be added to this quorum. Yet another evidence of the Church's growing international strength was the appointment of brethren from areas outside of Anglo-America. Beginning in 1975 these Church leaders were called from such diverse areas as the Netherlands, Germany, England, Japan, Korea, Philippines, Mexico, Argentina, and Brazil.

Beginning in 1984, some of the Seventy were called to serve for up to five years rather than for the traditional lifetime appointment. This arrangement, President Hinckley explained, would "provide a constant infusion of new talent and a much widened opportunity for men of ability and faith to serve in these offices."[9]

By 1989 the number in the First Quorum exceeded seventy and so a Second Quorum was formed. Those with five-year appointments became members of this quorum while those who were called for life were thereafter assigned to the First Quorum.[10] The Seven Presidents of the Seventy presided over both quorums (see D&C 107:95).

PATRIARCH TO THE CHURCH AND EMERITUS GENERAL AUTHORITIES

In 1833 Joseph Smith ordained his father to be a patriarch, "to hold the keys of blessing on the heads of all the members of the Church."[11] The Prophet later explained that wherever the Church is established, patriarchs should be ordained to bless the posterity of the Saints.[12]

This office first held by Joseph Smith, Sr., came to be known as the Patriarch to the Church. In accordance with revealed instructions, other patriarchs have been ordained as stakes have been established around the world (see D&C 107:39). Each of these was assigned to give blessings to those living within his particular stake, while the Patriarch to the Church had worldwide jurisdiction. His specific role was to give blessings to Church members residing in missions or in other areas where no stake patriarchs were available. The Patriarch to the Church did not have any presiding authority over the local patriarchs.[13]

In 1979 the First Presidency announced that "because of the large increase in the number of stake patriarchs and the availability of patriarchal service throughout the world," the office of Patriarch to the Church was being discontinued and Eldred G. Smith was honorably released and designated "Patriarch Emeritus."[14] Since that time, experienced brethren, often multilingual, have been called on a short-term basis to give patriarchal blessings in specified sections of the world where stake patriarchs are not available.

The first designation of "Emeritus General Authorities" had come the year before, in 1978. The First Presidency explained that this was done to "reduce somewhat the load of responsibility" carried by older or infirm brethren and to accord them "every honor and recognition" to which they were entitled.[15] Depending on independent circumstances, some Emeritus General Authorities were freed from all responsibilities and functioned in such specific assignments as temple president, visitors' center director, and so forth. Gradually, the practice developed of bestowing this title to members of the First Quorum of the Seventy following their seventieth birthday.

Eldred G. Smith served as Patriarch to the Church until 1979, when the Church began to rely solely on stake patriarchs to give patriarchal blessings. (Deseret News *photo)*

Follow the Brethren

At the organization of the Church in 1830, the Lord instructed the Saints to accept the Prophet's words "as if from mine own mouth" (D&C 21:5; see also D&C 1:38). A later revelation declared that whatever those in authority speak "when moved upon by the Holy Ghost shall be scripture" (D&C 68:4). Hence, Church members look to their leaders for inspired and authoritative guidance.

Not all groups of General Authorities possess the same jurisdiction. President J. Reuben Clark explained the distinction. Because the First Presidency and Quorum of the Twelve are sustained as "prophets, seers and revelators," they have "a special spiritual endowment in connection with their teaching of the people." In contrast, he continued, "Others of the General Authorities are not given this special spiritual endowment and authority covering their teaching; they have a resulting limitation." Specifically, "the President of the Church has a further and special spiritual endowment in this respect, for he is the Prophet, Seer, and Revelator for the whole Church. . . . [He] alone has the right to receive revelations for the Church, either new or amendatory, or to give authoritative interpretations of scriptures that shall be binding on the Church, or change in any way the existing doctrines of the Church. He is God's sole mouthpiece on earth."[16] Elder Marion G. Romney concurred: "What the presidency say as a presidency is what the Lord would say if he were here, and it is scripture."[17]

The Church's regular general conferences are important occasions when this inspired counsel may be received. As early as 1946, Elder Harold B. Lee urged the Saints to make the general conference report "the guide to their walk and talk during the next six months. These are the important matters the Lord sees fit to reveal to this people in this day."[18] Elder Spencer W. Kimball similarly encouraged Church members to get the printed report and "underline the pertinent thoughts and keep it with you for continual reference. No text or volume outside the standard works of the Church should [have] such a prominent place on your personal library shelves."[19]

Strengthening Local Leaders

With the worldwide growth of the Church, the General Authorities found it necessary to delegate more and more responsibility to local leaders. This same rapid growth, however, meant that those called

Presidency of Freetown-Wellington Branch, circa 1988. With the worldwide growth of the Church, the General Authorities sought ways to train and support local leaders. (LDS Church Archives)

to preside in the districts and branches as well as in the stakes and wards generally had little background in Church administration and activity. In Mexico City, for example, stake presidents during the early 1970s were comparatively young men in their thirties who had been members of the Church for only about ten years. This was in marked contrast to the typical stake president serving in the predominantly Latter-day Saint Intermountain West, who was in his fifties or sixties, had been a member of the Church all his life, and usually had previously served as a bishop and as a member of the stake high council. Therefore, the General Authorities gave special attention to the need for training these less-experienced local leaders to assume their increasingly weighty responsibilities.

Bishops had assumed a growing role as the shepherds of their flocks as well as administrators of ward activities. The *General Handbook of Instructions* listed fifty-eight distinct duties for bishops; in addition, bishops had to learn how to utilize effectively such new programs as social services and military relations. The average bishop spent about twenty-six hours per week in Church service, including twelve hours in meetings or attending other activities and eight hours in personal visits or interviews.[20] In the early 1970s approximately 32 percent of Church members resided in missions or in stakes within missions. Many bishops were, therefore, called with comparatively little training in Church leadership. In 1970 the General Authorities published a new program to help further qualify the thousands of bishops in the Church for their vital work. Although such training courses and printed bulletins provided valuable channels of communication and instruction from the General Authorities to local Church leaders, personal contact proved most effective.

Worldwide Supervision of Missions and Stakes

During the twentieth century, two new levels of administration had been developed—"areas" for missions, and "regions" for stakes. When missions were opened in continental Europe, their presidents were under the jurisdiction of the president of the British Mission, generally an Apostle, who was also known as president of the European Mission. This arrangement continued until 1929, when a separate president, not a General Authority, was called to preside over the British Mission. Like the presidents of the missions on the continent, he would serve under the direction of the European Mission president, who continued to be one of the Apostles.[21] Hence, Europe was the first part of the world to be organized into a mission area.

The appointments just after World War II of Elders Ezra Taft Benson and Matthew Cowley to direct the European and Pacific Missions, respectively, represented a continuation of this area supervision. In 1965 the world was divided into twelve large "areas," five in the United States and Canada and seven abroad. An Assistant to the Twelve or a member of the First Council of the Seventy served as a supervisor for each area under the direction of a member of the Twelve.[22]

Meanwhile, the number of stakes had continued to multiply, posing another administrative challenge. This was solved through the development of "regions," which had first been organized in 1936 to coordinate the functioning of the welfare program. In 1964, these units, composed of four to six stakes and renamed "priesthood regions," were realigned to serve expanded purposes. Additionally, a number of new regions were added for a total of seventy.[23]

Three years later, when the total number of stakes had reached 443, a further development occurred with the appointment of "regional representatives." The First Presidency explained that these brethren, who were not regarded as General Authorities, would "carry counsel to" and "conduct instructional meetings in groups of stakes or regions."[24] Initially, sixty-nine men were called as regional representatives. By the mid-1970s the number had doubled. Most had served as members of stakes presidencies, and many had also been mission presidents or members of one of the general priesthood committees. Most were assigned to regions near their homes, although a few had to travel long distances because of the need for their special language ability.

Regional representatives received instruction concerning priesthood and auxiliary programs at special seminars conducted in connection with the Church's general conferences in Salt Lake City. They then provided training in these programs to stake and ward leaders at regional meetings.

The Central America Area Presidency in 1994: (from left to right) Elders Joseph C. Muren, Carlos H. Amado, and Robert E. Wells. (Copyright Intellectual Reserve, all rights reserved)

In 1975 regions and stakes were placed under the direction of area supervisors for the first time. Several of the Assistants to the Twelve were assigned to move overseas and to personally direct the missions and regions in their assigned areas.[25] By the following year there were eleven of these brethren living abroad and serving as resident General Authority Area Supervisors. As these new units were stabilized, most of these area directors were able to return to Church headquarters.

In 1976, stakes in the United States and Canada were also placed under the jurisdiction of General Authority Area Supervisors, and the number of areas in these two countries was increased to nineteen.[26]

In 1977 the Twelve delegated to the First Quorum of the Seventy the immediate responsibility for the supervision of specific geographical areas. All area leaders were members of this quorum. At about this same time, the Seventies also received responsibility for directing the various ecclesiastical programs and departments at Church headquarters. This left the Twelve free to give broad attention to the Church's spiritual affairs worldwide. A further step in 1979 was the organization of councils to determine policy and give direction at various levels of Church organization.[27]

A significant development in 1984 was the appointment of area presidencies. The Church was divided into thirteen large geographic areas, seven in the United States and Canada and six elsewhere throughout the world. Each presidency consisted of a president and two counselors, all drawn from among the Seventy, who were to watch over and help build up the Church in their specific areas and report to the First Presidency and the Twelve (see D&C 107:34). Soon members of presidencies of areas outside the United States and Canada were assigned to live in their areas, giving these leaders the advantage of intimate contact with the Saints in their assigned areas. Membership in each presidency was rotated from time to time, giving the members broader perspective from experiences in various parts of the world. These area presidency assignments replaced the former Area Supervisors. With a presidency of three, rather than just a single General Authority heading each area, more responsibilities and decision-making power were delegated to this level. President Gordon B. Hinckley, then the Second Counselor in the First Presidency, indicated that with the Church's rapid international growth, it needed the flexibility that area presidencies could bring.[28] In later years, these areas divided and additional presidencies were formed. A decade later the regional representatives would be replaced by Area Authority Seventies and three additional Seventies quorums would be created.

Conferencegoers avoid the rain outside King's Hall at the inaugural area conference, in Manchester, England. (Deseret News *photo)*

Developments in Conference Patterns

Conferences had been another source of contact between the General Authorities and local leaders and Saints. Traditionally, conferences had been held in each stake four times a year (see D&C 20:61–62). As the number of stakes multiplied, the General Authorities were able to attend these conferences less frequently. Beginning in 1964, members of the four priesthood committees as well as members of auxiliary general boards were appointed to visit half of the stake conferences each year. Then, in 1968, General Authorities were assigned to attend only two conferences in each stake during the year, the other two being under the direction of the stake president. By 1975, regional representatives were given authority to conduct one conference in each stake annually.[29]

At the same time, bringing the leaders of these widespread units to the general conferences held at Church headquarters became an ever greater economic burden. In addition, it became more difficult to find seats in the Salt Lake Tabernacle for the throngs who traveled long distances to hear the messages of Church leaders. The Church, therefore, inaugurated the area conferences in 1971, sending a group of General Authorities to meet the Saints in a given part of the world.

Since the beginning of the twentieth century, Church auxiliaries had conducted annual conferences in Salt Lake City, at which they presented the coming year's programs and provided training and inspiration for local officers and teachers. However, at the MIA conference in 1975, President Spencer W. Kimball pointed out that only a very small proportion of local auxiliary leaders could afford to attend the annual conferences at Church headquarters and that existing facilities were inadequate to house all who should attend. Therefore, these auxiliary conferences were discontinued. Leadership training was provided instead in the regional meetings conducted by the regional representatives.

In 1977 general conferences were shortened from three to two days and were held on the first weekend of April and October. This meant that the spring conferences would not necessarily include April 6, the anniversary of the Church's organization and a traditional general conference date. Limiting the general sessions to the weekends facilitated attendance for stake presidents and others who often could not leave employment responsibilities during weekdays.[30]

Beginning in the 1970s, area conferences such as this one in Montevideo, Uruguay, provided spiritual strength to Church members around the world. (Copyright Intellectual Reserve, all rights reserved)

Beginning in 1979 the number of conferences held annually in each stake was reduced from four to two. This was done to ease the financial and time burdens on Church members. Only one of the conferences each year was conducted by a General Authority.

While conferences at the general and stake levels were being reduced, more emphasis was placed on conferences at intermediate levels. In addition to area conferences, regional or multiregional gatherings were held in sports arenas or other similarly large meeting facilities. These changes lessened the time Church leaders were required to spend holding conferences, but at the same time provided expanded contacts between Church members and the General Authorities. Additionally, the perfection of satellites and other communications media provided a new source of immediate contact between General Authorities and the far-flung membership of the Church and therefore reduced the need for Church leaders to travel so widely.

Latter-day Saints from around the world throng the Salt Lake Tabernacle during general conference to receive counsel and direction from Church leaders, circa 1980. (LDS Church Archives)

Responsibility for Church Programs

The General Authorities have been responsible not only for giving direction to Church units worldwide but also for administering the numerous and varied departments and committees at Church headquarters. In 1977 the First Presidency announced a delineation between responsibility for ecclesiastical and temporal matters, respectively: "The Lord has made it clear that the Council of the Twelve, under direction of the First Presidency, has special responsibility for administering the ecclesiastical affairs of the Church, including responsibility to direct the functioning of the newly organized First Quorum of the Seventy, the third governing quorum of the Church. Under the direction of the First Presidency, the Presiding Bishopric has been given the responsibility for administering the temporal affairs of the Church."[31] Areas to be administered by the Twelve included priesthood and auxiliary programs, as well as the missionary, temple and genealogy, and leadership-training activities. Departments under the Presiding Bishopric's jurisdiction included translation and distribution, physical facilities, data processing, financial, purchasing, membership records, and reporting. The mission of these "temporal" departments was to serve and support the ecclesiastical programs of the Church.[32]

Several behind-the-scenes agencies made a vital contribution to the success of better-known Church activities. The Legal Department's team of attorneys, at Church headquarters and abroad, handled tax status, legal recognition, and related problems. The Central Purchasing Department handled all Church buying, saving money through bulk purchasing and by eliminating unnecessary paperwork. The Church-operated Deseret News Press had become the Intermountain West's largest publisher of books, magazines, forms, and related materials. But in 1980, it phased out all commercial work and became the Church's Printing Services Division.[33]

Accurate membership records have helped Church leaders be aware of those for whom they are responsible (see Moroni 6:4). Before 1907, when members moved from one location to another, they were given their membership records to deliver in person to the new bishop or branch president. In that year, however, the practice began of sending the records to Church headquarters to be forwarded to the new wards or branches. In 1968 ward clerks began "auditing" records of Church members to verify accuracy and completeness. This information was then entered into a computer, which could automatically update records as new ordinances were performed and print ward lists of members, special lists by age groups, and so forth.[34]

Properly administering the sacred funds of the Church was commanded by revelation. Section 120 in the Doctrine and Covenants provided for a Council on the Disposition of Tithes composed of the First Presidency, Quorum of the Twelve, and Presiding Bishopric. This body approved financial budgets and strategies. A subcommittee, the Appropriation Committee, met weekly to consider and approve specific requests for expenditures.[35]

To provide continuity and more effective economic administration and to lessen the load carried by the First Presidency, the Church established several corporation entities: (1) The Corporation of the President of the Church administers legal and financial matters and holds tax-free properties mostly at Church headquarters. (2) The Corporation of the Presiding Bishopric holds ecclesiastical properties mostly away from Church headquarters. (3) In 1922 President Heber J. Grant organized Zions Securities Corporation to manage revenue-producing properties; on these strictly investment properties, the Church voluntarily pays taxes although it could generally claim a nonprofit exemption. (4) Cooperative Securities Corporation was set up during the Great Depression to coordinate the management of welfare program properties.[36]

Clarifying the roles of the General Authorities, modifying the pattern of holding conferences, utilizing modern tools such as the computer, and coordinating the services of the varied behind-the-scenes departments at headquarters all enabled the Church to keep up with its phenomenal growth and more effectively fulfill its worldwide mission.

Ezra Taft Benson's Leadership in Challenging Times

*D*uring the 1980s the Church faced a variety of challenges and opportunities. In the early years of this decade President Spencer W. Kimball gave dynamic leadership, preparing the Saints to meet these challenges. Following his death on November 5, 1985, the mantle of the presidency passed to eighty-six-year-old Ezra Taft Benson, the President of the Quorum of the Twelve. He had been called to the apostleship in 1943, at the same time as President Kimball.

President Benson's Earlier Life

Ezra Taft Benson was born in 1899 in Whitney, a small farming community in southeastern Idaho. He was named for his great-grandfather who had served as an Apostle under Brigham Young. "T," as the future Church president was familiarly known, was the first of eleven children. At age four, he began working on the family farm and at fourteen became the "man of the house" when his father left to serve in the Northern States Mission. He then attended the Oneida Stake Academy where he became a good friend of fellow student Harold B. Lee. In 1921 Ezra went to Logan to study at Utah State Agricultural College (later renamed Utah State University). Here, he met and fell in love with Flora Amussen, one of the more popular students on campus. Ezra left her to serve a mission in England under David O. McKay. When he returned, Flora did not feel that the time was quite right for

President Ezra Taft Benson (center), thirteenth President of the Church, with counselors Gordon B. Hinckley (left) and Thomas S. Monson. (Deseret News *photo*)

Sarah Benson and seven of her children at the time of her husband's mission. (The eighth child was born shortly thereafter.) Ezra is standing behind his mother. (LDS Church Archives)

their marriage. Feeling the need for additional spiritual maturity, she approached her bishop about serving a mission and was soon called to the Hawaiian Islands.[1]

Waiting two years for Flora gave Ezra time to complete his bachelor's degree at Brigham Young University. He graduated with honors and was voted "most likely to succeed."[2] Shortly after her return, and after a total of six years of courtship, they were married in the Salt Lake Temple on September 10, 1926, and immediately moved to Ames, Iowa. After a year of study at Iowa State College he earned a master's degree in agricultural economics. They then returned to the family farm in Whitney, and Ezra soon became a county agriculture agent. His work in this position became known throughout the state and led to his appointment as an agricultural economist and extension specialist in Boise, the state capital. During his nine years in Boise he helped organize local farmer cooperatives and became the secretary of the Idaho Cooperative Council. He also found time for Church service, becoming president of the Boise Stake in 1938.

His effective service in Idaho attracted national attention, and in 1939 he was invited to become the executive secretary of the National Council of Farmer Cooperatives in Washington, D.C. This post gave him contact with international government and agricultural leaders which would later proved valuable. Church activity remained an important part of his life. When the new Washington Stake was organized in 1940, he became its first president, calling Ernest L. Wilkinson as one of his counselors.

Ezra Taft Benson, missionary to England, in 1921. (LDS Church Archives)

During a visit to Salt Lake City in July 1943, Ezra Taft Benson was told President Heber J. Grant wanted to meet with him at his summer home. "Oh, I can't go up the canyon," Ezra protested. "I have a train to catch shortly." After being assured that the interview was important and that there was

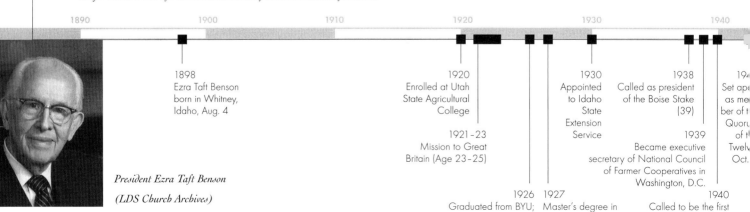

Major events in the life and administration of President Ezra Taft Benson

1890 1900 1910 1920 1930 1940

President Ezra Taft Benson (LDS Church Archives)

1898
Ezra Taft Benson born in Whitney, Idaho, Aug. 4

1920
Enrolled at Utah State Agricultural College

1921–23
Mission to Great Britain (Age 23–25)

1926
Graduated from BYU; married Flora Amussen (27)

1927
Master's degree in agricultural economics from Iowa State College

1930
Appointed to Idaho State Extension Service

1938
Called as president of the Boise Stake (39)

1939
Became executive secretary of National Council of Farmer Cooperatives in Washington, D.C.

1940
Called to be the first president of the Washington Stake (40)

19
Set ap as me ber of t Quoru of t Twelv Oct.

enough time, Ezra agreed to go. During the hour-long interview, the forty-three-year-old stake president was called to fill a vacancy in the Council of the Twelve.[3]

One of his most significant assignments came just over two years later when, at the close of World War II, he was called as president of the European Mission and given the specific assignment of supervising the distribution of welfare supplies and reopening missionary work in the countries of Europe.[4] Guided by inspiration, Elder Benson radiated love as he contacted the scattered Saints in these war-torn countries.

A unique opportunity came in 1952 when President-elect Dwight D. Eisenhower invited Ezra Taft Benson to become United States Secretary of Agriculture. President David O. McKay encouraged Elder Benson to accept the appointment, suggesting that serving in this national office would afford opportunities to further the Lord's work. At the cabinet's first meeting, President Eisenhower accepted Secretary Benson's suggestion that these meetings henceforth begin with prayer. In this position he tried to make decisions based on principle rather than political expediency. For this he was not always popular but was widely admired. Elder Benson was one of only two cabinet members who served throughout the entire eight years of the Eisenhower administration. Although Ezra later described his years as Secretary of Agriculture as a time of "cross fire," he nevertheless had traveled nearly a million miles in forty-four countries, making friends for the Church with his example of integrity and faith.[5] During a visit to Moscow in 1959, for example, he had an opportunity to share his testimony with a Baptist congregation. "I shall never forget that evening as long as I live," Benson would write later of the experience. "Seldom, if ever, have I felt the oneness of mankind and the unquenchable yearning of the human heart for freedom."[6]

Elders Spencer W. Kimball (left) and Ezra Taft Benson were called in 1943 as members of the Quorum of the Twelve and served together for some forty-two years. (Deseret News *photo*)

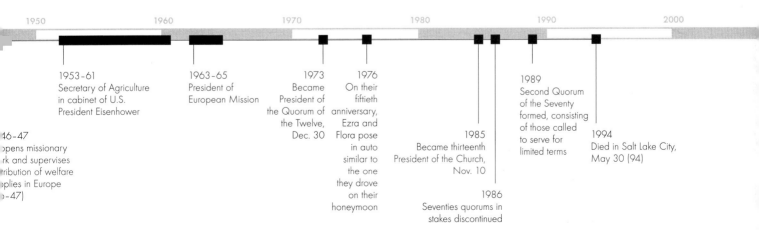

1950 1960 1970 1980 1990 2000

46-47
opens missionary
rk and supervises
ribution of welfare
plies in Europe
-47)

1953-61
Secretary of Agriculture in cabinet of U.S. President Eisenhower

1963-65
President of European Mission

1973
Became President of the Quorum of the Twelve, Dec. 30

1976
On their fiftieth anniversary, Ezra and Flora pose in auto similar to the one they drove on their honeymoon

1985
Became thirteenth President of the Church, Nov. 10

1986
Seventies quorums in stakes discontinued

1989
Second Quorum of the Seventy formed, consisting of those called to serve for limited terms

1994
Died in Salt Lake City, May 30 (94)

He returned to full-time Church service in 1961, and during the next quarter century Elder Benson fulfilled important assignments in the Quorum of the Twelve. These included presiding once again in Europe, supervising the work in Asia, and serving twelve years as president of the Twelve.

His 1983 book, *Come unto Christ*, included chapters entitled "What Manner of Men Ought We to Be?" "Lead Your Children to Christ," "Preach the Gospel to Every Nation," and "Feed My Sheep." These topics anticipated areas that President Benson would stress during his administration.

President Benson's Teachings

COME UNTO CHRIST

In 1985 as President Benson assumed his new responsibility, he called Gordon B. Hinckley and Thomas S. Monson to assist him as his counselors. At age fifty-eight, President Monson was the youngest man to be called to the First Presidency in over a hundred years. At the news conference where the new First Presidency was introduced, President Benson declared, "My heart has been filled with an overwhelming love and compassion for all members of our Heavenly Father's children everywhere. I love all our Father's children of every color, creed, and political persuasion." He emphasized that "the Lord, through President Kimball, has sharply focused on the threefold mission of the Church: to preach the Gospel, to perfect the Saints, and to redeem the dead. We shall continue every effort to carry out this mission." Specifically, he called for a renewed commitment to missionary work, indicating the Church's eagerness to carry the gospel to any parts of the world where doors might open. He also promised to give continuing emphasis to the family. At the conclusion of his comments, he stressed that the Church's ultimate purpose was to assist all people to "Come unto Christ, and be perfected in him" (Moroni 10:32).[7]

President Benson issued a special invitation to disaffected or less-active members to return to full fellowship in the Church. In their Christmas message of 1985, the First Presidency wrote, "We are aware of some who are inactive, of others who have become critical and are prone to find fault, and of those who have been disfellowshipped or excommunicated because of serious transgressions. To all such we reach out in love. . . . Come back. Come back and feast at the table of the Lord, and taste again the sweet and satisfying fruits of fellowship with the saints."[8]

EMPHASIS ON THE BOOK OF MORMON

President Benson frequently emphasized the importance of the Book of Mormon. He often quoted Joseph Smith's declaration that "the Book of Mormon was the most correct of any book on earth, and the keystone of our religion, and a man would get nearer to God by abiding by its precepts, than by any other book."[9] President Benson testified that this focus of his administration had been prompted by a spiritual experience he had in 1983: "As I participated in the Mexico City Temple dedication, I received the distinct impression that God is not pleased with our neglect of the Book of Mormon." He was convinced that it was through study of the Book of Mormon that individuals could gain a firm testimony of the restored gospel.[10] In his first general conference address as prophet, President Benson asserted that the Church was still under the condemnation pronounced by the Lord in 1831 for not using the Book of Mormon as they should (see D&C 84:54–57). He declared, "Now we not only need to *say* more about the Book of Mormon, but we need to *do* more with it. . . . The Book of Mormon has not been, nor is it yet, the center of our personal study, family teaching, preaching, and missionary work. Of this we must repent."[11]

In response, the prophet received numerous letters from Church members who accepted his challenge to read and study the Book of Mormon. During 1986, President Benson's first full year as President of the Church, the number of copies of the Book of Mormon distributed doubled from the previous year, reaching a total of 2,911,916. Fifteen percent of these contained photographs of individual members or families together with a brief written testimony addressed to nonmember friends or potential investigators of the Church.[12] In the April 1987 general conference, he called upon the Lord to bless the Saints with an "increased desire to flood the earth with the Book of Mormon."[13] Early in 1988, the book appeared for the first time in the Trukese, Papiamento, and Pahnpeian languages, bringing the total number of translations to eighty. More than half of these translations appeared for the first time in the 1980s.[14]

THE ROLE OF AMERICA AND THE CONSTITUTION

President Benson described America as "the Lord's base of operations in these latter days." He pointed out, "It was in America that the Book of Mormon plates were deposited. That was no accident. It was His design. . . . It was here where He organized His modern Church, where He, Himself, made a modern personal appearance." President Benson was convinced that God had "established a free people in this land as a means of helping to carry forward His purposes."[15] He often referred to the teachings in the Book of Mormon that America would be a choice land only as long as its inhabitants kept the commandments (see 2 Nephi 1:20).

He also stressed the divine origin of the United States Constitution (see D&C 101:80). He cited with approval Joseph Smith's description of the Constitution: "[It] is a glorious standard; it is founded in the wisdom of God. It is a heavenly banner."[16] He therefore frequently urged Latter-day Saints to study it and uphold its precepts.

BEWARE OF PRIDE

President Benson taught that pride had caused the destruction of the Nephites and in modern times continued to be the great stumbling block to Zion (see Moroni 8:27; D&C 38:39). "This is one of the major messages of the Book of Mormon," the Prophet emphasized. "In the scriptures there is no

Translations of the Book of Mormon have been done in clusters over the years. By 1988, the Book of Mormon had been printed in eighty languages. (Deseret News *photo)*

Elder Benson never hesitated to speak out on the subject of freedom. (LDS Church Archives)

such thing as righteous pride—it is always considered a sin." Disobedience, selfishness, and contentions are among the damning fruits of pride, he warned. "The antidote for pride is humility—meekness, submissiveness. It is the broken heart and contrite spirit."[17]

FAMILY MEMBERS' RESPONSIBILITY

In a series of talks, President Benson spoke of the unique responsibilities and opportunities of various family members—fathers, mothers, young men, and young women. Beginning with the October 1985 general conference, just a few weeks before the death of President Kimball, President Benson again used the Book of Mormon, this time as the basis of his message to fathers. "May we fathers teach our sons as the exemplary Book of Mormon fathers taught their sons," he admonished. "And may our sons, like Nephi, listen and obey, knowing that because of those teachings they too were born of goodly parents."[18]

The following April, President Benson directed his attention to the young men of the Church. "You are to be the royal army of the Lord in the last days," he told them in the general conference priesthood session. The prophet urged them to draw closer to their parents. He exhorted them to read the scriptures, especially the Book of Mormon, daily and diligently. He counseled them to obtain patriarchal blessings, attend meetings, participate in Scouting, attend seminary, and prepare for missionary service. "Currently, only a fifth of the eligible young men in the Church are serving full-time missions," President Benson lamented. "This is not pleasing to the Lord. We can do better. We *must* do better."[19]

He also counseled the young men on their family relationships: "Your most important friendships should be with your own brothers and sisters and with your father and mother. Love your family. Be loyal to them."[20]

Then, at the women's meeting in connection with conference six months later, President Benson addressed the young women, stating, "Give me a young woman who loves home and family, who reads and ponders the scriptures daily, who has a burning testimony of the Book of Mormon. . . . Give me a young woman who is virtuous and who has maintained her personal purity, who will not settle for less than a temple marriage, and I will give you a young woman who will perform miracles for the Lord now and throughout eternity."[21] On numerous other occasions, President Benson spoke to large groups of young people, conveying his love to them and urging them to utilize the Book of Mormon and live honorable, virtuous lives.

As part of a telecast to parents via the Church's satellite network in February 1987, President Benson addressed the mothers in Zion. He emphasized that there was no greater work than that of a mother. Referring to counsel given by David O. McKay, he explained that "Motherhood consists of three principal attributes or qualities: namely, (1) the power to bear, (2) the ability to rear, (3) the gift to love."[22] President Benson also encouraged mothers to stay at home and spend quality time with their children.

In October 1987, he again focused his attention on the fathers of the Church. "Fathers, yours is an eternal calling from which you are never released," he taught. "Callings in the Church, as important as they are, by their very nature are only for a period of time. . . . But a father's calling is eternal." After stressing the importance of providing leadership and material needs for the family, President Benson concluded: "A father's duty is to make his home a place of happiness and joy."[23]

LOTTERIES

Church leaders also took note of and gave counsel relative to other contemporary concerns. As a rapidly increasing number of states legalized and even sponsored public lotteries, Church leaders urged Latter-day Saints to oppose them. Echoing counsel given half a century earlier by President Heber J. Grant, the First Presidency publicly opposed this form of legalized gambling, pointing out that "all too often lotteries only add to the problems of the financially disadvantaged by taking money from them and giving nothing of value in return. The poor and the elderly become victims of the inducements that are held out to purchase lottery tickets."[24]

STATEMENT ON AIDS

During the 1980s Acquired Immune Deficiency Syndrome (AIDS) rapidly became a major health concern in many parts of the world. "Unlike some major epidemics of the past that were transmitted by polluted water, insect bites, and casual skin or respiratory contact," the First Presidency wrote concerning this issue, AIDS was most commonly transmitted through elicit sexual intimacy and through "illegal intravenous drug use. . . . We, with others, hope that discoveries will make possible both prevention and healing from this dread affliction," the Presidency continued. "But regardless of such discoveries, the observance of one clearly understandable and divinely given rule would do more than all else to check this epidemic. That is chastity before marriage and total fidelity in marriage. . . . Our concern for the bitter fruit of sin is coupled with Christ-like sympathy for its victims, innocent or culpable."[25]

In 1988, President Thomas S. Monson and Elder Russell M. Nelson negotiate with officials to receive permission for missionaries to work in the German Democratic Republic (Deseret News *photo*)

Organizational Changes

With the organization of the First Quorum of Seventy as a body of General Authorities in 1984, questions arose concerning the role of men holding the office of seventy at the stake level. These ambiguities ended in October 1986 when President Ezra Taft Benson announced that seventies quorums in the stakes were being discontinued. Most of the members of these groups were directed to affiliate with the elders quorums in their wards, while stake presidents were to recommend some for ordination to the office of high priest. Typically, there had only been a few seventies in a given ward, so these brethren lacked the priesthood fellowship enjoyed by elders and high priests. With this change, their needs would be more adequately met. Furthermore, seventies quorums had traditionally been linked with missionary work in the stakes. But with the discontinuation of these units at the stake level, instruction was given to more fully involve all Church members in local missionary work.

With the dissolving of these local quorums, the only seventies quorum that continued at that time was the First Quorum of the Seventy at the General Authority level. Two and a half years later, the Second Quorum of Seventy was also formed as a General Authorities body.

By 1987, the number of areas had increased to seventeen. In August of that year the First Presidency assigned these area presidencies to assume the function of the International Mission which was officially discontinued at that time.[26]

Doors Opened in Eastern Europe

Over the years President Ezra Taft Benson had spoken of the threat posed by "godless communism." As early as 1948 he asserted: "Communism, to my mind, is not merely an economic program. It is a total philosophy of life, utterly atheistic and utterly opposed to all we hold dear as a great Christian nation."[27] It was fitting that communism's domination of Eastern Europe came to an end during his administration. These climactic developments in world history at the end of the 1980s were anticipated by significant Church events.

In 1975 Elder Thomas S. Monson offered a dedicatory prayer in the German Democratic Republic (communist East Germany). Standing on a outcropping of rock overlooking the Elbe Valley, he petitioned "divine help" for the 4,000 faithful Saints living in that land, that they might enjoy, among other things, temple blessings. "Dear Father, let this be the beginning of a new day for the members of Thy Church in this land." Just then he heard a rooster crowing and a church bell far below. He noticed a ray of sun coming through the clouded sky. All suggested a new day truly was dawning.[28] President Spencer W. Kimball offered a similar prayer in Poland two years later.

Then in 1985, just ten years after Elder Monson's dedicatory prayer, the Freiberg Germany Temple was dedicated in the German Democratic Republic. This first temple behind the "Iron Curtain" was built following patient yet persistent negotiations by East German Church leaders and the Communist government authorities. In 1987 Premier Mikhail Gorbachev of the USSR called for reforms (*perestroika*) and increased openness (*glasnost*). The political climate was becoming more favorable for the expansion of the Church in central and eastern Europe.

President Thomas S. Monson described a key meeting on October 28, 1988, which led to missionaries being called from and being sent to East Germany: "That special morning the sunlight bathed the city of Berlin. It had been raining all night, but beauty prevailed." Seated around a large table with his visitors, Chairman Honecker, head of the communist East German government, began: "We know members of your Church believe in work; you've proven that. We know you believe in the family; you've demonstrated that. We know you are good citizens in whatever country you claim as home; we have observed that. The floor is yours. Make your desires known."

President Monson explained how 89,000 people attended the open house for the Freiberg Germany Temple, but the Church had no missionaries who could answer their questions. "The young men and young women whom we would like to have come to your country as missionary representatives would love your nation and your people. More particularly, they would leave an influence with your people which would be ennobling. Then," President Monson continued, "we would like to see young men and young women from your nation who are members of our Church serve as missionary representatives in many nations, such as in America, in Canada, and in a host of others. They will return better prepared to assume positions of responsibility in your land."

At length Chairman Honecker smiled and responded: "We know you. We trust you. We have had experience with you. Your missionary request is approved."[29]

In November of 1989, individuals were permitted to travel freely between East and West Berlin for the first time in several decades. Soon the infamous Berlin Wall was dismantled. Within a year, the communist regimes in East Germany and other eastern European countries toppled. These changes opened doors for the gospel to spread, and in the summer of 1990, missions opened in Poland, Czechoslovakia, and Hungary.[30]

Also in 1990, Yuri Dubinin, the Soviet ambassador to the United States, visited Utah. He met with Church leaders, visited Brigham Young University and the Missionary Training Center, and even spoke at a stake conference. He expressed appreciation for aid the Church had sent following a recent earthquake. He stressed that a new worldwide understanding needed to be based on "universal human values," and it must be achieved by peoples rather than by governments.[31]

The Freiberg Germany Temple became the first in what was then the Soviet bloc. (LDS Church Archives)

Missionary work, though on a very limited scale, had already begun in the USSR. In 1989, missionaries had begun teaching Russians who had crossed the border into Finland. Early in 1990, permission was received to send missionaries to Estonia and to

Leningrad and Vyborg in Russia. In the summer of that year, the new Helsinki East Mission was formed to supervise the work in Russia, headed by Gary Browning, a BYU professor of Russian literature. At first, missionaries were only permitted to enter as tourists and were required to live in hotels. During a visit to the Vyborg branch, President Browning was thrilled to hear six beautiful little girls singing "I Am a Child of God," in Russian. "The singing was angelic, as were their radiant, broadly smiling faces. As I watched and listened in awe, my heart filled with 'hosannas' for the blessing of this long-awaited day." In September 1990, the Leningrad branch became the first Church unit to be officially registered in the Soviet Union.[32]

Another giant stride forward in eastern Europe came in June 1991. During a three-week tour of Europe, the famed Mormon Tabernacle Choir gave concerts in Hungary, Czechoslovakia, Poland, and the Soviet Union. It was also heard by radio or seen on television throughout these countries. Following the Choir's performance at Moscow's Bolshoi Theater an announcement was made that the Church had been officially recognized in the Russian Republic.[33]

The following year, the first three missions would be organized within the former Soviet Union, at St. Petersburg (Leningrad) and Moscow, Russia, and at Kiev, Ukraine. Most Latter-day Saints had believed that the gospel would be taken to these lands someday, but probably not during their lifetimes. These momentous events during President Ezra Taft Benson's administration were regarded by many as no less than miraculous.

20

Howard W. Hunter and the Early 1990s

As the concluding decade of the twentieth century began, the Church witnessed continued growth and progress throughout the world. The Church made progress and provided humanitarian service in parts of the world that had not traditionally been centers of Latter-day Saint strength. Although Howard W. Hunter did not become President of the Church until 1994, he nevertheless exerted a major influence on earlier developments because of his service as President of the Quorum of the Twelve. As President, he left an indelible mark on the Church through his focus on the temple's central role in the lives of the Saints.

President Hunter's Earlier Life

Howard William Hunter was the first Church President to be born during the twentieth century—in Boise, Idaho, on November 14, 1907. Although his mother, Nellie, was a faithful Latter-day Saint who took Howard and his younger sister Dorothy to church, his father, Will, was not a member and did not allow the children to be baptized at age eight; he thought they needed to be old enough to decide for themselves when they were ready. When Howard's friends at church became deacons at age 12, he sat with them in meetings but felt left out because he could not pass the sacrament with them. Pleading with his father, Howard was finally given permission to be baptized five months after his twelfth birthday; eleven weeks later

Elder Howard W. Hunter shakes hands with mayor Teddy Kollek at the dedication of the Orson Hyde Memorial Garden in Jerusalem. Howard W. Hunter was instrumental in this project and the building of the BYU Jerusalem Center for Near Eastern Studies. (LDS Church Archives)

Howard in scouting uniform. (Photo courtesy Hunter family)

he was ordained a deacon.[1] His father joined the Church a few years later.

During his boyhood years he enjoyed spending time in the Idaho countryside, where he gained a love for animals, nature, and hard work. He became involved in Scouting and was only the second Boy Scout in Idaho to achieve the rank of Eagle. He loved music and learned to play the marimba, drums, saxophone, clarinet, trumpet, piano, and the violin. During his junior year of high school he organized his own dance band, Hunter's Croonaders. Soon after graduation, he and a few other musician friends formed a five-piece orchestra to play aboard a ship during a two-month cruise to Asia. They performed classical music during dinner, accompanied silent movies, and played for dances.

After returning to Idaho, opportunities for employment became increasingly scarce. Therefore, twenty-one-year-old Howard headed to southern California. He found employment performing as a musician, selling shoes, and eventually working in a bank. Even though he had been active in the Church during his youth in Idaho, it was in a Sunday School class in Los Angeles, California, that he experienced his "first real awakening to the gospel." He actively studied the lessons and participated in discussions. "I think of this period of my life as the time the truths of the gospel commenced to unfold. I always had a testimony of the gospel, but suddenly I commenced to understand."[2]

At a young adult Church activity, Howard met Clara May (Claire) Jeffs whom he married on June 10, 1931, in the Salt Lake Temple. As his wedding date approached, he decided to give up his career as a professional musician. "It was glamorous in some respects," Howard commented, "and I made good money, but the association with many of the musicians was not enjoyable because of their drinking and moral standards."[3]

Deciding he wanted to enter the legal profession, the young husband enrolled at Southwestern University, in Los Angeles, to finish his undergraduate work and to pursue a law degree. Continuing to work full time and taking classes in the evening, Howard determined that he would still fulfill his ecclesiastical and spiritual responsibilities. He received his degree in 1939.

Howard W. Hunter was called as bishop of the El Sereno Ward in 1940, during the time that more and more nations were becoming entangled in World War II. Even though his ward could not build their badly needed chapel during the war, Bishop Hunter nevertheless encouraged the members to participate in fund-raising projects so that the needed money would be available when construction became possible once again.

Bishop Hunter was released in 1946 and four years later was called as president of the Pasadena Stake. His

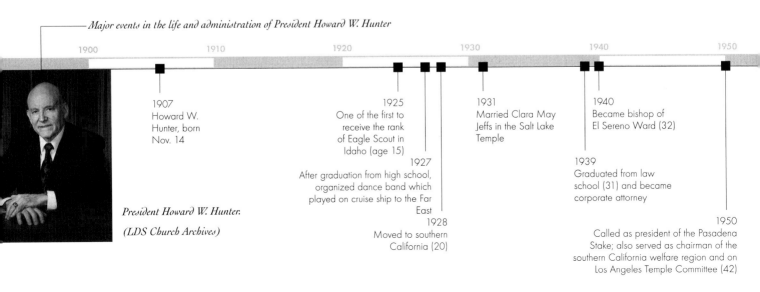

Major events in the life and administration of President Howard W. Hunter

1900 · 1910 · 1920 · 1930 · 1940 · 1950

President Howard W. Hunter. (LDS Church Archives)

1907
Howard W. Hunter, born Nov. 14

1925
One of the first to receive the rank of Eagle Scout in Idaho (age 15)

1927
After graduation from high school, organized dance band which played on cruise ship to the Far East

1928
Moved to southern California (20)

1931
Married Clara May Jeffs in the Salt Lake Temple

1939
Graduated from law school (31) and became corporate attorney

1940
Became bishop of El Sereno Ward (32)

1950
Called as president of the Pasadena Stake; also served as chairman of the southern California welfare region and on Los Angeles Temple Committee (42)

responsibility was not limited to his own stake, however. The General Authorities assigned President Hunter to take the lead in pioneering early-morning seminaries, to serve as chairman of the southern California welfare region, to act as priesthood advisor for regional youth activities, including music and dance festivals, and to play a key role in raising funds for the building of the Los Angeles Temple.[4] He was

HUNTER'S
Croonaders

As a junior in high school Howard W. Hunter organized his own dance band, Hunter's Croonaders. (Photo courtesy Hunter family)

invited to be present with President David O. McKay when the statue of the Angel Moroni was hoisted to the top of the temple's 257-foot tower.

Prior to the completion of the Los Angeles Temple, President Hunter's stake conducted regular excursions to the temples in St. George, Utah, and Mesa, Arizona. One of these visits to the Arizona Temple came on his forty-sixth birthday. After the Pasadena group had changed into white clothing, they gathered in the temple's chapel. The temple president called on Stake President Hunter to speak. "While I was speaking to the congregation," he later recalled, "my father and mother came into the chapel dressed in white. I had no idea my father was prepared for his temple blessings. . . . I was so overcome with emotion that I was unable to continue to speak." The temple president stepped to his side and explained to the group that Howard's parents had planned this as a birthday surprise. He accompanied his parents as they were endowed, and after witnessing their sealing, Howard then was sealed to them.[5]

As stake president, Howard W. Hunter generally attended general conferences in Salt Lake City. In October 1959, following the opening session of conference, President Hunter received a note asking him to go to President David O. McKay's office. His counselor reminded Howard that there was a vacancy in the Council of the Twelve. But President Hunter dismissed this remark and explained that he had been gathering some information for the First Presidency and that they likely wanted a report. He then walked to President McKay's office, confident that nothing out of the ordinary was going to happen. "Sit down, President Hunter," the Prophet directed, "I want to talk with you. The Lord has spoken. You are called to be one of his special witnesses, and tomorrow you will be sustained as a member of the Council of the Twelve." The Prophet put his arm around Howard and told him what this calling

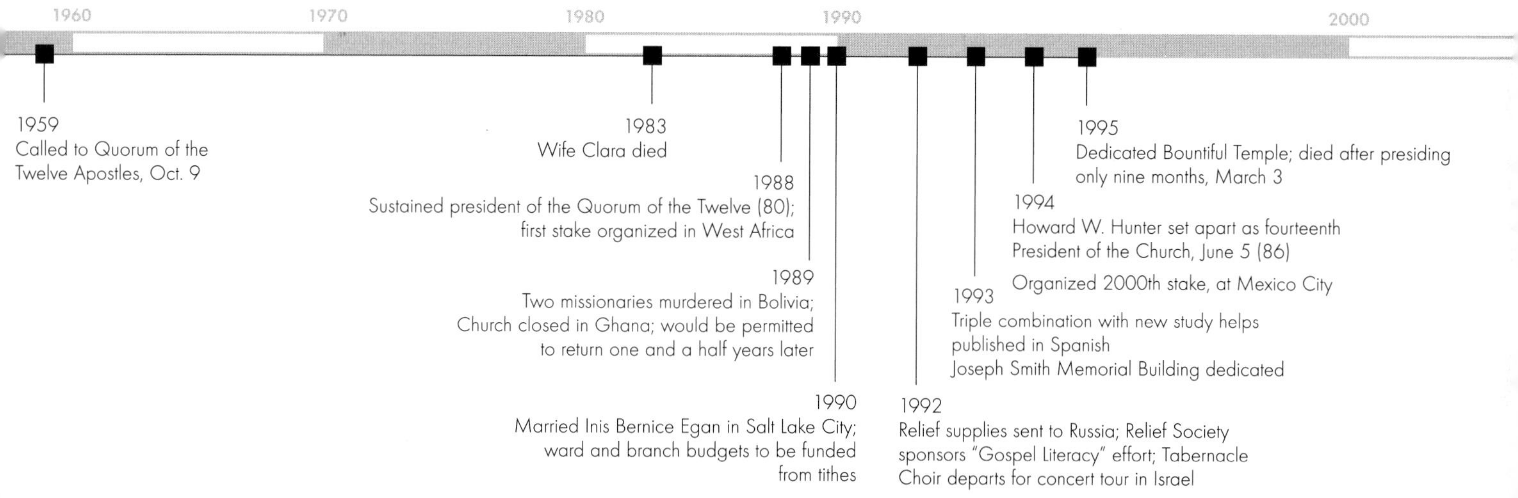
1960
1970
1980
1990
2000
1959
Called to Quorum of the Twelve Apostles, Oct. 9
1983
Wife Clara died
1988
Sustained president of the Quorum of the Twelve (80); first stake organized in West Africa
1989
Two missionaries murdered in Bolivia; Church closed in Ghana; would be permitted to return one and a half years later
1990
Married Inis Bernice Egan in Salt Lake City; ward and branch budgets to be funded from tithes
1992
Relief supplies sent to Russia; Relief Society sponsors "Gospel Literacy" effort; Tabernacle Choir departs for concert tour in Israel
1993
Triple combination with new study helps published in Spanish
Joseph Smith Memorial Building dedicated
1994
Howard W. Hunter set apart as fourteenth President of the Church, June 5 (86)
Organized 2000th stake, at Mexico City
1995
Dedicated Bountiful Temple; died after presiding only nine months, March 3

As an Apostle, Howard W. Hunter served as Church historian and later supervised the Historical Department of the Church. (Deseret News *photo)*

would mean in his life. President McKay told him that he could call and tell his wife, who was in Provo visiting their son, a student at BYU. When he called, President Hunter was so choked up that for several moments he was unable to explain to Claire what had happened.[6]

As a member of the Council of the Twelve, Elder Hunter played a key role in several Church programs. When Brigham Young University began building the Jerusalem Center in the early 1980s, Elder Hunter was assigned by the First Presidency to give close supervision and support to this project. Therefore, it was fitting that he was invited to dedicate this impressive edifice in May 1989.

Another of his assignments as a member of the Twelve was to serve as Church historian and recorder. He succeeded Joseph Fielding Smith who had filled that office for a half century. Elder Hunter took a personal interest in the functioning of the Church historian's office, encouraged efforts to improve the preserving of Church history, and played a key role in consolidating these efforts into the new Historical Department of the Church. In 1972, members of the Twelve were released from being the heads of Church departments, but Elder Hunter continued to serve as an advisor to the Historical Department.

Easing Burdens on Families

For some time, Church leaders had been concerned about the burden in time and money placed on families by the ever-growing programs of the Church. As early as 1978, the First Presidency declared, "We are most anxious that these requirements not become so heavy as to have an adverse effect on family life."[7] "There is concern," the Presidency later conceded, "lest some who are not able to meet these costs may withdraw themselves from full participation in the Church."[8] These concerns were echoed in at least four more official statements during the next few years. President Thomas S. Monson voiced the concern of the Brethren, saying, "In some respects, many of our youth activities in recent years have supplanted the home and family." He was worried that leaders increasingly felt that youth excursions "must be exotic to be successful"—resulting in mounting costs for parents.[9] Therefore, in 1990 Church leaders were grateful to announce that because of the members' faithfulness to the law of tithing and the payment of other offerings, ward and stake operational funds in the U.S. and Canada would come from the general Church funds.[10]

Elder Hunter's effective teaching of the principle of tithing had helped make this development possible. For example, to illustrate that tithing is simply returning to the Lord what is rightfully his, Elder Hunter referred to how, as a law student, he taught himself the difference between the crimes of larceny and embezzlement. "In order to memorize these distinctions, I pictured in my mind, to represent larceny, a masked burglar, sneaking about under the cover of darkness, taking that which was not his. To represent the theory of embezzlement I thought of a nontithepayer."[11]

Church leaders regarded the 1990 local budget program they were announcing as "but one of several carefully studied and prayerfully implemented steps taken by the Church to relieve the membership of financial burdens which some simply could not carry." First in this series of measures had been the consolidated meeting plan implemented in 1980 so "the time of Church members could be conserved and the cost of attending meetings reduced."[12] Next was the Church's increasing participation in the cost of constructing chapels. For years the Church had paid only half the cost, with the remainder being raised by the local congregations. Church headquarters then increased its share gradually until covering the total cost of construction. The third step was the elimination of the "per-capita welfare assessment," which members had previously been responsible for paying. President Thomas S. Monson was grateful that the needs of the poor could now be met through the "generous fast offerings" the Saints were paying. The final step was the implementation announced in 1990, "the local unit budget allowance program."[13] About these developments President Gordon B. Hinckley quipped, "In [the past] we would have thought the Millennium had come if we had received word that the Church would bear all of the costs of providing land, all of the costs incident to building construction, operation, and maintenance, let alone an activity and administrative budget allowance of forty dollars per year per individual, based on the number who attend sacrament meeting. It is not the Millennium," he conceded, "but this long hoped-for and prayed-for day has come. Though I have been a party to its inauguration, I still stand in awe at what has happened."[14]

Howard W. Hunter as a member of the Quorum of the Twelve Apostles. (LDS Church Archives)

The General Authorities warned local Church leaders that the new budget plan might require an adjustment in thinking. There would likely be a reduction in the amount of activities, and President Hinckley suggested that members use this as an opportunity to "look beyond the narrow boundaries of [their] own wards and rise to the larger vision of this, the work of God."[15]

About this same time the First Presidency became increasingly concerned about the "great and growing disparity in the cost of missions in various areas of the world," some costing as little as $100 per month with others as high as $750. Beginning in 1991, those supporting a missionary would contribute a fixed amount, originally set at $350.[16]

In a real sense, these budget changes implemented a principle of the law of consecration. Saints in affluent areas, through their faithful payment of tithes, subsidized Church activities for Saints living in less-prosperous circumstances. Likewise, those whose missionaries were serving in less-expensive areas helped to subsidize those whose missionaries were serving in more-costly locales.

Wider Geographical Horizons

During the early 1990s not only did the total number of members continue to grow, but the Church took significant strides in new and diverse geographical areas. The work in recently opened eastern Europe continued to grow. Black West Africa was another area of development. Over a thousand members attended the conference in 1988 when the first stake in this region was organized at Aba, Nigeria. For the first time in Church history, all the priesthood leaders in a stake were black.[17] Three years later, the Church received legal recognition in the Ivory Coast.[18]

Meanwhile, however, things were not going as well in another country of West Africa. In June 1989, after the Church had an official presence in Ghana for over a decade, the government unexpectedly announced that all Latter-day Saint activities were banned and that the twelve foreign Mormon missionaries, along with missionaries from three other religious groups, were to leave the country. Consequently, the Church chose to release its seventy-two native Ghanaian missionaries as well. These churches were banned for what was described as "conducting themselves in a manner that undermines the sovereignty of Ghana." A year and a half later, however, patient negotiations convinced

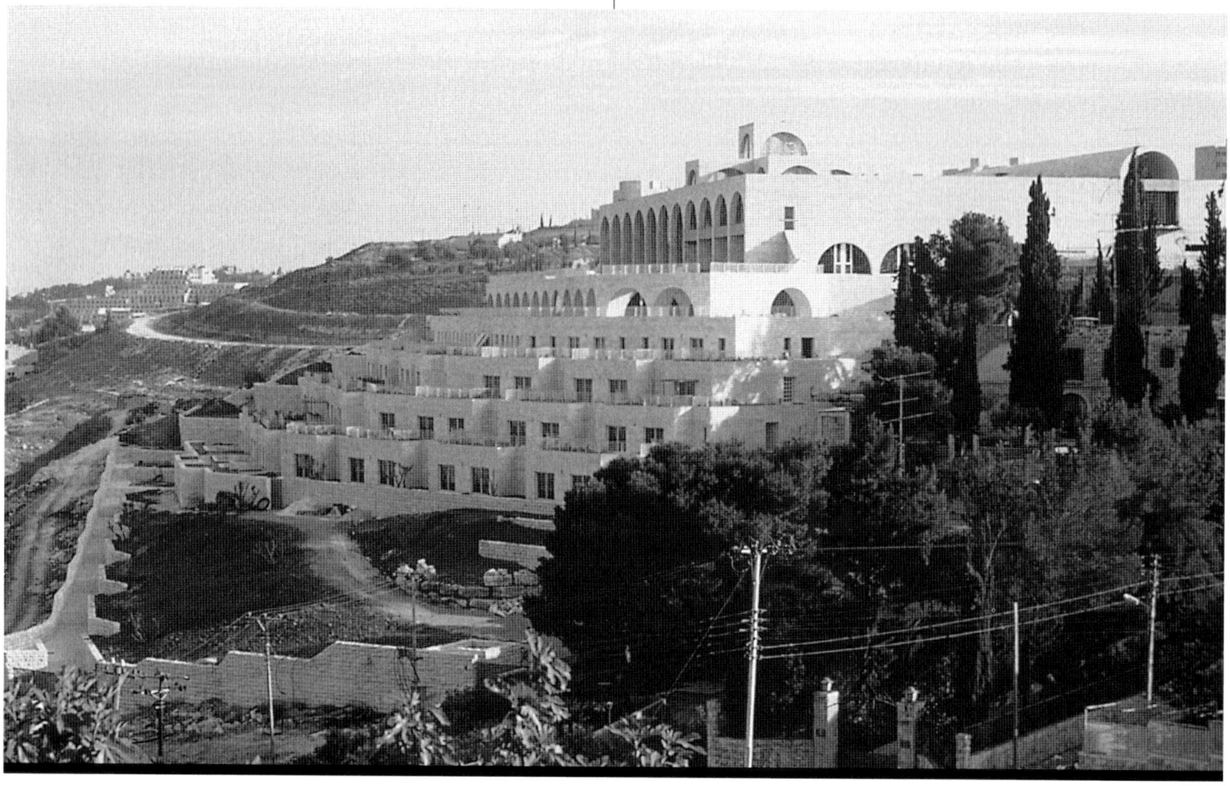

Elder Howard W. Hunter played a significant role in the creation of the BYU Jerusalem Center for Near Eastern Studies. The beautiful building would facilitate student groups touring the Holy Land. (Copyright Intellectual Reserve, all rights reserved)

government officials that Latter-day Saints really were exemplary and patriotic citizens and the Church was permitted to resume its activity in Ghana.[19]

Although the ban had halted most Church activities in Ghana, in many ways it actually strengthened the West African Saints. Less than four months after it was lifted, stakes were organized at Accra and Cape Coast. When the mission was reopened, the seventy-two local missionaries were contacted to see if they would like to resume their proselyting service. Three were out of the country, but remarkably, all of the remaining sixty-nine chose to complete their missions. One of the elders, Ebenezer Owusu, fasted and prayed during the interim that he might be worthy to resume his mission if the opportunity arose. As he waited he read *Jesus the Christ, Teachings of the Prophet Joseph Smith, Gospel Principles,* and the *Book of Mormon Institute of Religion Manual* each twice, and the Book of Mormon twenty times.[20]

In January 1991 the Gulf War focused the world's attention on the Middle East. Many Latter-day Saints were among the military personnel sent to that region. They returned with an increased awareness of the challenges faced by people in that part of the world. The BYU Jerusalem Center prospered despite tensions in the region.

On the day after Christmas in 1992, the Tabernacle Choir left for a 12-day concert tour to the Holy Land. Performances in Jerusalem and Tel Aviv were sold out. With the help of Israeli technical crews, the Choir's weekly "Music and the Spoken Word" broadcast came from BYU's Jerusalem Center, rather than from the "Crossroads of the West." Choir officials were delighted to learn that the managing director of the Jerusalem Symphony Orchestra and the head of music at the Israel Broadcast Authority had been fans of the Tabernacle Choir since their youth.[21]

During these same years, the Church was having a mixed experience in Latin America. Growth in the area continued to be more rapid than any other in the world. This progress, however, did not come easily.

In Chile, five Latter-day Saint chapels were damaged by bombs in 1986, and another destroyed in 1990. These attacks appeared to have been linked to anti-American sentiment. Even worse, two missionaries from Utah serving in Bolivia were murdered in 1989. The following year, two Peruvian missionaries, serving in their own country, were also shot to death. All four killings appeared to have been perpetrated by revolutionary terrorists.[22] Precautions were taken, and despite these tragedies missionary work went forward.

On a more positive note, in June 1993, after more than a century of activity in Mexico, the Church was finally officially registered as a religious organization by the government. This meant that the Church would enjoy all rights not permitted under earlier constitutions, including the ownership of property. In announcing this development, government officials gratefully acknowledged the many contributions made by the Mormon community in Mexico.[23]

Later the same year, the Church published a new Spanish edition of the triple combination. This publication made available for the first time in a language other than English the improved study helps that were part of the 1981 edition of the Book of Mormon, Doctrine and Covenants, and Pearl of Great Price. The 260-page "Guide to the Scriptures" incorporated the most helpful material drawn from 1,225 pages of the Topical Guide, the Bible Dictionary, and other helps in the English edition.

Humanitarian Efforts Worldwide

From the beginning, Church members had been taught to help one another (see D&C 38:35; 42:30; 52:40). The Church's welfare program was organized during the 1930s to facilitate these efforts. Over the years, as individuals or as a group, the Latter-day Saints had rendered valued assistance at times of local disasters or emergencies. The closing decades of the twentieth century witnessed the Church's involvement in "humanitarian aid" on a more global scale.

AID AT TIMES OF DISASTER

During the early 1980s a severe drought hit much of northeastern Africa, causing the malnutrition and death of millions of people in several countries. Elder M. Russell Ballard, of the First Quorum of the Seventy, and Glenn L. Pace, managing director of Welfare Services, were assigned to visit Africa in March 1985 and inspect conditions to see what the Church might do to assist the multitudes of starving people. Through special fasts during that year, Latter-day Saints donated more that $11 million for this cause. Early in January 1986, President Ezra Taft Benson traveled to Washington, D.C., and personally reported to U.S. President Ronald Reagan on these efforts.[24]

Early in 1992, eighteen hundred boxes of food and vitamins were sent to three newly created branches in Russia and Estonia. About half of the supplies went to Church members, and the remainder to other needy people in the area. Other boxes of supplies were sent directly to schools, hospitals, senior citizens' homes, and children's relief agencies. This project was financed mostly by donations from Latter-day Saints in Europe, but about two and a half tons of milk and a supply of vitamins came from the Church's welfare program in America.[25]

During the decade from 1985 to 1995, Latter-day Saint humanitarian efforts involved 2,340 separate projects in 137 countries at a total value of $162.5 million. Since 1985, Church humanitarian aid has included 9,800 tons of food, 894 tons of medical supplies, and 20,798 tons of surplus clothing.[26]

To provide the clothing needed for these relief projects, the First Presidency established the Deseret Industries "sort center" in Salt Lake City. It occupied two stories of a large building and employed 130 disadvantaged workers who otherwise would likely be unemployed. Each day they would sort about 45 tons of clothing, binding it into 125-pound bales for shipment.

Much of this humanitarian aid was initially distributed by experienced organizations not necessarily affiliated with the Church. However, in 1996 the Church created Latter-day Saint Charities, a charitable, nonprofit corporation to help "deliver humanitarian aid to poor and needy people of the world." The Church was then able to give much of this assistance directly to those in need, although in

The interior of the Joseph Smith Memorial Building at Chistmastime. (Photo courtesy John Luke)

some cases, other agencies continued to help with distribution.[27]

GOSPEL LITERACY

Closely related to these efforts was the "Gospel Literacy" program. Pioneered by the Church Educational System in the 1970s, it was adopted by the Relief Society in 1992 as part of its 150th anniversary commemoration. Missionaries and other volunteers taught basic reading skills to those who needed them, and then encouraged all to study the gospel in order to improve their skills and their lives. A couple serving a mission in Africa reported that they taught members to read in homes, on patios, or even under trees. A sister in Chicago didn't write letters to her friends because she didn't know how. As she learned the basics of spelling and grammar, she not only was able to write letters, but she also gained self-confidence in the process. One literacy missionary commented: "Every class we taught was a teacher's payday as class members, individually and collectively, read scriptures and sang hymns and other songs."[28] In some parts of the world local leaders gained the ability to read Church magazines and manuals for the first time. A branch president in Bolivia remarked that before he learned to read, his life was like a closed book. But when he gained this skill, opportunities had become like an open book.[29]

The Joseph Smith Memorial Building

Ever since the Hotel Utah had opened under Church sponsorship in 1911, it had been a landmark in downtown Salt Lake City. It was located across the street from Temple Square and on the same block as the Church headquarters. During the later twentieth century, however, several newer hotels had opened, and the cost of keeping this facility competitive became prohibitive for the Church. Therefore, after seventy-six years of service the Hotel Utah closed in 1987. During the next six years and at a cost of $42 million, this landmark hotel was structurally upgraded and completely renovated and refurbished to serve a completely new purpose. It was remodeled to include a chapel to be used by two wards and a branch, offices for the Church's Public Affairs Department, banquet facilities, a distribution center, and two restaurants. It also included large rooms with 133 computer terminals where visitors from all over the world were able free of charge to search the Church's family history databases for information on their own pedigrees.

The renovated structure was renamed the Joseph Smith Memorial Building. It was dedicated on June 27, 1993, the 149th anniversary of the Prophet Joseph's martyrdom. President Gordon B. Hinckley noted: "It is appropriate that we have on this block a beautiful memorial to the Prophet Joseph Smith, from whose calling and work has sprung all that the Church is today."[30]

A unique feature of the building was the 500-seat theater. On its thirty-one-by-sixty-two-foot screen, visitors saw a fifty-three-minute film, *Legacy*, dramatizing the trials and triumphs of the early Latter-day Saints as they sought to establish Zion. Produced by Academy Award winner, Kieth Merrill, the film used the experiences of a typical Latter-day Saint family to trace Church history from its origins in 1830 to the placing of the Salt Lake Temple's capstone in 1892.[31]

President Hunter's Focus on the Temple

Ever since becoming a General Authority, Howard W. Hunter had been closely involved in the Church's genealogical, or family history, program. In 1964 he had become President of the Church's Genealogical Society. It was under his direction that computers were first used to "manage and process names for temple ordinance work."[32] Over a period of several years, he was involved in key decisions which helped to refine and expedite genealogical procedures. These included the creation of the Pedigree Referral Service and the development of a system of branch genealogical libraries.[33]

Following the death of President Ezra Taft Benson, Howard W. Hunter was set apart on June 5, 1994, as the fourteenth President of The Church of Jesus Christ of Latter-day Saints. At the press conference where President Hunter was presented as the Church's new leader, he introduced the theme which would become the hallmark of his brief administration. He invited "the members of the Church to establish the temple of the Lord as the great symbol of their membership and the supernal setting for their most sacred covenants. It would be the deepest desire of my heart to have every member of the Church temple worthy. I would hope that every adult member would be worthy of—and carry—a current temple recommend, even if proximity to a temple does not allow immediate or frequent use of it. Let us be a temple-attending and a temple-loving people."[34]

President Hunter again sounded this theme that same year at the conclusion of the October general conference: "Let us make the temple, with temple worship and temple covenants and temple marriage, our ultimate earthly goal and the supreme mortal experience."[35]

The early 1990s had brought new strides in temple building. After a six-year lull, two new temples were announced in 1990. They would be built in Orlando, Florida, and Bountiful, Utah; both were subsequently dedicated by President Howard W. Hunter. By the end of President Hunter's administration, eleven more temples would be announced, and construction on the Bogotá Colombia Temple, announced nine years earlier, would finally be under way. These new temples included two in Europe and three in Latin America.

Although Howard W. Hunter served only briefly as President of the Church, he succeeded in focusing the Saints' attention on the importance of temples. In this way, he had as much lasting impact as many who had the opportunity to serve for longer periods of time.

Some Important Milestones

During the early 1990s, the Church passed several significant milestones. For example, early in May 1991 the 500,000th full-time missionary received his call. The cumulative total had stood at only 60,000 in 1950 and had almost doubled from 264,000 in 1980.[36]

Another milestone was reached when the 20,000th local unit (ward or branch) was created in December 1992. These were found in 144 nations or territories. Sixty-seven percent were wards and the remainder were branches. The thousandth of these units had been organized in 1927. The 5,000 mark was not reached until 1970, and the 10,000 mark in 1980.[37]

On December 11, 1994, it was fitting that President Howard W. Hunter personally organized the 2,000th stake of the Church in Mexico City. In 1975 he had gone there as a member of the Twelve and organized the five existing stakes into fifteen. On no other occasion in Church history had ten new stakes been organized in a single city at the same time. The 1,000th stake in the Church had been organized in 1979 at Nauvoo. Thus, the number of stakes had doubled in just fifteen years. During the early 1990s three stakes were created outside the United States for every one within.[38]

Another kind of milestone was the publication in 1991 of the five-volume *Encyclopedia of Mormonism*. Published by Macmillan in New York City and edited by Daniel H. Ludlow, a former dean of religious education at Brigham Young University, the encyclopedia contained 1,200 articles by 738 different authors on Latter-day Saint history, doctrine, and practice.[39]

After presiding over the Church for not quite nine months, President Howard W. Hunter died on March 3, 1995. Fittingly, his last public appearance was at the dedication of the Bountiful Utah Temple two months earlier. During his brief administration and during his years of service in the Quorum of the Twelve, President Hunter had left his stamp on various key Church activities. Whether through his refining of the Church's Family History Program, his shepherding Brigham Young University's Jerusalem Center to dedication, or his helping the Church to focus on the temple, lives of Latter-day Saints around the world were blessed by his ministry.

President Howard W. Hunter (center) with counselors Gordon B. Hinckley (left) and Thomas S. Monson at a temple dedication. (Deseret News *photo)*

The Administration of Gordon B. Hinckley: The Church Comes Out of Obscurity

A prophesy in the preface of the Doctrine and Covenants declared that the Church would ultimately be brought "forth out of obscurity and out of darkness" (D&C 1:30). Perhaps no President of the Church came to his office with more administrative experience than did Gordon B. Hinckley. Building on this preparation President Hinckley helped the Church to come "out of obscurity" as he met the press and traveled extensively to visit the Saints worldwide.

President Hinckley's Earlier Life

Gordon Bitner Hinckley was born June 23, 1910, in Salt Lake City. In contrast to the stamina he would exhibit later in life, as a toddler he was quite frail—susceptible to earaches, asthma, allergies, and other illnesses. The dense coal smoke which blanketed the city during the winter was not good for him, so the family decided to move out into the country. On the farm young Gordon learned to work hard and developed his skills as a carpenter and all-around handyman.

Soon after becoming a deacon, the twelve-year-old boy attended a stake priesthood meeting and sat on the back row. He was moved when he heard the congregation stand and sing with power, "Praise to the man who communed with Jehovah! / Jesus anointed that Prophet and Seer."[1] "Something happened within me as I heard those men of faith sing," he later reflected. "It touched my heart. It gave me a feeling that was

President Gordon B. Hinckley and his wife, Marjorie, are met with great fanfare in Shenzhen, China. President Hinckley was the first Church President to visit mainland China. (Deseret News *photo*)

difficult to describe. I felt a great moving power, both emotional and spiritual. I had never had it previously in terms of any Church experience. There came into my heart a conviction that the man of whom they sang was really a prophet of God."[2] In 1986 Elder Boyd K. Packer noted, "Even today, more than six decades later, [President Hinckley] cannot tell of that experience without slipping a finger under his glasses to prevent a tear from rolling down his cheek."[3]

In 1928 Gordon began his studies in English at the University of Utah. As the Great Depression spread, so did an atmosphere of cynicism. Gordon questioned many assumptions, even "in a slight measure" the faith of his parents. Nevertheless, he gratefully acknowledged, "The testimony which had come to me as a boy remained with me and became as a bulwark to which I could cling during those very difficult years."[4]

Gordon B. Hinckley, approximately age twelve. (Photo courtesy Hinckley family)

Following graduation from the "U," he was planning to study journalism at Columbia University. These plans were changed, however, when he accepted a call to the British Mission. During the Depression, relatively few were able to afford a mission, so accepting this call represented a substantial sacrifice for Gordon and his family. Arriving in England, he was assigned to serve in the Preston area.

As a new missionary, Elder Hinckley had little success, so he wrote home stating that he didn't want to waste his own time or his father's money, especially during the Depression. His father responded: "Dear Gordon, I have your recent letter. I have only one suggestion: forget yourself and go to work." His father's wise advice prompted Gordon to seek the solitude of his room and pour out his heart to the Lord. Years later he indicated: "That July day in 1933 was my day of decision. A new light came into my life and a new joy into my heart. The fog of England seemed to lift, and I saw the sunlight. Everything good that has happened to me since then I can trace back to the decision I made that day in Preston."[5]

Later, Elder Hinckley was transferred to London where he became the assistant to Elder Joseph F. Merrill of the Council of the Twelve, who at that time presided over all the missions of Europe. Working closely with this respected Church leader gave the young missionary valuable experiences that strengthened his confidence. Addressing skeptical

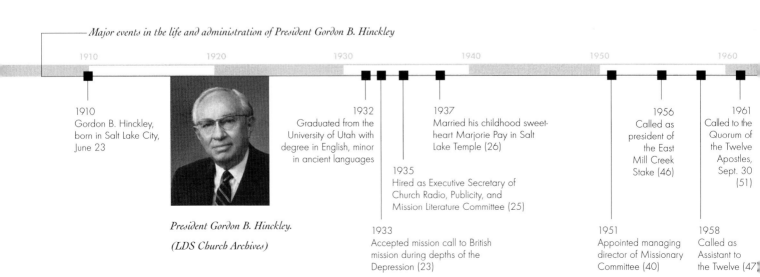

Major events in the life and administration of President Gordon B. Hinckley

1910 1920 1930 1940 1950 1960

1910
Gordon B. Hinckley, born in Salt Lake City, June 23

President Gordon B. Hinckley. (LDS Church Archives)

1932
Graduated from the University of Utah with degree in English, minor in ancient languages

1933
Accepted mission call to British mission during depths of the Depression (23)

1935
Hired as Executive Secretary of Church Radio, Publicity, and Mission Literature Committee (25)

1937
Married his childhood sweetheart Marjorie Pay in Salt Lake Temple (26)

1951
Appointed managing director of Missionary Committee (40)

1956
Called as president of the East Mill Creek Stake (46)

1958
Called as Assistant to the Twelve (47)

1961
Called to the Quorum of the Twelve Apostles, Sept. 30 (51)

and even hostile crowds in Hyde Park helped to develop Elder Hinckley's skills as a public speaker. He was given responsibility for the mission's publications and was assigned to develop a series of filmstrips that the missionaries could use in teaching.

When Elder Hinckley was released from his mission, President Merrill assigned him to personally visit with the First Presidency about the critical need for teaching materials in missionary work. Accordingly, on August 20, 1935, twenty-five-year-old Gordon met with Heber J. Grant and his counselors, J. Reuben Clark and David O. McKay. He was given fifteen minutes to present his message, but as the Presidency raised questions, the interview was lengthened another hour.

Even though Gordon was reviving his interest in further studies at Columbia University, he was once again asked to set these plans aside. Two days after his interview with the Brethren, President McKay called and invited him to work with the newly constituted Church Radio, Publicity, and Mission Literature Committee. The committee consisted of six members of the Twelve, and the young returned missionary was to work closely with them as their executive secretary.

He was assigned to work in an unfurnished office. He was able to scrounge a dilapidated table from a missionary associate. It had a warped, cracked top and one short leg under which Gordon had to place a block of wood for stability. He brought his own typewriter from home and had to justify his request for even a single ream of paper. From this humble beginning would grow the Church's extensive media and public affairs programs.

In 1937 he married his neighborhood sweetheart, Marjorie Pay. They would become the parents of five children. That same year he became a member of the Sunday School General Board. Then in 1946, he was

Gordon B. Hinckley as executive secretary of the Church Radio, Publicity, and Mission Literature Committee. (Photo courtesy Hinckley family)

called into the Millcreek Stake presidency where he served for the next twelve years, the last two as president.

For over two decades as an employee at Church headquarters he wrote scripts for radio programs and

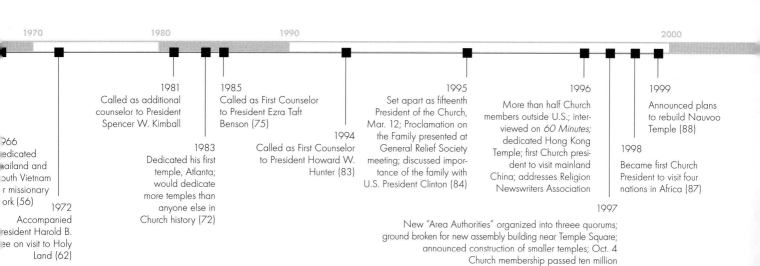

1970 1980 1990 2000

966 edicated ailand and outh Vietnam r missionary ork (56)

1972 Accompanied resident Harold B. ee on visit to Holy Land (62)

1981 Called as additional counselor to President Spencer W. Kimball

1983 Dedicated his first temple, Atlanta; would dedicate more temples than anyone else in Church history (72)

1985 Called as First Counselor to President Ezra Taft Benson (75)

1994 Called as First Counselor to President Howard W. Hunter (83)

1995 Set apart as fifteenth President of the Church, Mar. 12; Proclamation on the Family presented at General Relief Society meeting; discussed importance of the family with U.S. President Clinton (84)

1996 More than half Church members outside U.S.; interviewed on *60 Minutes;* dedicated Hong Kong Temple; first Church president to visit mainland China; addresses Religion Newswriters Association

1997 New "Area Authorities" organized into threee quorums; ground broken for new assembly building near Temple Square; announced construction of smaller temples; Oct. 4 Church membership passed ten million

1998 Became first Church President to visit four nations in Africa (87)

1999 Announced plans to rebuild Nauvoo Temple (88)

In 1958 Elder Hinckley was assigned to supervise the Church in Asia, a land that he came to love dearly. (Deseret News *photo*)

other presentations, produced filmstrips, and organized Church exhibits at worlds fairs. As the Swiss Temple was being planned, President David O. McKay personally assigned Brother Hinckley to consider how the temple endowment could be presented in many languages. Meeting regularly with the Prophet, he developed a system which used motion pictures.

In 1958 Gordon B. Hinckley was called as a General Authority, as an Assistant to the Twelve. In this capacity he continued to supervise the missionary department. When the worldwide Church was divided into twelve areas, each to be supervised by a General Authority, Elder Hinckley was assigned to Asia. Elder Hinckley gladly accepted this assignment even though this would entail traveling "halfway around the world . . . where the Church was [still] in its infancy."[6] He also served under Elder Harold B. Lee on the General Priesthood Committee as it planned what would become known as priesthood correlation.

In 1961 Elder Hinckley was called to become a member of the Quorum of the Twelve, one of the "special witnesses of the name of Christ in all the world" (D&C 107:23). As an Apostle, Elder Hinckley traveled widely, including an around-the-world tour in 1964. Two years later during the Vietnam War he visited Saigon and dedicated that land for the preaching of the gospel. During his travels he met with world leaders, conducted conferences, dedicated chapels, visited missions, and in other ways worked "to build up the church, and regulate all the affairs of the same in all nations" (D&C 107:33).

In 1981 Elder Hinckley became a third counselor to President Spencer W. Kimball. Because both of the other counselors were in poor health, a heavy load fell on President Hinckley's capable shoulders. This situation would be repeated during the next dozen years, requiring President Hinckley to provide the primary direction of the Church's day-to-day affairs.

Speaking at the October 1985 general conference, President Hinckley rejoiced in the experiences he had at temple dedications during that year. "I have looked into the faces of tens of thousands of Latter-day Saints. Their skins are of varying colors and hues. But their hearts beat as one with testimony and conviction concerning the truth of this great restored work of God. I have heard their testimonies spoken with sincerity. I have listened to their prayers. I have heard them lift their voices in anthems of praise. I have seen their tears of gratitude. I have known of their sacrifices made in appreciation for the blessings that have come to them."[7]

When he dedicated the Manila Philippines Temple, for example, he recalled how in 1961 he had helped open missionary work in the Philippines and that there was only one native member in the entire country. In just twenty-three years, Church membership had passed one hundred thousand, and these members could now enjoy the blessings of the temple. In South Africa he contrasted the highly publicized racial tensions of that country with the harmony among various ethnic groups as the faithful Saints assembled within the temple. At the dedication of the Freiberg Germany Temple, the Saints rejoiced that a new day had dawned, "the sun was shining," and happiness and joy had replaced a feeling of gloom.[8]

All these experiences helped to prepare Gordon B. Hinckley for the even greater responsibility that he was to assume. On March 12, 1995, following the death of Howard W. Hunter, he was set apart as the fifteenth President of the Church in this dispensation.

Proclamation on the Family

For some time Church leaders had been concerned about the erosion of traditional family values. Therefore, in the fall of 1995, the First Presidency and Council of the Twelve Apostles issued "The Family: A Proclamation to the World." Noting that this is only the fifth such proclamation issued in the entire history of the Church, Elder Henry B. Eyring concluded that "we can understand the importance our Heavenly Father places upon the family."[9]

At a time when the necessity of formal marriage commitment was being questioned and when even same-sex marriages were being promoted by some people, the proclamation affirmed that "marriage between a man and a woman is ordained of God and that the family is central to the Creator's plan for the eternal destiny of His children." Furthermore, it stated that "sacred ordinances and covenants available in holy temples" enable us to perpetuate our family relationships beyond the grave. In contrast to the declining moral standards of the world, the proclamation declared that "God has commanded that the sacred powers of procreation are to be employed only between man and woman, lawfully wedded as husband and wife."

In a day when almost half of all children do not grow up in a home where both father and mother are present, the First Presidency and the Twelve declared that "children are entitled to birth within the bonds of matrimony, and to be reared by a father and a mother who honor marital vows with complete fidelity. Happiness in family life," the proclamation continued, "is most likely to be achieved when founded upon the teachings of the Lord Jesus Christ." Keys to success include "faith, prayer, repentance, forgiveness, respect, love, compassion, work, and wholesome recreational activities." The proclamation also answered questions about the roles of men and women, declaring that fathers should provide support and protection to their families, while "mothers are primarily responsible for the nurture of their children."

THE FAMILY

A PROCLAMATION TO THE WORLD

The Proclamation on the Family, printed in the November 1995 issue of the Ensign. *(Photo courtesy LDS Church)*

The proclamation warned that those who violate sacred covenants or do not fulfill family responsibilities "will one day stand accountable before God."[10] Speaking in a general conference, President Hinckley lamented that there were some who in anger abuse their wives and children. "No man who engages in such evil and unbecoming behavior is worthy of the priesthood of God. No man who so conducts himself is worthy of the privileges of the house of the Lord. . . . If there be any such men within the hearing of my voice," declared President Hinckley, "as a servant of the Lord I rebuke you and call you to repentance."[11]

The Proclamation on the Family concluded by calling upon government officials everywhere to promote measures to strengthen the home and family. On November 13, 1995, about two months after the proclamation was issued, President Hinckley had the opportunity of spending a half hour with U.S. President Bill Clinton at the White House in Washington, D.C. The Prophet presented him a copy of the proclamation; this led to a discussion on the family. "It is our feeling that if you're going to fix the nation," counseled President Hinckley, "you need to start by fixing families. That's the place to begin." The leaders discussed, among other things, the importance of parents' involvement in their children's lives. After giving the Clintons bound copies of their family histories and describing the Church's family home evening program, President Hinckley suggested that President Clinton "get Hillary and Chelsea and sit down with those books and have a family home evening."[12]

President Hinckley and the Media

With his many years of experience in working with the media, President Gordon B. Hinckley was well aware of the importance of communicating the Church's message clearly. An example was the new Church logo adopted in December 1995. It was designed so that the words "Jesus Christ" were the most prominent feature in the heart of the Church's official name.

An unusual opportunity came to President Hinckley when he was invited to become the subject of a profile on the popular television magazine program, *60 Minutes.* Mike Wallace, the show's host, came to Salt Lake City to interview him. The potential impact on the public's attitudes about the Church was great; this made the interviews intense, but President Hinckley responded freely. For several hours, Wallace asked difficult and probing questions. In response to a question about women's roles, the President insisted that "my wife is my companion. In this Church the man neither walks ahead of his wife

President Hinckley guides Mike Wallace, host of 60 Minutes, *around Temple Square in 1996. President Hinckley took many opportunities to help the Church gain favorable public recognition.* (Deseret News *photo)*

nor behind his wife, but at her side. They are coequals in this life in a great enterprise." When asked how he received revelation, President Hinckley referred to Elijah's experience with the "still, small voice." He then added "that the things of God are understood by the Spirit of God, and one must have and seek and cultivate that Spirit, and there comes understanding and it is real. I can give testimony of that."[13]

Mike Wallace said of President Hinckley, "Generally speaking, he's first rate, but compared with other eighty-five-year-olds, he is incredibly responsive. There was no question that he found difficult or unpleasant. He came to talk."

"Frankly, nearly everything about this assignment surprised me," Wallace later reflected. "I was surprised by Gordon Hinckley's humor and his candor, neither of which I expected. We raised the issues that were on the minds of the skeptics, he was willing to answer every question, and his answers were reasonable."[14]

The telecast aired on Easter Sunday evening, April 7, 1996. As President Hinckley closed general conference earlier that afternoon, he shared some of his feelings about this experience. "I recognized that if I were to appear, critics and detractors of the Church would also be invited to participate. I knew we could not expect that the program would be entirely positive for us. On the other hand, I felt that it offered the opportunity to present some affirmative aspects of our culture and message to many millions of people. I concluded that it was better to lean into the stiff wind of opportunity than to simply hunker down and do nothing. . . . We have no idea what the outcome will be—that is, I don't. We will discover this this evening when it is aired in this valley. If it turns out to be favorable, I will be grateful. Otherwise, I pledge I'll never get my foot in that kind of trap again."[15] President Hinckley had nothing to fear; response to the program was very positive.

With this experience behind him, President Hinckley was encouraged to accept other invitations to tell the world about the restored Church. In March 1997 he addressed twenty-three hundred listeners at the Los Angeles World Affairs Council. President Hinckley pointed out to this California audience that the Church had played a key role in the history of the Golden State. The Mormon Battalion was involved in two notable developments—the treaty which made California part of the United

President Hinckley is greeted by local Church authorities at a conference in Chile. (Deseret News *photo)*

States and the discovery of gold. He noted that the Church now was the second largest faith group in California and the seventh largest nationwide. At the conclusion of President Hinckley's remarks, the audience, which included diplomats, local and state officials, and other dignitaries, gave him a standing ovation.[16]

In November 1997 he appeared before the Religion Newswriters Association's annual convention at Albuquerque, New Mexico. He offered a "panoramic view of the Church." Although fifty years earlier 55 percent of Latter-day Saints had lived in Utah, only 17 percent now lived there. He pointed out that a new Church member was "more likely to be a Latino in Mexico or Argentina than a white male in St. Louis." He emphasized that Latter-day Saints "embrace such diversity." He insisted that Mormons truly are Christians. "No one believes more literally in the redemption wrought by the Lord Jesus Christ." He indicated that the Church's two major challenges both resulted from its rapid growth—construction of meetinghouses and training of leaders. The Church was building approximately one new chapel every day, but this was still not enough. He gratefully acknowledged the service of fifty thousand missionaries worldwide who served selflessly "at an age when most young men are prone to think only of themselves."[17]

In September 1998, President Hinckley was once again on television, this time appearing on CNN's *Larry King Live.* In contrast to *60 Minutes,* which was recorded in advance and then edited, this broadcast was completely live. He responded to interviewer Larry King's probing questions as well as to others called in by viewers. When asked why people were attracted to the Mormon faith, President Hinckley responded: "Many people are looking for something they can hang onto, an anchor to which they can attach their lives. . . . It isn't always easy to be a member of this Church," he concluded, "it is demanding, but it is wonderfully fruitful, and has a tremendous effect upon people."[18]

Getting Out with the Saints

Speaking at a general conference early in his administration, President Gordon B. Hinckley expressed, "I have a desire to get out with the Latter-day Saints across the world, to look into your faces, to shake your hands wherever possible, to share with you in a more personal and intimate way my feelings concerning this sacred work, and to feel of your spirit and your love of the Lord and His mighty cause."[19]

During his first three years as President of the Church, President Hinckley visited Latter-day Saints

President Hinckley listens to a children's choir during his 1998 trip to Africa. (Deseret News *photo)*

on every continent except Antarctica. He traveled to western Europe twice, to the Holy Land, to Mexico four times, to Central America, twice to South America, to Asia, to Australia and New Zealand, to the islands of Polynesia, and to Africa. No other Church President had traveled so far during a comparable period. He visited some fifty countries, conducted at least 350 meetings, and addressed audiences totaling over 1.5 million. These international travels were made more convenient when Jon M. Huntsman, a Utah industrialist, placed a personal jet at President Hinckley's disposal.

In mid-May 1996, President Hinckley left for a two-week trip to Asia. He was able to visit people with whom he had become closely associated during his assignment to the Orient nearly four decades earlier. These reunions were characterized by "hearty hugs, lingering handshakes and tear-filled eyes."[20] President Hinckley admitted, "I had difficulty holding back the tears in seeing these men and women of faith who have remained true to the work of the Lord."[21]

After brief visits to Japan, Korea, and Taiwan, he arrived in Hong Kong where he dedicated the Church's forty-eighth temple. The timing was important—just over one year before the British colony of Hong Kong would revert to Chinese jurisdiction. In the dedicatory prayer, President Hinckley petitioned, "May the blessings of freedom continue to be enjoyed by those who live here and, in a particular way, we pray that future events may be conducive to the growth and strengthening of Thy work."[22]

Gordon B. Hinckley became the first Church President to visit mainland China. The day following the Hong Kong Temple dedication, he and his party traveled just over the border to Shenzhen to visit a cultural center recreating villages from different regions of China. The idea for this center grew out of its creator's visit to the Church's Polynesian Cultural Center (PCC) in Hawaii. For the previous ten to fifteen years, personnel at the PCC had assisted their Chinese counterparts to develop this facility. More than five hundred costumed dancers and other performers lined the walks as President Hinckley's party toured the center.[23]

Later, that afternoon, President Hinckley flew to Cambodia where, in the evening at Phnom Penh, he addressed a fireside attended by 439—more than half of whom were investigators. The next morning, standing on a hillside overlooking the Mekong River, he dedicated Cambodia for the preaching of the gospel. That same day he traveled to Ho Chi Minh City (formerly Saigon) and Hanoi in Vietnam. In both locations he met with small groups of local Latter-day Saints. In Hanoi, he met Professor Nguyn Huy Phan, who for some time had been coordinating the Church's humanitarian aid to his country, particularly in the form of medical supplies and expertise. Here President Hinckley also offered an "addendum" to his 1966 prayer, dedicating the entire country of Vietnam.[24]

In February 1998, Gordon B. Hinckley became the first Church President to visit Nigeria, Ghana, Kenya, and Zimbabwe. At his first stop, in Nigeria, he addressed over a thousand priesthood bearers in one meeting and then 12,417 people in a general session. During a meeting at Accra, Ghana, his announcement of the first temple in West Africa was received with joyous applause. He also visited South Africa, where he told his listeners not to emigrate just because there had been some difficulties in their land, but that "the Church is spreading forth over the earth, to build Zion wherever it goes for the people who live there." On this trip he traveled a total of 24,700 miles, nearly the distance around the world, his longest trip so far.[25]

The Pioneer Sesquicentennial Celebration

During 1996–97 the Saints celebrated the sesquicentennial, or the 150th anniversary, of the Mormon pioneers. "Faith in Every Footstep" was the motto chosen for the pioneer commemoration. On February 4, 1996, one group braved temperatures of twelve degrees below zero at Nauvoo to commemorate Brigham Young's exodus.[26] Then on July 13, President Gordon B. Hinckley dedicated the reconstructed Kanesville Tabernacle (in present-day Council Bluffs, Iowa), where the First Presidency was reorganized in December of 1847 with Brigham Young as the second President of the Church. President Hinckley also addressed a group gathered for the reenactment of the Mormon Battalion's enlistment and departure.

President Hinckley was back on the Missouri River on April 18, 1997, where he dedicated the new "Mormon Trail Center at Historic Winter Quarters" in the outskirts of Omaha, Nebraska. He admitted that he had never looked at Avard Fairbanks's statue at that site of a pioneer family burying their baby without being "deeply touched. I never get over it. I think it is ingrained very deeply in me a respect and love and appreciation for those who 150 years ago moved over this trail."[27] Beginning the next day, the sesquicentennial wagon train left the Omaha area to reenact the one-thousand-mile trek to the Salt Lake Valley. During the next three months, hundreds of individuals joined the train to ride in covered wagons, pull handcarts, or to just simply walk along parts of the 1847 trail. Along the way, they were honored by state and local officials who paid tribute to the exploits of the early Mormon pioneers.[28]

An estimated fifty thousand welcomers gathered around the "This Is the Place" monument to greet the wagon train as it emerged from Immigration Canyon into the Salt Lake Valley on July 22. Looking over these 1997 "pioneers," President Hinckley quipped, "You look as if you've come a thousand miles."[29]

The media, both print and electronic, showed a great interest in the Pioneer Sesquicentennial Celebration. They particularly were eager to follow the day-by-day experiences of the wagon train recreating the early pioneers' trek. "In 1997, the Church received more national and international media coverage than all the other years in Church history combined," asserted Elder M. Russell Ballard, who had chaired the sesquicentennial celebration and believed this publicity had benefitted the Church around the world.[30]

The celebrations were not limited to the United States, however. The one hundred Latter-day Saints living in Krasnoyarsk, Siberia, constructed two traditional pioneer handcarts. On a frigid Saturday in February the members took turns pulling them through the main streets of their city. The carts were transported by train from one major city to another across Russia and Ukraine. At each stop local members paraded them through their city. Finally, one of the carts was flown to the United States, where it joined the wagon train for the last leg of its journey to the Salt Lake Valley.

*The sesquicentennial wagon train was greeted into the Salt lake Valley on July 22, 1997, by a crowd of some fifty thousand. (*Deseret News *photo)*

Some 8,500 persons converged on the grounds of the Mexico City Temple to commemorate the accomplishments of not only the Utah pioneers, but also of the pioneers in Mexico. During the summer there were pioneer parades in such diverse places as Rome, Italy, and Charleroi, Belgium.[31]

"Is there a lesson in the pioneer experience for us today?" asked Elder Ballard. "I believe there is. The faith that motivated the pioneers of 1847 as well as pioneers in other lands was a simple faith centered in the basic doctrines of the restored gospel, which they knew to be true. That's all that mattered to them, and I believe that is all that should matter to us."[32]

Curriculum Restructured

In 1998 the Melchizedek Priesthood and Relief Society began studying a completely revised

The vast interior of the new Conference Center under construction. When completed, the building will hold twenty-one thousand conference attenders. (Deseret News *photo*)

curriculum. The objective was to promote spirituality, service, and leadership, and "to help members and leaders put gospel truths to work more effectively in their lives."[33]

On the first Sunday of each month, Melchizedek Priesthood quorum or group leaders led discussions focusing on learning priesthood duties and planning action to carry them out. At the same time in Relief Society meetings, members of the presidency taught lessons on the duties of women and the society's work. Elder Jeffrey R. Holland, who with Elder Dallin H. Oaks developed the curriculum, hoped that priesthood and Relief Society leaders would see such instruction "as an extension of their leadership."[34]

President Hinckley specifically directed that the teachings of the Latter-day prophets be the basis of the new curriculum. Beginning with the teachings of Brigham Young, these lessons were studied on the second and third Sundays of each month. The standard works continued to be studied in Sunday School Gospel Doctrine classes; the new series built on this scriptural foundation, showing how God has continued to guide His people through inspired leaders.

President Gordon B. Hinckley and his wife, Marjorie, at the Mexico City Temple. (LDS Church Archives)

Fourth-Sunday lessons, entitled "Teachings for Our Time," considered current topics as outlined by the First Presidency and the Twelve; they were based primarily on these leaders' own recent teachings. Two lessons each year were to be outlined by stake or mission leaders. Occasional fifth-Sunday lessons were taught by members of ward bishoprics or branch presidencies. Thus leaders at both general and local levels were able to direct attention to matters of urgent current concern.

Practical application was to be the theme of all these lessons. Even though husbands and wives generally met separately, they often were studying the same lessons. This new system would enhance follow-up discussions at home focusing on how the principles studied could be put into practice.

Growth Around the World

As the twentieth century was drawing to a close, the Church was continuing to grow worldwide. It was adding about a million new members every three years, passing the ten million mark early in November 1997. Another milestone had been reached in February of the previous year, when for the first time there were more members outside of the United States than there were within that country—the traditional base of the Church.

To administer to this growing membership, refinements were made in the Church's organization. In 1995 the 284 regional representatives were released and replaced by 117 new "Area Authorities." These new leaders were high priests who continued in their existing employment, lived in their own homes, and served for a period of approximately six years. Unlike the regional representatives, who had been assigned only to stakes in a specific region, Area Authorities could serve anywhere in the broader "area" as assigned by the area presidency. Their expanded assignments included presiding at stake conferences, creating or reorganizing stakes, and in a few cases, even serving in area presidencies.[35]

Two years later, the Area Authorities were ordained to the office of Seventy and became known as "Area Authority Seventies." Although they were not General Authorities, they became members of three new quorums of Seventy: the Third Quorum (Europe, Africa, Asia, Australia, and the Pacific), the Fourth Quorum (Mexico, Central America, and South America), and the Fifth (the United States and

Canada). President Hinckley explained that this arrangement gave them "a quorum relationship presided over by the Presidents of the Seventy."[36]

Another response to the Church's growth took a more tangible form. At the opening of the April 1996 general conference, President Hinckley lamented that the Salt Lake Tabernacle on Temple Square was not able to accommodate the ever larger throngs. He announced plans to build a twenty-one-thousand-seat assembly building on the block north of Temple Square called the Conference Center. It would not be a sports arena, but rather would be designed to accommodate general conferences as well as other large meetings and activities. Ground was broken for the new facility on July 24, 1997, as part of the Pioneer Sesquicentennial Celebration.[37] Construction on the auditorium section of the building was planned so that the April 2000 general conference could be held there.

Perhaps President Hinckley will be remembered most for his involvement in temple building. Even before becoming President of the Church, he had dedicated more temples than anyone else in Church history, participating in the dedication or rededication of all but five of the Church's operating temples. He introduced some unique innovations in temple design, including plans to construct dozens of "smaller temples" around the world. Plans to build one of these temples at Palmyra, New York—the birthplace of the Church—brought the total number of temples in service or being planned to one hundred.

22

Temples to Dot the Earth

Temple building and temple activity have always been important and unique characteristics of the Latter-day Saint religion. This was likewise true of the Lord's people in earlier dispensations. Nevertheless, the later twentieth century witnessed remarkable developments in this sacred service, an unprecedented number of temples having been constructed around the world. The Saints viewed these developments as a beginning of the fulfillment of prophesies that temples would eventually dot the earth. In 1856 President Brigham Young declared: "To accomplish this work there will have to be not only one temple but thousands of them, and thousands and tens of thousands of men and women will go into those temples and officiate for people who have lived as far back as the Lord shall reveal."[1]

The House of the Lord

Latter-day Saints regard their temples as significantly different from ordinary chapels or other houses of worship. The scriptures, both ancient and modern, describe temples as unique places of revelation and communion between God and man (see Exodus 25:8, 22; D&C 109:5; 124:27–28). This function of temples suggests the importance of personal worthiness as a requirement for those who enter. The Lord promised: "And inasmuch as my people build a house unto me in the name of the Lord, and do not suffer any unclean thing to come

The Salt Lake Temple on a winter morning, circa 1911. (LDS Church Archives)

The Kirtland Temple, completed in 1836, was designed for general worship and educational purposes. It was here that the prophet Elijah restored the keys required for temple ordiancnes. (Deseret News *photo)*

Major events related to temple work, 1836–94

1830 1840 1850 1860 1870 1880 1890 1900

1836
Kirtland Temple dedicated; sealing keys restored

1840
Baptisms for the dead inaugurated

1842
Endowment for the living given in Joseph Smith's private office

1846
Nauvoo Temple dedicated

St. George Temple (Photo courtesy Darrel Chamberlain)

1877
St. George Temple dedicated; endowments for the dead

1893
Salt Lake Temple dedicated

1894
Genealogical Society organized

into it, that it be not defiled, my glory shall rest upon it" (D&C 97:15–17).

Elder James E. Talmage of the Council of the Twelve suggested that temples have a second major function, explaining that a temple "is characterized not alone as the place where God reveals Himself to man, but also as the House wherein prescribed ordinances of the Priesthood are solemnized."[2]

Elder Boyd K. Packer declared that "temples are the very center of the spiritual strength of the Church." This strength is not only available to the Church as a whole, Elder Packer emphasized, but also to individual Latter-day Saints: "When members of the Church are troubled or when crucial decisions weigh heavily upon their minds, it is a common thing for them to go to the temple. It is a good place to take our cares. In the temple we can receive spiritual perspective. There, during the time of the temple service, we are 'out of the world.'"[3]

An early photograph of the Nauvoo Temple. (LDS Church Archives)

The endowment is at the heart of temple worship. Elder Talmage defined the endowment as a course of instruction that reviews important phases of the history of mankind, including the creation of the world, the fall of Adam and Eve, and conditions we face in the present world. It teaches the plan of salvation, he explained, including "the absolute and indispensable condition of personal purity and devotion to the right in the present life, and a strict compliance with Gospel requirements."[4] Elder Packer explained that "the instruction given in the endowment provides a firm perspective, a point of reference by which a person may gauge all his learning and wisdom, both spiritual and temporal; by which he may gather things together, determine their true meaning and significance, and fit them into their proper places."[5]

Early Latter-day Temples

Elder James E. Talmage believed that because "there is a definite sequence of development in the dealings of God with man throughout the centuries," there must be a "direct revelation of temple plans" for each dispensation.[6] Therefore, the temple buildings themselves, even in the latter-day dispensation, constitute a tangible record of God's progressive revelations concerning the scope of temple work.

An important precedent was set in Kirtland when the Lord directed that the first temple of this dispensation be built "not after the manner of the world," but according to a pattern which he would reveal. Because the "House of the Lord" in Kirtland was built before temple ordinances were restored, the Lord directed that it be designed for general worship and educational purposes (see D&C 95:13; see also verses 14–17). It wasn't until one week following the dedication of this temple that the Prophet Elijah restored the sealing keys so important in temple work (see D&C 110:13–16).

With these priesthood keys, the Prophet Joseph Smith first taught the doctrine of baptism for the dead in 1840.[7] Shortly afterwards, he also introduced the temple endowment and performed "sealings" or marriages for eternity. Thus, when the Nauvoo Temple was built, it not only followed the pattern of the Kirtland Temple—two large auditoriums, one above the other, for general purposes—but also added a baptismal font in the basement and specialized rooms for additional ordinances on the attic storey.[8] As enemies of the Church forced the Saints to flee to the West, both of these temples were lost, the Nauvoo Temple eventually being destroyed.

Within a few days of the pioneers' arrival in the Salt Lake Valley, Brigham Young designated the site where a new temple would stand, and the city was laid out from that point. During the forty years of the Salt Lake Temple's construction, three other Utah temples were erected and dedicated. The earliest of these, in St. George (dedicated in 1877), followed the Nauvoo pattern. But as further revelation expanded the Saints' understanding about the importance of temple ordinances, specific facilities needed to be provided, making the temples much more than merely places for general worship. Thus, the temples in Logan, Manti, and Salt Lake City (all completed during the last two decades of the nineteenth century) placed a greater emphasis on the endowment by providing rooms on the main floor where different phases of man's eternal life were taught as part of the presentation.

The next four temples—Hawaii, Alberta, Arizona, and Idaho Falls, all built during the first half of the twentieth century—represented Church expansion in the Intermountain West and also in the Pacific. These temples were smaller than the previous four because they did not include the large upper-level meeting room but rather provided only rooms designed for presenting temple ordinances. Hence they represented a complete shift from the Kirtland Temple, designed only for general meetings, to a concept of temples intended solely for ordinances.

First "Overseas Temples"

Following the close of World War II, Church authorities felt a growing need to make temple blessings more widely available. Providing these ordinances in Spanish at the Arizona Temple in 1945 was only the first step.

During the early 1950s Church leaders considered the possibility of building temples abroad. Many Church members had assumed that temples would be built only in central areas of "gathering." Nevertheless, at a historic meeting in the Salt Lake Temple on April 17, 1952, the First Presidency and Quorum of the Twelve, following extensive and prayerful consideration, decided to build temples in Europe.[9] The following year President David O. McKay announced plans to build a temple in Switzerland and indicated that it would be "but the first of several such temples" for the benefit of the far-flung membership of the Church. He also noted that by building smaller temples it would be possible to build more of them.[10] The construction of this first "overseas" temple marked a major turning point in Church history. Previously, the European Saints had felt they needed to "gather" to America, where they could receive their temple blessings. Now they realized that they could heed the General Authorities' counsel to stay where they were, build up the Church in their own lands, and enjoy all the benefits of the gospel program, including temple blessings, in Europe. Another innovation with the Swiss Temple was the use of motion pictures. These films, which Gordon B. Hinckley had helped to develop, made it possible to present the endowment as effectively in one room as in the series of four separate rooms required in earlier temples. The Swiss Temple was also the first truly multilingual temple in which English was not the basic language. The use of films made it easier to present the endowment in the several languages spoken by the patrons of this temple.

Following the 1952 decision to build a temple in Europe, the presidents of the missions there had agreed that it should be located in or near Bern, the

Major events related to temple work, 1911–present

1910 1920 1930 1940 1950

1911
One millionth endowment for the dead performed

1919
Hawaii Temple dedicated

The Hawaii Temple.
(Photo courtesy Darrel Chamberlain)

1938
Genealogical Society began using microfilms

1941
Ten millionth endowment for the dead performed

195
Swiss Temple dedicate
first "overseas" temp
and first to use film

capital of Switzerland. President McKay approved a location, but despite several months of negotiations with the site's owners, no definite agreement could be reached. "Finally, during a sleepless night in October" the Swiss Mission president, Samuel E. Bringhurst, recalled, "the thought occurred that perhaps there was a reason for the delay, and that we should pray for a decision, and leave the matter with the Lord." He therefore asked all the missionaries to fast, "that we might receive a decision concerning the proposed temple site." The following day he was notified that the property was no longer for sale. Though disappointing, this decision received so quickly "was a wonderful testimony to all of us."[11]

The mission president reported these developments to President McKay, who replied: "As I read your letter stating that all effort had failed and a negative decision had been rendered, I was not surprised, but at first disappointed; however, strangely enough, my disappointment soon disappeared and was replaced by an assurance that the Lord will overrule all transactions for the best good of his Church, not only in Switzerland but throughout Europe."[12]

Meanwhile, President Bringhurst and his real estate agent found another property site in the Bern area. As they walked over the site, they felt that it was the place the Lord intended for the temple to be built. They later learned why; the construction of a new highway preempted a key section of the original site. The new property included twice the area and was purchased for half the cost.

President David O. McKay and Church leaders at the Swiss Temple. (LDS Church Archives)

At the dedication of the Swiss Temple in 1955, President David O. McKay specifically acknowledged gratitude to the Lord for answering prayers for guidance in selecting the site and for "overruling matters that brought about the consummation of this beautiful temple."[13]

At about this same time, steps were taken to obtain a temple site in the South Pacific. In 1954 President McKay appointed Wendell B. Mendenhall, who was then directing the Church's Pacific building program, to confidentially investigate possible locations in New Zealand. Elder Mendenhall looked over various properties but did not feel satisfied that he had seen the temple site yet. He was then impressed that the temple should be located adjacent to the Church college then under construction near Hamilton. "The Church facilities for construction were already there, and that was the center of the population of the mission. Then, in my mind, I could

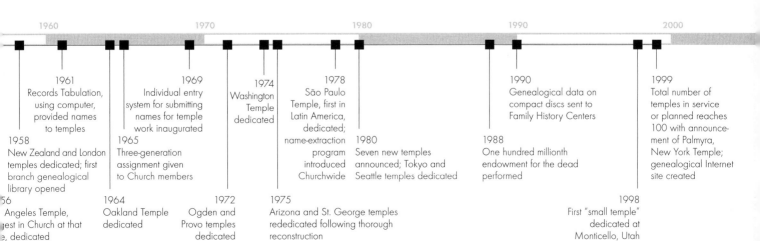

1960 1970 1980 1990 2000

56 Angeles Temple, gest in Church at that e, dedicated

1958 New Zealand and London temples dedicated; first branch genealogical library opened

1961 Records Tabulation, using computer, provided names to temples

1964 Oakland Temple dedicated

1965 Three-generation assignment given to Church members

1969 Individual entry system for submitting names for temple work inaugurated

1972 Ogden and Provo temples dedicated in Utah

1974 Washington Temple dedicated

1975 Arizona and St. George temples rededicated following thorough reconstruction

1978 São Paulo Temple, first in Latin America, dedicated; name-extraction program introduced Churchwide

1980 Seven new temples announced; Tokyo and Seattle temples dedicated

1988 One hundred millionth endowment for the dead performed

1990 Genealogical data on compact discs sent to Family History Centers

1998 First "small temple" dedicated at Monticello, Utah

1999 Total number of temples in service or planned reaches 100 with announcement of Palmyra, New York Temple; genealogical Internet site created

Members plant trees on the grounds of the New Zealand Temple in 1958. The New Zealand Temple was the second overseas temple built by the Church. (Deseret News *photo)*

see the area even before I arrived, and I could envision the hill where the temple should stand."

About ten days later Elder Mendenhall met President McKay at the site. "After we stepped from the car and were looking around," he recalled, "President McKay called me to one side. By the way he was looking at the hill, I could tell immediately what was on his mind. I had not said a word to him. He asked, 'What do you think?' I knew what his question implied, and I simply asked in return, 'What do you think, President McKay?' And then in an almost prophetic tone he pronounced, 'This is the place to build the temple.' "

The owners of this choice hill had previously indicated that they did not wish to sell their property. One morning, following President McKay's departure from New Zealand, Elder Mendenhall again met with them. They still were not willing to sell. By afternoon, however, he had convinced them to change their minds, but their attorney "over-priced the property considerably." Following an hour of negotiation the attorney agreed to reconsider the property's value. The selling price he then proposed was identical "to the penny" with the amount Mendenhall earlier had determined the Church should be willing to pay. By that evening, the contracts were signed.[14] The New Zealand and London temples, both dedicated in 1958, were similar in design and function to the Swiss Temple.

Larger Temples in North America

Meanwhile, the Los Angeles Temple, dedicated in 1956, was the largest such structure the Church had built so far. Like earlier temples, it was designed to present the endowment in a series of rooms with muraled walls; however, the temple was later modified to present these instructions using film as did the Swiss Temple. It was the first temple in the twentieth century to contain a large "solemn assembly" room on the upper floor and to feature a statue of the angel Moroni atop its tower—the only other temple to have these at the time was the Salt Lake Temple. The angelic figure reminded Latter-day Saints of the restoration of the gospel (see Revelations 14:6) and the coming forth of the Book of Mormon as a second witness of Jesus Christ. The construction of the Los Angeles Temple represented extensive Latter-day Saint progress in southern California.

The Saints in northern California often spoke of what they regarded as a prophetic statement concerning a temple in their area. During the summer of 1924 Elder George Albert Smith was in San Francisco attending regional Boy Scout meetings. On that occasion he met with the presidents of the small branches in Oakland and San Francisco—the extent of the Latter-day presence in the Bay Area at that time. From the Fairmont Hotel, high atop San Francisco's Nob Hill, they had a panoramic view of the bay and the hills beyond. One of the branch presidents present later recalled how Elder Smith gazed out on the majestic scene: "I can almost see in vision a white temple of the Lord high upon those hills," Elder Smith exclaimed, "an ensign to all the world travelers as they sail through the Golden Gate into this wonderful harbor. . . . A great white temple of the Lord will grace those hills."[15]

The Los Angeles Temple. (Photo courtesy Darrel Chamberlain)

The influx of Latter-day Saints to California during the 1920s and 30s led to the organization of a stake at San Francisco in 1927 and another at Oakland in 1934. A building committee was formed in the mid-1930s to locate a temple site in the area envisioned by Elder Smith. As the relative merits of several sites were weighed, "one particular spot always seemed to impress us as 'the one,'" Eugene Hilton, the committee's chairman later recalled. Although the desired site was not for sale, two others offered free of charge were still turned down. Just after World War II started, however, the owners of the choice site found that their plans for developing it were blocked because necessary building materials had become restricted. They therefore sold the land to the Church. Hilton, who by this time had become stake president, regarded this as an answer to prayer.[16] The Oakland Temple, dedicated in 1964, featured two large rooms where the endowment could be presented simultaneously on film to separate groups.

The Provo and Ogden temples, both dedicated in 1972, served Latter-day Saints living along the Wasatch Front and relieved pressure on the Salt Lake Temple. The Washington D.C. Temple, dedicated two years later in the United States capital, was one of the largest the Church had built. These three temples each had six large rooms where separate groups could receive the endowment instructions at once. With this efficient design, the Provo Temple became the most productive in the Church in terms of the number of vicarious ordinances performed for the dead. The Washington D.C. Temple, like the Los Angeles Temple, was built with an upper priesthood assembly room and a statue of the angel Moroni.

In the early 1970s, the Arizona and St. George temples were remodeled to present the endowment by film. So thorough was their reconstruction that in 1975 these temples were reopened for public open houses and then rededicated, the first time this had ever been done. The Hawaii and Logan temples were similarly remodeled and rededicated later in the decade.

Worldwide Expansion in Temple Building

The year 1975 also brought the announcement of three new temples in diverse locations—the São Paulo Temple, in Brazil, the first in South America; the Tokyo Temple, the first in Asia; and the Seattle Washington Temple, the first in the Pacific Northwest.

Latter-day Saints in these and other scattered areas around the world had eagerly looked forward to a time when they might have a temple and temple blessings closer at hand. In São Paulo, for example, when President Spencer W. Kimball announced plans for the future temple, "a gasp" could be heard from the large congregation that had assembled for an area conference and "tears filled the eyes of many. They openly wept for joy."[17] In 1977 plans were announced for the Mexico City Temple and in 1978 for the Jordan River Temple in the southern part of the Salt Lake Valley. The pace quickened substantially in 1980 with the simultaneous announcement of seven new temples. They were to be built in Atlanta (first in the southeastern United States), Argentina, Chile, Australia, Tonga, Tahiti, and Western Samoa. President Spencer W. Kimball declared: "There now begins the most intense period of temple building in the history of the Church. . . . We look to the day when the sacred ordinances of the Church, performed in the temples, will be available to all members of the Church in convenient locations around the globe."[18]

The Hong Kong Temple, dedicated in 1996, was innovative in its combination of classrooms, chapel, and temple into a single structure. (LDS Church Archives)

Consistent with this expectation, Church leaders in the early 1980s would announce plans to construct yet more temples, including the Freiberg Germany Temple behind the Iron Curtain in East Germany. Completion of these new temples would bring the total to forty-seven; there were only fifteen temples in service when President Kimball began his administration. Furthermore, for the first time in the Church's history, temples would be located on every continent.

This increase in the number of temples was made possible by building much smaller structures, as President David O. McKay had anticipated over a quarter-century earlier. The largest of these new temples would be only the size of a typical stake center, about twenty-eight thousand square feet.[19]

As the 1980s came to a close, several beautiful temples were being constructed in North America. These included the Portland, Las Vegas, Toronto, and San Diego temples. They were larger, having fifty to eighty thousand square feet.

New Concepts in Temple Design During the 1990s

During the 1990s new temples continued to be announced and built. Among these were two which represented new and distinct concepts in temple design. Church leaders felt a sense of urgency to have a temple dedicated and functioning in Hong Kong before the British colony returned to Chinese jurisdiction in 1997. During a visit in 1992, President Hinckley could not find a suitable site because of the difficulty of obtaining real estate in this crowded city. One night during this visit, he had a most unusual experience. "Something very interesting came into my mind," he recorded in his diary. "I did not hear a voice with my natural ears. But into my mind there came the voice of the Spirit. It said, 'Why are you worried about this? You have a wonderful piece of property where the mission home and the small chapel stand. They are in the very heart of Kowloon, in the location with the best transportation. . . . Build a building of [several] stories. It can include a chapel and classrooms on the first two floors and a temple on the top two or three floors.' . . . I relaxed and went back to sleep."[20] The temple was built according to President Hinckley's concept, having a public entrance leading to the chapel and mission

The Monticello Utah Temple was dedicated in 1998. The first "small" temple, it contained facilities for all ordinances necessay for salvation, but it could be run at a much lower cost. (LDS Church Archives)

offices and a separate temple entrance. When the seven-story edifice was dedicated in 1996, Gordon B. Hinckley, now President of the Church, testified: "If ever I felt the inspiration of the Lord at any time in my life, it was in connection with this building."[21]

Another new concept in temple design was introduced in Vernal, Utah. For the first time the Church transformed an existing older building into a temple. The exterior of the former stake tabernacle was renovated, and temple facilities were constructed inside. This temple was dedicated in 1997. Two years later, this concept was employed once again, this time in Copenhagen, Denmark. Church architects planned to remodel the historic Latter-day Saint chapel where Elder Joseph Fielding Smith had met with missionaries being evacuated from Europe in 1939.

Perhaps the most far-reaching development in temple building was announced by President Gordon B. Hinckley at the October 1997 general conference: "I believe that no member of the Church has received the ultimate which this Church has to give, until he or she has received his or her temple blessings in the house of the Lord. . . . But there are many areas of the Church that are remote, where the membership is small and not likely to grow very much in the near future. Are those who live in these places to be denied forever the blessings of the temple ordinances?" the Prophet asked. The answer was to build much smaller temples in such areas. They would be built to "temple standards," and would accommodate baptisms for the dead, the endowment, sealings, and all other necessary ordinances.

Such temples would be presided over and staffed by local Saints. Where possible, they would be located adjacent to existing chapels in order to share such facilities as parking lots. They could be constructed economically in just a few months. One of these small temples could be built for about the same cost as simply maintaining a larger temple for one year.[22]

The first of these small temples was dedicated at Monticello, Utah, in 1998. Meanwhile, President Hinckley had announced the goal of having at least thirty of these newer temples in service by the end of the year 2000. These plus other temples would bring the total to well over one hundred.

Prior to this time, many families in widely scattered parts of the world had sacrificed most of their material possessions in order to make the once-in-a-lifetime trip to the nearest temple. As the new temples began to dot the earth, such sacrifices increasingly became unnecessary. Derek Metcalfe, director of temples, anticipated that a new kind of sacrifice would now be required. "As more temples are built worldwide, the sacrifice will be one of time, as members attend local temples with far greater frequency."[23]

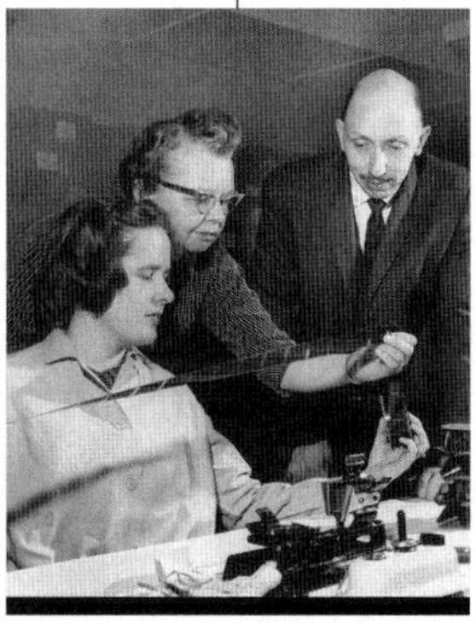

Workers inspect microfilm at the Genealogical Library in 1964. (Deseret News *photo*)

At the April 1999 conference, President Gordon B. Hinckley made the surprise announcement of plans to reconstruct the Nauvoo Temple. Built on the original site, its exterior would look exactly like the 1846 structure, and its interior would contain modern temple facilities.

Progress in Family History

As early as 1842 Joseph Smith had warned that "the earth will be smitten with a curse unless there is a welding link of some kind or other between the fathers and the children. . . . For we without them cannot be made perfect; neither can they without us be made perfect" (D&C 128:18). The Prophet also taught that "the greatest responsibility in this world that God has laid upon us is to seek after our dead," and "those Saints who neglect it" do so "at the peril of their own salvation."[24] The Latter-day Saints consequently went to work seeking genealogical records of their forbears.

In 1888 the Deseret News created the "Latter-day Saints' Genealogical Bureau" to promote the cooperative sharing of information. Then in 1894 President Wilford Woodruff in general conference emphasized, "We want the Latter-day Saints from this time to trace their genealogies as far as they can, and to be sealed to their fathers and mothers. Have children sealed to their parents, and run this chain through as far as you can get it. . . . This is the will of the Lord to his people."[25]

In November of that same year a group of top Church leaders met and organized the Genealogical Society of Utah with the purpose of establishing and maintaining a genealogical library for the use of Church members and others and of disseminating information on genealogical matters.[26]

Although the society during the early years of the twentieth century was a comparatively small operation, one of its leaders, Nephi Anderson, in 1912 envisioned a much greater future: "I see the records of the dead and their histories gathered from every nation under heaven to one great central library in Zion—the largest and best equipped for its particular work in the world. Branch libraries may be established in the nations, but in Zion will be the records of last resort and final authority. . . . Then, as temples multiply, and the work enlarges to its ultimate proportions, this Society, or some organization growing out of this Society, will have in its care some elaborate, but perfect system of exact registration and checking, so that the work in the temples may be conducted without confusion or duplication."[27]

Use of microfilm was the first step toward fulfilling Anderson's prophecy. Genealogical Society cameras filmed vital records all over the world, making available information that otherwise would likely have remained inaccessible. This project began in the eastern United States just before the outbreak of World War II. Expansion overseas had to wait until the years immediately following the close of the conflict. Microfilming was carried on in Europe, Latin America, the South Pacific, the Far East, and even behind the Iron Curtain in eastern Europe. By the end of 1980, the Society's library included 1,024,000 hundred-foot rolls of microfilm, equivalent to 4,927,000 volumes of three hundred pages each. At that time it was acquiring records from thirty-six countries.[28]

The advent of microfilm also made the establishment of branch libraries practical. Established in 1964, soon there were hundreds of branches in many parts of the world. Microfilm copies of materials in the main library could be circulated inexpensively as needed.[29] In 1968 some 140,000 patrons used the facilities of the main library in Salt Lake City, while 212,000 utilized the branches. Thus from its humble beginnings, the Church's Genealogical Society grew in stature and holdings to become recognized internationally as one of the major genealogical organizations of the world.

The Genealogical Society Building, circa 1948. (Deseret News *photo*)

The computer became an even more indispensable tool in genealogical research. When in 1961 more names were needed for the temples, Genealogical Society employees extracted vital information from selected parish and civil records. These names were then automatically alphabetized and printed by the computer.

In 1969 Church members were authorized to send individual names of ancestors for computer processing. Heretofore only names grouped into families had been accepted for temple work. This greater freedom allowed the Saints to accelerate their genealogical activity, so many more names were added to the Church's growing computerized International Genealogical Index.

Over the years the Genealogical Society sponsored classes, published instructions, and in other ways sought to stimulate Church members' involvement in genealogical activity. In 1965, Church leaders challenged individuals to fill out family group forms for the seven families in the first three generations of their pedigrees. During the following year, those who had completed this assignment were challenged to complete the eight family group forms corresponding with the fourth generation of their pedigrees. Church officials hoped that this practical experience with actual genealogical forms might spark an interest in further family research. The resulting collection of family group data came to be known as the Ancestral File™.[30]

In 1974, Church leaders encouraged Latter-day Saints to keep a personal or family "book of remembrance," a sacred history of spiritual, ecclesiastical, or other significant experiences. The Saints were also to see that temple blessings were made available to members of their immediate as well as direct-line ancestral families and to record these ordinances in their book of remembrance.[31]

By the mid-1970s, more than three million endowments for the dead were being performed annually, but less than one million names were being supplied by the Latter-day Saints' own genealogical research. Although the General Authorities wanted to increase the amount of temple work, they felt an even greater need to expand the Saints' role in providing names for temple ordinances. Therefore, in 1978 they began calling Church members to assist in the "extraction" of names from genealogical records and preparing them for temple ordinances.[32]

Because Latter-day Saints' ancestral lines often overlapped, and research became more difficult beyond the fourth generation, Church leaders found that work beyond this point was best done by the whole Church working together rather than by

The Granite Mountain Record Vault was completed in 1963 to store the Church's vast holdings of genealogical information on microfilm. (Deseret News *photo*)

individual families. Rather than several individual members searching endless hours for the same genealogical information, "extraction" volunteers were assigned to copy all the names from primary vital records. These names were then alphabetized by the computer in "telephone book" fashion for easy reference.[33] The Saints' involvement in this "extraction" program would help achieve the goal of each temple district supplying its own names for temple ordinance work.[34]

In 1985 the Church opened its new $8.5 million genealogical library across the street west of Temple Square. The new five-story structure was described as "undoubtedly the largest, most modern and best-equipped genealogical library in the world."[35] Elder Richard G. Scott, executive director of the Genealogical Department, explained: "This building has been designed to accommodate the use of the most modern technology available and forthcoming. This will, when in place, make genealogical research more doable by the average member."[36] Eight years later, when the Joseph Smith Memorial Building was opened a block away, it contained even more facilities for genealogical research.

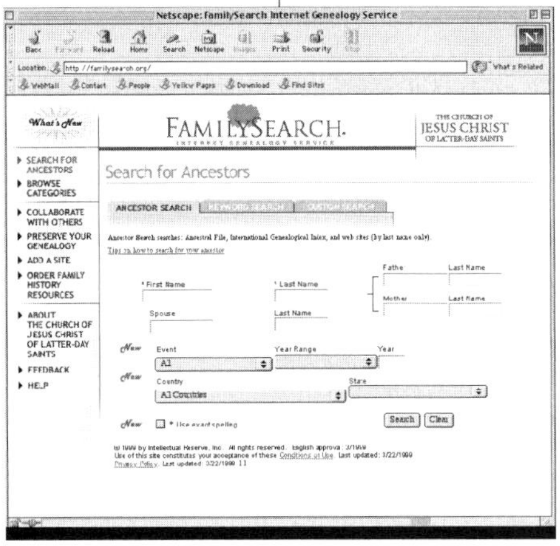

When the Church made www.familysearch.org *available to the public in May 1999, it quickly became one of the most popular sites on the Internet, receiving one hundred million hits on the first day.*

Elder Boyd K. Packer looked forward to the time when the computer would make clearing names for temple ordinances as easy as making an airplane reservation over the phone.[37] Still, many Church members continued to view genealogy as being difficult and complicated. Elder James E. Faust of the Quorum of the Twelve explained, "We are trying to simplify and demystify the seeking and finding of our ancestors. We are also hoping to make it easier for everyone with little training to find his or her own forefathers and receive the temple ordinances in their behalf."[38] Therefore, simpler family group sheets, pedigree charts, and name submission procedures were implemented. In 1987 the Church officially changed the name "Genealogy" to "Family History." Ward consultants were called to go to members' homes to help them with their family history research. A new motto arose: "Take an ancestor to the temple."

Significant strides in family history work during the 1980s and 1990s were directly related to the greatly expanded use of the computer. In 1986 the Church developed the Personal Ancestral File® (PAF), a software program for personal computers, which enabled individuals to organize and print their genealogical records, share information electronically, and even submit data on diskette for temple work or to the Church's growing geneaological files.

At about 3,000 local Family History Centers™ (formerly branch genealogical libraries) computers assisted patrons to find information more quickly. Beginning in 1990, the Church supplied each center with a set of compact discs, each containing up to 5 million names or the equivalent of 320,000 pages of information. This FamilySearch® database contained the International Genealogical Index (IGI), Ancestral File™, the catalog of Salt Lake City's Family History Library, and other resources. A few years later, a computerized program, TempleReady™, enabled Church members at their local Family History Centers™ to check for duplication as they cleared names for temple ordinance work.

These family history resources became available on a much broader basis in May 1999 when the Church launched a new website, www.familysearch.org. When President Hinckley officially announced the website, he indicated that during the previous eight-week trial period there had been over 200 million hits, "without any promotion or requested publicity, . . . making it one of the most sought-after sites on the Internet, even before its formal launch."[39] This free service received 100 million hits from all over the world on the day following the official public announcement. This site not only provided genealogical information, but it also created a forum where individuals could contact others researching their own family lines.

Reflecting on the impressive capacity of the computer and related technology to facilitate the work, Elder Boyd K. Packer declared: "When the servants of the Lord determine to do as He commands, we move ahead. As we proceed, we are joined at the crossroads by those who have been prepared to help us. They come with skills and abilities precisely suited to our needs. And, we find provisions; information, inventions, help of various kinds, set along the way waiting for us to take them up. It is as though someone knew we would be traveling that way. We see the invisible hand of the Almighty providing for us."[40]

The San Diego California Temple, dedicated in 1993, was the forty-fifth temple in this dispensation. The acceleration of genealogical work at the end of the twentieth century has been matched by an increase in temple building and temple ordinances performed. (Photo courtesy Darrel Chamberlain)

23

The Destiny of the Church

As the "Latter-day Saint Century" drew to its close, the Church had come a long way from its relatively obscure circumstances in 1900. Rather than there being only about 250,000 members, most in the valleys of the Rocky Mountains, by the year 2000 there were eleven million Latter-day Saints, more than half located outside of the United States. The Church of Jesus Christ of Latter-day Saints had become one of the six largest faith groups in the United States. Instead of there being only four temples, all in Utah, there were well over a hundred (including those announced or under construction), found on every continent. In contrast to the Church's being in debt a century earlier, the complete cost of building chapels and local programs in 2000 could be covered by general Church funds. At the dawning of the twentieth century, the Mormons were generally misunderstood and sometimes even persecuted. In many parts of the world a century later, however, they were generally respected members and even leaders of their communities.

At the Church's sesquicentennial conference in 1980, Elder Bruce R. McConkie spoke of the Church's progress to date and of its future destiny. Using symbolic terms, he likened the Church's achievements to standing on a majestic and glorious mountain peak: "From where we stand, on the peak of 150 years of progress, the view is glorious indeed." But, he continued, "Our joy and rejoicing is not in what lies below, not in our past—great and glorious as that is—but in our present and in

The Christus *at Temple Square in Salt Lake City.*
(Copyright Intellectual Reserve, all rights reserved)

our future. . . . From the top of the peak . . . we can look forward, crest upon crest, to the Zion of God which one day will be ours if we walk in the course charted by those who have gone before."[1]

In another talk four years later, Elder McConkie declared that "the Church is like a great caravan—organized, prepared, following an appointed course." Although there may be difficulties along the way, he conceded, "Ahead is the celestial city, the eternal Zion of our God, where all who maintain their position in the caravan shall find food and drink and rest."[2]

Church leaders have consistently taught that the Saints must be prepared for this glorious destiny. Joseph Smith recorded that in 1823 the angel Moroni instructed him "that the preparatory work for the second coming of the Messiah was speedily to commence; that the time was at hand for the Gospel in all its fullness to be preached in power, unto all nations that a people might be prepared for the Millennial reign."[3]

Since this time, Church programs have been designed to help the Saints with this preparation. In the 1960s, for example, priesthood correlation committee members received a special assignment. President N. Eldon Tanner, a counselor in the First Presidency, told them: "Brethren, we are sending you out to the conferences of this Church. . . . You go out and prepare the people for the second coming of Jesus Christ."[4] One of those present testified, "We sat there with those chills just going up and down our spines when we heard a prophet say this."[5]

Prophecies in the Doctrine and Covenants and other scriptures speak of future challenges through which the Church and Saints must first pass before the Second Coming. The consistent message is "a voice of warning" to prepare "for that which is to come" (D&C 1:4, 12). "We are in a program of defense," Elder Harold B. Lee insisted. "The Church of Jesus Christ was set upon this earth in this day '. . . for a defense, and for a refuge from the storm, and from wrath when it should be poured out without mixture upon the whole earth' (D&C 115:6). . . . [Therefore we are instructed] to move forward, that we consolidate to make more efficient, and more effective the work of the priesthood, the auxiliaries, and the other units in order that we may conserve our time, our energy, and our efforts toward the prime purpose for which the Church itself has been organized."[6]

President Hugh B. Brown, a counselor to David O. McKay in the First Presidency, similarly and emphatically declared:

> It seems to me that of all the signs of the times (and they are ominous and on every side) this is one of the significant signs of the times—that the Church of Jesus Christ, the kingdom of God, is massing its forces, getting ready for that which is to follow. . . .
>
> I want to say to you, brethren, that in the midst of all the troubles, the uncertainties, the tumult and the chaos through which the world is passing, almost unnoticed by the majority of the people of the world, there has been set up a kingdom, a kingdom over which God the Father presides, and Jesus the Christ is the King. That kingdom is rolling forward, as I say, partly unnoticed, but it is rolling forward with a power and a force that will stop the enemy in its tracks while some of you live.
>
> Do you want to be among those on the side of Christ and his apostles?[7]

Zion must be established on earth before Christ comes again. An 1834 revelation outlined what is required: "It is expedient in me that mine elders should wait for a little season for the redemption of Zion—That they themselves may be prepared, and that my people may be taught more perfectly. . . . But first let my army become very great, and let it be sanctified before me" (D&C 105:9–10, 31).

Tremendous growth during the twentieth century has made the Lord's army "very great." But the Church has not yet filled the earth as the ancient prophet Daniel foresaw (see Daniel 2:26–45). The approximately eleven million Latter-day Saints only represent about 0.18 percent of the world's estimated six billion inhabitants. Obviously there is room and need for further growth.

Is the Lord's "army," or Church, sufficiently sanctified? Available statistics do not measure worthiness or sanctification directly. Nevertheless, faith and devotion are reflected in the levels of Church activity. There has been substantial progress during the twentieth century in such matters as church attendance, missionary service, tithe-paying, and temple ordinances performed. Yet here again there is ample room for further improvement.

Latter-day Saints in the twentieth century should find the Church's progress thrilling. "There was never a brighter day than today in the history of The Church of Jesus Christ of Latter-day Saints," affirmed President Gordon B. Hinckley. "There was never a season when the work of the Lord prospered as it now prospers. . . . I marvel at what is happening in the growth and expansion of this work. And yet I know that what we see today is but the scratching of the surface of far greater things yet to come."[8] Truly the kingdom is rolling forth.

Still much more remains to be accomplished. Each Church member has the opportunity and responsibility to contribute to the kingdom's forward momentum. The challenge to all Latter-day Saints, then, is to catch the vision of the Church's mission and destiny, that they may help to realize the fulfillment of the Prophet Joseph Smith's inspired petition in Doctrine and Covenants 65:6, in which he prayed, "May the kingdom of God go forth, that the kingdom of heaven may come, that thou, O God, mayest be glorified in heaven so on earth."

Chronology

1901 Elder Heber J. Grant is sent to open the Japanese Mission

President Lorenzo Snow dies in Salt Lake City at age eighty-seven, October 10

Joseph F. Smith becomes President of the Church, October 17

Juvenile Instructor becomes the official organ of the Sunday School

1902 Bureau of Information is opened on Temple Square

New edition of the Pearl of Great Price is approved

Children's Friend is first published by the Primary

1903 Carthage Jail becomes the first of several important Church history sites purchased by the Church

1904 U.S. Senate committee opens hearings on Elder Reed Smoot's election as senator

President Joseph F. Smith issues "Second Manifesto," banning all new plural marriages

Society for the Aid of the Sightless is organized

1905 Elders John W. Taylor and Matthias Cowley resign from the Quorum of the Twelve because of a disagreement with Church leaders over plural marriage

LDS Hospital is opened in Salt Lake City

Monument is dedicated at Joseph Smith's birthplace in Sharon, Vermont

1906 President Joseph F. Smith becomes first Church President to visit Europe

Sunday School conducts first classes for adults

1907 Elder Reed Smoot is allowed to retain seat in the Senate

Church issues "Address to the World" to correct misunderstandings

President Joseph F. Smith announces that the Church is out of debt

1908 General Priesthood Committee is appointed

Weekly ward priesthood meetings and specific ages for ordination to offices of the priesthood are introduced

1909 Weekly ward priesthood meetings commenced

First Presidency issues statement entitled "Origin of Man"

1910 *Utah Genealogical and Historical Magazine* is inaugurated

1911 YMMIA adopts the Boy Scout program

One millionth endowment for the dead is performed

1912 Exodus of Mormon colonists during Mexican Revolution

First seminary is established near Salt Lake City

Correlation Committee appointed to reduce duplication among auxiliaries

1915 *Jesus the Christ*, by Elder James E. Talmage, is published

Relief Society Magazine is instituted

First Presidency issues statement entitled "The Father and the Son"

1917 Saints' support of the war effort leads to an improved public image

Church Administration Building is occupied

1918 President Joseph F. Smith receives a vision of the redemption of the dead, October 3

President Joseph F. Smith dies in Salt Lake City at age eighty, November 19

Heber J. Grant becomes President of the Church, November 23

Hawaii Temple is dedicated

Church membership reaches half a million

Wheat stored by the Relief Society is sold to alleviate World War II shortages

1920 Elder David O. McKay tours missions of the world (1920–21)

Church decides to close its academies

Correlation-Social Advisory Committee coordinates priesthood and auxiliaries, stressing that the auxiliaries are to be helps to the priesthood

1922 Primary Children's Hospital is opened

1923 Los Angeles stake is organized, the first outside the Intermountain area

Alberta Temple is dedicated

1924 Conference is broadcast on radio for the first time

1925 South America is dedicated and a mission is opened

Missionary home in Salt Lake City opens

1926 First institute of religion is opened at the University of Idaho

1927 The Alberta Temple is dedicated

1928 The Hill Cumorah is purchased by the Church

Priesthood Auxiliary Movement is launched, simplifying Church activities by uniting priesthood and auxiliary meetings

The one hundredth stake is organized

1929 Stock market crash leads to the Great Depression

Tabernacle Choir network broadcasts begin

MIA magazines are merged

Religion Classes and the Primary are combined

Czechoslovak Mission is opened, the first in Eastern Europe

1930 Church celebrates its centennial

1931 Church's junior colleges, except Ricks, are transferred to states

Aaronic Priesthood youth correlation program is outlined

1933 Churchwide program is launched to reactivate Aaronic Priesthood adults

1935 Harold B. Lee called to formulate Churchwide welfare program

Radio, Publicity, and Mission Literature Committee is formed with Gordon B. Hinckley as executive secretary

1936 General welfare committee and regions formed

Stake missions instituted

Shortwave radio sends First Presidency message to Europe

1937 President J. Reuben Clark challenges Saints to store a year's supply of food, clothing, and other supplies

President Heber J. Grant visits missions in Europe

Cooperative Securities Corporation is organized to hold title and coordinate welfare projects

The Missionary's Handbook and LeGrand Richard's proselyting outline are published

1938 Boards of Church schools are consolidated

Deseret Industries is created

Genealogical Society begins using microfilm

1939 Missionaries are evacuated from Europe as World War II breaks out

1940 Missionaries are evacuated from the South Pacific

1941 Assistants to the Twelve are appointed

Japan attacks Pearl Harbor, December 7

Ten millionth endowment for the dead is performed

1942 Church meetings are curtailed anticipating restrictions on travel

1945 End of World War II

President Heber J. Grant dies in Salt Lake City at age eighty-eight, May 14

George Albert Smith becomes President of the Church, May 21

1946 Elder Ezra Taft Benson reopens the missionary work in Europe

Elder Matthew Cowley reopens the missionary work in the Pacific

Elder Spencer W. Kimball is named head of the Indian Committee

1947 Pioneer centennial

"This Is the Place" monument is dedicated

Church membership reaches one million members

1949 General conference telecasts begin

1950 LDS Girls program taken over by YWMIA

Indian Student Placement Program is implemented Churchwide

Building missionaries begin erecting schools in the Pacific

Early-morning seminaries are pioneered in southern California

1951 President George Albert Smith dies in Salt Lake City at age eighty-one, April 4

David O. McKay becomes President of the Church, April 9

1952 President David O. McKay tours European, South African, Latin American, and Pacific missions of the Church (1952–55)

First official proselyting outline is published by the Church

1953 Elder Ezra Taft Benson serves as Secretary of Agriculture in cabinet of U.S. President Eisenhower (1953–61)

1955 Swiss Temple is dedicated

Temple films are introduced

1956 First student stake is organized at BYU

1958 Auckland Stake is formed in New Zealand, the first outside of the United States and Canada

First branch genealogical library is opened

1959 Tabernacle Choir tours Europe

1960 Manchester Stake is formed, the first in Europe

1961 Mexico City Stake is formed, the first in Latin America

Worldwide mission presidents' seminar is held

Missionary language training begins at BYU

Computers are used for the first time to provide names for temple ordinances

1962 Curriculum for children, youth, and adults is outlined

1963 Priesthood committees are established to give direction to home teaching, missionary, genealogical, and welfare activities

1964 Church hosts a pavilion at New York World's Fair

Ward priesthood executive committees and correlation councils are formed

1965 Family home evening manuals are published

Missions are organized into areas for administrative purposes

Church members are assigned to fill out three-generation sheets

1966 Home-study seminary pilot program is inaugurated

1967 Regional representatives are first called

1970 President David O. McKay dies in Salt Lake City at age ninety-six, January 18

Joseph Fielding Smith becomes President of the Church, January 23

Five hundredth stake is organized

Tokyo Stake is organized, the first in Asia

Johannesburg Stake is organized, the first in Africa

Aaronic Priesthood and YMMIA are consolidated

1971 First area conference is held in Manchester, England

1972 President Joseph Fielding Smith dies in Salt Lake City at age ninety-five, July 2

Harold B. Lee becomes President of the Church, July 7

Public Communications Department is organized

1973 President Harold B. Lee dies in Salt Lake City at age seventy-four, December 26

Spencer W. Kimball becomes President of the Church, December 30

1974 Seventies quorums' and stake missions' leadership are combined

1975 Regions and stakes become parts of areas

Auxiliary conferences at Church headquarters are discontinued

1976 Two visions are added to standard works of the Church

First Quorum of the Seventy is organized

Assistants to the Twelve become members of the First Quorum of the Seventy

1977 General conferences are shortened to two days

1978 All missionaries begin receiving training at Missionary Training Center near BYU

President Spencer W. Kimball receives revelation extending priesthood to all worthy males

BYU performing group tours the Soviet Union

Emeritus status is given to designated General Authorities

Name extraction program is introduced Churchwide

1979 One thousandth stake is organized at Nauvoo

New edition of the King James Version of the Bible published with LDS study aids

Office of Patriarch to the Church is discontinued

Stake conferences are cut from two to four per year

1980 Sesquicentennial of the Church organization is commemorated

Ward meetings are consolidated

1981 Church installs an extensive satellite system

1984 Area presidencies are organized

Some Seventies are called to three-to-five-year terms

1985 President Spencer W. Kimball dies in Salt Lake City at age ninety, November 5

Ezra Taft Benson becomes President of the Church, November 10

1986 Seventies quorums in stakes are discontinued

1988 First stake in West Africa is organized

One hundred millionth endowment for the dead is performed

1989 Second Quorum of the Seventy is formed, consisting of those called to serve for limited terms

BYU Jerusalem Center is dedicated by President Howard W. Hunter

Church is closed in Ghana for a period of one and a half years

1990 Ward and branch budgets are funded entirely from tithes

Genealogical data recorded on compact discs is available at Family History Centers

1991 Tabernacle Choir tours European countries including Czechoslovakia, Hungary, Poland, and the Soviet Union

1992 Relief Society sponsors "Gospel Literacy" effort

Tabernacle Choir tours Israel

1993 "Triple Combination" with new study helps is published in Spanish

Joseph Smith Memorial Building is dedicated

1994 President Ezra Taft Benson dies in Salt Lake City at age ninety-four, May 30

Howard W. Hunter becomes President of the Church, June 5

Two thousandth stake is organized in Mexico City

1995 President Howard W. Hunter dies in Salt Lake City at age eighty-seven, March 3

Gordon B. Hinckley becomes President of the Church, March 12

The Family: A Proclamation to the World is first presented at General Relief Society meeting

Area Authorities replace regional representatives

1996 More than half of Church members live outside the United States

President Gordon B. Hinckley is interviewed on *60 Minutes*

President Gordon B. Hinckley dedicates the Hong Kong Temple and becomes the first Church President to visit mainland China

1997 Area Authorities are ordained to the office of Seventy and are grouped into the Third, Fourth, and Fifth quorums

Pioneer sesquicentennial is commemorated

Ground is broken for new assembly building across from Temple Square

Plans are announced to build smaller temples

Church membership passes ten million

1998 President Hinckley tours Africa and is the first Church President to visit four African countries

First "small temple" is dedicated at Monticello, Utah

1999 Plans are announced to rebuild the Nauvoo Temple

Total number of temples in service or planned reaches one hundred with announcement of the New York Temple, in Palmyra

Church makes genealogical Internet site available to public

Notes

Chapter 1

1. Lorenzo Snow, *Deseret Evening News*, January 1, 1901, p. 5.
2. Lorenzo Snow, as quoted in Eliza R. Snow, *Biography and Family Record of Lorenzo Snow* (Salt Lake City: Deseret News Co., 1884), pp. 7–9.
3. Ibid., p. 46.
4. Brigham Young, as quoted in Preston Nibley, *The Presidents of the Church* (Salt Lake City: Deseret Book Co., 1974), p. 156.
5. Lorenzo Snow, as quoted in LeRoi C. Snow, "Raised from the Dead," *Improvement Era* 32 (September 1929): 885.
6. See Lorenzo Snow, as quoted in Reed C. Durham and Steven H. Heath, *Succession in the Church* (Salt Lake City: Bookcraft, 1970), pp. 103–4.
7. LeRoi C. Snow, "An Experience of My Father's," *Improvement Era* 36 (September 1933): 677.
8. Ibid.
9. Allie Young Pond, as quoted in ibid.
10. Francis M. Lyman, as quoted in ibid.
11. Journal History, September 13, 1898, p. 2.
12. See Durham and Heath, *Succession in the Church*, pp. 97–98.
13. Harold B. Lee, in Conference Report, April 1970, p. 24.
14. Spencer W. Kimball, in Conference Report, April 1970, pp. 118–19.
15. John A. Widtsoe, *Evidences and Reconciliations* (Salt Lake City: Bookcraft, 1960), p. 264.
16. Joseph Fielding Smith, *The Life of Joseph F. Smith* (Salt Lake City: Deseret News Press, 1938), pp. 310–11.
17. Ibid., p. 311.
18. Leonard J. Arrington, *Great Basin Kingdom* (Cambridge, Massachusetts: Harvard University Press, 1958), pp. 400–401.
19. See ibid., pp. 400–403.
20. LeRoi C. Snow, "The Lord's Way Out of Bondage," *Improvement Era* 41 (July 1938): 401.
21. Ibid., p. 439.
22. Lorenzo Snow, as quoted in ibid.
23. Ibid., p. 440.
24. Lorenzo Snow, as quoted in ibid.
25. B. H. Roberts, *A Comprehensive History of the Church*, 6 vols. (Salt Lake City: The Church of Jesus Christ of Latter-day Saints, 1930), 6:359.
26. Lorenzo Snow, as quoted in ibid.
27. Ibid., 6:360.
28. Heber J. Grant, in Conference Report, October 1903, p. 7.
29. Lorenzo Snow, as quoted in Roberts, *A Comprehensive History of the Church* 6:377.
30. Ibid., 6:379; emphasis in original.
31. Lorenzo Snow, as quoted in Susa Young Gates, "Biographical Sketches: Mrs. Elizabeth Claridge McCune," *Young Woman's Journal*, 9 (August 1898): 339.
32. George Q. Cannon, as quoted in J., "Biographical Sketches: Jennie Brimhall and Inez Knight," *Young Woman's Journal* 9 (June 1898): 245.
33. Inez Knight, as quoted in "Our Girls," *Young Woman's Journal* 10 (June 1899): 187.
34. Inez Knight, "Our Girls," *Young Woman's Journal* 9 (June 1898): 416.
35. See, for example, Journal History, January 19, 1899, pp. 2–5; see also Frederick Jackson Turner, *The Frontier in American History* (New York: Holt and Co., 1920).
36. See James R. Clark, *Messages of the First Presidency of The Church of Jesus Christ of Latter-day Saints*, 6 vols. (Salt Lake City: Bookcraft, 1965–75), 4:165.
37. Lorenzo Snow, as quoted in Roberts, *A Comprehensive History of the Church* 6:377.
38. *Millenial Star*, September 15, 1921, p. 585.

Chapter 2

1. Doctrine and Covenants, Official Declaration—1.
2. Thomas G. Alexander, *Mormonism in Transition: History of the Latter-day Saints, 1890–1930* (Chicago: University of Illinois Press, 1986), p. 18.
3. In B. H. Roberts, *A Comprehensive History of the Church*, 6 vols. (Salt Lake City: The Church of Jesus Christ of Latter-day Saints, 1930), 6:334.
4. See ibid., 6:134–37.
5. Alexander, *Mormonism in Transition*, p. 19.
6. See Russell R. Rich, *Ensign to the Nations* (Provo, Utah: Brigham Young University Publications, 1972), pp. 472–73.
7. Francis T. Plimpton at Amherst College, as quoted in *Reader's Digest*, June 1958, p. 142.
8. See Alexander, *Mormonism in Transition*, p. 27.
9. Joseph F. Smith, in Conference Report, April 1904, p. 75.
10. John W. Taylor, as quoted in Joseph Fielding Smith, *Life of Joseph F. Smith* (Salt Lake City: Deseret News Press, 1938), p. 379.

11. B. H. Roberts, *A Comprehensive History of the Church* 6:407–8.
12. Charles W. Nibley, *Reminiscences of Charles W. Nibley* (Salt Lake City; Nibley Family, 1934), p. 125.
13. See Alfred Henry Lewis, "The Viper on the Hearth," *Cosmopolitan*, March 1911, pp. 439–50.
14. Joseph F. Smith, in Conference Report, October 1907, p. 5.
15. Rudger Clawson, *Millenial Star* 72 (July 28, 1910): 476, as cited in Gilbert W. Scharffs, *Mormonism in Germany* (Salt Lake City: Deseret Book Co., 1970), p. 54.
16. See James B. Allen and Glenn M. Leonard, *The Story of the Latter-day Saints* (Salt Lake City: Deseret Book Co., 1992), p. 477.
17. See Roberts, *A Comprehensive History of the Church* 6:435–41.
18. See Alexander, *Mormonism in Transition*, pp. 249–50; for a thorough discussion of the Spaulding theory see Kent P. Jackson, *Manuscript Found: The Complete Original "Spaulding Manuscript"* (Provo, Utah: Religious Studies Center, Brigham Young University, 1992).
19. See Roberts, *A Comprehensive History of the Church* 1:v–vi, x.
20. Theodore Roosevelt, "Mr. Roosevelt to the Mormons," *Collier's*, April 15, 1911, p. 28; reprinted in *Improvement Era* 14 (June 1911): 715–18.
21. Charles C. Goodwin, as quoted in Roberts, *A Comprehensive History of the Church* 6:477–78.

Chapter 3

1. Joseph F. Smith, as quoted in Preston Nibley, *The Presidents of the Church* (Salt Lake City: Deseret Book Co., 1974), p. 187.
2. Joseph Fielding Smith, *Life of Joseph F. Smith* (Salt Lake City: Deseret News Press, 1938), p. 164.
3. Ibid., p. 170.
4. Ibid., p. 290; see also pp. 281–91 for more information about President Joseph F. Smith's struggles in this area.
5. Joseph F. Smith, in Conference Report, April 1907, p. 7.
6. Joseph F. Smith, as quoted in Francis M. Gibbons, *Joseph F. Smith* (Salt Lake City: Deseret Book Co., 1984), p. 244.
7. From an interview with David F. Boone, March 2, 1999.
8. See B. H. Roberts, *A Comprehensive History of the Church*, 6 vols. (Salt Lake City: The Church of Jesus Christ of Latter-day Saints, 1930), 6:426–30.
9. Ibid. 1:iii.
10. Ibid. 1:33, fn. 8.
11. Truman Madsen, *Defender of the Faith* (Salt Lake City: Bookcraft, 1980), p. 357.
12. See Smith, *Life of Joseph F. Smith*, pp. 425–27; see also Conference Report, October 1911, pp. 29–30.
13. See ibid., pp. 427–28.
14. Ibid., p. 397.
15. See Rey L. Pratt, "History of the Mexican Mission," *Improvement Era* 15 (April 1912): 493, 498.
16. W. Ernest Young, *The Diary of W. Ernest Young* (Salt Lake City: Walter Ernest Young, 1973), pp. 135–36.
17. Anthony W. Ivins, as quoted in Thomas C. Romney, *The Mormon Colonies in Mexico* (Salt Lake City: Deseret Book Co., 1938), pp. 226–27.
18. Joseph F. Smith, in Conference Report, October 1915, p. 8.
19. Joseph F. Smith, as quoted by Serge F. Ballif, in Conference Report, October 1920, p. 90.
20. John W. Taylor, as quoted in *Temples of the Most High*, comp. N. B. Lundwall (Salt Lake City: Bookcraft, 1993), p. 165.
21. Joseph F. Smith, as quoted in ibid., p. 166.
22. Joseph F. Smith, as quoted by Reed Smoot, in Conference Report, October 1920, p. 137.
23. Ibid.
24. See Jill Mulvay Derr, et al., *Women of Covenant* (Salt Lake City: Deseret Book Co., 1992), pp. 206–9.
25. See ibid., pp. 210–13.
26. See ibid., p. 205.
27. Quoted in *Improvement Era* 19 (February 1916): 369.
28. Joseph F. Smith, in Conference Report, April 1917, p. 3.

Chapter 4

1. See *Deseret News Weekly*, April 17, 1852, p. 2.
2. See *Deseret News Weekly*, April 9, 1894.
3. In James R. Clark, comp., *Messages of the First Presidency of The Church of Jesus Christ of Latter-day Saints*, 6 vols. (Salt Lake City: Bookcraft, 1965–75), 3:282.
4. See Thomas G. Alexander, *Mormonism in Transition: History of the Latter-day Saints, 1890–1930* (Chicago: University of Illinois Press, 1986), pp. 152–53.
5. Joseph F. Smith, in Conference Report, April 1906, p. 3.
6. J. Golden Kimball, in ibid., p. 19.
7. Joseph F. Smith, in Conference Report, April 1907, p. 6.
8. B. H. Roberts, "Seventy's Council Table," *Improvement Era* 11 (November 1907): 63.
9. See Clark, comp., *Messages of the First Presidency* 4:195.
10. Ibid. 2:288.
11. Joseph F. Smith, in Granite Stake Presidency, *Home Evening Bulletin*, January 1927, p. 43.
12. See Clark, comp., *Messages of the First Presidency* 4:338–39.
13. "The Origin of Man," in ibid. 4:195.
14. Ibid. 4:205.
15. "The Father and the Son," in ibid. 5:34.
16. See John R. Talmage, *The Talmage Story: Life of James E. Talmage* (Salt Lake City: Bookcraft, 1972), pp. 154–59.
17. See ibid., p. 172.
18. James E. Talmage, in ibid., p. 184.
19. Ibid., p. 183.
20. Ibid., p. 185.
21. In Clark, comp., *Messages of the First Presidency*, 4:195.
22. Mark E. Peterson, "The Publications of the Church," an address given to seminary and institute teachers at Brigham Young University, July 8, 1958, p. 1.
23. Society for the Aid of the Sightless, Minutes, Historical Department Archives, The Church of Jesus Christ of Latter-day Saints (hereafter cited as Church Archives), pp. 1–2.

24. See Carol Anne Schuster, "LDS Church Services to the Blind Through the Society for the Aid of the Sightless: The Talmage Era" (master's thesis, Brigham Young University, 1972), pp. 21–50.
25. *Deseret News*, October 11, 1880, p. 2.
26. Doctrine and Covenants, 1921 edition, p. xx; see also Alexander, *Mormonism in Transition*, pp. 281–82.

Chapter 5

1. See Francis M. Gibbons, *Heber J. Grant: Man of Steel, Prophet of God* (Salt Lake City: Deseret Book Co., 1979), p. 13.
2. In Heber J. Grant, *Gospel Standards*, comp. G. Homer Durham (Salt Lake City: Improvement Era, 1969), p. 11.
3. Ibid., p. 343.
4. Heber J. Grant, "Learning to Sing," *Improvement Era* 3 (October 1900): 889.
5. See Heber J. Grant, Diary, December 20, 1931, MS, Church Archives.
6. Heber J. Grant, in Conference Report, October 1922, pp. 2–3.
7. James R. Clark, comp., *Messages of the First Presidency of The Church of Jesus Christ of Latter-day Saints*, 6 vols. (Salt Lake City: Bookcraft, 1965–75), 2:348.
8. Heber J. Grant to Mrs. Parley Fenn, February 13, 1931, MS, Church Archives.
9. Joseph Anderson, *Prophets I Have Known* (Salt Lake City: Deseret Book Co., 1973), p. 25.
10. Ibid., p. 30.
11. Heber J. Grant, "Settlement," *Improvement Era* 44 (January 1941): 9, 56.
12. Heber J. Grant, as quoted in Emerson R. West, *Profiles of the Presidents* (Salt Lake City: Deseret Book Co., 1972), p. 232.
13. Clark, comp., *Messages of the First Presidency* 5:291.
14. Gibbons, *Heber J. Grant*, pp. 174–75.
15. Joseph F. Smith, as quoted in Grant, *Gospel Standards*, p. 196.
16. See discussion on the Social Advisory Committee in chapter 4.
17. Heber J. Grant, in Conference Report, October 1919, p. 17.
18. See James B. Allen, "Personal Faith and Public Policy: Some Timely Observations on the League of Nations Controversy in Utah," *BYU Studies* 13 (Autumn 1973): 77–98.
19. Clark, comp. *Messages of the First Presidency* 5:245.
20. Ibid. 5:250.
21. Ibid. 5:260.
22. Joseph F. Smith, in Conference Report, October 1908, p. 8.
23. Heber J. Grant to the president of the Association Against the Prohibition Amendment, May 31, 1930, First Presidency letterbooks, Church Archives.
24. Kirk H. Porter and Donald Bruce Johnson, *National Party Platforms*, 1840–1964 (Urbana: University of Illinois Press, 1966), pp. 332; see also pp. 348–49.
25. Heber J. Grant, in Conference Report, October 1933, p. 6.
26. George F. Richards, in Conference Report, October 1935, p. 30.
27. Heber J. Grant to Leo J. Muir, September 22, 1941, Muir Papers, Brigham Young University Library.
28. Heber J. Grant, in Conference Report, April 1942, p. 11.
29. George Albert Smith, in Conference Report, October 1943, p. 47.
30. *Deseret News*, May 11, 1968, p. 1.
31. Howard W. Hunter, as quoted in Eleanor Knowles, *Howard W. Hunter* (Salt Lake City: Deseret Book Co., 1994), p. 71.
32. Joseph Smith, *Teachings of the Prophet Joseph Smith*, sel. Joseph Fielding Smith (Salt Lake City: Deseret Book Co., 1938), p. 363.
33. A. Theodore Tuttle, "South America: Land of Prophecy and Promise," *Improvement Era* 66 (May 1963): 352–60.
34. First Presidency statement, in Conference Report, April 1930, p. 3.
35. B. H. Roberts, *A Comprehensive History of the Church*, 6 vols. (Salt Lake City: The Church of Jesus Christ of Latter-day Saints, 1930), 6:537.

Chapter 6

1. Joseph F. Smith, in Conference Report, October 1915, p. 4.
2. See Thomas G. Alexander, *Mormonism in Transition: History of the Latter-day Saints, 1890–1930* (Chicago: University of Illinois Press, 1986), p. 169.
3. See Board of Education minutes, March 15, 1920, MS, Church Archives.
4. Ibid., February 3, 1926.
5. See Heber J. Grant, in Conference Report, April 1926, p. 4.
6. See Board of Education minutes, February 3 and March 18, 1926.
7. See Jerry C. Roundy, *Ricks College: A Struggle for Survival* (Rexburg, Idaho: Ricks Collge Press, 1976), pp. 113–51.
8. Joseph F. Merrill, "Brigham Young University, Past, Present and Future," *Deseret News*, December 20, 1930, section 2, p. 3.
9. See *Enrollment Resume 1963–1964* (Provo, Utah: Brigham Young University, 1965), p. 2.
10. See I. L. Williamson, "On the Existing Relationship Between Religious Seminaries and Public High Schools in the State of Utah," report to the Utah State Board of Education, January 8, 1930; see also Journal History, May 3, 1930, p. 4, and September 24, 1931, p. 3, MS, Church Archives; see also Board of Education minutes, November 4, 1931.
11. J. Wylie Sessions, from an interview with author, July 29, 1965.
12. See G. Homer Durham, "University Religious Training and the LDS Deseret Clubs," *Weekday Religious Education* 1 (March 1937): 1–2.
13. Ernest L. Wilkinson and W. Cleon Skousen, *Brigham Young University: A School of Destiny* (Provo, Utah: Brigham Young University Press, 1976), p. 207; see also the discussion in chapter 3.
14. George H. Brimhall, as quoted in ibid., p. 212.
15. Ibid., p. 211.

16. Joseph F. Smith, "Philosophy and the Church Schools," *Juvenile Instructor* 55 (April 1911): 209.
17. See Ernest L. Wilkinson, ed., *Brigham Young University: The First One Hundred Years*, 4 vols. (Provo, Utah: Brigham Young University Press, 1975), 2:262–69.
18. J. Reuben Clark Jr., as quoted in Clark, comp., *Messages of the First Presidency of The Church of Jesus Christ of Latter-day Saints*, 6 vols. (Salt Lake City: Bookcraft, 1965–75), 6:45–55.
19. See Wilkinson, *Brigham Young University: The First One Hundred Years* 2:360.
20. See *Utah Economic and Business Review*, December 1974, p. 58, citing U.S. Government census data.
21. E. L. Thorndike, "The Origin of Superior Men," *Scientific Monthly* 56 (May 1943): 424–33; see also "Utah Holds High Rank as Birthplace of Scientists," *Improvement Era* 43 (October 1940): 606.

Chapter 7

1. Thomas G. Alexander, "The Economic Consequences of the War: Utah and the Depression of the Early 1920s," *Dependent Commonwealth* (Provo, Utah: Brigham Young University Press, 1974), pp. 57–89.
2. See Conference Reports, April 1928, pp. 3–4, and April 1934, 4–5.
3. Stephen L Richards, in Conference Report, October 1933, p. 65.
4. Heber J. Grant, in ibid., 5; see also Sylvester Q. Cannon's comments, ibid., pp. 33–35.
5. Stephen L Richards, in Conference Report, October 1934, p. 36.
6. See J. Reuben Clark Jr., in Conference Report, April 1935, p. 93.
7. See Glen L. Rudd, *Pure Religion* (Salt Lake City: The Church of Jesus Christ of Latter-day Saints, 1995), p. 4.
8. Sylvester Q. Cannon, in Conference Report, October 1930, p. 103.
9. James R. Clark, comp. *Messages of the First Presidency of The Church of Jesus Christ of Latter-day Saints*, 6 vols. (Salt Lake City: Bookcraft, 1965–75), 5:331–34; for a discussion of President Clark's role in formulating the welfare plan, see Michael D. Quinn, *J. Reuben Clark: The Church Years* (Provo, Utah: Brigham Young University Press, 1983), pp. 251–78.
10. Harold B. Lee, in Francis M. Gibbons, *Harold B. Lee: Man of Vision, Prophet of God* (Salt Lake City: Deseret Book Co., 1993), p. 125.
11. Harold B. Lee, *Church News*, August 26, 1961, p. 8.
12. Ibid.
13. See "An Important Message from the First Presidency," *Improvement Era* 39 (May 1936): 305.
14. See *Deseret News*, June 9, 1936, p. 1.
15. Heber J. Grant, in Conference Report, October 1936, p. 3.
16. J. Reuben Clark Jr., in Conference Report, April 1937, 26.
17. David O. McKay, in Conference Report, October 1936, p. 103.
18. J. Reuben Clark Jr., *A Discussion of the Church Welfare Plan* (pamphlet, 1939) pp. 15–36.
19. See J. Reuben Clark Jr., as recounted by John A. Widtsoe in an interview with Lauritz G. Petersen, December 1, 1940, written summary in Church Archives.
20. Heber J. Grant, as quoted in William E. Berrett, "Teaching by the Spirit" and "Revelation," addresses given at Brigham Young University, June 27, 1966, and June 27, 1956.
21. Wilford Woodruff, as quoted in Harold B. Lee, in Conference Report, April 1943, p. 126.
22. Harold B. Lee, in ibid.
23. Harold B. Lee, in Conference Report, April 1941, p. 121.
24. Melvin J. Ballard, as quoted by Harold B. Lee, in Bryant S. Hinckley, *Sermons and Missionary Services of Elder Melvin Joseph Ballard* (Salt Lake City: Deseret Book Co., 1949), p. 121.
25. J. Reuben Clark Jr., in Conference Report, October 1942, p. 57.
26. See Brian Q. Cannon, "Mormons and the New Deal: The 1936 Presidential Election in Utah," *Utah Historical Quarterly* 67 (Winter 1999): 4–22.
27. Heber J. Grant, diary, April 7, 1937, MS, Church Archives.
28. Clark, comp. *Messages of the First Presidency* 6:18.
29. Heber J. Grant to J. Harold Long, August 23, 1934, First Presidency letterbooks, Church Archives; see also Heber J. Grant, in Conference Report, October 1919, pp. 13–14.
30. First Presidency statement, *Deseret News*, November 29, 1941; compare *Deseret News*, June 25, 1963; see also David O. McKay, "On Unionism," *Improvement Era* 40 (August 1937): 496.

Chapter 8

1. In "Priesthood Quorums," *Improvement Era* 31 (January 1928): 257.
2. Joseph F. Smith, in Conference Report, April 1906, p. 3.
3. *In the Realm of Quorum Activity* (Salt Lake City: Deseret News Co., 1931), p. 3.
4. Melvin J. Ballard, "New Priesthood-MIA Plan," *Improvement Era* 31 (June 1928): 744–45; see also p. 794.
5. See Council of the Twelve circular letter, November 11, 1927, in *Juvenile Instructor* 61 (November 1927): 620–21.
6. See James R. Clark, comp. *Messages of the First Presidency of The Church of Jesus Christ of Latter-day Saints*, 6 vols. (Salt Lake City: Bookcraft 1965–75), 5:267–68.
7. Minutes of the Aaronic Priesthood Convention, April 4, 1931, p. 3, MS, Church Archives.
8. See ibid., pp. 4, 9–10.
9. Joseph F. Smith, as quoted in General Priesthood Committee minutes, December 12, 1911, p. 265, Church Archives.
10. See "What They Say: A Collection of Sentiments of the Value of Y.M.M.I.A.," *Improvement Era* 28 (May 1926): 687.
11. See *Instructor's Manual Aaronic Priesthood*, 1936, pp. 7–8; see also *Deseret News, Church Section*, June 6, 1936, p. 4; *Improvement Era* 36 (November 1933): 812.
12. See *Church News*, September 18, 1982, p. 10.
13. See *Deseret News*, April 6, 1931, p. 1; see also Daniel J. Lang, in Mission Annual Reports, 1933, p. 240.
14. Heber J. Grant to Leah Widtsoe, October 13, 1933,

in First Presidency letterbooks, MS, Church Archives.

15. Letter from J. Golden Kimball to the Seventies, January 31, 1934, in First Quorum of the Seventy Circular Letters 1860–1978, MS, Church Archives.

16. Circular letter from Rudger Clawson to stake presidents, April 24, 1936, MS, Church Archives.

17. See *Deseret News, Church Section,* March 4, 1939; July 17, 1937.

18. First Presidency to Joseph Fielding Smith, Stephen L Richards, and Albert E. Bowen, January 1939, MS, Church Archives.

19. J. Reuben Clark Jr., "Memorandum of Suggestions," MS, Church Archives.

20. See Genealogical Society of Utah, board minutes, 5:159; see also *Improvement Era* 43 (August 1940): 480.

21. See Gilbert Scharffs, *Mormonism in Germany* (Salt Lake City: Deseret Book Co., 1970), pp. 80–81; see also Joseph M. Dixon, "Mormons in the Third Reich," *Dialogue* 7 (Spring 1972): 80–90; see also reports by German mission presidents in Mission Annual Reports, 1933–1939, MS, Church Archives.

22. Wallace F. Toronto, in Mission Annual Reports, 1937, p. 186; see also *Deseret News, Church Secton,* August 14, 1937, pp. 2, 6, 8.

23. See Arthur Gaeth, "Children of Adversity," *Improvement Era* 41 (June 1938): 338.

24. See Near East Mission Manuscript History, March 4, 1902; October 18, 1927; May 31, 1933, Church Archives.

25. See Glen R. Stubbs, "A Biography of George Albert Smith" (Ph.D. dissertation, Brigham Young University, 1974), p. 343.

26. First Presidency letter, January 18, 1935, in *Improvement Era* 38 (March 1935): 134.

27. Spencer W. Kimball, "The Reconstitution of the First Quorum of the Seventy," *Ensign* 6 (November 1976): 9.

28. J. Reuben Clark Jr., in Conference Report, April 1941, pp. 94–95.

Chapter 9

1. Alfred C. Rees and M. Douglas Wood, Mission Annual Reports, 1938, pp. 256, 736, MS, Church Archives.

2. M. Douglas Wood, in West German Mission Manuscript History, August 26, 1939, Church Archives.

3. Norman G. Seibold, from a taped interview with Joseph F. Boone.

4. M. Douglas Wood, in West German Mission Manuscript History, August 26, 1939, Church Archives.

5. Norman G. Seibold, from a taped interview with Joseph F. Boone.

6. M. Douglas Wood, from an interview with author, February 3, 1978; see also M. Douglas Wood, in Conference Report, April 1940, pp. 78–81; David F. Boone, "The Worldwide Evacuation of Latter-day Saint Missionaries at the Beginning of World War II" (master's thesis, Brigham Young University, 1981), pp. 35–43.

7. Martha Toronto Anderson, *A Cherry Tree Behind the Iron Curtain* (Salt Lake City: Martha Toronto Anderson, 1977), p. 32.

8. See ibid., pp. 31–32.

9. Franklin J. Murdock Oral History, interviews by Gordon Irving (1973), pp. 54–55, Oral History Program, Church Archives.

10. J. Reuben Clark Jr., in Conference Report, April 1940, p. 20.

11. See Gilbert Scharffs, *Mormonism in Germany* (Salt Lake City: Deseret Book Co., 1970), pp. 104–5.

12. Ibid., p. 111.

13. See Lee A. Palmer to the Presiding Bishopric, September 21, 1944, LeGrand Richards Papers, Church Archives.

14. First Presidency circular letter, January 17, 1942, in *Improvement Era* 45 (February 1942): 74.

15. Harold B. Lee, in Conference Report, April 1943, p. 128.

16. J. Reuben Clark Jr., in Conference Report, October 1939, p. 11; see also D. Michael Quinn, *J. Reuben Clark: The Church Years* (Provo, Utah: Brigham Young University Press, 1983), pp. 201–3.

17. J. Reuben Clark Jr., "In Time of War," *Improvement Era* 42 (November 1939): 657.

18. Heber J. Grant, in James R. Clark, comp, *Messages of the First Presidency of The Church of Jesus Christ of Latter-day Saints,* 6 vols. (Salt Lake City: Bookcraft, 1965–75): 6:96.

19. Ibid. 6:141.

20. First Presidency message read by J. Reuben Clark Jr., in Conference Report, April 1942, pp. 90–96.

21. See Joseph Boone, "The Roles of The Church of Jesus Christ of Latter-day Saints in Relation to the United States Military, 1900–1975," (Ph.D dissertation, Brigham Young University, 1975), pp. 548–52; see also Richard Maher, *For God and Country: Memorable Stories from the Lives of Mormon Chaplains* (Bountiful: Horizon Publishers, 1976).

22. Ibid., pp. 698–99.

23. Ezra Taft Benson, in Conference Report, April 1945, p. 109.

24. See Lowell Eliason Call, "LDS Servicemen in the Philippine Islands" (master's thesis, Brigham Young University, 1955).

25. See Melden J. Smith, "An Escape from Death," *Improvement Era* 49 (September 1946): 568, 580.

26. Roy W. Doxey, *Prophecies and Prophetic Promises from the Doctrine and Covenants* (Salt Lake City: Deseret Book Co., 1969), pp. 97–98.

27. Harold B. Lee, in Conference Report, October 1942, p. 73.

Chapter 10

1. As cited in *The Teachings of George Albert Smith,* ed. Robert and Susan McIntosh (Salt Lake City: Bookcraft, 1996), p. xix.

2. See Glen R. Stubbs, "A Biography of George Albert Smith, 1870 to 1951" (Ph.D. dissertation, Brigham Young University, 1974), pp. 55–57.

3. George Albert Smith, as quoted in ibid., p. 83.

4. George Albert Smith, "Your Good Name," *Improvement Era* 50 (March 1947): 139.

5. George Albert Smith, as quoted in Bryant S. Hinckley, "Superintendent George Albert Smith," *Improvement Era* 35 (March 1932): 295.

6. Ibid.

7. See J. Reuben Clark Jr., "Our Dwindling Sovereignty," address a the University of Utah, February

13, 1952, in *Stand Fast by Our Constitution* (Salt Lake City: Deseret Book Co., 1962), p. 118; see also James B. Allen, "J. Reuben Clark, Jr., on Sovereignty and International Organizations," *BYU Studies* 13 (Spring 1973): 117–42; Stanly A. Taylor, "J. Reuben Clark, Jr., and the United Nations," ibid., pp. 185–95.

8. Frank B. Jex, "As I Saw the Church in Holland," *Improvement Era* 49 (June 1946): 400.

9. Ezra Taft Benson, *Church News,* March 23, 1946, p. 6.

10. Hugh B. Brown, *Church News,* August 25, 1948, p. 8.

11. George Albert Smith, in Conference Report, October 1947, pp. 5–6.

12. See Sheri L. Dew, *Ezra Taft Benson: A Biography* (Salt Lake City: Deseret Book Co., 1987), p. 197.

13. Harold Lundstrom and Albert L. Zobell Jr., "Ezra Taft Benson Called to European Mission," *Improvement Era* 49 (February 1946): 67.

14. As quoted in Frederick W. Babbel, *On Wings of Faith* (Salt Lake City: Bookcraft, 1972), p. 46.

15. Ezra Taft Benson, in Conference Report, April 1947, p. 153.

16. Babbel, *On Wings of Faith,* pp. 7–8.

17. Ibid., p. 36.

18. Ezra Taft Benson, in Conference Report, April 1947, p. 154.

19. Ezra Taft Benson, *A Labor of Love: The 1946 European Mission of Ezra Taft Benson* (Salt Lake City: Deseret Book Co., 1989), p. 63.

20. See Joseph Anderson, *Prophets I Have Known* (Salt Lake City: Deseret Book Co., 1973), p. 103.

21. Ezra Taft Benson, special report to the First Presidency, October 22, 1946, European Mission Manuscript History, p. 70, Church Archives.

22. See Richard Ranglack, *Church News,* November 24, 1945, pp. 5, 9.

23. Cornelius Zappey, as quoted in Babbel, *On Wings of Faith,* p. 76.

24. Ibid.

25. Babbel, ibid., p. 132.

26. Ibid., pp. 148–49.

27. See Ezra Taft Benson, in Conference Report, April 1947, pp. 152–57; see also Babbel, *On Wings of Faith,* pp. 25–26.

28. See Babbel, *On Wings of Faith,* pp. 126–38.

29. See ibid., p. 168.

30. See ibid., pp. 129–30.

31. Harrison T. Price, "A Cup of Tea," *Improvement Era* 65 (March 1962): 161; see also Spencer J. Palmer, *The Church Encounters Asia* (Salt Lake City: Deseret Book Co., 1970), pp. 65–69; Boyd K. Packer, in Conference Report, April 1975, p. 155.

32. Matthew Cowley, as quoted in Henry A. Smith, *Matthew Cowley: Man of Faith* (Salt Lake City: Bookcraft, 1954), p. 160.

33. See *Church News,* June 1, 1946, p. 1; see also *Church News,* June 15, 1946, pp. 2–3.

Chapter 11

1. See *Church News,* April 12, 1947, p. 1; see also statement by Spencer W. Kimball, as quoted in James R. Clark, comp., *Messages of the First Presidency of The Church of Jesus Christ of Latter-day Saints,* 6 vols. (Salt Lake City: Bookcraft, 1965–75), 6:256–58.

2. See Melvin K. Johnson, "A History of the Temple Square Mission of The Church of Jesus Christ of Latter-day Saints to 1970" (master's thesis, Brigham Young University, 1971), pp. 50–51; see also David K. Jacobs, "The History of Motion Pictures Produced by The Church of Jesus Christ of Latter-day Saints" (master's thesis, Brigham Young University, 1967), pp. 69–99; *Church News,* October 5, 1949, pp. 1, 12–13.

3. See *Church News,* March 3, 1945, p. 5; January 26, 1946, p. 1; and October 25, 1947, p. 1; see also George H. Fudge Oral History, pp. 1–3, Oral History Program, Church Archives; Doyle L. Green and Albert L. Zobell Jr., "A Period of Progress," *Improvement Era* 53 (April 1950): 273.

4. See Richard L. Evans, in Conference Report, April 1948, p. 166.

5. See *Church News,* May 11, 1946, p. 1.

6. Ralph W. and Emma B. Evans, "The Navajo-Zuni Mission," MS, Church Indian Committee files, p. 3, Church Archives.

7. See *Church News,* November 10, 1945, p. 1.

8. Spencer W. Kimball, in Conference Report, April 1947, pp. 144–45.

9. Spencer W. Kimball, in *Church News,* February 19, 1977, p. 3; compare December 20, 1947, p. 9.

10. Golden R. Buchanan Oral History volume 2, interview by William G. Hartley, 1974, Church Archives, pp. 3, 4.

11. See ibid., pp. 3–12.

12. In James R. Clark, comp., *Messages of the First Presidency* 6:265–67.

13. David O. McKay, in *Church News,* April 11, 1951, p. 10.

Chapter 12

1. David O. McKay, as quoted in Llewelyn R. McKay, *Home Memories of President David O. McKay* (Salt Lake City: Deseret Book Co., 1956), p. 213.

2. Jennette Evelyn Evans McKay, as quoted in ibid., pp. 5–6.

3. John Smith, as quoted in Preston Nibley, *The Presidents of the Church* (Salt Lake City: Deseret Book Co., 1974), p. 312.

4. David O. McKay, "A Personal Testimony," *Improvement Era* 65 (September 1962): 628.

5. David O. McKay, *Cherished Experiences from the Writings of David O. McKay,* comp. Clare Middlemiss (Salt Lake City: Deseret Book Co., 1970), pp. 182–83.

6. McKay, "A Personal Testimony," p. 629.

7. Bryant S. Hinckley, "David O. McKay," *Improvement Era* 35 (May 1932): 443.

8. Hugh J. Cannon, as quoted in David O. McKay, *Cherished Experiences from the Writings of David O. McKay,* comp. Clare Middlemiss, p. 98.

9. David O. McKay, in ibid., pp. 57–63.

10. See ibid., pp. 70–76.

11. See ibid., pp. 80–81.

12. Ibid., pp. 86–90.

13. David O. McKay, in Conference Report, April 1951, p. 157.
14. David O. McKay, "The World Needs to Be Saved from Dominating Instincts," *Instructor* 97 (June 1962): 181.
15. David O. McKay, in Conference Report, October 1936, p. 103.
16. David O. McKay, *Cherished Experiences of the Writings of David O. McKay,* comp. Clare Middlemiss, pp. 108–9.
17. See J. E. McCulloch, *Home: The Savior of Civilization* (Washington, D.C.: The Southern Co-operative League, 1924), p. 42.
18. See *Church News,* January 22, 1955, p. 2.
19. David O. McKay, in *Church News,* January 29, 1955, p. 2.
20. In James B. Allen and Glen M. Leonard, *The Story of the Latter-day Saints* (Salt Lake City: Deseret Book Co., 1992), p. 584.
21. See Jerry C. Roundy, *Ricks College: A Struggle for Survival* (Rexburg, Idaho: Ricks College Press, 1976), pp. 168–72, 178–85.
22. Ernest L. Wilkinson and W. Cleon Skousen, *Brigham Young University: A School of Destiny* (Provo, Utah: Brigham Young University Press, 1976), p. 433.
23. See ibid., pp. 591–92.
24. Ernest L. Wilkinson, remarks at Brigham Young University devotional assembly, March 9, 1971, p. 7.
25. See William E. Berrett, "A General History of Weekday Religious Education: The Seminaries and Institutes of Religion," MS, Church Educational System Archives.
26. See *Church News,* December 1, 1973, p. 12.
27. See Leon R. Harshorn, "Mormon Education During the Bold Years" (Ph.D. dissertation, Stanford University, 1965), pp. 185–88.
28. Neal A. Maxwell, *"Seek Learning by Study and by Faith": Report for 1971 from Commissioner of Education of the Church of Jesus Christ of Latter-day Saints,* (Salt Lake City: The Church of Jesus Christ of Latter-day Saints, 1971), p. 1.
29. See ibid., p. 3.

Chapter 13

1. See Thomas F. O'Dea, "Mormonism and the Avoidance of Sectarian Stagnation," in *Religion in America,* ed. George C. Bedell, 2d edition (New York: Macmillan, 1982), pp. 296–320.
2. Bruce R. McConkie, in Conference Report, Mexico City Area Conference, 1972, p. 45.
3. See James E. Faust, "This Is Our Day," *Ensign* 29 (May 1999): 19.
4. Gordon B. Hinckley, "Here We Will Build Our Zion," *Ensign* 3 (August 1973): 6.
5. Victor L. Brown, in Conference Report, April 1967, p. 35.
6. See *Church News,* October 6, 1965, p. 11.
7. Victor L. Brown, in Conference Report, April 1967, p. 36.
8. See Doyle L. Green, "The Church Sends Its Message to the World Through the Unified Magazine," *Improvement Era* 72 (August 1969): 4–7.
9. From Harold W. Burton, in an interview with author, January 28, 1964; see also Summary of Projects as of April 3, 1956, Building Committee Papers, Church Archives.
10. See David W. Cummings, *Mighty Missionary of the Pacific: The Building Program of the Church* (Salt Lake City: Bookcraft, 1961).
11. Henry D. Moyle, in address to special bishop's session of general conference, April 5, 1963.

Chapter 14

1. *A Systematic Program for Teaching the Gospel* (Salt Lake City: Deseret News Press, 1952), p. 6.
2. See LeRoi Snow, "The Missionary Home," *Improvement Era* 31 (May 1928): 552–54.
3. Ernest J. Wilkinson, from taped interview with the author.
4. See *Church News,* February 15, 1969, pp. 8–10; December 15, 1973, p. 3; January 3, 1976, p. 3; September 9, 1978, p. 10.
5. See Gordon B. Hinckley, in *Church News,* April 26, 1947, pp. 4–5.
6. See *Church News,* July 14, 1973, p. 5.

Chapter 15

1. First Presidency letter, as quoted by Harold B. Lee, in Conference Report, April 1963, pp. 82–83.
2. Harold B. Lee, in ibid, September 1961, pp. 77–79.
3. Harold B. Lee, in *Genealogical Devotional Addresses—1968* (Provo, Utah: Brigham Young University Press, 1968), p. 55.
4. Harold B. Lee, in Conference Report, September 1961, p. 79, 81.
5. Ibid., p. 80.
6. Harold B. Lee, in Conference Report, October 1962, p. 72.
7. See Harold B. Lee, in Conference Report, September 1961, p. 80.
8. See *Priesthood Home Teaching Handbook* (Salt Lake City: Deseret News Press, 1963), preface and pp. 1–2.
9. *Suggested Outlines for Stake Priesthood Leadership Meetings* (1964), p. 9, in Church Archives.
10. David O. McKay, in Conference Report, April 1964, p. 5; see also James E. McCulloch, *Home, The Savior of Civilization* (Washington, D.C.: The Southern Cooperative League), p. 42.
11. Heber J. Grant, *Gospel Standards,* comp. G. Homer Durham (Salt Lake City: *Improvement Era,* 1941), p. 155.
12. David O. McKay, as quoted by Marion G. Romney, in Conference Report, October 1962, p. 78.
13. Harold B. Lee, in Conference Report, April 1973, p. 130.
14. Wilford Woodruff, *Discourses of Wilford Woodruff,* comp. G. Homer Durham (Salt Lake City: Bookcraft, 1990), pp. 267–68.
15. Joseph F. Smith, *Gospel Doctrine* (Salt Lake City: Deseret Book Co., 1986), p. 302.
16. James R. Clark, comp., *Messages of the First Presidency of The Church of Jesus Christ of Latter-day Saints,* 6 vols. (Salt Lake City: Bookcraft, 1965–75), 4:338, 339.
17. From the *Home Evening Handbook* (1936), as quoted by Ezra Taft Benson, in Conference Report,

October 1947, p. 26.
18. Harold B. Lee, in Conference Report, October 1964, p. 84.
19. Ibid., p. 137.
20. Ibid., p. 87.
21. David O. McKay, as quoted in *Family Home Evening Manual,* 1965, (Salt Lake City: Deseret News Press, 1965), p. iii.
22. *Family Home Evening Manual* (Salt Lake City, Deseret News Press, 1967), pp. iii–iv.
23. See *Church News,* October 10, 1970, p. 3.
24. *Church News,* February 26, 1966, p. 3.
25. David O. McKay, in Conference Report, April 1969, p. 8.
26. First Presidency circular letter, April 14, 1969, quoted in *My Kingdom Shall Roll Forth* (Salt Lake City: The Church of Jesus Christ of Latter-day Saints, 1979), p. 114.
27. See *Church News,* December 31, 1966, pp. 8–9; May 3, 1969, p. 4.
28. See *Church News,* June 23, 1973, p. 3; June 30, 1973, p. 6.
29. Thomas S. Monson, "Correlation Brings Blessings," *Relief Society Magazine,* April 1967, pp. 246–47.

Chapter 16

1. Joseph Fielding Smith, in Conference Report, April 1930, p. 91.
2. John Smith, as quoted in *Improvement Era* 53 (April 1950): 315.
3. See Joseph Fielding Smith, "History and Historical Records," *Utah Genealogical and Historical Magazine* 16 (April 1925): 52–53; see also Joseph Fielding Smith, "Libels of Historians," *Improvement Era* 10 (December 1906): 103–4; Leonard J. Arrington, "Joseph Fielding Smith: Faithful Historian," *Dialogue* 7 (Spring 1972): 21–24.
4. Ethel G. Reynolds, as quoted in Bryant S. Hinckley, "Joseph Fielding Smith," *Improvement Era* 35 (June 1932): 459.
5. Joseph Fielding Smith, in Conference Report, April 1970, p. 114.
6. Joseph Fielding Smith, as quoted in Joseph Fielding McConkie, *True and Faithful: The Life Story of Joseph Fielding Smith* (Salt Lake City: Bookcraft, 1971), p. 74.
7. Harold B. Lee, as quoted in Marion G. Romney, "Harold B. Lee, Apostle of the Lord," *Improvement Era* 56 (July 1953): 522.
8. Harold B. Lee, in Conference Report, Mexico and Central America Area Conference, August 1972, pp. 48–49.
9. Stephen L Richards, as quoted by Harold B. Lee, in Conference Report, April 1952, p. 126.
10. Harold B. Lee, in ibid., pp. 126–27.
11. Harold B. Lee, in Conference Report, October 1972, pp. 19–20.
12. Harold B. Lee, as quoted in *Church News,* July 15, 1972, p. 3.
13. *Church News,* September 4, 1971, p. 13.
14. See *Church News,* August 28, 1971, p. 5.
15. See *Church News,* January 29, 1972, p. 3.
16. See *Church News,* September 30, 1972, p. 3.
17. See *Church News,* April 14, 1973, p. 3; May 31, 1975, p. 3.
18. Harold B. Lee, in Seminar for Regional Representatives, October 1971, pp. 4–5.
19. See *Church News,* February 24, 1968, p. 10.
20. *Health Services Handbook* (Salt Lake City: The Church of Jesus Christ of Latter-day Saints, 1971), pp. 2–3.
21. See *Church News,* July 31, 1971, pp. 3, 12; see also July 21, 1973, p. 7; August 18, 1973, pp. 5, 13.
22. *Church News,* September 14, 1974.
23. See *Church News,* October 4, 1969, p. 3.
24. See *Social Services Handbook* (Salt Lake City: The Church of Jesus Christ of Latter-day Saints, 1971), p. 7.
25. Harold B. Lee, as quoted in ibid., pp. 7–8.
26. See Marvin J. Ashton, "The Church Focuses on Social and Emotional Problems," *Ensign* 1 (January 1971): 30–31; see also Robert L. Simpson, "Help Available Here," *Ensign* 3 (December 1973): 56.
27. See *Church News,* October 20, 1973, p. 4.
28. See *Church News,* August 19, 1972, pp. 7–12.
29. See *Church News,* June 27, 1970, p. 6.
30. See Harold B. Lee, *Ye Are the Light of the World* (Salt Lake City: Deseret Book Co., 1974), p. 349.

Chapter 17

1. Spencer W. Kimball, as quoted in Edward L. and Andrew E. Kimball Jr., *Spencer W. Kimball* (Salt Lake City: Bookcraft, 1977), pp. 169–70.
2. Spencer W. Kimball, in Conference Report, October 1943, p. 15.
3. Ibid., p. 16.
4. Spencer W. Kimball, as quoted in Kimball and Kimball, *Spencer W. Kimball,* p. 195; see also pp. 172–95.
5. Spencer W. Kimball, *One Silent Sleepless Night* (Salt Lake City: Bookcraft, 1975), pp. 35, 51.
6. Boyd K. Packer, "President Spencer W. Kimball: No Ordinary Man," *Ensign* 4 (March 1974): 4.
7. See Robert L. Simpson, in Conference Report, October 1975, p. 17.
8. Spencer W. Kimball, in *Church News,* January 5, 1974, p. 14.
9. Spencer W. Kimball, in Conference Report, April 1974, p. 4.
10. W. Grant Bangerter, in Conference Report, October 1977, p. 38.
11. Spencer W. Kimball, " 'When the World Will Be Converted,' " *Ensign* 14 (October 1974): 5, 7, 14.
12. Ezra Taft Benson, as quoted by W. Grant Bangerter, in Conference Report, October 1977, pp. 38–39.
13. See *Church News,* April 13, 1974, p. 17.
14. *Church News,* September 17, 1977, p. 3.
15. See *Church News,* October 29, 1977, p. 3.
16. See *Church News,* July 15, 1978, p. 5; see also August 11, 1979, pp. 8–10. 17. Spencer W. Kimball, as quoted in *Church News,* January 6, 1979, p. 4.
18. Bruce R. McConkie, "The New Revelation on Priesthood," in *Priesthood* (Salt Lake City: Deseret Book Co., 1981), p. 127.
19. Spencer W. Kimball, as quoted in *Church News,* January 6, 1979, p. 4.
20. Bruce R. McConkie, "New Revelation on the

Priesthood," p. 128.
21. Ibid.
22. Spencer W. Kimball, *Faith Precedes the Miracle* (Salt Lake City: Deseret Book Co., 1972), p. 230.
23. Spencer W. Kimball, *The Miracle of Forgiveness* (Salt Lake City: Bookcraft, 1969), pp. 168–69.
24. Spencer W. Kimball, *The Teachings of Spencer W. Kimball,* ed. Edward L. Kimball (Salt Lake City: Bookcraft, 1982), pp. 613–14.
25. Spencer W. Kimball, "God Will Not Be Mocked," *Ensign* 4 (November 1974): 7.
26. Spencer W. Kimball, *Marriage and Divorce* (Salt Lake City: Deseret Book Co., 1976), p. 19; see also pp. 7–10.
27. See ibid., p. 10.
28. See U.S. Government, Department of Health and Welfare, Public Health Service, Center for Disease Control, "Abortion Surveillance, 1977," p. 33.
29. First Presidency statement, in *Church News,* January 27, 1973, p. 7.
30. *Priesthood Bulletin* (Salt Lake City: The Church of Jesus Christ of Latter-day Saints, February 1973), p. 2.
31. Spencer W. Kimball, "President Kimball Speaks Out on Morality," *Ensign* 10 (November 1980): 97.
32. First Presidency statement, in *Church News,* October 30, 1976, p. 2.
33. *The Church and the Proposed Equal Rights Amendment: A Moral Issue* (pamphlet circulated with Church magazines, March 1980), pp. 19–20.
34. Spencer W. Kimball, in *Church News,* September 23, 1978, pp. 3, 10.
35. Bruce R. McConkie, "A New Commandment," *Ensign* 6 (August 1976): 7.
36. Boyd K. Packer, "Scriptures," *Ensign* 12 (November 1982): 53.
37. See *Church News,* February 2, 1980, p. 3.
38. See "New Generation of Meetinghouses," *Ensign* 11 (November 1981): 108–10.
39. Spencer W. Kimball, in Conference Report, April 1978, p. 4.

Chapter 18

1. Harold B. Lee, in Conference Report, September 1967, pp. 103–4.
2. Bruce R. McConkie, "Succession in the Presidency," *Speeches of the Year, 1974* (Provo, Utah: Brigham Young University Press, 1975), pp. 22–23.
3. Spencer W. Kimball, ". . . To His Servants the Prophets," *Instructor* 95 (August 1960): 257.
4. Spencer W. Kimball, in Conference Report, October 1976, p. 10.
5. See J. Reuben Clark Jr., in Conference Report, April 1941, pp. 94–95.
6. David O. McKay, in *Church News,* June 17, 1961, p. 3.
7. See Spencer W. Kimball, in Conference Report, October 1975, pp. 3–4.
8. Spencer W. Kimball, in Conference Report, October 1976, p. 10.
9. Gordon B. Hinckley, in Conference Report, April 1984, p. 4.
10. See Thomas S. Monson, in Conference Report, April 1989, p. 22.
11. Joseph Fielding Smith, *Essentials in Church History,* 25th ed. (Salt Lake City: Deseret Book Co., 1979), pp. 141–42.
12. See Joseph Smith, *Teachings of the Prophet Joseph Smith,* sel. Joseph Fielding Smith (Salt Lake City: Deseret Book Co., 1938), p. 151.
13. John A. Widtsoe, *Priesthood and Church Government* (Salt Lake City: Deseret Book Co., 1954), pp. 269–70.
14. See N. Eldon Tanner, in Conference Report, October 1979, p. 25.
15. N. Eldon Tanner, in Conference Report, October 1978, p. 23.
16. J. Reuben Clark Jr., in *Church News,* July 31, 1954, pp. 9–10.
17. Marion G. Romney, in Conference Report, April 1945, p. 90.
18. Harold B. Lee, in Conference Report, April 1946, p. 68.
19. Spencer W. Kimball, *In the World But Not of It,* Brigham Young University Speeches of the Year, September 12, 1967 (Provo, Utah: Brigham Young University Press, 1967).
20. See *Church News,* October 31, 1970, pp. 3, 5.
21. See Andrew Jenson, *An Encyclopedic History of the Church* (Salt Lake City: Deseret News Publishing Co., 1941), pp. 237–38.
22. See *Church News,* June 19, 1965, pp. 3–5.
23. See *Church News,* December 28, 1963, p. 6.
24. First Presidency letter, as quoted in Conference Report, October 1967, pp. 25–26.
25. See *Church News,* May 3, 1975, pp. 3, 12; May 17, 1975, p. 3.
26. See *Church News,* June 26, 1976, p. 7.
27. See N. Eldon Tanner, in Conference Report, April 1979, p. 119.
28. See *Church News,* July 1, 1984, p. 3.
29. See Conference Report, November 2, 1974, p. 13.
30. See "General Conferences to Be Two-day Conferences," *Ensign* (February 1977): 91–92.
31. *Church News,* February 5, 1977, p. 8.
32. See ibid., pp. 8–9.
33. See *Church News,* January 2, 1971, p. 9; May 3, 1980, p. 14.
34. See *Church News,* May 30, 1964, p. 9; November 2, 1968, pp. 8–9, 12.
35. See Richard Edgley and Wilford G. Edling, "Finances of the Church," in *Encyclopedia of Mormonism* (New York: Macmillan Publishing Co., 1992), 2:508–9.
36. See John A. Widtsoe, *Priesthood and Church Government* (Salt Lake City: Deseret Book Co., 1938), pp. 256–57; see also Harold B. Lee, address at welfare conference session, October 3, 1970, pp. 1–2.

Chapter 19

1. See Sheri L. Dew, *Ezra Taft Benson: A Biography* (Salt Lake City: Deseret Book Co., 1987), pp. 46–48, 77–79, 88.
2. Ibid., p. 87.
3. Ezra Taft Benson, as quoted in ibid., p. 174.
4. See chapter 10.
5. See Ezra Taft Benson, *Cross Fire: The Eight Years with*

Eisenhower (New York: Doubleday, 1962).

6. Ezra Taft Benson, as quoted in Dew, *Ezra Taft Benson: A Biography,* p. 344.

7. Ezra Taft Benson, as quoted in *Church News,* November 17, 1985, pp. 3, 7.

8. First Presidency statement, in *Church News,* December 22, 1985, p. 3.

9. Joseph Smith, in *History of the Church* 4 (Salt Lake City: Deseret Book Co., 1966), 461.

10. Ezra Taft Benson, *The Teachings of Ezra Taft Benson* (Salt Lake City: Bookcraft, 1988), p. 51.

11. Ezra Taft Benson, "The Cleaning of the Inner Vessel," *Ensign* 16 (May 1986): 5–6.

12. See *Church News,* March 14, 1987, p. 3.

13. Ezra Taft Benson, "The Book of Mormon and the Doctrine and Covenants," *Ensign* 17 (May 1987): 85.

14. *Church News,* January 9, 1988, p. 3.

15. Ezra Taft Benson, *The Teachings of Ezra Taft Benson,* p. 571.

16. Joseph Smith, as quoted by Ezra Taft Benson, in Conference Report, April 1948, p. 84.

17. Ezra Taft Benson, in Conference Report, April 1989, pp. 3, 6.

18. Ezra Taft Benson, in Conference Report, October 1985, p. 49.

19. Ezra Taft Benson, in Conference Report, April 1986, pp. 55, 57; emphasis in original.

20. Ezra Taft Benson, in Conference Report, p. 56.

21. Ezra Taft Benson, "To the Young Women of the Church," *Ensign* 16 (November 1986): 84.

22. Ezra Taft Benson, *The Teachings of Ezra Taft Benson,* p. 513.

23. Ezra Taft Benson, in Conference Report, October 1987, pp. 59–62.

24. First Presidency statement, "Church Opposes Government-Sponsored Gambling," *Ensign* 16 (November 1986): 104–5.

25. First Presidency statement, in *Church News,* May 28, 1988, p. 7.

26. See *Church News,* September 26, 1987, p. 5.

27. Ezra Taft Benson, in Conference Report, April 1948, p. 85.

28. Thomas S. Monson, in Conference Report, April 1989, p. 67.

29. Ibid., pp. 68–69; see also *Church News,* November 12, 1988, pp. 3–4.

30. See *Church News,* March 3, 1990, pp. 3, 8–9.

31. Yuri Dubinin, as quoted in *Church News,* May 5, 1990.

32. Gary L. Browning, "Out of Obscurity: The Emergence of The Church of Jesus Christ of Latter-day Saints in 'That Vast Empire' of Russia," *BYU Studies* 33 (1993): 680; see also Bruce Van Orden, *Building Zion: The Latter-day Saints in Europe* (Salt Lake City: Deseret Book Co., 1996), pp. 292–93.

33. See *Church News,* September 29, 1990, pp. 3, 5.

34. See *Church News,* June 29, 1991, pp. 3, 12; July 6, 1991, pp. 3, 8–10.

Chapter 20

1. Eleanor Knowles, *Howard W. Hunter* (Salt Lake City: Deseret Book Co., 1994), p. 38.

2. Howard W. Hunter, as quoted in ibid., p. 71.

3. Ibid., p. 81.

4. See Richard O. Cowan and William E. Homer, *California Saints: A 150-Year Legacy in the Golden State* (Provo, Utah: Brigham Young University Religious Studies Center, 1996), pp. 329–33.

5. Howard W. Hunter, as quoted in Eleanor Knowles, *Howard W. Hunter,* p. 135.

6. David O. McKay, as quoted in ibid., p. 144.

7. First Presidency, as quoted in Boyd K. Packer, "Teach Them Correct Principles," *Ensign* 20 (May 1990): 89–90.

8. First Presidency letter, as quoted in ibid., p. 90.

9. Thomas S. Monson, "The Lord's Way," *Ensign* 20 (May 1990): 93–94.

10. See *Church News,* November 25, 1989, p. 3.

11. Howard W. Hunter, Conference Report, April 1964, p. 34.

12. Thomas S. Monson, "The Lord's Way," p. 92.

13. See ibid., p. 92.

14. Gordon B. Hinckley, "Rise to a Larger Vision of the Work," *Ensign* 20 (May 1990): 95–96.

15. Ibid., p. 97.

16. First Presidency, as quoted in *Church News,* December 1, 1990, p. 3; see also pp. 3–4.

17. See *Church News,* May 21, 1988, p. 6.

18. *Church News,* May 25, 1991, pp. 3–4.

19. See *Church News,* June 24, 1989, p. 12; see also December 8, 1990, p. 5.

20. Ebenezer Owusu, in interview by E. Dale LeBaron in Nairobi, Kenya, on July 18, 1992. Copy in LeBaron personal files.

21. In *Church News,* January 2, 1993, pp. 3, 13.

22. See *Church News,* May 4, 1986, p. 14; May 27, 1989, p. 4; August 25, 1990, p. 4; December 22, 1990, p. 4.

23. See *Church News,* July 17, 1993, pp. 3–4.

24. See *Church News,* April 14, 1985, p. 19; January 12, 1986, p. 3.

25. In *Church News,* March 30, 1991, p. 3.

26. See Thomas S. Monson, "Our Brother's Keepers," *Ensign* 28 (June 1998): 33–39.

27. In *Church News,* November 2, 1996, p. 3.

28. Hermine B. Horman, in *Church News,* December 30, 1995, p. 13; see also "Church Efforts to Improve Literacy," *Ensign* 23 (October 1993): 79–80.

29. From an interview with author, May 1974.

30. Gordon B. Hinckley, as quoted in *Church News,* June 26, 1993, p. 6.

31. See *Church News,* June 19, 1993, pp. 8–10.

32. James B. Allen, et al., "Hearts Turned to the Fathers: A History of the Genealogical Society of Utah, 1894–1994," *BYU Studies* 34 (1994–95): 303; see also p. 174.

33. See Eleanor Knowles, *Howard W. Hunter,* pp. 187–92.

34. Howard W. Hunter, as quoted in *Church News,* June 11, 1994, p. 14.

35. Howard W. Hunter, in Conference Report, October 1994, p. 118.

36. See *Church News,* May 4, 1991, pp. 3, 7.

37. See *Church News,* December 19, 1992, p. 4.

38. See *Church News,* December 17, 1994, p. 3, 8.

39. See *Church News,* December 7, 1991, p. 7; May 9, 1992, p. 11.

Chapter 21

1. *Hymns of The Church of Jesus Christ of Latter-day Saints* (Salt Lake City: The Church of Jesus Christ of Latter-day Saints, 1985), no. 27.
2. Gordon B. Hinckley, as quoted in Sheri L. Dew, *Go Forward with Faith: The Biography of Gordon B. Hinckley* (Salt Lake City: Deseret Book Co., 1996), p. 35.
3. Boyd K. Packer, "President Gordon B. Hinckley, First Counselor," *Ensign* 16 (February 1986): 5.
4. Gordon B. Hinckley, as quoted in Dew, *Go Forward with Faith: The Biography of Gordon B. Hinckley,* p. 47.
5. Ibid., p. 64.
6. Henry D. Moyle, as quoted by Marjorie Hinckley, in ibid., p. 208.
7. Gordon B. Hinckley, in Conference Report, October 1985, p. 71.
8. Ibid., p. 72.
9. Henry B. Eyring, "The Family," *Ensign* 28 (February 1998): 10.
10. "The Family: A Proclamation to the World," *Ensign* 25 (November 1995): 102; see also Henry B. Eyring, "The Family," pp. 10–18.
11. Gordon B. Hinckley, in Conference Report, October 1996, p. 92.
12. Gordon B. Hinckley, in *Church News,* November 18, 1995, p. 3.
13. Gordon B. Hinckley, in Conference Report, October 1996, pp. 66–72.
14. Mike Wallace, as quoted in Dew, *Go Forward with Faith: The Biography of Gordon B. Hinckley,* pp. 541, 543.
15. Gordon B. Hinckley, in Conference Report, April 1996, p. 115.
16. See *Church News,* March 15, 1997, pp. 3, 7.
17. Gordon B. Hinckley, as quoted in *Church News,* September 20, 1997, p. 5.
18. *Church News,* September 12, 1998, p. 13.
19. Gordon B. Hinckley, as quoted in Conference Report, October 1995, p. 92.
20. See *Church News,* May 25, 1996, p. 3.
21. Gordon B. Hinckley, in ibid.
22. *Church News,* June 1, 1996, p. 4.
23. See *Church News,* June 1, 1996, pp. 3, 5.
24. See *Church News,* June 8, 1996, pp. 3, 5.
25. See *Church News,* February 28, 1998, pp. 3–6.
26. See *Church News,* February 10, 1996, pp. 3, 8–9.
27. Gordon B. Hinckley, as quoted in ibid., p. 3.
28. See *Church News,* April 26, 1997, pp. 3–9.
29. Gordon B. Hinckley, in *Church News,* July 26, 1997, pp. 3, 5.
30. M. Russell Ballard, as quoted in *Church News,* December 27, 1997, p. 8.
31. See *Church News,* March 8, 1997, pp. 8–10; March 15, 1997, p. 11; July 19, 1997, p. 3; August 30, 1997, pp. 6, 12.
32. M. Russell Ballard, in Conference Report, April 1997, p. 81.
33. Don L. Searle, "Major Curriculum Changes in Priesthood and Relief Society," *Ensign* 27 (December 1997): 7.
34. Jeffrey R. Holland, as quoted in ibid., p. 8.
35. See *Church News,* August 5, 1995, p. 3.
36. Gordon B. Hinckley, in Conference Report, April 5, 1997, p. 4; see also *Church News,* August 2, 1997, pp. 3–4.

Chapter 22

1. Brigham Young, in *Journal of Discourses,* 26 vols. (London: Latter-day Saints' Book Depot, 1854–1886), 3:372.
2. James E. Talmage, *The House of the Lord* (Salt Lake City: Bookcraft, 1962), p. 17.
3. Boyd K. Packer, *The Holy Temple* (Salt Lake City: Bookcraft, 1980), pp. 177, 180.
4. Talmage, *The House of the Lord,* p. 100.
5. Packer, *The Holy Temple,* p. 45.
6. Talmage, *The House of the Lord,* p. 110.
7. See Joseph Smith, *Teachings of the Prophet Joseph Smith,* sel. Joseph Fielding Smith (Salt Lake City: Deseret Book Co., 1976), p. 179.
8. See Stanley Kimball, "The Nauvoo Temple," *Improvement Era* 66 (November 1963): 974–82.
9. See Richard O. Cowan, *Temples to Dot the Earth* (Salt Lake City: Bookcraft, 1989), p. 157.
10. See *Church News,* April 11, 1953, p. 7.
11. Samuel E. Bringhurst, in *Church News,* September 17, 1955, p. 4.
12. Quoted in Marba C. Josephson, "A Temple Is Risen to Our Lord," *Improvement Era* 58 (September 1955): 624–25.
13. See David O. McKay, "Dedicatory Address Delivered at Swiss Temple Dedication," *Improvement Era* 58 (November 1955): 795.
14. Allie Howe, "A Temple in the South Pacific," *Improvement Era* 58 (November 1955): 811–13; see also Wendell B. Mendenhall, in Conference Report, April 1955, p. 5.
15. George Albert Smith, as quoted in Harold W. Burton and W. Aird MacDonald, "The Oakland Temple," *Improvement Era* 67 (May 1964): 380–81.
16. Eugene Hilton, "Temple Hill," in *Triumph,* a souvenir brochure commemorating the opening of the East Bay Interstake Center in January 1959 (published by the Hayward, Oakland-Berkeley, and Walnut Creek stakes of The Church of Jesus Christ of Latter-day Saints, 1959), pp. 10, 19.
17. In *Church News,* March 8, 1975, p. 3.
18. Spencer W. Kimball, as quoted by Jay M. Todd, "Report of the Regional Representatives' Seminar," *Ensign* 10 (May 1980): 99.
19. See *Church News,* April 4, 1981, p. 3.
20. Sheri L. Dew, *Go Forward with Faith: The Biography of Gordon B. Hinckley* (Salt Lake City: Deseret Book Co., 1996), p. 481.
21. Gordon B. Hinckley, as quoted in ibid., p. 552.
22. Gordon B. Hinckley, "Some Thoughts on Temples, Retention of Converts, and Missionary Service," *Ensign* 27 (November 1997): 49.
23. "Church Launches Worldwide Temple-Building Emphasis with Announcement of Seven New Temples," *Ensign* 10 (May 1980): 102.
24. Joseph Smith, *Teachings of the Prophet Joseph Smith,*

sel. Joseph Fielding Smith, p. 356; see also p. 193.

25. Wilford Woodruff, as quoted in James R. Clark, comp., *Messages of the First Presidency of The Church of Jesus Christ of Latter-day Saints,* 6 vols. (Salt Lake City: Bookcraft, 1965–75), 3:256–57.

26. See Merrill S. Lofthouse, "A Glance Backward—Historical Sketch of the Genealogical Society," *Improvement Era* 72 (July 1969): 14–17.

27. James B. Allen, et al., "Hearts Turned to the Fathers: A History of the Genealogical Society of Utah, 1894–1994," *BYU Studies* 34 (1994–95): 53.

28. See *Church News,* April 11, 1981, p. 22.

29. See *Church News,* January 18, 1964, pp. 8–9.

30. See *Church News,* March 13, 1965, p. 3.

31. See *Priesthood Genealogy Handbook,* (Salt Lake City: The Church of Jesus Christ of Latter-day Saints, 1974), pp. 6–7.

32. See Spencer W. Kimball, in Conference Report, April 1978, p. 4; see also *Church News,* April 22, 1978, p. 3.

33. See J. Thomas Fyans, in Conference Report, October 1978, pp. 39–40.

34. See *Church News,* December 31, 1978, p. 8.

35. David M. Mayfield, *Church News,* October 20, 1985, p. 5.

36. Richard B. Scott, ibid.

37. See Boyd K. Packer and Howard W. Hunter, *That They May Be Redeemed,* (Salt Lake City: The Church of Jesus Christ of Latter-day Saints, 1977).

38. James E. Faust, as quoted in *Church News,* July 4, 1987, p. 10.

39. Gordon B. Hinckley, as quoted in *Church News,* May 29, 1999, p. 3; see also June 7, 1999, p. 6.

40. Boyd K. Packer, as quoted by Earl C. Tingey, in Conference Report, April 1991, p. 33.

Chapter 23

1. Bruce R. McConkie, in Conference Report, April 1980, pp. 97–99.

2. Bruce R. McConkie, in Conference Report, October 1984, p. 105.

3. Joseph Smith Jr., *History of the Church of Jesus Christ of Latter-day Saints,* 2d ed. rev., 7 vols. (Salt Lake City: Deseret Book Co., 1960), 4:537.

4. Paul F. Royall, "Every Man in His Place . . . ," Brigham Young University six-stake fireside address, January 3, 1965, (Provo, Utah: Division of Continuing Education, 1965), p. 12.

5. Ibid.

6. Harold B. Lee, in Conference Report, September 1961, p. 81.

7. Hugh B. Brown, in Conference Report, October 1967, pp. 115–16.

8. Gordon B. Hinckley, in Conference Report, April 1987, pp. 67, 69.

Index

C

N

O

P

Q

R

S